Detective Fiction and the Rise of the Japanese Novel, 1880–1930

Harvard East Asian Monographs 346

Detective Fiction and the Rise of the Japanese Novel, 1880–1930

Satoru Saito

Published by the Harvard University Asia Center
and distributed by Harvard University Press
Cambridge (Massachusetts) and London, 2012

Printed in the United States of America

The Harvard University Asia Center publishes a monograph series and, in coordination with the Fairbank Center for Chinese Studies, the Korea Institute, the Reischauer Institute of Japanese Studies, and other faculties and institutes, administers research projects designed to further scholarly understanding of China, Japan, Vietnam, Korea, and other Asian countries. The Center also sponsors projects addressing multidisciplinary and regional issues in Asia.

Library of Congress Cataloging-in-Publication Data

Saito, Satoru, 1973–
Detective fiction and the rise of the Japanese novel, 1880-1930 / Satoru Saito.
pages cm. -- (Harvard East Asian monographs ; 346)
Includes bibliographical references and index.
ISBN 978-0-674-06586-4
1. Japanese fiction--Meiji period, 1868-1912--History and criticism. 2. Japanese fiction--Taisho period, 1912-1926--History and criticism. 3. Japanese fiction--Western influences. 4. Detective and mystery stories, Japanese--History and criticism. I. Title.
PL726.6.S285 2012
895.6'308720904--dc23

2011048240

Index by the author

♾ Printed on acid-free paper

Last figure below indicates year of this printing

22 21 20 19 18 17 16 15 14 13 12

To M

Acknowledgments

Were it not for the goodwill of a great number of people, this book would not have been possible. I am most indebted to my advisor at Columbia University, Tomi Suzuki, who never hesitated to offer her time and critical acumen for as long as I have known her. I cannot express how fortunate I feel to have her as my mentor and how invaluable her insights have been in shaping this project.

Haruo Shirane also spent countless hours in helping me through this project and in guiding me through my academic career to date. His thirst for knowledge and dedication to the field continue to be an inspiration for me. Paul Anderer's warm support and guidance have been indispensable, as has his ability to tease out the deepest implications of an argument with so much eloquence. His comments brought form to ideas that lay nebulous and dormant in my mind and now occupy the pages of this book. Marilyn Ivy's seminar on detective fiction and Japanese modernity jump-started my project, and her theoretical vigor quickly became a model that I still seek to emulate.

My dissertation research in Japan, which forms the foundation of this book, was conducted through the generous assistance of the Japan Foundation Doctoral Dissertation Fellowship. While there, Komori Yōichi of Tokyo University took time out of his busy schedule to shed light on the value of finding a balance between critical theory and historical knowledge in articulating the conceptual frameworks of my project. The Junior Fellowship in Japan Studies from the Weatherhead East Asian Institute allowed me to focus my energies on writing in my final year at Columbia University. The generous support of Rutgers University and the Department of Asian Languages and Cultures made subsequent research trips to Japan possible, as I was completing this project as an assistant professor. I appreciate the willingness of Waseda University's Toeda Hirokazu to share his vast knowledge of Japanese literature and to facilitate my research in Japan on these occasions.

My colleagues at Rutgers—Ching-I Tu, Richard Simmons, Youngmee Cho, and Janet Walker—provided me with a nurturing environment in which to develop both as a researcher and a teacher. I am especially indebted to Paul Schalow who has given me support at every juncture to guide me through the long process of revising the dissertation into this book and to Senko Maynard whose productivity in and dedication to research have truly been inspirational.

My friends and colleagues Joy Kim, Christina Laffin, Sharon Pacuk, Torquil Duthie, Mathew Thompson, Dennis Frost, Indra Levy, and Michael Scanlon all read through various drafts of this project and provided numerous suggestions. I am thankful to have such dedicated and fun-loving people as colleagues. They have made my days as a graduate student and an assistant professor not only productive but also greatly enjoyable.

An earlier version of Chapter 1 appeared under the same title in the *Journal of Japanese Studies*, vol. 36, no. 1 (Winter 2010). I am grateful for Martha Walsh and the anonymous readers of the article for providing insightful suggestions. A fragment of Chapter 6 was given as a presentation and published as "Detecting the Unconscious: Edogawa Ranpo and Narratives of Modern Experience," in *Literature and Literary Theory*, Proceedings of the Association for Japanese Literary Studies, Vol. 9 (2008).

I am indebted to William Hammell of the Harvard University Asia Center for his belief in this project and for his efforts in seeing it through to the end. I thank the anonymous readers for the press whose reports gave the manuscript the final push and insights necessary to bring it to completion.

And last but certainly not least, my deepest gratitude goes to Tomoko Sakomura who has been there for me always.

Contents

	Conventions	x
	Introduction	1
1	The Novel's Other: Detective Fiction and the Literary Project of Tsubouchi Shōyō	17
2	Allegories of Detective Fiction: Kuroiwa Ruikō and the Refashioning of a Meiji Subject	60
3	Of Crimes and Punishments: The Tribulations of Meiji Students in the Writings of Japanese Naturalism	111
4	Mysteries of the Modern Subject: The Detective and the Detective Fiction Framework in the Writings of Natsume Sōseki	156
5	Rhetoric of Disavowal: "Secrets and Liberation" and the Specters of the West	197
6	Detecting the Unconscious: Edogawa Ranpo and the Emergence of the Japanese Detective	235
	Epilogue: The Detective, the Masses, and the State	277

Reference Matter

	Works Cited	285
	Index	295

Conventions

Unless otherwise noted, all translations are mine. For names of Japanese authors and scholars working in the Japanese language, I have listed the surname first followed by the first name. For authors who use pen names, I refer to them by their pen names, which normally takes the place of their first names, and not by their surnames. There are a few exceptions when I refer to a full pen name by its surname portion (e.g., Futabatei Shimei, but not Edogawa Ranpo) as dictated by academic customs in Japan. I have used the surname for the purposes of citation in all cases. Throughout the book, I use single quotations to denote scare quotes in order to distinguish them from words, phrases, and sentences that are citations, which are denoted by double quotations. For convenience, I have included the plot summaries of the lesser-known works in the footnotes.

Detective Fiction and the Rise of the Japanese Novel, 1880–1930

Introduction

In January 1888, just as Japan was set to consolidate itself as a modern state with the promulgation of the constitution in February 1889 and the opening of the Diet in November 1890, the journalist and political activist Kuroiwa Ruikō (1862–1920) began the serialization of *Hōtei no bijin* (A beauty in court), a translation of Hugh Conway's *Dark Days* (1884), in the newspaper *Konnichi shinbun*. Over the course of the next five years, Ruikō would take advantage of American dime novel collections, such as the Seaside Library and Lovell's Library, that began to flood the Japanese market in the latter half of the 1880s and serialize more than twenty translations of Western detective stories in various newspapers. Many of these stories were French in origin by such authors as Émile Gaboriau (1832–1873) and Fortuné du Boisgobey (1821–1891) that depicted the glamorous world of French high society and the sensational secrets lurking within it. By introducing such works to the Japanese reading public, Ruikō catered to their exotic interest for the foreign to single-handedly fashion "the golden era of detective novels" in Japan.[1]

1. Takagi, *Shinbun shōsetsushi kō*, 70. Ruikō's overwhelming popularity can be observed in the following figure: when Ruikō left the newspaper *Miyako shinbun* to start his own paper *Yorozu chōhō* in November 1892, much of the former's readership followed Ruikō to the latter, and by the next month the readership of the *Miyako shinbun* had decreased from 27,000 to 7,000, and the *Yorozu chōhō* could boast a healthy circulation of 35,000 (the figure is from Itō Hideo, *Kuroiwa Ruikō: tantei shōsetsu no ganso*, 135).

No doubt prompted by Ruikō's success, the journal *Kokumin no tomo* (The nation's friend) made the following comments in the opening editorial of its May 3, 1893 issue:

> The age of *Maihime* and *Saikun* has disappeared like a dream, and the age of the detective novel or the railroad novel has arrived. For four or five years, the literary world that wore the air of unexpected spring has withered, and we can only see birds resting on leafless branches. Everything has a period of development and inactivity; has today become a period of inactivity? . . . Today, the literature of our country has deteriorated. Detective novels or railroad novels, as spiritual sustenance of our society, do not even serve as a humble meal. Our citizens desire animated literature that will raise their heads, boil their blood, and severely shake their backbones.[2]

Most likely written by Tokutomi Sohō (1863–1957), the editor-in-chief of the highly influential journal, this editorial entitled "Bungaku shakai no genjō" (Present state of the literary world) vehemently criticizes "detective novels" for having emaciated the spirit of Japanese society in the Meiji period (1868–1912) and blames their overwhelming popularity for the decline of the literary world. Thus, it pitted detective fiction squarely against the novel, which was conceived as a new form of fictional narrative with Western influence in the latter half of the 1880s and was exemplified, at least according to *Kokumin no tomo*, by Mori Ōgai's *Maihime* (The dancing girl; 1890) and Tsubouchi Shōyō's *Saikun* (The wife; 1889). And in this battle, detective fiction seemed to have the upper hand, forcing proponents of the novel such as Ken'yūsha, the dominant literary group of the period and an ardent opponent of detective fiction, to take drastic action: to "fight one evil with another" by publishing its own detective fiction series in January of the same year the above editorial appeared.[3]

---

2. "Bungaku shakai no genjō," *Kokumin no tomo*, May 3, 1893, 1, 4. The term "railroad novel" used in the passage refers to fictional stories that were geared toward the masses for pure entertainment purposes and can be considered a derogatory synonym for detective fiction. General index to *Meiji bungaku zenshū* lists two instances of this term's use. In both instances, the term is used in conjunction with "detective novel" to describe the state of the Meiji literary world in the 1890s. For actual passages, see Izumi, "Obakezuki no iware shōshō to shojosaku," 349, and Masaoka, "Bunkai yatsuatari," 266.

3. The phrase "fight one evil with another" is from the following anecdote written in the 1927 memoir by Ken'yūsha member Emi Suiin (1869–1934): "At that time [1893], detective novels were in fashion. The translations by Kuroiwa Ruikō were spreading with great momentum. . . . 'With detective novels growing ram-

Given the severity of *Kokumin no tomo*'s charges against detective fiction, it was fitting that Ruikō responded immediately with his side of the story in an editorial entitled "Tantei-dan ni tsuite" (On detective stories), which appeared in the May 11, 1893 issue of *Yorozu chōhō*, the newspaper he had founded a year prior. Ruikō writes:

> In our country, there are occasionally people who think detective stories as something that should be observed from the interest of literature, give them names like "detective novels" [*tantei shōsetsu*], and even attempt at criticisms that detective novels are ruining the literary world. However, a detective story [*tantei-dan*] is a detective story and not a novel, and even if the author squeezed it out from his imagination as if he were writing a novel, it is still one type of "story" and cannot be called a "novel." Therefore, the novel and the detective story have different territories and are not harmful to each other. I have seen and know that in countries like the United States, the detective story, alongside the rapidly developing novel, occupies a different path and develops without conflicting or fighting [with the novel].[4]

Whereas the supporters of the novel deny the literary value of detective fiction and view its popularity as an evil to be defeated, Ruikō rejects any claim that detective fiction is literature and argues that they are two distinct narrative forms which have nothing to do with each other and, therefore, should not be in competition or in conflict.[5] According to him, it is the supporters of the novel who coined the phrase "detective novel" in the first place to create the illusion that detective fiction exists within the realm of literature.

If we take Ruikō's word in assessing the state of this dispute over detective fiction, then we must admit that detective fiction is falsely accused of a crime it has not committed. But despite his fervent denial, Ruikō also does not forget to hint at the possibility of the connection and fluidity between the two genres when he comments later in the editorial that "there are detective stories that have advanced and joined the

---

pant, the sales of pure literature are deteriorating. So let's fight one evil with another and publish detective novels and sell lots of them at a low cost.' This insistence of Shun'yōdō [a publishing house] was brought to [Ozaki] Kōyō's place. And so Kōyō at once recruited a death squad from the company" (Emi, *Jiko chūshin Meiji bundan shi*, 180). The series was short lived, ending in February 1894, as it did nothing to quench Ruikō's popularity.

4. Kuroiwa, "Tantei-dan ni tsuite."

5. Ruikō states later in the article: "I have occasionally translated detective stories, not for literature, but for the newspaper. . . . [Detective stories] are not novels but serials [*tsuzukimono*], not novels but news" (ibid.).

ranks of the novel, and there are also emotional [*ninjōteki*] novels that have the same composition as detective stories."[6] And such a comment must have stung the supporters of the novel, for an exemplar of such a fluidity between genres had made its appearance in Japan: the translation of Fyodor Dostoevsky's *Crime and Punishment* (1866) by Uchida Roan (1868–1929), published in two installments as *Tsumi to batsu*, the first in November 1892 and second in February 1893. Sharing important characteristics with the detective story yet undeniably literary, this work radically problematized the fundamental difference between the two genres, especially because Roan's translation exhibited characteristics that emphasized the detective fiction elements present in the Russian original. Indeed, given the time frame of Roan's translation, the vehement criticism of detective fiction in *Kokumin no tomo* also begins to appear as a defense mechanism on the part of the supporters of the novel to repress the reality of the intimate connection and inherent fluidity between the two genres.

But importantly, the crisis of genres between detective fiction and the novel quietly yet powerfully brought about by Roan's *Tsumi to batsu* was, in fact, already present in the story of their birth—that is, in the nascent stages of their emergence in the latter half of the 1880s.[7] As I explore in Chapter 1 of this book, the intricate connection between the two genres can be clearly discerned in the literary project of Tsubouchi Shōyō (1859–1935), whose *Shōsetsu shinzui* (The essence of the novel; 1885–1886) not only articulated the theoretical and technical foundations on which modern Japanese literature would develop but also provided the criteria against which detective fiction would be criticized. Yet, at the same time, Shōyō was also one of the very first to experiment with the detective fiction genre in Japan, translating the American detective story writer Anna Katharine Green's *XYZ* as *Nisegane tsukai* (The counterfeiter) in the last months of 1887. Appearing a month or so before Ruikō's first adaptation *Hōtei no bijin*, *Nisegane tsukai* reveals that the emergence of detective fiction via translations of Western detective stories was not an isolated phenomenon of popular culture but had in-

6. Ibid.

7. The timing of the emergence of the two genres in Japan already suggests a different relationship between detective fiction and the novel from that in the West where their formative periods do not overlap historically. For a discussion of this relationship in the Western context, see D. A. Miller, *The Novel and the Police*, especially 50–51.

stead much to do with the articulation of the notion of the modern novel, which would have far-reaching ramifications in the development of fictional narratives in modern Japan.

It is the extent, nature, and development of this connection between detective fiction and the modern novel that is the subject of this book. As such, this book does not attempt to provide a literary history of Japanese detective fiction nor is its primary focus the examination of this genre within the larger sociocultural developments of Japanese modernity, especially since such approaches have yielded much scholarship in recent years, both in Japan and in the United States.[8] Rather, this book sheds light on the deep structural and conceptual similarities between detective fiction and the novel in prewar Japan through a series of close reading of literary texts by canonical writers of Japanese literature—Tsubouchi Shōyō, Shimazaki Tōson (1872–1943), Tayama Katai (1871–1930), Natsume Sōseki (1867–1916), Akutagawa Ryūnosuke (1892–1927), Tanizaki Jun'ichirō (1886–1965), and Satō Haruo (1892–1964)—and of Japanese detective fiction, Kuroiwa Ruikō and Edogawa Ranpo (1894–1965). In so doing, I hope to illustrate that the interactions between the two genres, implicated in these texts, were not marginal occurrences but instead critical moments of literary engagement. It is to posit a genealogy within modern Japanese literature that comes into shape through these interactions—from the latter half of the 1880s on the dawn of the first detective fiction boom driven by Ruikō's translations to the 1920s when the second detective fiction boom took place with Edogawa Ranpo tak-

8. For example, Uchida Ryūzō's *Tantei shōsetsu no shakaigaku* (Sociology of the detective novel; 2001) has provided a comparative examination of Japanese detective fiction within the international history of the genre, and *Tantei shōsetsu to Nihon kindai* (Detective novel and Japanese modernity; 2004) has collected essays by prominent scholars that discuss the role detective fiction played in the various developments of Japanese modernity. Outside of Japan, Mark Silver's *Purloined Letters: Cultural Borrowing and Japanese Crime Literature, 1868–1937* (2008) has provided a much needed English-language analysis of the issues and themes of prewar Japanese detective fiction from the perspective of this genre as an act of "cultural borrowing," and Sari Kawana's *Murder Most Modern: Detective Fiction and Japanese Culture* (2008) has elucidated the relationship between Japanese detective fiction and a variety of contemporaneous cultural discourses, including science and abnormal sexuality, and, in so doing, framed detective fiction within the larger sociocultural developments of modern Japan from the prewar to the postwar period.

ing the lead through his original detective stories—that I employ the term "the Japanese novel" in this book.

At the heart of such interactions is one of the primary preoccupations of modern Japanese literature: the tribulations of the student and its later incarnation—the intellectual—as emblematic subjects within Japan's modernization process. I contend that the detective fiction genre provided the Japanese authors with structural and conceptual frameworks, both explicit and implicit, through which to examine and critique the nature and implications of this overarching process. Loosely defined in terms of the classical Western tradition introduced by Edgar Allan Poe (1809–1849) and institutionalized by Arthur Conan Doyle (1859–1930), detective fiction tells a story of a detective who uses his powers of observation and deduction based on his rational intellect and scientific knowledge to identify and capture a criminal. In this sense, detective fiction operates under the larger dynamic of secret and exposure that characterizes many modern fictions, both in the West and in Japan. But what distinguishes detective fiction within this dynamic is the articulation of a specific subject position occupied by the detective who represents the subject's epistemological desire to understand the Other as the object of knowledge, where the knowledge as truth of the crime is posited as undiscovered, concealed, or withheld from the subject. Importantly, this epistemological desire finds legitimacy in the detective's status as an agent of the state—however aloof and eccentric he may appear in the examples of classical Western tradition—who employs his intellect in the name of authority for the good of the state and its people.

And it is here that the detective intersects squarely with the Japanese student and intellectual in modern Japan through its symbolic value within the critical ideologies of the nation's modernization as Westernization process. By taking up matters of rationality, justice, and science among others, detective fiction positioned itself perfectly within the social-evolutionary rhetoric of *bunmei kaika* (civilization and enlightenment), an aggressive strategy by the Meiji government and intellectuals to import all aspects of Western civilization to Japan that posited Western nations as 'civilized' and 'enlightened' in opposition to the 'uncivilized' and 'unenlightened' Japan.[9] As such, it functioned as a site where these

9. Characterized by its all-encompassing nature, *bunmei kaika* affected not only the elites of Meiji Japan but also its ordinary citizens, especially those in large cities. As Nakanome Tōru writes: "From customs and habits such as hairstyles (cropped hair), clothing (Western dress), and diet (beef *nabe*) and the rapid devel-

epistemological and moral issues regarded as central to Japan's nation building and Westernization process were explored and as a vehicle through which they were popularized. Through its protagonist, the detective, who "celebrated the triumph of science and reason, and embodied the certainty of *shinpo* [progress]," detective fiction provided its readers with a hero who symbolized how Western knowledge can be utilized for the good of the nation.[10] That is, the detective became an emblem of success within the ideology of *risshin shusse* (rising in the world) that drove ambitious youths of Meiji Japan and beyond to seek success through education, in general, and Western learning, in particular.[11] In such a way, the detective and his story exerted their influence through their appeal within the binary opposition between Japan and the West, not necessarily as historical reality, but as promoted by the critical ideologies of modern Japan that effectively interpellated its students and intellectuals as subjects, a process that was not only reflected in but also reproduced and renewed through its literary formations.[12]

---

opments in transportation and communication systems such as the railroads and postal service to the thought and education that subsumed the works of Fukuzawa Yukichi, the school system, and new media such as public speeches, the newspaper, and journals—the full-scale mobilization of Westernization in all aspects of sociocultural phenomena and the [resulting] confusion of values . . . the world of *bunmei kaika* was like a huge theater where comedies and tragedies surrounding these aspects were performed" ("Bunmei kaika no jidai," 214).

10. Kawana, *Murder Most Modern*, 9.

11. As Maeda Ai has discussed at length, this ideology finds its origin in the two bestsellers of the early Meiji period, namely, Nakamura Masanao's *Saigoku risshi-hen* (a translation of Samuel Smiles's *Self-help*; 1870–1871) and Fukuzawa Yukichi's *Gakumon no susume* (Encouragement of learning; 1872–1876), both of which espoused the notion of human equality and the universal potential to succeed in life through learning. For details, see Maeda, "Meiji risshin shusse shugi no keifu."

12. In this sense, this book examines the ways in which literary texts function to shape a certain collective consciousness or what Raymond Williams has called "structures of feeling." On this concept, Williams writes: "The term is difficult, but 'feeling' is chosen to emphasize a distinction from more formal concepts of 'world-view' or 'ideology.'. . . It is that we are concerned with meanings and values as they are actively lived and felt, and the relations between these and formal or systematic beliefs are in practice variable (including historically variable). . . . We are talking about characteristic elements of impulse, restraint, and tone: specifically affective elements of consciousness and relationships: not feelings against thought, but thought as felt and feeling as thought: practical con-

But even despite the undeniable symbolic appeal of its protagonist that makes detective fiction appear as an overdetermined genre whose emergence was all but guaranteed in Meiji Japan, this was not the case, for there is another side to the story of its birth that needs to be taken into account: the historical relationship between the detective and the paradigmatic sociopolitical landscape of the early Meiji period buttressed by the Freedom and People's Rights movement (Jiyū minken undō). Touting Western Enlightenment ideals of human freedom and liberty and calling for the establishment of a constitution and a representative form of government, this liberal political movement spread throughout Japan in the latter half of the 1870s. But as government suppression heightened in the early 1880s, the movement steadily deteriorated, especially when its radical members, mostly affiliated with the Liberal Party (Jiyūtō), turned to violence out of frustration and desperation.

Significantly, the government use of so-called *tantei* or detectives played a major role in the movement's deterioration, with the introduction of detectives in 1881 marking a turning point in its fate.[13] Infiltrating political parties and conventions disguised as activists, government detectives spied on and sometimes even framed activists for crimes they did not commit. In so doing, they quickly and firmly established their reputation as enemies of the people, as the editorial "Tantei-ron" (On detectives), which appeared in the political newspaper *Jiyū shinbun* in April 1883, clearly indicates: "A political detective is not something that should ever exist in a peaceful society ruled by an emperor. And because it is an evil existence that should be abhorred and detested, the ministers of the government should never lend their ears to it."[14] It was in

---

sciousness of a present kind, in a living and inter-relating continuity" (*Marxism and Literature*, 132).

13. The government use of detectives officially began in November 1881 when the Department of Finance issued a state detective expense of 10,000 yen to the Metropolitan Police Department (Obinata, *Tennō-sei keisatsu to minshū*, 77). Coming just after the Crisis of 1881, when a public uproar ignited in response to a political scandal forcing the government to promise the opening of the Diet in 1890, this measure was a direct result of the government's realization of the power of public opinion formed through newspapers and political conventions during this turbulent era of damning articles and inciting orations. For an overview of the Crisis of 1881, see Huffman, *Creating a Public*, 112–20.

14. "Tantei-ron," *Jiyū shinbun*, April 12, 1883. The essay appeared a day after the reporting of the unethical nature of a government detective in the Takada Incident, in which over twenty members of the Liberal Party were falsely

such a way that the word *tantei* became known in Japan, often being substituted by its derogatory variant *mittei* (spy) and appearing as villains in the fictional narratives of the 1880s.

Given such a negative connotation, the overwhelming popularity of Ruikō's detective stories—and the popularity of the detective as fictional hero—only around ten years after the introduction of the historical detective as villain in Japanese society begins to appear as an astounding turn of events rather than as a natural course of history within the nation's modernization and Westernization process. Not surprisingly then, the emergence and blossoming of detective fiction via translations of Western detective stories in the late 1880s required a successful amelioration and radical transformation of the negative connotations associated with the figure of the detective. As I illustrate in Chapter 2, Ruikō's detective stories cleverly utilized existing discourses that were popular during the period to redirect the resentment felt toward government detectives by those involved in or supportive of the Freedom and People's Rights movement, ultimately supplanting and refashioning the historical detective as villain with the fictional detective as hero *for* the people.

But as popular as Ruikō's detective stories were, suggesting their ideological influence, I would argue that a sense of deep ambivalence characterized the relationship between the detective and the Japanese student/intellectual—at least, as portrayed by the self-proclaimed voice, the novelist—within the major literary developments of modern Japan. No doubt reflecting the condition of the detective's birth in Meiji Japan, such ambivalence also had much to do with the difficulties of the Japanese student and intellectual in finding productive ways to participate in society as emblems of modernization and Westernization that they were supposed to embody. In other words, while the archetypal protagonist of the literary works I have selected—many of which are pivotal works within the development of modern Japanese literature—shares with the detective his desire to understand the Other as an object of knowledge, these works invariably fail to describe how he converts such desire into utility for the nation, as did the detective story. And if the detective symbolized the individual's success to embody the Western values and ideals that Japan sought hard to import and incorporate within the context of nation-building, then the failure to find social success in society as a productive member rendered the subject as the detective's opposite, the

charged of planning a coup d'état and assassinations of ministers. For an overview of Takada Incident, see Morinaga, *Saiban jiyū minken jidai*, 84–90.

criminal. Indeed, the dangers of failing to embody these ideals are already suggested by Futabatei Shimei's *Ukigumo* (Drifting clouds; 1887–1889), often considered the first modern novel in Japan, through the protagonist Bunzō, whose dismissal from his official post leads him on a path to delusion and madness. And it was *Crime and Punishment*, introduced in Japan in the early 1890s through Roan's translation, that took these failures to the next level, by suggesting the potential of the fallen student to turn to violent crime when he becomes alienated from society as a result of his divergence from the path to success.

The various permutations of the Japanese intellectual's struggle within the framework of *risshin shusse* ideology that manifests itself within the spectrum of the opposition between the detective and the criminal—*Crime and Punishment* providing one powerful example—constitute the primary subject matter of Chapters 3, 4, and 5. In addition to considering the Meiji reception of *Crime and Punishment*, Chapter 3 examines the works of Japanese Naturalism, which emerged as the dominant literary trend after the Russo-Japanese War (1904–1905), and, in particular, its pivotal works, *Hakai* (Broken commandment; 1906) by Shimazaki Tōson and *Futon* (The quilt; 1907) by Tayama Katai. While being influenced by the heterogeneous literary developments of the 1890s, the two works share critical narrative structures with *Crime and Punishment*, not only in their employment of the dynamic of secret and exposure but also in the way such dynamic unfolds through an act of confession that, in turn, results in the subjects' banishment from the society in which they had hoped to succeed. Through the analysis of such similarities that make it possible to frame these works as successors to the Russian masterpiece, Chapter 3 reconsiders the fate of the stories' marginalized protagonists—a *burakumin* and a woman—within the struggles of Japanese writers to find imaginary solutions for the aspiring intellectuals in a society where *risshin shusse*, as the central ideological cog of the educated class in the Meiji period, was quickly collapsing.

If the pivotal works of Japanese Naturalism in their own ways exercised strategic negotiations of the problems facing the Japanese intellectual, then Natsume Sōseki, whose works are examined in Chapter 4, utilized the dynamic of secret and exposure to tackle the issue of the Japanese intellectual head on. And he did so by positing the criminality of the intellectual in modern society as a likely and logical, if not an inherent, trait. Importantly, it is here that the deep-seated ambivalence toward the detective in modern Japan manifests itself most extremely. While he extensively criticized the detective as the most evil of all professions—often comparing him to the criminal—Sōseki could not help but write stories about detectives and engage more seriously than any other writer in modern Japan on their potential as metaphors, utilizing them to elucidate the fate of the modern individual caught in a rapidly changing world of self-interest and over-analysis. In so doing, Sōseki reconsidered the role of the intellectual for the nation in post–Russo-Japanese War Japan when nation-building received new focus through the production of a modern citizenry fit for Japan's new position as one of the international powers. As we shall see, Sōseki's exploration involved the intellectual's inability to find a place for himself within the nation-building process as a productive citizen that Western education should have offered him, as manifested in his portrayals of subjects who could be understood to be *kōtō yūmin*, or "upper-class vagabonds" characterized by their unproductive existence.

Such explorations would continue in the Taishō period (1912–1926) after Sōseki's works finally began the process of actively connecting the critical undercurrents of modern Japanese literature with the detective fiction genre, bringing the contours of the Japanese novel into sharp focus. The prime example in this regard was a special issue of the magazine *Chūō kōron* (Central review) titled "Himitsu to kaihō" (Secrets and liberation) in 1918, which contained stories organized under the rubric of "new artistic detective novels" written by the likes of Tanizaki Jun'ichirō, Akutagawa Ryūnosuke, and Satō Haruo. As I argue in Chapter 5, these stories whose focus still remain on the criminal explore the potentially criminative power that Western ideals exercised on Japanese intellectuals and thereby provide a suture between the criminal and the detective that most vividly manifests itself in Satō's "Shimon" (The fingerprint) in which the protagonist turns detective in order to exonerate himself of a murder that he may have committed unknowingly. In such ways, these stories took the exploration of the link between Western education and criminality to its extremes—in a manner similar to *Crime and Punishment*—to expose the fundamentally fragmented nature of the Japanese intellectual who is torn between his belief in Western ideals and his existence within Japanese society.

And I would argue that it was only through such negotiations between the detective and the criminal enacted by the major writers of modern Japan that a Japanese detective could finally emerge as hero in the figure of Edogawa Ranpo's Akechi Kogorō to bring about the second detective fiction boom in the 1920s. Ranpo's early stories, examined in Chapter 6, reflected the process through which they emerged, telling how the educated and apolitical subjects from the country become implicated in the detective fiction framework in one way or another. Thus, these stories engaged with the central issue of the Japanese novel explored through its relationship to the detective fiction genre, positing the detective as a savior of the Japanese subject whose relationship to the rapidly changing external reality of the modern metropolis was becoming more and more tenuous each day, especially after the Great Kantō Earthquake of 1923 that devastated much of the Tokyo-Yokohama region and spurred a major reconstruction of the urban landscape.

Significantly, the second detective fiction boom brought on by the popularity of Ranpo's detective stories occurred under similar sociopolitical climate as the first. Both booms took place after the spread of liberal political movements—the aforementioned Freedom and People's Rights movement and the so-called Taishō Democracy from the 1910s to the early 1920s—which, in turn, were followed by a new system of political representation with the institution of voting in 1890 and of universal male suffrage in 1925. But while these movements could be said to have obtained their goals, such successes came after vehement suppression of these movements and were coupled with despotic measures by the government, which sought to curb any meaningful political activity on the part of its citizens. These measures were the 1887 Public Order Ordinance (Chian jōrei), which banned 570 activists from the capital and prohibited political assemblies, and the 1925 Maintenance of Public Order Act (Chian iji hō) whose vague language made it easily applicable—and was, in fact, liberally applied—to control and punish any activity that might be deemed politically subversive.

On the one hand, this historical connection between liberal political movements (especially as it relates to enfranchisement) and the detective fiction booms makes sense considering the theoretical underpinnings of democracy. Despite his unofficial nature, the private detective—the primary protagonist of the Western detective fiction tradition—is "a shrewd agent of authority" who demonstrates the surveying and controlling powers of the state and suggests how such authority "has already been deeply internalized in diffused form by the general public" to the extent that the private detective represents the public's active role in reproducing the efforts of the state to capture and punish the violators of its laws.[15] And if the private detective suggested the participation on

15. First citation from Takahashi, "'Tantei shōsetsu' ga inpei suru mono," 54; second citation from Uchida Ryūzō, *Tantei shōsetsu no shakaigaku*, 38.

the part of citizens in the state machinery as it relates to the disciplinary powers of the state, then voting is a participation on the part of citizens in the state machinery as it confers the rights of the people to the state as an agent of the people's will. The detective is an agent of the state, but, at the same time, he is made possible theoretically by the authority granted by the people to the state. Coupled with the ineptitude of the police as the official agents of the state that is comically portrayed in the detective stories of Conan Doyle and Poe, the private detective as coming from the side of the public reiterates this power relationship between the state and its citizens (that is often felt as reversed) by suggesting that the state cannot provide the necessary disciplinary actions without the help of its citizens. Thus, the detective story celebrates democracy and the rights of citizens as powerful constituents of state machinery.

On the other hand, the despotic measures taken by the Japanese government in conjunction with liberal political movements complicate this understanding. In a sense, the democratic movements functioned as foils to highlight the despotic measures coupled with such movements as violations of the basic tenets of democracy that made citizens keenly aware of their alienation from the state. Indeed, we could argue that it is precisely because authority comes at them from without in reality that there arises a need for the detective who celebrates such authority to emerge in the fictional world and for the detective story as "an ideological act in its own right, with the function of inventing imaginary or formal 'solutions' to unresolvable social contradictions," to use Fredric Jameson's formulation.[16] And Jameson's use of the word "unresolvable" seems particularly fitting for Japan's case, which was significantly different from the advanced Western nations that may experience moments of the government's despotic eruptions in the course of its democratic development, for such a contradiction was not just a facet of the development of Japan as a modern state but rather an inherent and constitutive part of the Japanese state and its political system. Crystallized in the foundational framework of the Meiji Constitution, Japanese democracy was a fraud at its source to the extent that the rights of the Japanese citizen were not taken as inherent and inviolable but granted by the graces of the emperor.[17]

---

16. Jameson, *The Political Unconscious*, 79.

17. Delineating the power of the government and guaranteeing specific rights of its people, the constitution, as the most basic and necessary component of a democratic society, most often represents a contract between the state and its

As the above examples make clear, a variety of contradictions, sociopolitical and historical in nature, confronted the modern Japanese subject, necessitating a literary/imaginary resolution in the fictional world. This book seeks to elucidate how the dynamic of the detective story, whether consciously evoked or unconsciously evocative, offered ways for Japanese writers to imagine such resolutions and what the nature of these resolutions were. And it does so through the examination of specific works to consider their sociopolitical function as "an ideological act," to heed Jameson's formulation. But while such considerations have taken literary studies in recent years toward what is often called a 'sociology of literature,' I focus primarily on the literary texts themselves with the belief that it is possible to contribute to the consideration of narrative form as an ideological act through such methodological emphasis.

As Hans Robert Jauss has argued, the text, by existing within a spe-cific historical moment and sociopolitical environment, presents itself to readers within the "horizon of expectations" that is constructed through their prior experiences as discursive and historical subjects, and thus: "the psychic process in the reception of a text is, in the primary horizon of aesthetic experience, by no means only an arbitrary series of merely subjective impressions, but rather the carrying out of specific instructions in a process of directed perceptions that can be comprehended according to its constitutive motivations and triggering signals."[18] A liter-

---

citizens. Sovereignty resides with the people, thereby indicating that the authority of the government, at least in theory, is conferred by the people to the state so that the latter can act as agents of the people's will. But such was not the case for Japan. Despite being the fruit of the Freedom and People's Rights movement, the Meiji Constitution was also a product of ultimate compromise, for the constitution was not presented as a birthright of the people but as being conferred by the grace of the emperor. That is, while the opening of the Diet the year following the promulgation of the constitution in February 1889 may have theoretically signaled the arrival of representation as an act of conferring of authority by the people to their representatives in accordance with the democratic process, it did not, or could not, trump the constitution that guaranteed the Diet possible in the first place.

18. Jauss, *Toward an Aesthetic of Reception*, 23. From the perspective of the author, such a horizon makes for difficulty, particularly in a detective story where the unexpected is expected. As discussed in detail in Chapter 6, the flooding of Western detective stories, by constructing a well-developed set of expectations on the part of the readers, presented a challenge for Japanese writers in producing detective stories that were original. But, at the same time, such expectations enabled Japanese writers, and Ranpo in particular, to use the formal and thematic

ary text adopts various narrative strategies in the process of its production in order to guide and manipulate the reader's interpretation of the text in a systematic manner, and it is the understanding of these strategies in literary production, which are most often consciously enacted by the author but not necessary so, that must be the first steps in talking about the reception of literary texts.[19] Thus, the methodological focus of this book, first and foremost as previously mentioned, is the close reading of texts in order to reveal the often implicit and contradictory strategies of a literary text—including its narrative forms, symbolic mappings, and intertextual evocations—that engage the readers to respond in a specific manner.

What Jauss calls the "horizon of expectations" does not merely connote the formal negotiations between the text and its reader, however, and is also constituted by numerous extra-textual factors including the sociohistorical conditions of the text's consumption as well as paratexts that provide an interpretative framework for the text's consumption. And it is here that theory meets history in the case of Japan during the period in question, for the formation of the Japanese novel significantly began during the zenith of an interpretative paradigm that utilized such paratexts consciously and actively. This was the allegorical mode of literary production and consumption that dominated the 1880s, which, as I argue in Chapter 2, played a major role in the emergence of detective fiction in the late 1880s. Similar to the contradictory ambivalence embodied in the emergence of detective fiction in Japan, the allegorical interpretative paradigm grew out of the desire to fight for the materialization of Western ideals in Japan and of the need to combat the despotic

---

elements of Western stories as foils against which they could construct stories that countered reader expectations.

19. In this sense, detective fiction is a particularly suitable subject for the investigation of the ways in which a reader responds to a text. Often considered one of the most rigid literary genres, detective fiction relies heavily on a common set of formal and cultural codes, conventions, and presuppositions—which are formed through the readers' previous encounters with its 'members'—in the production of meaning. The authors utilize these codes and expectations, or the "horizon of expectations" that inform us of the ways in which a given story might be interpreted by the readers, which are manipulated, suspended, and/or thwarted in the course of the story. And while the detective fiction genre may have strict rules and codes to be recognized as such, every story challenges and bends these rules and codes, leading to the formation of a new "horizon of expectations" within the readers.

measures of censorship by the Meiji government during the Freedom and People's Rights movement.

Although the allegorical mode of literary production and consumption is often understood to have faded away with the rise of modern Japanese literature buttressed by Shōyō's *Shōsetsu shinzui* as the foundational work that sowed the seeds of the realistic novel in Japan, I argue that the allegorical mode remained a quiet yet powerful undercurrent of the modern Japanese literary environment, placing itself in constant negotiation with the realistic mode. And at the center of this negotiation was the detective story, which not only offered the detective as the allegorical double of the Japanese student/intellectual, but also mediated, by functioning as a conceptual, structural, and organizational nexus, the tenuous relationships between literature and society as well as subject and authority that made literary texts significant as political acts, whether consciously or not, to authors and readers alike. Through the mapping of such connections and relationships, I hope to reconsider and shed new light on the understanding of what we now call modern Japanese literature.

ONE

The Novel's Other: Detective Fiction and the Literary Project of Tsubouchi Shōyō

Tsubouchi Shōyō's first-person narrative "Tane hiroi" (Gleaning the seeds) opens with a writer who travels to the Kansai region to relieve writer's block and, while crossing Lake Biwa on a steamboat, overhears a private conversation between two strangers. Serialized from October 1, 1887 in the *Yomiuri shinbun* with which he was closely affiliated, the story deviates significantly in both content and form from his previous efforts to embody the notion of the novel that he had come to espouse. As one of the strangers (a woman named Osumi) recounts her hard life to the other (a man named Masa), the narrator becomes completely engrossed and follows the strangers from place to place in hopes of eavesdropping the entirety of the tale. But before we get to the end of her story, the readers are told that everything was just a dream, and, in this sense, "Tane hiroi" follows the tradition in the vein of *Kinkin sensei eiga no yume* (Mr. Glitter 'n Gold's dream of splendor; 1775), in which Kinbei, who is from the country, dreams of the rise and fall of his fortunes in Edo. Unlike this latter work, a *kibyōshi* picture book from the preceding Edo period (1600–1867), however, "Tane hiroi" does not end with the awakening of the protagonist. Rather, the story continues after the dream to tell the narrator's discovery that Osumi's life story, which he had dreamed to overhear, was actually a story—a *tsuzukimono* (serial)—that he had read in the newspaper during his recent trip.

The development of the newspaper medium will be discussed in more detail in the course of this chapter, but for now let us note that *tsuzukimono* emerged in the late 1870s when news began appearing over a multiple number of installments in story format. The favorite theme of *tsuzukimono* was the crime story based on actual cases, and, in particular, those involving immoral and often amorous women called *dokufu-mono* (poisonous women tales), that focused on the criminal and told the events leading up to the crime.[1] Given its penchant for the spectacular and the scandalous that were made even more so through fictional embellishments, *tsuzukimono* quickly caught the interest of readers and, by the early 1880s, its various forms, including adaptations of Edo fiction in *jitsuroku-mono* style (sensational stories mixing facts and fiction), had become a dominant narrative form in Meiji Japan.[2]

It was such proliferation of *tsuzukimono* and of these adaptations, in particular, that Shōyō criticized and set as his explicit objects of reform in his introduction to *Shōsetsu shinzui*:

> With the restoration, writers of *gesaku* [so-called frivolous works] faded for a bit and so narrative fiction [*shōsetsu*] deteriorated, but recently it has seen a great revival . . . and thus various stories and tales are published and compete with each other on their novelty. The situation has reached such extremes that even newspapers and magazines carry adaptations of really old fiction, and the momentum being thus, the number of fictional stories of this country today knows no limit, being in the tens of millions. . . . From the long past, the custom of our country has been to think of fiction as one means of instruction, but while it has been proclaimed over and over that its object is to discipline evil and to encourage good, [people] in actual practice only enjoy bloody and cruel or extremely ob-

---

1. For an English-language examination of *dokufu-mono*, see Marran, *Poison Woman*. For a comprehensive discussion of the development of *tsuzukimono* during the Meiji period, see Honda, *Shinbun shōsetsu no tanjō*.

2. As a result of the popularity of *tsuzukimono*, newspapers, whose primary purpose was the reporting of facts, were caught in a quandary, both seeking to maintain their claim as providers of truthful facts and needing to reflect readers' demand for the sensational and the scandalous in order to sell. In fact, newspaper serialization, discontinuation of serialization, and the completion of the story in the form of *yomihon* (literally, "reading books," which were fictional stories produced for entertainment) would be a common course of development for *dokufu-mono*. For example, "Torioi Omatsu no den" (The story of actress Omatsu), serialized in *Kanayomi shinbun* from December 10, 1877 and said to have been the work that brought popularity to the genre, discontinued its serialization on January 11, 1878, stating that the story would be made into a *yomihon*. For more information, see Oku, *Sukyandaru no Meiji*, 75.

scene stories, and it is rare to see people who even give a glance to a plot that is more serious. . . . And because they follow the trends of society, [the authors] cannot shed the pretext of intending to encourage good, so they distort human feelings, bend social conditions, and create impossible plots to incorporate the object of encouraging good.[3]

Lamenting the state of narrative fiction, which was gaining popularity at the cost of quality in Meiji society, this passage criticizes the predilection of contemporary authors and readers for immoral stories that distort reality and calls for their reform. According to Shōyō, whose treatise was one of the first organized efforts in the world to argue for the artistic value of narrative fiction, the key to such reform was the rejection of the didactic framework (*kanzen chōaku* or "encouraging virtue and chastising vice"), which prevents the accurate portrayal of the true subjects of the novel that are made clear by the treatise's most famous proclamation: "The principal object of the novel is human feelings [*ninjō*]; social conditions [*setai*] and customs [*fūzoku*] come next" (68).

When considered within Shōyō's critical position toward extant Meiji narratives exemplified by *tsuzukimono*, "Tane hiroi" presents itself as a contradictory work within his literary project that exposes his ambivalence toward the literary genre he sought to reform through *Shōsetsu shinzui*. As suggested by the plot summary of the story given above, the ending of "Tane hiroi" demands a radical reinterpretation on the part of readers in making sense of the story. No longer is the work just about a writer who eavesdrops on a strange conversation to use it as the "seed" for his next story, but it also becomes a story that suggests the powerful effect that *tsuzukimono* exercises on the imagination of its readers and the allure of the act of eavesdropping that is at the source of such imagination. To the extent that it is a dream, the narrator is free to assume any character position that he desires within the story-world. Yet, the narrator of "Tane hiroi" finds himself in the position of an eavesdropper within the conspiratorial framework between the narrator and the reader of *tsuzukimono*: the identification of the narrator-as-character of "Tane hiroi" was with the gaze of the narrator-as-perspective, who, standing outside the story's events, perceived and described the private affairs of individuals as if he were an eavesdropper existing inside the story-world.

But while it may appear as a contradiction and an aberration within Shōyō's literary project, there is no denying that "Tane hiroi" took up the

3. Tsubouchi, *Shōsetsu shinzui*, 40–42. All subsequent references to this source will appear in the text in parentheses.

project's primary themes, namely, the desire to penetrate the private lives of people and the role of eavesdropping as an act, perspective, and technique that enables the fulfillment of such desire.[4] Indeed, it was, as I argue in this chapter, Shōyō's need to legitimate his relentless pursuit of these themes in Meiji society—that is, to dissociate the novel from a similar emphasis expressed as desire to eavesdrop by the narrators of *tsuzukimono* and "Tane hiroi" alike—that led to his experimentation with the detective fiction genre. Through the examination of his theoretical and fictional works in conjunction with the translated detective story *Nisegane tsukai*, this chapter reconsiders Shōyō's literary project and makes clear the nature of the intricate connection between the novel and the detective story in their nascent stages of emergence. In so doing, this chapter illustrates how the detective story assisted in the establishment of a modern authorship suitable for the age of *bunmei kaika*, by functioning as a tool to address the inherent contradiction between Shōyō's articulation of the novel based on the notion of the moral author and the potential of his endeavor to evoke the immoral eavesdropper.

Shōsetsu shinzui *and the Two Gazes of the Novelist*

Although the most famous passage in *Shōsetsu shinzui* is undoubtedly the aforementioned proclamation on "human feelings," "social conditions," and "customs," we must also recognize that this statement, which epitomizes the commitment to verisimilitude and criticism of didactic framework that are often seen as the backbone of Shōyō's treatise, was nothing new. As early as 1821, Tamenaga Shunsui (1790–1843), the pioneer of *ninjōbon* (books on human feelings), used the phrase *ninjō setai* to describe the proper subjects of depiction for narrative fiction in the preface to his first work *Akegarasu nochi no masayume* (Prophetic dream after the morning crow).[5] As Peter Kornicki has noted, moreover, various Meiji writers, including Kanagaki Robun (1829–1904), were naming the terms *ninjō* and *setai* as the goals of fiction during the late 1870s and early 1880s.[6] These precedents clearly set Shōyō's rhetoric within a pre-existing paradigm es-

---

4. In his seminal work on *Shōsetsu shinzui*, Kamei Hideo argues that one of the most distinctive characteristics of Shōyō's literary theory "even if we compare it to the contemporaneous theories of the novel in English [was its emphasis on] the private realm and the 'interior' [*naimen*] as the reason of being for the novel" (*"Shōsetsu" ron*, 134).

5. Hiraoka, *Nihon kindai bungaku no shuppatsu*, 18.

6. Kornicki, *The Reform of Fiction in Meiji Japan*, 33–35.

tablished, in particular, by *ninjōbon* and suggest his attempt to utilize an indigenous model in developing his notion of the modern novel.[7] Indeed, as I hope to show, the significance of Shōyō's literary project had less to do with new terms or even new ways to construct fictional narratives and more to do with a new strategy to establish the social importance of the novel and its author, which was fundamental to the negotiation between past traditions of Japanese fiction and the newly emergent Western novels in the Meiji period.

The underpinnings of such an ideological project manifest themselves most clearly in the way that Shōyō couches the term *ninjō* within the visual dichotomy between the exterior (seen) and the interior (unseen), a dichotomy ubiquitous in the treatise. After the aforementioned proclamation, for example, Shōyō rearticulates *ninjō* as *jōyoku* (passions) and *hyaku-hachi bonnō* (108 earthly desires) and proposes their natural conflict with *dōri* (reason) and *ryōshin* (conscience) within the individual as the true subject of the novel, identifying the task of the novelist as relentless exploring and exposing of such conflict:

> Humans should have two phenomena, external actions that manifest on the outside and thoughts that are hidden on the inside. . . . The likes of actions that can be seen on the outside have been depicted for the most part, but the likes of the thoughts that are contained on the inside can be diffuse, and it is rare to succeed in their depiction. To pierce the depth of this *ninjō* and to depict, in detail without missing anything, the inner workings of the inside of hearts . . . and to make human feelings manifest vividly—this is to be the duty of our novelists (69–70).

Significantly, Shōyō primes the vectored interpretation of this goal of the novel and the novelist by positioning it within the rhetoric of *bunmei kaika* and "the framework of Herbert Spencer's theory of social Darwinism, which lay behind many Meiji period notions of modernization and westernization."[8] Rather than simply positing the Western novel as the

---

7. Literary scholars have pointed out Shōyō's use of the terms *ninjō* and *setai*, among other factors, to discuss the fluidity that exists between the fictional narratives of the Edo and Meiji periods. For example, in recent years, Jonathan Zwicker has argued: "To take *Shōsetsu shinzui* as the starting point for investigating the semantic history of *shōsetsu* in Japanese not merely severs—artificially—this history at its midpoint, it also and perhaps more importantly misrecognizes the fact that this was the framework within which Shōyō was himself, quite self-consciously, working" (*Practices of the Sentimental Imagination*, 158).

8. Tomi Suzuki, *Narrating the Self*, 20.

most advanced form of narrative fiction that Japanese writers should strive toward and ultimately surpass—no doubt echoing the popular slogan *oitsuke oikose* (to catch up and surpass) that was used to promote *bunmei kaika*—Shōyō instead delineates sociohistorical causes to explain the evolution of narrative forms, beginning with mythology and ending with the novel as the dominant art form of present society. And it is in the latest shift in this evolutionary process, "the decline of theater" and the blossoming of "the true novel," that the dichotomy between the interior and exterior takes on explanatory power as the central cog of his ideological project (61). In an "uncivilized and unenlightened society," Shōyō argues, people do not have much power to reason so their internal thoughts and emotions are expressed outwardly, and, thus, theater, which is a narrative form based on external expressions, flourishes (61). But the novel takes over "when the intellect advances" because, in an age of reason, "one tries to suppress one's passions and tries not to show [them] clearly on one's face" (62).[9]

By promoting the link between the objectives of the novel with the preconditions of its emergence in such a manner, Shōyō establishes the unique social position of the novel and the novelist in "the age of reason/civilization" (*kaimei no yo*) (56). On the one hand, the flourishing of the novel becomes a sign that a society and its people have embraced reason and, thus, are 'civilized' and 'enlightened.' In this sense, Shōyō's treatise posits the production of fictional narratives that fit his articulation of the novel as a way to demonstrate the 'civilized' and 'enlightened' nature of Meiji Japan, and, as such, fictional writing, which was traditionally considered a frivolous pastime for entertainment of women and children, becomes elevated into a national project.[10] On the other hand, to the extent

---

9. It can be argued that the developmental understanding of the novel is inconsistently applied in the course of *Shōsetsu shinzui*. For example, Shōyō argues that Bakin's *Hakkenden* is a less developed work of fiction than *Genji monogatari*. However, this can be seen as Shōyō's complex strategy to reconstruct the lineage of Japanese fiction in terms of native and not Chinese-influenced works. Atsuko Ueda provides a discussion of this strategy in her *Concealment of Politics, Politics of Concealment*, 28–33.

10. For more information on the understanding of fiction prior to *Shōsetsu shinzui*, see Tomi Suzuki, *Narrating the Self*, 15–32. We should note that the rise of the political novels in the early 1880s also played a significant role in changing the public's view toward fictional narratives precisely because political novels, as a vehicle to spread the ideals of the Freedom and People's Rights movement,

that Shōyō's evolutionary view of narrative forms posits the suppression of passions by reason and the resulting cessation of their external expression in *actual* human beings as historical preconditions for the development of the novel, the task of the novelist rhetorically becomes what laypersons can no longer do in the society in which they live: to understand what is going on underneath the appearances of others. Fittingly, such an ideological framing of the novelist as a solver of a real-world problem finds support in the oft-cited phrases of *Shōsetsu shinzui*—"observe passively" (*tada bōkan shite*) and "depict as it is" (*arinomama o mosha suru*)—that present the novelist, albeit only figuratively, as an external observer who maintains critical distance from the object of depiction (71).

The privileged position of the novelist in the modern age in conjunction with the novelist's façade as an observer, then, makes the detective the perfect metaphor for the novelist and, by extension, the narrator. Not only is the criminal, the object of the detective's gaze, an extreme example of an individual who must suppress external manifestations of the interior through reason (as self-interest that such manifestations would lead to exposure), but the *myth* of the master detective is also founded upon his ability to read internal thoughts and emotions by means of external appearances and behavior. We only need to recall the famous scene in Edgar Allan Poe's "The Murders in the Rue Morgue" (1841) in which the detective Auguste Dupin reads the thoughts of the narrator, leading the latter to exclaim: "Tell me, for Heaven's sake . . . the method—if method there is—by which you have been enabled to fathom my soul in this matter."[11]

Such a scene, which would be repeated in Arthur Conan Doyle's Sherlock Holmes tales, posits the detective as a master novelist, if we were to follow Shōyō's definition. Of course, it is not the detective but the psychologist to whom Shōyō explicitly likens the novelist in *Shōsetsu shinzui*, urging the creation of characters according to "the logic of psychology" (70).[12] But either way, the analogy does not seem to be a rigor-

---

made clear the value of fictional narratives as educational tools and political motivators.

11. Poe, "The Murders in the Rue Morgue," in *The Short Fiction of Edgar Allan Poe*, 180.

12. During his first and second year at Tokyo University, Shōyō attended psychology classes that focused primarily on the teachings of the evolutionary psychologist Alexander Bain (1818–1903). For Shōyō's early influences, including that of Bain, see Ochi, "*Shōsetsu shinzui* no botai."

ous one, for the primary task of the novelist as articulated in *Shōsetsu shinzui* lies not in being a true detective or a psychologist—that is, in understanding one's interior through external appearances and behavior and, more specifically, in constructing a code that will make the exterior *legible* as effects of the interior—but rather in portraying the internal shift of thoughts and emotions in his characters as an entity with full access to them.[13] The novelistic gaze, which 'observes' the interior, does not do so through the senses but through the power of imagination as an authority that offers imaginary or fictional access to a barrier 'created' by the breakdown of correspondence between interior and exterior.

But fittingly when considering the emphasis Shōyō places on the presentation of the novelist as an external observer, Shōyō's use of the dichotomy between interior and exterior in *Shōsetsu shinzui* extends beyond the confines of what I have called the novelistic gaze to demarcate another level of the apparent and the hidden. Here the detective becomes a more apt metaphor than the psychologist; whereas a psychologist's task is focused on the understanding of human psyche, the detective's task is not restricted to connecting a person's interior with the exterior. The detective had some dirty work to do as well. He had more hands-on tasks of collecting evidence, disguising himself to infiltrate the world of crime, eavesdropping on conversations, and, in most general terms, prying into people's private lives and discovering their secrets. And the same seems to be the case for Shōyō's novelist:

> To freely dissect people's hearts, which would be impossible in reality, to enter the bedroom of a dignitary's wife, which is not to be entered without good reason, and write about her behavior and actions, or to depict the situations inside [the house] without considering whether the gates or sliding doors are closed—these are the freedoms of a novelist (149–50).

As this passage reveals, the novel operates on two different but interrelated levels of the invisible or the inaccessible, which Shōyō delineates without differentiation here. On the one hand, the novel "dissect[s] people's hearts" to make visible the *ninjō* that is hidden beneath the exterior.

---

13. Shōyō writes: "So if [the novelist] wants to create a person and depict feelings, then [the novelist] should first stipulate temporarily that this person already possesses what is called passion. If such and such event were to take place to give this or that stimulation, what kind of feelings would be awoken in this person? Or would there be certain differences in the workings of such feelings, not to mention the nature of this person, according to his past education and the temperament of his occupation?" (74).

On the other hand, the novel reveals the private affairs of people—the actions and behavior of a woman in her bedroom or goings-on behind closed doors—that those who are not family members or close acquaintances are restricted from knowing in real life. In this passage, then, Shōyō conflates the interior with the private life of individuals, thereby representing the epistemological dichotomy between interior and exterior as a spatial dichotomy between the public and the private.[14]

Through the dual metaphor of the interior and the exterior, *Shōsetsu shinzui* presents the novelist as a bearer of two distinct gazes, which had contrasting literary significances in Meiji Japan. Rarely seen in fictional narratives of and before Meiji Japan but prevalent in Western fiction, a gaze that penetrates and portrays in detail the interior thoughts and emotions of characters is the explicit centerpiece in Shōyō's articulation of what constitutes a modern novel. Not only does he make this gaze the characteristic privilege of the novelist but he also makes the need for this gaze the necessary condition for the emergence of the novel as the dominant narrative form of a given society in the first place.[15] In contrast, the explicit manifestation of the gaze that penetrates into the private lives of characters was a carry-over from and a staple of Edo-period fiction, most notably the works of *ninjōbon*. Extensive depictions of the inner thoughts and feelings of characters being all but non-existent, this tradition most often presented the narrator as "an expressive subject who positions himself on the borderline that differentiates the inside and the outside of the scenes of a story-world [and] from there . . . 'peeps' and 'eavesdrops' on the actions and behavior of characters."[16]

Like his recycling of the terms *ninjō* and *setai* as the primary goals of the novel, these two gazes of the novelist make evident that Shōyō's conceptualization of the novel involved an intricate negotiation between

14. As we will see in the next section, the spatial dichotomy between the public and the private had particular sociohistorical significance in the Meiji period that went beyond literary theory and narrative perspective.

15. As Maeda Ai states: "Meiji fiction gained the qualification as a modern novel when the narrator who talks about the interior of the Other was positioned solidly in the story-world" ("Meiji no hyōgen shisō to buntai," 6).

16. Komori, *Kōzō to shite no katari*, 166. Komori uses this explanation to compare the narrator of Futabatei Shimei's *Ukigumo*, especially of the narrator in its first section, to the archetypal narrators of *ninjōbon*, but, as many scholars attest, *Tōsei shosei katagi*, discussed below, employs a similar narrator. For an example of such a discussion regarding the similarity of the narrator in these two works, see Yamada Yūsaku, *Gensō no kindai*, 116–30.

Japanese tradition, as exemplified by *ninjōbon*, and the Western realistic novel. In this sense, Shōyō's decision to mix the old with the new in his first full-length fiction *Tōsei shosei katagi* (Manners and lives of contemporary students; 1885–1886), about a group of students at a private Tokyo school, is hardly surprising. At the most basic level, *Tōsei shosei katagi*, by telling the story of the student-protagonist Komachida Sanji and his relationship to the geisha Tanoji, mixes the new subject of the Meiji novel—the student—with the archetypal heroine of Edo fiction, the geisha. But more significantly, such mixing extends to the core of the story, on the level of narrative development and narration: to the extent that Sanji's attraction to Tanoji comes into conflict with his 'rational' awareness that he would be better off without Tanoji, *Tōsei shosei katagi* explores how *ninjō* as passions come into conflict with and are ultimately suppressed by reason.

Yet, despite this choice to implement the new objective of the novel, Shōyō nonetheless chooses to employ the paradigmatic narrator of the pre-existing fictional narratives described above. Given the characteristics of such a narrator not to describe the inner thoughts and feelings of characters, however, it was natural, if not necessary, that satisfying the new objective of the novel through such a narrator proved itself as a difficult undertaking. For example, while the narrator of *Tōsei shosei katagi* occasionally makes visual observations in a similar manner to "how Sherlock Holmes deduces personal data from things like clothes that are observed by the eye," the conclusions drawn from these observations remain superficial—such as age and social class—rarely divulging information regarding the internal state of characters.[17] Thus, these attempts, rather than being sincere efforts on the part of Shōyō to produce a code to make the interior decipherable by means of the exterior, suggest his strategy to shed light on the limitations of this type of narrator and thereby pave the way for the emergence of a new narrator who embodies the privileged gaze of the novelist. In fact, after another such attempt at a detective's analysis, the narrator concludes that "it is an arbitrary opinion based upon the observation of the author" and thereby relativizes the possible accuracy of his observation and the benefit of these attempts at being a detective.[18]

---

17. Yamada Yūsaku, *Gensō no kindai*, 133–34.

18. Tsubouchi, *Tōsei shosei katagi*, 228. Yamada Shunji discusses this topic by incorporating the work of Kamei Hideo in his essay "*Tōsei shosei katagi* ni okeru 'sakusha' no ichi," 11.

The story's extensive use of dialogue, which is another characteristic of Edo fictions and reflective of the restrictions placed on the story's narrator, also presents Shōyō with difficulties in reconciling the old and the new. On the one hand, the use of dialogue supported by narration is certainly a legitimate method, on the level of literary expression, to indirectly construct the internal turmoil of characters. On the other hand, dialogue, as an interchange of individual utterances through which characters attempt to express and share their internal passions, is precisely what has become difficult in "the age of reason" according to Shōyō's understanding of *ninjō* in *Shōsetsu shinzui*. That is, if the text allows individual utterances by a character to give readers the sense of truthfully expressing internal thoughts and feelings, then it does so at the risk of presenting the character as an individual who is, at best, a bad representative of the age and, at worst, someone who is lacking in reason, the advancement of which prevents the expression of his or her internal passions.

And of course, the subject of this work—the students—are the modern rational individuals *par excellence* not only because of their knowledge of Western values and culture but also because they, having left their communities and flocked to the city for the purpose of education, represent the indecipherability of human beings in the modern age as they confront one another as complete strangers in the metropolis. In this sense, the illegibility of human beings, which founds Shōyō's theory of the novel, is the flip side of Walter Benjamin's comment that the detective story emerges with "the obliteration of the individual's traces in the big-city crowd" that results from urbanization in the modern age.[19] Significantly for the case of early Meiji Japan, the materialization of this condition was sudden and substantial, thanks to the prompt lifting of restrictions on travel that was in effect during the Edo period coupled with new opportunities in the big cities after the Restoration. And as Shōyō highlights in the opening paragraph of *Tōsei shosei katagi*, the student was one of the most conspicuous groups in this process: "Saying that it is a metropolis, various people come from all directions, but above all others the most numerous are rickshaw drivers and students. . . . Everywhere there are drivers and students. There is a sign for a boarding house there; a lantern for a rickshaw house here. There is a private school for

19. Benjamin, "The Paris of the Second Empire in Baudelaire," 43.

Western learning in the side streets; there are rickshaws waiting for passengers at the intersections."[20]

Given the theoretical hurdles associated with combining old literary perspectives with the new themes and goals of the novel, how does the narrator of *Tōsei shosei katagi* attempt to depict *ninjō*? An example of such an attempt can be seen in Shōyō's employment of a specific form of speech, namely, confession—an act in which the external speech sincerely describes the internal thoughts and feelings of a character—exemplified in Section 13 of the text when Komachida confesses to Tanoji his thoughts regarding their relationship. Importantly, it is here that the narrator becomes most like a character who is eavesdropping on a private conversation outside "sliding doors," as the identities of the interlocutors are not disclosed, designated only as "man" and "woman," and the narrator, besides the few stage-direction-like comments inserted parenthetically within the dialogue, disappears in his narration.[21]

In this scene, then, Shōyō juxtaposes the incidence of the character's attempt at a sincere expression of the interior with the narrator's penetration into the private and thereby utilize the eavesdropping gaze of the narrator to take on the function of enhancing the *appearance* of the confession's truthfulness and earnestness. More specifically, the narrative technique in this scene actively invokes a barrier between the interlocutors and the narrator through its continuous 'failure' to provide the readers with visual cues, and, in so doing, confession as a voluntary expression of the interior by a character becomes reframed and reclaimed as a 'hidden' interior that is actively exposed by the narrator who penetrates the barrier via the act of eavesdropping. Through the employment of this narrative technique, moreover, Shōyō actively places the narrator in the position of the unknowing, promoting the façade that the narrator and the readers share the same knowledge regarding what is being 'overheard.' Thus, this scene reiterates the receptive framework of *ninjōbon*, which, as Yamada Shunji has noted, consisted of "a kind of fictitious community where [readers] can form a conspiratorial relationship with the narrator that they had met in the process of weaving a text."[22]

---

20. Tsubouchi, *Tōsei shosei katagi*, 223.

21. As Yamada Shunji notes, a similar technique was employed in Tamenaga Shunsui's *Shungyō hachiman gane* (1836–1838) ("*Tōsei shosei katagi* ni okeru 'sakusha' no ichi," 10).

22. Ibid.

Considering its profound implications within Shōyō's discussion of the novel and the novelist in *Shōsetsu shinzui*, it was only natural that the act of eavesdropping, highlighted in the above example from *Tōsei shosei katagi*, would quickly become a major preoccupation in his fictional writings. As his next work *Imotose kagami* (Mirror of marriage; 1885–1886) clearly illustrates, Shōyō's experimentation with eavesdropping was broad in scope, not confined to the realm of literary practices and narrative techniques that he explored in his first work. Instead, it involved a negotiation with the rapid sociohistorical changes taking place in Meiji Japan, which imbued this old practice with new conceptual significances that would bring to light the fundamental contradiction within Shōyō's articulation of the modern novel.[23]

Eavesdropping and the Paradox of the Novel in Imotose kagami

Written during a similar time frame as *Tōsei shosei katagi*, *Imotose kagami* in many ways is a complement to its immediate predecessor.[24] Whereas

---

23. Of course, eavesdropping not only served as a commonly used technique of past and contemporary Japanese fictions but also constituted, as Ann Gaylin illustrates, a fundamental part of the novel (she states: "Eavesdropping has existed in the novel as long as the novel has existed"), most notably in nineteenth-century novels such as Emily Brontë's *Wuthering Heights*, the sensational novels by Wilkie Collins, and the numerous novels by Honoré de Balzac (*Eavesdropping in the Novel from Austen to Proust*, 1). This fact, it could be argued, was significant for Shōyō's literary project that grasped literary development within an evolutionary framework, for, to the extent that it was a common narrative technique in both Western and Japanese fictional narratives, eavesdropping provided evidence of the 'evolutionary' link between the two.

24. *Imotose kagami* tells the story of the bureaucrat Misawa Tatsuzō who hopes to wed Oyuki, a refined daughter of a high government official. Upon discovering that Oyuki has no feelings for him, he instead marries Otsuji, a fish dealer's uneducated daughter whom he fancied as a student. Soon after, during a business trip to Kansai, Misawa encounters a woman named Sawae whom his father had wronged in the past by not repaying a debt that her daughter Kouno (who has since died) had paid on his behalf. Shocked by her story, Misawa vows to rescue Wakazato, Sawae's younger daughter, who has been sold to a Nezu brothel as a result of the debt of Misawa's father. Upon returning to Tokyo, Misawa contacts Wakazato to convince her to let him pay for her freedom. Because of her husband's repeated lateness in coming home and a letter sent to him by a mysterious woman (Wakazato), Otsuji begins to worry that Misawa is having an affair. Realizing her feelings, Misawa explains to her the story of

the narrator of the former insisted on maintaining its position as an outside observer and an eavesdropper—even employing specific narrative techniques to emphasize such a position—the narrator of *Imotose kagami* is not as adamant, freely moving from transmissions of characters' conversations to depictions of their internal thoughts and feelings in the form of internal monologues. While the employment of the privileged gaze of the novelist may mitigate the story's need to use eavesdropping as a narrative technique like its predecessor, this is not to say that *Imotose kagami* does not share the interest in the notion of eavesdropping with *Tōsei shosei katagi*. Rather, the exploration of the concept of eavesdropping occurs elsewhere in *Imotose kagami*, its most striking quality being the central role played by eavesdropping not as narrative perspective but as concrete story-events for plot development. Overhearing a conversation between Otsuji and Oyuki makes the protagonist Misawa believe that Oyuki has no interest in him and decides to marry Otsuji; listening in on a conversation of gossiping servants at a restaurant about Oyuki's unhappy marriage to Tanuma, a friend of Misawa, forces Misawa to realize his mistake about Oyuki's feelings for him and pushes him to harbor misdirected resentment toward Otsuji. And it is the reporter's eavesdropping of a conversation between Otsuji's sister Oharu and the geisha Wakazato that leads to a false gossip-column account of the intention behind their meeting and to the story's tragic ending as Misawa is dismissed from his official post and Otsuji commits suicide.

Given such prevalence of eavesdropping, it is not surprising that this characteristic of *Imotose kagami* did not go unnoticed by Shōyō's contemporaries. In his essay "*Imotose kagami* o yomu" (Reading *Mirror of marriage*; 1887), Ishibashi Ningetsu (1865–1926), one of the leading literary critics of the Meiji period, objects to Shōyō's repeated use of eavesdropping as "one method of abbreviation," going as far as to state that the story "begins with eavesdropping, ends with eavesdropping, and it is possible to say that the story's central framework is found in eaves-

---

Wakazato, but, egged on by her sister Oharu, Otsuji continues to harbor her suspicions, ultimately enlisting Oharu to go to the brothel to talk to Wakazato. While there, a newspaper reporter in the next room overhears Oharu's conversation with Wakazato and prints an article regarding Misawa's infidelity with Wakazato. As a result of this article, Misawa is forced to leave his government post, and he, in turn, realizes Otsuji's involvement and divorces her. Devastated by this turn of events, Otsuji kills herself.

dropping."[25] While Ningetsu's objection may be warranted, his criticism that the act of eavesdropping functions as a 'lazy' way for Shōyō to develop the story seems to miss the import of this act within *Imotose kagami*. As many scholars have noted, the act of eavesdropping in *Imotose kagami* provides information to characters in general and to Misawa in particular, inciting specific reactions, both internal and external, that determine the course of the narrative.[26] Or to put it in terms of Shōyō's literary theory, the various acts of eavesdropping enable the production of causal relationships between story-events where a peek into the *private* world of others causes *internal* turmoil between *ninjō* and reason, which, in turn, leads to *external* action, and, in so doing, Shōyō synthesizes the two realms that are to be the proper subject of the novel: the interior and the private.

But crucial here is the fact that external actions arrived through such course of development produce one tragedy after another in *Imotose kagami* precisely because information obtained through the various acts of eavesdropping turn out more often than not to be false, as highlighted by the source of all tragedies in the story, namely, the eavesdropping by Misawa of a private conversation between Oyuki and Otsuji. In this conversation, Oyuki tells Otsuji that she does not like Misawa, stating: "I hate people like that. Even if father and mother told me to become his wife, I have . . . no intention of becoming his wife."[27] Upon hearing these harsh words, Misawa gives up his hope of marrying Oyuki and turns his interest toward Otsuji. And as we later discover, Oyuki's mother, who had been hoping to wed Oyuki to Misawa, was also eavesdropping on this conversation, and she too abandons her plan to pursue Misawa as Oyuki's husband. But as we later learn through the peculiar narrative technique

25. Ishibashi, "*Imotose kagami* o yomu," 8. First appearance in *Jogaku zasshi*, January 29, 1887.

26. In his discussion of *Imotose kagami*, Maeda Ai states that the act of eavesdropping in this work functions as "a device that expands the conflict between the 'exterior' and the 'interior' and accelerates the misunderstanding and mistrust not only by Misawa but by all the characters in the story" ("Meiji no hyōgen shisō to buntai," 9). In a similar fashion, Komori Yōichi states that eavesdropping in this story functions as that which "not only produces misunderstanding, but also provides the opportunity for people who have been grasped by the feeling of jealousy to make a false step from 'reason' that they should have preserved" (*Kōzō to shite no katari*, 189).

27. Tsubouchi, *Imotose kagami*, 185. All subsequent references to this source will appear in the text in parentheses.

of the "magic mirror"—named as such in the text—that reflects the true thoughts of a person, Oyuki had in fact been hoping to become Misawa's wife.[28] The magic mirror reveals:

> When I first heard about this [her mother trying to marry her to Misawa], I was so happy that I could jump, but I was embarrassed to show my feelings. And if Misawa wasn't handsome, then there would be no reason to be embarrassed, but I didn't want people to say that I took fancy to his appearance, so I behaved myself and acted as if it was nothing. And when Otsuji said this and that [about Misawa], I said such bad things that were not in my heart because I didn't want her to vie for his attention (217).

As disclosed to the readers some chapters later in such a manner, it was because Oyuki saw Otsuji as her rival for Misawa's affection and was embarrassed to admit her feelings for him that she said what she said about Misawa on that fateful day. In short, Oyuki lied out of self-interest.

Importantly, other narrative details frame Oyuki's falsehood—and succeed in making others believe it as true—as a behavior in accordance with her disposition, which is explicitly characterized as indecipherable. For example, when the narrator introduces her for the first time: "The older sister [Oyuki] was by nature prudent and had a character short on affability from the beginning. So even on occasions when she was deeply happy, her happiness was not conspicuous to the eyes of others, and on occasions when she was very angry, she endured and did not express it in words" (178). And a comment by Oyuki's servant girl Okama regarding Oyuki's reaction to her mother's suggestion that she wed Tanuma instead of Misawa: "Oh, what a strange girl! I have no idea if she's unhappy or happy. With her proud temperament, she might be feigning ignorance regarding her [marriage] to Tanuma because, although she is happy inside, she feels ashamed to be seen by others as such" (216).

Not only do these passages present Oyuki as a person who is difficult to understand, but they also present her as a person who actively suppresses her internal emotions from manifesting on the outside because of the belief that to do so would be embarrassing or shameful. Although the text of *Imotose kagami* does not explain how she has come to hold this belief (except perhaps to say it was "by nature"), we must note the undeniable resemblance between the description of Oyuki's disposition and *Shōsetsu shinzui*'s description of the changes that take place as a soci-

---

28. For details on the "magic mirror," see Maeda, "Meiji no hyōgen shisō to buntai," 10–11.

ety enters into 'civilization and enlightenment.' The following is the longer version of a previously cited fragment regarding this change:

As mental capacities advance, people suppress their passions, trying not to display them frankly on their faces. For example, even when they are very angry, they deliberately soften their expressions and converse calmly; or even when they are extremely sad, they sometimes don't shed a tear. Human feelings change in such a way, and passionate behaviors and appearances gradually disappear (62).

Oyuki then is an indecipherable figure—the 'mystery' to be solved—who is, at least in *Imotose kagami*, the closest embodiment of an individual in "the age of reason" that Shōyō describes in his *Shōsetsu shinzui*.[29] Through the awkward technique of the magic mirror, Shōyō singles out and emphasizes Oyuki's indecipherability, suggesting that even a novelist—whose uncanny ability to penetrate through external appearances that have become impenetrable for the ordinary man in the age of reason sets him apart in society—cannot access her internal thoughts and emotions without the help from the un-modern supernatural tool.

But *Imotose kagami* does not turn out as tragically as it does simply because of Oyuki's indecipherability. It is also the result of Misawa's belief, and to certain extent the belief of Oyuki's mother, that he had understood Oyuki's feelings through his eavesdropping of the conversation between Oyuki and Otsuji. For, the fact that such eavesdropping leads to his decision to marry Otsuji and not Oyuki requires his rejection of the possibility that Oyuki may have ulterior motives (which she does) for saying what she said. As highlighted by his comment after he overhears the conversation, the rejection is subconscious and instantaneous, for such a possibility does not even occur to Misawa: "I see, Oyuki hates me

29. This marks the seemingly obvious but nonetheless peculiar conflation between the object of desire and of knowledge that will have profound effects on the development of the Japanese novel. Although I argued earlier in this chapter that the student presents himself as an emblem of the illegibility of human beings because of his education and of his uprooted condition, it is the woman who is actually presented as a mystery in *Imotose kagami* as well as in other canonical works of modern Japanese literature, including Osei in *Ukigumo* and Yoshiko in *Futon*. Within the context of this argument, the woman as mystery is a result of a projection of the suspicion that the student has for his own kind, a suspicion whose admission would force the student to realize that he is not only a subject of suspecting but also inevitably the object of suspicion. This issue of projection will resurface in the course of the development of the Japanese novel, and I will revisit this issue in the conclusion to Chapter 6.

to this extent on the inside [*naishin*]" (185). To put it in terms of *Shōsetsu shinzui* once again, Misawa believes the external actions (words) of Oyuki as a reflection of her internal feelings, an 'anti-modern' belief that goes against the understanding of human beings as indecipherable in the age of reason. Fittingly, the text makes sure to emphasize the gap that exists between the gullible Misawa and duplicitous others driven by self-interest. For example, after visiting Oyuki's house where Misawa reencounters Otsuji, Misawa's friend Tanuma praises Otsuji and recommends that Misawa take her for his wife, a recommendation which Misawa takes to heart. However, we later find out that this recommendation was a ploy to prevent Misawa from courting Oyuki whom Tanuma hopes to have—and soon takes—as his wife.[30]

Shōyō also provides examples of instances in which truthful utterances are met with suspicion, reiterating the state of communicative breakdown or uncertainty that characterizes the world of *Imotose kagami* and, by extension, contemporary society. Upon realizing that Otsuji has begun to harbor suspicions that he is having an affair, Misawa confesses his involvement with Wakazato to her by explaining the story of his father's wrongdoing to Wakazato's family and by reading the letter written by Wakazato to prove that he is merely trying to help Wakazato leave the brothel. But these efforts do not dissolve Otsuji's suspicions because the letter, despite merely thanking Misawa for his "kindness" (*goshinsetsu*), can be interpreted in more than one way. The narrator states: "Depending on the reader's interpretation, the word 'kindness' can mean 'humanity' [*gi*] or 'love' [*ai*]" (226). Although the narrator leaves Otsuji's interpretation of this word as a mystery, her subsequent actions show that it was the latter. That is, while Misawa made an honest confession, Otsuji doubts its truthfulness due to the multiple possibilities for interpretation inherent in language.

In *Imotose kagami*, Shōyō presents a world where an accurate assessment of whether a certain utterance is true or false proves difficult. The act of eavesdropping by various characters produces scenes that are exemplary of such a state of communication breakdown where the desire of the eavesdropper to know and the eavesdropped to hide his or her true feelings or thoughts are at irreconcilable odds. Through these eavesdropping scenes in which the truth-value of information has a negative

---

30. In his social ambition and duplicity, Tanuma can be seen as the forerunner to Honda Noburu in *Ukigumo*. For passages that portray Tanuma's character, see Tsubouchi, *Imotose kagami*, 213–16.

relationship to how it is obtained (through an act of eavesdropping) and where it originates (behind closed doors), *Imotose kagami* problematizes the epistemological validity of the conflation of the private and the interior, all the while synthesizing them causally on the level of plot through the act of eavesdropping.

This problematization then functions to undermine the narrative technique employed in the critical scene of *Tōsei shosei katagi* that juxtaposes the confessions of characters with the narrator who presents the story as if he were an eavesdropping character. In this previously discussed scene, a conscious attempt is made to augment the *appearance* of truthfulness and earnestness of the confession by presenting it as a conversation behind "sliding doors" captured through the act of eavesdropping. In *Imotose kagami*, the opposite is the case: eavesdropping, rather than being the means to access truthful information, is exposed as an act that only produces the *illusion* of such access precisely because of the way in which the information is obtained. And if *Imotose kagami* points out the shortcoming of eavesdropping as an act that leads to truthful information, then it presents such shortcoming as a *social* disease by ending the string of eavesdropping by various characters with an act of eavesdropping as a professional task. This, of course, is the eavesdropping by a newspaper reporter of a conversation between Oharu and Wakazato that leads to a false report in a gossip-column account, called *zappō*, of the relationship between Misawa and Wakazato directly responsible for the story's tragic end.

Developing rapidly from the early 1870s, the newspaper, as many have argued, functioned as the most effective medium for the inculcation of the public on the ways of *bunmei kaika*.[31] The Newspaper Ordinance (Shinbunshi jōrei) issued in July 1871 made this function of the newspapers explicit, stating that "the goal of the newspaper should be the guiding of people's wisdom" which meant "breaking stubbornly narrow minds to guide them to the state of civilization and enlightenment."[32] One newspaper that took this official guidance to heart, at least on the surface, was the *Yomiuri shinbun*, whose inaugural issue on November 2, 1874 contained the following announcement: "This newspaper intends to take up matters that will serve as a lesson for women and children so

31. There was a popular song in the early Meiji period that went: "To those who don't know *bumei kaika*, boil a newspaper and make them drink it" (cited in Nakanome, "Bunmei kaika no jidai," 220).

32. Reprinted in Matsumoto and Yamamuro, *Genron to media*, 410.

please earnestly arrange nearby matters that are of benefit into a story and send it to us with your name and place."[33] Befitting this didactic intention and its target—the ordinary citizens of Tokyo and its surroundings—the *Yomiuri* deviated from both the *kanbun*-style writing and the focus on political, economic, and foreign matters that were found in such newspapers as the *Yokohama Mainichi shinbun* (first issue, December 8, 1870), *Tōkyō Nichinichi shinbun* (first issue, February 21, 1872), and *Yūbin Hōchi shinbun* (first issue, June 10, 1872), and employed colloquial language to take up news around town. These differences in the *Yomiuri* and the newspapers above would later lead to the distinction between *koshinbun* (small newspapers) and *ōshinbun* (large or prestige newspapers), named as such for the size of the paper that was used.[34]

And it was within the numerous *koshinbun* that quickly blossomed in the latter half of the 1870s that the *zappō* (literally, "miscellaneous report") column emerged to become their mainstay, attracting the interest of the general public. Consisting of reports that might be thought of as a combination of today's tabloid news and neighborhood gossip, *zappō* columns ran stories of a public and private nature—from crime reports to acts of infidelity and from admonition of superstitions to commemoration of filial piety—that were sent in by readers or were gathered by reporters called *tanbōsha*. The targets (or victims) of such news included not only the rich and the famous or geishas and prostitutes but also ordinary people from next door. The panoptic intention of this gossip column can be discerned, for example, in the first issue of the *Yomiuri shinbun*, which warned the readers that "all things good and bad will be known by the newspaper so you won't even be able to have a fight between husband and wife carelessly."[35] This warning was no lie, as reports by eavesdropping neighbors exposing the minutiae of everyday life filled the pages day after day while others wrote in letters expressing the fear

---

33. *Yomiuri shinbun*, November 2, 1874.

34. It has been traditionally understood that the readership of *koshinbun*, which targeted the ordinary citizen, and *ōshinbun*, which targeted the intellectuals, did not overlap until the mid-Meiji 10s, but Yamada Shunji suggests that there were many people who read both *koshinbun* and *ōshinbun*. For details, see Yamamoto, *Shinbun to minshū*, 43–55 and Yamada Shunji, *Taishū shinbun ga tsukuru Meiji no "Nihon,"* 35–36.

35. *Yomiuri shinbun*, November 2, 1874.

that any criminal or immoral act would be discovered by the newspaper for all the world to read.[36]

Within the discursive construct of *zappō* columns, correspondents and reporters alike were to spy on the private lives of people and expose the good and evil (but mostly evil) that had previously gone unnoticed with the newspaper passing judgments based on its position as the harbinger of *bunmei kaika*. The result was that the *zappō* column fostered—and legitimated as socially responsible and culturally productive—the desire to transgress the boundary between public and private spheres and expose what lay behind closed doors. But this is not to say that the production of such desire was the sole doing of the newspapers. Rather, such desire—as well as Shōyō's seemingly obsessive exploration of the topic of eavesdropping—must also be considered in conjunction with the radical changes taking place in the early Meiji period regarding the significance of private and public spheres that provided the conceptual framework within which the desire of the eavesdropper exerted its power.

The primary impetus behind this change took the form of government intervention via various regulations—most systematic of which was the Ordinance of Transgressions and Negligence (Ishiki kaii jōrei) issued in Tokyo prefecture on November 13, 1872—that prohibited such things as sale of erotic prints, nudity, mixed bathing, display of tattoos, urination, and fighting in public spaces.[37] And it was through articulation of the spaces where these regulations took effect—the sphere of enforcement—that the public/private distinction, which was undifferentiated in the Edo period for the most part, became emphasized and bifurcated. Makihara Norio states:

> For the common people, there was still not a clear differentiation between the inside and outside of a house, and the alley was nothing but an extension of the earthen entrance [*doma*]. Therefore, if "the focus of the regulations was on the streets—to make peaceful streets, clean streets, and 'civilized' streets"—then this meant the exfoliation of the streets as a "public" space from a community where the house and the alley were fused. The streets were no longer owned by the people, and "private life" became gradually confined into the house.[38]

---

36. For examples of such letters, see Yamada Shunji, *Taishū shinbun ga tsukuru Meiji no "Nihon,"* 199–219.

37. For details of the ordinance, see Ogi, Kumakura, and Ueno, *Fūzoku sei*, 3–29.

38. Makihara, "Bunmei kaika ron," 256.

Through restrictions placed on acts performed in the streets, including small alleyways, people were forced to differentiate between a space where regulations would be applied and a space where they would be free to continue their 'uncivilized' customs. To the extent that these regulations were primarily concerned with the view (as it relates to the vision and to the opinion) of the Westerner, this differentiation was fundamentally visual in nature.[39] Whether something was considered public—and, thus, restricted by law—or private was determined first and foremost by what was accessible to the eyes of strangers, officials, and Westerners. Thus, public space became a stage where the Japanese would perform according to the externally determined criteria of decorum and the private a realm to where 'uncivilized' activities were expelled.[40]

As this overview makes clear, government regulations and *zappō* columns were intimately linked in their utilization of the rhetoric of *bunmei kaika* to actively construct and separate the private and public spheres in the 1870s and beyond. If government regulations sought to remove 'uncivilized' activities from the public realm, then the *zappō* column emerged as their flip side, exposing the 'uncivilized' activities that had been expelled to the private realm and making them into public spectacle for the purposes of education and entertainment. And if the regulations strengthened the demarcation between public and private spheres through their prohibition of certain activities in specific areas, then the *zappō* columns did the same by presenting the private sphere as something that required transgression and exposure.[41] Indeed, we could argue

---

39. A prime example of the visual nature of these regulations can be seen in one of the earliest and most detailed regulations of the early Meiji, which related to the issue of skin exposure, whether it involved taking off one's shirt in public or mixed bathing. And it was the characteristic of Japanese people not to be sensitive about nudity that impressed or surprised the Westerners most. For details on regulations on nudity and its relationship to the Western gaze, see Imanishi, *Kindai Nihon no sabetsu to sei bunka*, 129–80. Also see Oku, *Bunmei kaika no minshū*, 5–13, 159–67.

40. The need on the part of the government to show Westerners that Japan was a civilized nation stemmed largely from Japan's desire to renegotiate the unequal treaties, which Japan was forced to sign with the Western nations during the late Edo and early Meiji periods.

41. But this is not to say that the government was satisfied with merely regulating what happened on the street, as the door-to-door surveys (*toguchi chōsa*) by police officers went into full effect in 1876. As a report made by the Tokyo police in 1879 reveals, this practice was intended not only to monitor the identi-

that the visual barrier necessitated by the government regulations produced a prohibitive rift between the inside and the outside, and this rift (as Lacanian distance) in turn produced the desire to know what existed on the inside. In this context, the eavesdropper, as a presence existing at the boundary between the public and the private—literally, under the eaves just outside house walls—functions as the marker that actively produces and reproduces the demarcation between public and private spheres. For, while the eavesdropper satisfies the desire to transgress the barrier by gaining access to what is going on behind the barrier, he also refuses to penetrate the barrier directly via physical or visual means, thereby maintaining his distance to the object of desire. Instead of being a direct penetration of the barrier, the access gained through eavesdropping is a *linguistic substitution* via auditory means of a visual desire.

That such a nonvisual 'gaze' succeeded in addressing the desires of the reading public can be surmised from the growing popularity of *koshinbun* from the late 1870s into the 1880s—fueled by *zappō* columns and their longer, more narrative and fictional form *tsuzukimono* discussed earlier in this chapter—as its counterpart *ōshinbun* deteriorated.[42] In treating the subject of eavesdropping, then, Shōyō's *Imotose kagami* took up a subject and a discursive framework that had become embedded within the popular consciousness of his readers through their encounter with the *zappō* column on a daily basis. As we have seen, however, the story's position on eavesdropping is a highly negative one, and it seems only fitting that Shōyō sought to explicitly make this point the moral thrust of the story through a narrator's intrusion near the end of the story:

> There is nothing more sinful than overhearing [*tachigiki*] . . . it is the same as eavesdropping [*nusumigiki*] on an important secret without the person's consent. Even if one does not become a criminal by law, what is it but a theft of morality? In the world of today in which one is free in general to do as he pleases as long as one does not violate the rights of others, does one have to endure the finger pointing of others into private matters relating to one's intimate affairs? (241).

---

ties and occupations of people living in a specific address but also to determine their characters and beliefs. For the details of this practice, see Obinata, *Nihon kindai kokka no seiritsu to keisatsu*, 200–203.

42. In 1880, daily circulation of *ōshinbun* (36,024) accounted for 42 percent and *koshinbun* (49,410) 58 percent of Tokyo newspapers. In 1885, the number was 28 percent for *ōshinbun* (28,686) and 72 percent for *koshinbun* (73,924) (figures are from Tsuchiya, *Taishūshi no genryū*, 157).

Although Shōyō goes on to discuss the evils of eavesdropping from a variety of angles—from human psychology to the structure of Japanese houses—the cited passage, which begins the rant on eavesdropping as an immoral act, frames the ensuing discussion within the ethical framework of privacy.[43] Employing the fashionable terminology of the Freedom and People's Rights movement, the passage posits the private sphere as an untouchable space where one should be "free [*jiyū*] in general to do as he pleases" as long as what occurs behind closed doors "does not violate the rights [*kenri*] of others." In so doing, Shōyō indirectly criticizes the *zappō* columns and the 'gaze' of the eavesdropper that they promote, offering a different understanding of the private sphere in the process. Rather than being a space for 'uncivilized' and 'unenlightened' activities that need to be exposed and admonished (*zappō* columns) or hidden away from view (government regulations), Shōyō presents the activities of the private sphere in positive terms as an "important secret" and "intimate affairs" and, thus, as something to be respected.

But Shōyō runs into a problem here, for the goal of the novel is precisely to expose what happens in the most private of the private, and, in this sense, a respect for privacy is exactly what the novel does not have. As we have seen, Shōyō's notion of the novel is founded upon the detailed depiction of the private lives of its characters, which he couches in the rhetoric of relentless exposing by a novelist who "observe[s] passively" and "depict[s] as it is." Albeit metaphorical, these epitomes of Shōyō's realism prescribe the treatment of characters as if they were real human beings and present the novelist as an eavesdropper regardless of

---

43. The rant continues as follows: "Unlike the people of other countries who live in solid stone houses and lock their doors without fail, people of our country live in houses that are thin-walled and bunched up closely . . . not to mention the sliding doors and paper doors, if one decides to eavesdrop, it is easy to know the private affairs of others. So people of our country, since they are not sages, cannot gain a sense of relief, and they cannot even talk to themselves from the fear of being heard by others. . . . After all, I wouldn't think to criticize the act of overhearing so much if it remained with the hearing of truths, but overhearing is for the most part mishearing, and from the old days, to become falsely accused of a crime is normally the result of a mistake in overhearing. . . . when overhearing, everyone holds his breath with all his effort, worries not to be noticed by others, and listens with all his might. Thus, the mind is probably in a frenzy, missing parts here and there, and upon encountering places that are hard to understand or hear, he thinks that it is probably this way or that way with groundless suspicion and bias" (241–42).

whether the narrator assumes a perspective of the eavesdropper, as was the case in *Tōsei shosei katagi*. Thus, such a diatribe draws attention to this potential of the novelist and, by extension, the inherently paradoxical nature of Shōyō's formulation of the novel, which Maeda Ai has succinctly described as "the contradiction between modern civil ethics that respects the privacy of individuals and the logic of a modern novel that delves boldly into the internal life of individuals."[44]

By bringing attention to this paradox of the novel, *Imotose kagami*'s vehement criticism of eavesdropping may appear to be an instance of Shōyō shooting himself in the foot. But I would argue that it is also possible to see it as the opposite: the moral criticism of eavesdropping not only evokes the paradox of the novel but also represents Shōyō's attempt to resolve this paradox. Might not the structure of *Imotose kagami*—the over-reliance on eavesdropping for narrative development followed by an extensive narrator's intrusion that criticizes this act from all angles—be seen as Shōyō's attempt to foreground and tackle this paradox? By telling a story in which the various acts of eavesdropping lead to misinformation and ultimately tragedy, the narrator positions himself to explicitly criticize such acts and the invasion of privacy that they represent, thereby retaining his moral high ground all the while suggesting his difference from the eavesdropping characters in the story. The aforementioned problematization of the conflation between the private and the interior on the part of the characters makes clear their inability to cut through appearances despite their desire, unlike the novelist who is, by Shōyō's definition, someone who can do precisely what they as ordinary people cannot do. The eavesdropping characters assert, albeit negatively, the privileged position occupied by the novelist in the age of reason.

In 'chastising' the act of eavesdropping as a 'vice' in order to inculcate his readers, however, Shōyō also seems to be walking a fine line between implementing the educational role of the novel, which he espouses in *Shōsetsu shinzui*, and operating within the framework of *kanzen chōaku*, which he vehemently criticizes in the same treatise.[45] No doubt, Shōyō is treading dangerous waters, but when we consider the following passage from *Shōsetsu shinzui*, we see the way in which the rejection of the

---

44. Maeda, "Noberu no mosaku," 306–7.

45. Atsuko Ueda provides an insightful discussion of the significance of *kanzen chōaku* during the Meiji period (*Concealment of Politics, Politics of Concealment*, 44–48).

didactic framework that paves the way for the realistic novel gives rise to a new type of a moral framework. Shōyō writes:

Because this society in which we live still is in the position of half-civilization, there are many cruel people, and occasionally there are obscene incidents. If, just because one selfishly disliked these [people and incidents], one disregarded them, the story that will be depicted would be a thing that is based on the author's ideals and cannot be said to be the conditions of the period. . . . Obscene love stories should be written, cruel incidents should be told, but when one writes these [stories] it requires that the author's heart is pure and unmotivated. . . . If the author himself enjoys exposing and writing about secret love affairs, the inner thoughts of the author will unknowingly manifest themselves on the page, and discerning readers will not be able to persevere and will stop reading (136–37).

In this passage criticizing contemporary Meiji fictions for employing the didactic framework as a moral license to tell obscene or immoral stories, we see that Shōyō's concern does not lie with their content (the immoral incidents or behaviors that are depicted within the narrative) but in their execution (the authorial attitude toward the objects of depiction). In order to present a realistically depicted story, Shōyō admits that "obscene" and "cruel" incidents, which are part of contemporary Japanese society, need to be taken up. His qualm with extant narratives of Meiji Japan exemplified by *tsuzukimono*—the objects of his reform—is the lack of distance shown by the authors in depicting these incidents, as reflected in the eavesdropping narrator who fosters a conspiratorial relationship with the readers. According to him, the "author's heart" must be "pure" and "unmotivated" in describing these incidents, a sentiment that is echoed in his introduction to the second half of *Tōsei shosei katagi* where he writes: "However vulgar and base in nature the human feelings, social conditions, or words [that are depicted in the story] may be, if their spirit is not vulgar, then [one] should not denounce them as base."[46]

---

46. Tsubouchi, *Tōsei shosei katagi*, 331. Indeed, such belief expressed by Shōyō went beyond paratexts and literary theories, for he had consciously been incorporating the world of *zappō* columns and *tsuzukimono* into the world of the novel. For example, Maeda Ai hypothesizes that the romance between Komachida and Tanoji may have been influenced by the newspaper serial "Asao Yoshie no rireki" (The life of Asao Yoshie), which appeared in *Tōkyō e'iri shinbun* from April 26 to August 5, 1882 (Maeda, "Gesaku bungaku to *Tōsei shosei katagi*," 116–33). And in *Imotose kagami*, Shōyō explicitly notes in the text (203) that he had gained the idea for the story of Wakazato's mother Sawae—of how she was wronged by

But how are we to recognize whether the author's "spirit" is "vulgar" or not? According to Shōyō, such a determination is an easy one for "discerning readers" because "the inner thoughts of the author will unknowingly manifest themselves on the page." But this comment certainly does not provide us with a method to discern the immorality or non-immorality of a given text on the practical level of fiction writing and reading. As we have seen, the extensive narrative intrusion in *Imotose kagami*, which criticizes the act of eavesdropping, attempts to maintain the author's "pure" and "unmotivated" stance toward what he narrates and provides an example of the difference in authorial stance between the novel and contemporary fictional narratives whose author "enjoys exposing and writing about secret love affairs." In so doing, the modern novel—whose emergence depends, according to Shōyō, on the rejection of the didactic framework—gives birth, paradoxically, to a moral author whose nonvulgar "spirit" is guaranteed by the critical distance he keeps from the content of his depiction.

Such 'resolution' of the paradox of the novel in *Imotose kagami* seems to have not been a satisfactory one for Shōyō, however. Clearly discernable from his relentless pursuit of the subject of eavesdropping in his fictions, the paradox of the novel continued to be a fundamental theoretical problem of his literary project. And it was, I would argue, the preoccupation with this paradox and the search for the moral "spirit" that prompted his experimentation with the detective fiction genre in *Nisegane tsukai*.

Nisegane tsukai *and the Transformation of a Bungling Detective*

"Let us leave aside its value as a novel, but from the point of view of the impression it leaves, there is nothing more interesting."[47] So Shōyō writes in his introduction to *Nisegane tsukai*, the translation of *XYZ* (1883) by

---

Misawa's father, forcing Sawae to sell Wakazato's services to a brothel—from a serialized report entitled "Geigi no kontan" (Complicated circumstances of a geisha), which appeared in the *zappō* column of *Yomiuri shinbun* during February 1884. Shōyō's incorporation of the world of *zappō* and *tsuzukimono* into the world of the novel could be understood as an attempt to present a "vulgar" story in a non-vulgar manner.

47. Tsubouchi, *Nisegane tsukai*, 662. All subsequent references to this source will appear in the text in parentheses.

Anna Katharine Green (1846–1935). Appearing on November 27, 1887 in the *Yomiuri shinbun*, this first installment foreshadows the sentiment expressed by the *Kokumin no tomo* editorial in 1893 (discussed in the Introduction): detective fiction, while interesting as a form of entertainment, has no literary value, even or especially in a country which has just begun its path toward the modern novel. No doubt Shōyō, who had just completed his *Shōsetsu shinzui*, in which he reconsidered the cultural role of fiction and sought to position the Western realistic novel as the model toward which Japanese authors should strive, had to be careful of the examples he posited. He did not want Japanese authors to mistake *Nisegane tsukai* for an exemplar of the novel he sought. But unlike in the *Kokumin no tomo* editorial, Shōyō does not see this example of detective fiction as an useless form of entertainment. Arguing that plot must come before the investigation of *ninjō* because a good plot is what makes people read, Shōyō concludes the first installment of *Nisegane tsukai* with the proclamation to embark on his translation of Green's highly "interesting" text in order to "study the workings of plot" as a part of his training to become a novelist (662).[48]

Significantly, as the plot from which Shōyō sought to learn clearly reveals, Anna Katharine Green's *XYZ* is, in short, a *failed* detective story, and its narrator-detective no Sherlock Holmes.[49] True, he solves a crime

---

48. Shōyō uses a citation from a French writer in his argument: "Eight or nine out of ten animals of reading society read with their eyes. There are barely any that read with their hearts. If an author hopes for a good reputation, he should put tangible things first and intangible *ninjō* second. More specifically, put plot before unsurfacing. The first thing to do is to change what lies immediately before their eyes" (661).

49. *XYZ* tells a story of a government detective who is dispatched to Brandon, Massachusetts, on a money counterfeiting case to investigate suspicious letters being mailed to "X.Y.Z." and picked up by a mysterious recipient at its post office. There, the narrator discovers a letter—with code-like language designating a meeting place and a password ("counterfeit")—that he alters so that he can take the place of the intended recipient to rendezvous with the letter's sender in the garden of the millionaire Benson's mansion on the night it will host a costume ball. Acting as the letter's recipient, the narrator makes the appointment and successfully infiltrates the ball, but he soon realizes his mistake. The plot involving the letter turns out not to concern a counterfeiting scam but the reuniting of Benson and his disowned son Joe, assisted by Joe's brother Hartley and sister Carrie. Before the narrator can rectify the situation, however, Hartley escorts him to the library for a meeting with Benson who quickly drops dead upon entering the room after drinking from the wineglass that was on the table.

in this story—the murder of the millionaire Benson—but this crime has no relationship to the money counterfeiting case that the government ordered him to investigate and is encountered as a consequence of a critical misstep in his treatment of the suspicious letters addressed to "X.Y.Z." In a flash, the narrator decides that one of these letters is the letter he is looking for, although the narrator (as well as the readers) should already recognize at this point that the lead which brought him to this town was a false one, as the letters that caught the authorities' attention—the letters that are picked up every night by the same individual who is not the mysterious recipient of *the* letter—were unrelated to the counterfeiting case. Nonetheless, the narrator proceeds to alter the meeting place designated in the letter so that he, and not its intended recipient, will rendezvous with the letter's sender at the costume ball held at Benson's mansion. Thus, while it is true that this rash decision enables the narrator to solve a murder case, the accomplishment is nothing but an accidental result of the narrator's misunderstanding and mishandling of evidence. In fact, such incompetence on the part of the detective would be the norm in this story, promoting the understanding of the narrator-detective as a dupe rather than a hero.

As such, it is no wonder that Green's *XYZ* employs a first-person narrative to tell a confessional story, for it is this mode of narration that is particularly suited to depict the sense of self-reflection—including the feeling of shame—that might naturally arise in the process of recounting such ineffectiveness on the part of the detective. In the course of the narrative being told at a future time when the narrator has had a chance to reflect upon his past actions, a clear distinction develops between the *narrated* self, the rash detective, and the *narrating* self who is repenting the actions of the former self. The following comment at the story's end succinctly summarizes the narrator's feeling regarding his involvement in the Benson affair: "I was too much ashamed of the curiosity which was the mainspring of my action to publish each and every particular of my conduct abroad."[50]

Hartley immediately arrives at the scene, and the narrator understands all. Hartley, thinking that the narrator was Joe, has framed him for the murder of their father. In the investigation that follows, Hartley cleverly guides the discussion to incriminate his brother, but the narrator reveals his identity by discarding his disguise and incriminates Hartley for the murder of his father instead.

50. Green, *XYZ*, 97. All subsequent references to this source will appear in the text in parentheses.

Given the archetypal nature of Green's first-person narrative, it seems quite fitting that Shōyō decided to translate this story when he did, for, as Komori Yōichi notes, 1887 was the year when a sudden interest in the first-person narration form arose among Japanese writers.[51] While the specific import of this form for Shōyō will be discussed a bit later, it is clear from his literary endeavors in 1887 that he was one of the first and most enthusiastic writers of the boom in first-person narration. In January 1887, he published the essay "Jitsuden ron" (Theory of autobiography), which called for the writing of autobiographical confessions, and, from October 1 to November 9, 1887, he serialized "Tane hiroi," with which we began this chapter, in the *Yomiuri shinbun*, just prior to his serialization of *Nisegane tsukai*.[52] Moreover, two translations of Edgar Allan Poe's stories—"The Black Cat" and "The Murders in the Rue Morgue"—by Aeba Kōson (1855–1922) appeared in the supplementary issues of the *Yomiuri shinbun* in the late months of 1887 when *Nisegane tsukai* was being serialized in the main issues of the same paper, the latter of these stories suggesting the intimate connection between Japanese authors' interests in first-person narration and detective fiction.[53]

But Shōyō surprises us given such historical circumstances: rather than continuing his experimentation with the first-person narrator, Shōyō replaces Green's first-person narrator with the third-person in the process of translation. Green's *XYZ* is a recounting of the narrator's past investigation. In contrast, *Nisegane tsukai* is told as an unfolding of a continuous present, and Shōyō takes care in his translation to eliminate the narrative framework of self-reflection, which constitutes Green's text. No longer

---

51. Komori, *Kōzō to shite no katari*, 301.

52. In 1889, moreover, Shōyō would posit the detective explicitly as a metaphorical double of the ideal narrator/novelist, a connection implicit in his *Shōsetsu shinzui*, by stating that the first-person narrator "should be like an observant detective" who provides "objective observations and subjective feelings" of what he/she sees and hears ("Eikoku shōsetsu no hensen," 5).

53. Other works appearing in 1887 that employ or discuss the first-person narration were Morita Shiken's essay "Shōsetsu no jijotai kijutsutai" (First person narration and descriptive style of the novel; September 1887), Shiken's translation *Kinro monogatari* (The tale of the golden donkey; January–February 1887), Yoda Gakkai's original work *Kyōbijin* (Chivalrous beauty; July and November 1887), and Aeba Kōson's essay "Jiden o kakubeshi" (Write an autobiography; June 1887). For Komori's complete analysis of the first-person narration during the Meiji 20s, including an illuminating discussion of Aeba's translations of Poe's stories, see Komori, *Kōzō to shite no katari*, 301–54.

present in *Nisegane tsukai* is the aforementioned ending of *XYZ*, in which the narrator-detective expresses his shame for the curiosity that led to his involvement in the Benson's case. Also eliminated are the many clues in Green's text that suggest curiosity as the motivating force behind the narrator-detective's actions. For example, the narrator employs phrases such as "moved by a sudden impulse" (9), "seized by an intense desire" (18), and "so my adventurous curiosity decided" (19) at critical junctures of the narrative to describe how something beyond his control is pushing him to delve deeper and deeper into the mystery at hand.[54] In Shōyō's translation, however, these phrases are nowhere to be seen, replaced in all instances by a variation of the verb *omoitsuku* (to think of), which is less nuanced to say the least (668, 674, 675).

As these changes in the translation should make clear, Shōyō suppresses any evidence of curiosity's grasp on the narrator—and the resulting shame—all the while presenting a story whose original had curiosity as its driving force.[55] Unlike the narrator-detective of Green's text, Kurisu Masamichi, the protagonist of *Nisegane tsukai*, is not motivated by his sense of curiosity and is presented as a consummate professional: he does what is expected of him by the government. The fact that he goes astray from his original mission is not his fault but rather his fortune. This point is emphasized in the introduction to *Nisegane tsukai* where Shōyō has this to say about the story: "because the occupation of the secret detective, in always looking to detect and expose criminals, requires that he disguise appearances or sneak into people's houses to investigate hidden things, there are times when he unexpectedly discovers

---

54. Fittingly, the first of these examples occurs when the narrator is altering the meeting place designated in the letter at the post office.

55. Here we must say that Shōyō makes a conscious decision not to employ *Nisegane tsukai* as a work that represents his notion of the novel, which aspires to describe realistically the inner conflict between reason and desire. But it is also true that Shōyō made some changes to Green's text in order to better position *Nisegane tsukai* within his understanding of the novel. For example, as Takahashi Osamu notes, Shōyō casts Sadamune (Hartley in *XYZ*) as a son of the millionaire Amako (Benson) and his mistress, and a half-brother of Jōjirō (Joe) and Karuko (Carrie). Takahashi interprets this change as Shōyō's way to provide a framework within which Sadamune's ill will toward Jōjirō can be understood: "Shōyō's translation consciously creates a psychological drama between half-brothers and positions this 'conflict' as the 'coherent thread' that flows beneath the novel. This should be interpreted as a direct reflection of Shōyō's novelistic method" ("'Hon'yaku' to iu jiko genkyū," 78–79).

secret wrongdoings" (662). In this way, Shōyō replaces *XYZ*'s textual framework of shame regarding the detective's curiosity with a paratextual framework through which the readers will view the actions of Kurisu's involvement in the murder of the millionaire Amako (Benson in *XYZ*) not as a shameful accident but as a characteristic, albeit extraordinary, consequence of a detective doing his duty.

But Shōyō does more than offer such an interpretative framework constructed via paratexts. Through making other changes to Green's text, Shōyō emphasizes Kurisu's sense of duty and delineates what this duty of the detective entails. After altering the letter addressed to "123" (X.Y.Z. in the original) with the intention of taking the place of its proper recipient, Kurisu goes to the train station to gather information on the wealthy Amako family whose garden is to be the meeting place between the mysterious stranger and the "counterfeiter." Here is Kurisu's train of thought regarding his decision:

> Since my duty [*yakume*, written as *shokushō* which is a more official word meaning "charged function"] is to gather information that may be of use, however uncertain it might be, and to determine without exception whether they are fact or fiction, I must do that without fail. Generally where people gather, rumors of famous people flow, so a waiting room at a train station would be perfect. I will mix in with the crowd and listen (670–71).

In contrast, the corresponding section in Green's text runs as follows: "business is business, and no clue, however slight or unpromising in its nature, is to be neglected when the way is as dark as that which lay before me" (13). As this comparison reveals, Shōyō explicitly uses the word "duty," highlighting the awareness on the part of Kurisu regarding what he is expected to do, which in this instance is the collecting of rumors surrounding the suspect through the act of eavesdropping and the determining of their truthfulness. In addition to this delineation of the expected actions of the detective's duties, Shōyō emphasizes the detective's sense of duty, expressed in the phrase "I must do that without fail."

No doubt, the collection of rumors through eavesdropping is but one of many actions a detective is expected to take in the course of his investigation. Considering the importance that eavesdropping has within Shōyō's understanding of the novel, however, it is no surprise that the emphasized relationship between the demands of the profession and this act can be seen elsewhere as well. Upon visiting the Amako estate in order to be hired as a guard to serve at the costume ball, Kurisu overhears a conversation between Sadamune (Hartley in *XYZ*) and Karuko

(Carrie), although Kurisu does not know to whom the voices belong. First, a look at the corresponding section from *XYZ*:

> The sound of voices reached my ear from the next room. A man and woman were conversing there in smothered tones, but my senses are very acute, and I had no difficulty in overhearing what was said.
>
> "Oh, what an exciting day this has been!" cried the female voice. "I have wanted to ask you a dozen times what you think of it all. Will he succeed this time? Has he the nerve to embrace his opportunity, or what is more, the tact to make one? Failure now would be fatal. Father—" (21–22).

And here is *Nisegane tsukai*:

> From the next room leaked voices of people whispering. Straining his ears to listen, he realized that it was the voices of a man and a woman conversing stealthily, but Kurisu by nature had good ears, which was indeed a necessary professional trait, so although the voices were faint they were clearly audible.
>
> The woman's voice said, "Really, there was not a day that I worried like today. Although I wanted to ask you, I couldn't because there's an ear on every wall. So I worried alone. . . . What do you think? Will he accomplish it successfully? I cannot but worry. A great opportunity like this will not come again, but will he do it boldly? Even if he has the courage to do so, he must also have tact or else he will be exposed before . . . Father" (677; ellipses in the original).

That Shōyō sought to augment the element of eavesdropping in Green's text can clearly be seen in the changes he makes in the passage. Made explicit in the translation is the awareness on Karuko's part of the possibility that her conversation with Sadamune may be eavesdropped. But even more important for our purposes here is the alteration Shōyō makes in the role played by the detective in the scene. While the text of *XYZ* makes the narrator a passive listener who overhears the conversation, Shōyō's translation gives Kurisu an active role: although he has good ears, Kurisu must make the decision to listen actively ("straining his ears") to ascertain what is being said in the next room. Moreover, Shōyō presents Kurisu's acute hearing as a necessary qualification for being a detective, intimating that eavesdropping is a crucial function of the profession.

Indeed, this connection between the duty of the detective and the act of eavesdropping goes beyond Shōyō's alterations. In both *XYZ* and *Nisegane tsukai*, the detective is an eavesdropper. It is who he is and all he does. And this is nowhere clearer than in the second half of the story when Kurisu infiltrates the costume ball disguised as Jōjirō (Joe in *XYZ*), the second son of Amako and the mysterious recipient of the letter that Kurisu has altered. While his choice to impersonate the suspect may appear as a clever way to get into the heart of the criminal gang and to take on an active role in the investigation, it does nothing of the sort. Once he dons the costume provided by the suspect, Kurisu, despite his desire to ask questions that will lead him to the truth of the case, is forced to become a completely passive subject, for to speak would mean that he would be exposed as a fake. Thus, he becomes a listener to a barrage of disguised partiers who accost him at every turn to discuss the sordid affairs surrounding the Amako family with the understanding that he is Jōjirō.[56] This situation clearly marks Kurisu as an eavesdropper to the extent that eavesdropping is an intrusion by a third party on a dialogue that is taking place within an 'I-you' relationship where those involved are unaware of the existence of a third party who is neither a *recognized* addresser nor an addressee of utterances in a dialogue.

At this point in the discussion, it is easy to see that the intrusion by a third party on an 'I-you' relationship is what drives the entire narrative of *Nisegane tsukai*, for the root of all 'evil' in the story, its Pandora's box—the letter—also exists within this structure of eavesdropping. The letter is a statement made by its sender to be communicated to its recipient, and, in this regard, it is the same as an utterance in a dialogue made possible within an 'I-you' relationship. Thus, a letter that is read by a third party shares the same fate as an utterance overhead by an eavesdropper. Or rather, an intercepted letter is an example *par excellence* of the structure of eavesdropping. The eavesdropper is provided with some extra-linguistic factors—emotions and accents that can be discerned from the voice, for example—that assist him/her in giving meaning to what is being said. Moreover, the eavesdropper always has the context of the scene of a conversation, which enables him/her to interpret certain utterances within the flow of a dialogue between interlocutors. But such factors do not exist in the case where a letter is read by a third party, for the letter is a monologue that is always out of context, its place of writing always different from the statement it makes.

And now, the mechanism of *Nisegane tsukai* that is produced as the result of the changes effected by Shōyō in the process of translation of Green's text begins to surface. On the one hand, Green's *XYZ* presents

---

56. The sordid affairs of the Amako family involve the story of how Jōjirō became estranged from the family after he was accused of the theft of Amako's money and bonds. Kurisu's conversations with family members suggest that it was not Jōjirō but Sadamune who was guilty of this theft. The knowledge of this family story then serves to promote the understanding of Sadamune as an evil person who is deceitful and disloyal to his father and, thus, capable of patricide.

eavesdropping as an act where the detective-narrator's curiosity manifests itself, and, in this sense, the feeling of shame that he experiences at the end of the story is a direct result of his repeated indulgence in this act, which reflects his desire to pry into people's private lives in the name of the law. On the other hand, there is no judgment passed in *Nisegane tsukai* on the actions of the detective Kurisu, either by the detective himself or by the third-person narrator. Instead, Shōyō highlights eavesdropping as a crucial function of the detective and presents him as an exceptional eavesdropper whose actions are not dictated by his curiosity but by the demands of his profession. It is not that the detective wants to eavesdrop; it is just that he must. Through the presentation of the detective as the rightful and fitting subject of eavesdropping whose motivation derives from his sense of duty to expose the truth of the case at hand, Shōyō provides an example of the moral and objective gaze that is required of the novel's narrator who must explore and depict the most interior and private without any 'personal' interest or investment: the detective becomes the metaphorical double of the ideal narrator and, by extension, the novelist.

But Shōyō's strategy to establish the foundations for the novel in Meiji Japan through the articulation of a new type of writer—the novelist—went beyond the promotion of such doubling, extending to the employment of practical strategies to establish the narrator as the authorial substitute of the novelist at the level of the text. And here again, the shift in perspective from first- to third-person narration plays a critical role. As a mode of narration in which the narrator is assumed to exist as a character within the story-world, the first-person narration must adhere to the limited perspective of the narrator who lacks the privileged gaze of the novelist to cut through appearances. Because of this characteristic, the first person posits itself as a suitable mode of narration for the detective story whose success is highly dependent on the ability of its narration to maintain suspense as the primary mechanism of readers' enjoyment. Most often, such narration takes the form of what Komori Yōichi calls "the companion-style," where the narrator is not the detective but rather his sidekick, a clueless observer—exemplified by Watson of Sherlock Holmes tales—who only knows to record everything without understanding the significance of anything and, thus, is incapable of divulging the case's mysteries ahead of the detective.[57]

57. Komori, *Kōzō to shite no katari*, 332. The narrator of Poe's Dupin trilogy also employs this type of first-person narration, as Meiji readers would have

Of course, Green's *XYZ* does not employ such a sidekick, for the detective himself is a clueless observer who does not pose a threat as narrator to destroy the suspense of the text as Dupin or Holmes might. This characteristic of *XYZ*, thus, makes the story conducive for a reformulation into third-person narration because there is no need to deal with the narrator-sidekick who would become a superfluous narrative element after such a change in narrative perspective, enabling the translator to focus on maintaining suspense critical to the detective story. In this sense, Shōyō's *Nisegane tsukai* can be seen, as Takahashi Osamu does, as Shōyō's attempt to utilize the generic demands of detective fiction to achieve the limited third-person narration that he deemed necessary for the development of the modern novel.[58] But if such was the case, then I would also argue that this attempt involved Shōyō's engagement with *XYZ* not as a typical detective story but as a parodic text keenly aware of the narrative dynamic and implications of the classical detective story, as manifested not only in the fact that the story's narrator is the once-clueless detective but also in the way he comes to solve the Benson case.

After the death of Benson, Joe—or rather the man in a yellow domino who is believed to be Joe—is accused of poisoning Benson based on the testimony of his servant who claims to have seen the man in a yellow domino holding the wineglass in which the poison was poured. But such an accusation, of course, does not trouble the narrator-detective who simply takes off the yellow domino to reveal his identity to the crowd and clears the accusation against him. It is not because the narrator is not Joe and, thus, does not have a motive for killing Benson that suspicion against the narrator is cleared. In fact, Hartley, upon seeing a total

---

known through Kōson's translation of Poe's "The Murder in the Rue Morgue" in December 1887. This type of narration would also be employed in Futabatei Shimei's "Aibiki" (The rendezvous; 1888) and "Meguriai" (The encounter; 1888), translations of Ivan Turgenev that had a major impact on the future generation of Japanese writers.

58. Takahashi understands *Nisegane tsukai* within the development of Shōyō's notion of the modern novel that finds its fruition in the 1889 story *Saikun*, a story that employs the limited third-person narration. He states: "It can be said that to consciously translate the detective novel *XYZ*, which employs a first-person narration that necessitates by nature a methodological construction of a restricted scope of consciousness, into *Nisegane tsukai* as a third-person narration was the ultimate experiment in theory of expression by Shōyō to achieve a stable 'place of narration' based upon the 'perspective' of third-person narration, which was necessary for the modern novel" ("'Hon'yaku' to iu jiko genkyū," 83).

stranger appear from under the yellow domino, accuses the narrator of having been sent by Joe to commit this crime. Rather, suspicions against the narrator are cleared by the fact of his being a government detective and, hence, of his being someone who is 'incapable' of committing such a crime *irrespective* of the evidence that may have incriminated the man in the yellow domino. Applying his authority—that is, his reliability as a witness—to full effect, the narrator turns the circumstantial evidence of the servant's testimony, which had been used against the man in the yellow domino, to incriminate Hartley: the narrator testifies that it was Hartley who told him to inspect the wineglass to determine whether Benson had gone to bed or not and thereby holds Hartley accountable for trying to frame him for Benson's murder.

In *XYZ*, then, it is not the actions of the detective that lead to the actual solving of the case but merely the fact that the narrator-detective disguises himself as Joe while maintaining his authority/identity as a government official that proves critical, for this authority guarantees the truthfulness of the first-person witness account that he *experienced* as Joe's double. But significantly, it is precisely this authority that the narrator himself problematizes through his *other* first-person narrated account, namely, his confession that is *XYZ*, as highlighted by the previously cited ending of the original work. The first time around, this passage was read as evidence of the narrator's deep sense of shame regarding his curiosity that motivated him to get involved in the Benson affair, which had nothing to do with the counterfeiting case. This time around, however, let us focus somewhere else, namely, his admission that he did not tell us everything. Why? Because he was "too much ashamed." What he 'left' out, we will never know, although it might actually change our interpretation of his story. In fact, this might be the reason for his 'omissions.' The ending of Green's text reminds us that the narrator who exists in the storyworld is hypothetically bound to the same sense of self-interest that 'prevented' *Imotose kagami*'s Oyuki from expressing her true feelings about Misawa. While the autobiographical recounting style of narration may 'ensure' the reality of the experiences it tells by claiming direct experience, it also exposes the possibility of their untruthfulness, omissions, and manipulations, putting into question the very authority that it invokes regarding the truthfulness of the narration's content and the sincerity of its presentation.[59]

---

59. Thus, *XYZ*'s narrator-detective reveals the inherent artificiality of the first-person narrated story, including the sharing of perspectives between the

The employment of the third-person narration in *Nisegane tsukai* forecloses such possibilities of doubt arising on the part of the readers regarding the reality and authenticity of the detective's story by acting as a metalanguage that exists outside the story-world. And here the novel and the detective conspire to legitimate each other's authority. On the one hand, the detective draws on his authority as a government official to function as an example of an 'objective' and 'moral' bearer of the gaze of the eavesdropper or voyeur that Shōyō deemed necessary in the narrating of the modern novel. On the other hand, the third-person narration, in describing the actions of the detective from an extra-diegetic position, functions as an authority that ensures, in turn, the authority of the detective and his 'objective' and 'moral' nature. The production of the figure of the detective as the metaphorical double of the 'moral' and 'objective' novelist simultaneously involves the emergence of the third-person narrator as an authority figure who ensures such morality and objectivity on the part of the detective.

But this is not to say that Shōyō expected the shift in narrative perspective to be enough for such an emergence, as it can be surmised from the paratextual moves that he made in the process of translation—including a title change—which function strategically to establish the authority of the narrator all the while maintaining key aspects of a detective story intact. *XYZ*, the title of Green's text, is the 'name' of the recipient of the mysterious letters, the 'name' that the detective-narrator assumes in order to infiltrate Benson's costume ball. It is a fitting title, no doubt, for it reflects the desire on the part of the detective to experience an alternative subjectivity—the criminal—and, as such, is at the source of the detective's curiosity. In contrast, the title of Shōyō's translation has a double meaning: it is the reason that Kurisu was sent to investigate as well as the password included in the letter that becomes the critical clue drawing Kurisu into the Amako affair. And the title change,

---

narrator and the reader that assists in the production of suspense by enabling the readers see what the narrator sees and join the latter in analyzing the case that unfolds before them. While the text may promote the sense that the narrator and the readers are going through the investigation together, this conspiratorial relationship is only a result of the conscious and active directing and misdirecting of the readers by the first-person narrator. As Rosemary Jann writes of Conan Doyle's first-person narrator: "since Watson narrates all Holmes's cases after the fact, in the telling he must suppress his knowledge of how they turned out in order to re-create the puzzlement and surprise he felt at the time" (*The Adventures of Sherlock Holmes*, 24).

as Takahashi Osamu states, had an important effect of prompting the story to be read in a certain way: "The readers will read the story by bringing together the various information given in the novel around the word '*nisegane tsukai*' with the expectation that at some point the whole picture of '*nisegane tsukai*' will be made clear and that they will be given clues to that end."[60] To the extent that to "bring together the various information" around the word "*nisegane tsukai*" is exactly what Kurisu does in his investigation, the change in title functions to reinforce the sharing of perspective and expectation—the conspiratorial relationship—between Kurisu and the readers that may have been mitigated by the shift from *XYZ*'s first-person narration to *Nisegane tsukai*'s third-person narration.

At the same time, *Nisegane tsukai*'s third-person narrator distances himself from this conspiratorial relationship between the detective and the readers by utilizing to full effect the fact that this work, first and foremost, is a work of translation. As many scholars have noted, 1887 was the year in which the translation industry saw its first prewar peak after a sudden boom the previous year.[61] Naturally, this phenomenon brought on a number of essays regarding the nature of translation in various media including the *Yomiuri shinbun*, in which Takada Sanae's "Hon'yaku no kairyō" (Reform of translation; March 26, 1887) and Ryōgoku Dōjin's "Hon'yaku-sho no dokusha ni ichigen su" (A word to the readers of translations; October 25, 1887) appeared. Driven by desire to improve the level of translation in Meiji Japan, these essays like many others attacked the loose adaptation–style of translation that was customary at the time for being insincere to the original text and immature as a work of translation.

Interestingly, Shōyō, who was no doubt aware of these criticisms, nonetheless employs a variety of such criticized translation techniques in the early pages of *Nisegane tsukai*'s main text, explicitly situating the narrator as a Japanese translator who is introducing an American work to his Japanese readers. Like many translations at the time, *Nisegane tsukai* substitutes Japanese names for Western names; it also emphasizes the substitution as a conscious decision on the part of the translator, in both the translator's introduction and the main text: "for convenience,

---

60. Takahashi, "'Hon'yaku' to iu jiko genkyū," 78.

61. For example, see the chart constructed by Hirata Yumi that plots the number of literary works in the National Diet Library by year ("'Onna no monogatari' to iu seido," 179). Takahashi Osamu also discusses the relationship between *Nisegane tsukai* and translation in "'Hon'yaku' to iu jiko genkyū," 84–85.

I will make it a Japanese name and call him Kurisu Masamichi" (665). Moreover, the narrator begins the story in a comparative mode, likening Washington D.C. to Tokyo of "our country" as well as explaining the American postal system to provide the readers with the cultural knowledge necessary to digest this foreign text (663–64).

Yet, despite these changes to reframe the story for the Japanese readers, Shōyō does not forget to make the claim that he has decided to translate Green's text "as it is" (*arinomama*) in the introduction (663), evoking his use of the same phrase in *Shōsetsu shinzui* regarding the presentation of the novelist as an external observer who "depict[s] as it is" (*arinomama o mosha suru*). Although it can be argued that such a comment by Shōyō reveals his understanding of translation at the time, it also plays an important role in establishing the authority of the narrator via the translator. That is, the phrase "as it is" emphasizes the translator's role as a mediator who stands in between the Western text and the Japanese readers, passively relaying information from the former to the latter. In this sense, the translator evokes the eavesdropper who also stands at the border of information and its wanting consumers, but, unlike the eavesdropping narrator who tries to convey the sense that he and the readers are sharing the same information, the narrator-as-translator, as seen in above examples, underscores his difference from the readers. To the extent that the Japanese readers of the general public have no access to the original text nor can they understand it, the third-person narrator-as-translator is placed in a privileged position of the knower who provides access to the usually inaccessible. And within the context of *bunmei kaika*, the translation of a Western text allows for the presentation of the content of Kurisu's story—of prying into people's private lives—not as entertainment but as something important for the education of the Japanese reading public.[62] Like the detective and in contradistinction to the eavesdropper, the translator promotes the understanding of the novelist as an authorial figure by providing information inaccessible to the readers through the use of his special skills and through emphasizing education and duty as opposed to curiosity and entertainment as his motivating factors.

But here, we must also recognize the precarious position in which the translator finds himself, a position that evokes the eavesdropper in

62. Or to put it in another way, translating is a mode of narration that presupposes and projects the existence of privileged information worth translating on the other side rather than a simple tale for entertainment.

another way. As mentioned above, various foreign books—whether classics from the past or recently published pulp fiction—flooded into Japan toward the end of the 1880s, and we can imagine that Japanese intellectuals were lacking in the knowledge of Western literary histories and of the source countries that would assist in contextualizing and understanding the 'meaning' of these texts: appearing all at once, these books must have seemed to the Japanese readers as being out of time and place. And such sociohistorical conditions most likely had some influence on Shōyō's decision to translate a first-person narrative into a third-person one, for it must have been difficult for him to be interpellated by the "you" that is addressed by the "I" in Green's *XYZ*. Like the narrator-detective whom he will rename Kurisu Masamichi, Shōyō usurps a text that was not 'intended' for him and intrudes upon an 'I-you' relationship in an attempt to decipher the meaning of a text whose context he has no way of knowing fully. In so doing, Shōyō attempts to synthesize the two extremes of writing—the first-person narration that 'ensures' the reality of its events by recounting the personal experiences of the narrator and a work of translation in which the translator knows nothing about the reality of story events—to produce a narrative that mediates the two realities that are Japan and the West.

☙

Central to Shōyō's strategy to reform the extant fictional narratives of Meiji Japan was the articulation of a 'moral' gaze of the novelist, which differed from the 'vulgar'—nonobjective and emotionally invested—gaze embodied in such stories. As a rightful and fitting subject of eavesdropping whose actions are dictated by his sense of duty to expose the truth of the case at hand, the figure of the detective enables the explicit articulation of the 'objective' and 'moral' nature of this gaze. Thus, he personifies the theoretical difference emphasized by Shōyō between the modern novel and the objects of his reform, offering itself as a metaphorical surrogate of the novelist.[63] At the same time, Shōyō's rendering of the detective story enabled him to do much more than legitimize the task of the novelist metaphorically. By the shift from first- to third-person narration

---

63. Of course, this does not mean that the readers, through their identification with the detective, must adopt the 'objectivity' and 'morality' of this gaze. Rather, the figure of the detective merely offers a justification, an apology, for the curiosity that drives the reading process.

as well as through the narrator establishing himself explicitly as a translator, *Nisegane tsukai*'s narration extricates itself from the conspiratorial relationship with the readers promoted by *XYZ*'s narration and asserts its role as a metalanguage that treats the story events as objects of knowledge. In the process, the third-person narrator emerges as an authority figure who, as someone occupying the position of the knower, simply relays 'reality' to the readers in an 'objective' manner, all the while maintaining the conspiratorial relationship necessary to entice the readers in the reading process through the surrogate of the detective. The translated detective story presented itself as a perfect tool to legitimize the inherent contradiction in Shōyō's articulation of the novel as a medium that promotes itself as the harbinger of 'civilized' and 'enlightened' values, including that of privacy, and, yet, draws its reason for being in the desire to penetrate what has become impenetrable in the age of modernity.

As history would have it, however, it was not Tsubouchi Shōyō but Kuroiwa Ruikō who would maximize this potential of the Western detective story for the Japanese translator and novelist to carve out the authorial position and perspective necessary within Shōyō's formulation of the novel.[64] As we will discuss in detail in the next chapter, the content of Ruikō's stories reflects this connection, as he introduced to the Japanese readers a world filled with characters who were gossipers, eavesdroppers, and, most of all, those who sought to penetrate the private lives and internal thoughts of the characters. Quite ironically, considering the 1893 editorial of *Kokumin no tomo* with which we began this book, Ruikō's detective stories functioned as the immediate heirs to the legacy of Shōyō's literary project, and it could be argued that the popularity and dissemination of the detective story in the late 1880s and the early 1890s was what made possible the rise of the novel as a socially viable and respectable art form in Meiji Japan. Indeed, as Nakayama Akihiko points out, the rhetoric and terminology of *Shōsetsu shinzui*, or what Nakayama

---

64. *Saikun*, published in January 1889 in *Kokumin no tomo* marked Shōyō's last serious attempt to write narrative fiction, but he would continue to dabble with translations of Western stories, including his *Daisagishi* (The swindler), a story with a mystery-novel flavor which was serialized during 1892 in the *Miyako shinbun*. Interestingly enough, the *Miyako shinbun* at this time was looking for works that would successfully fill the void created by Ruikō when he left the newspaper in August of the same year and quickly approached Shōyō. For details of Shōyō's *Daisagishi*, see J. Scott Miller, *Adaptations of Western Literature in Meiji Japan*, 77–110.

calls "Shōyō-esque clichés," only began to manifest themselves in the Japanese literary histories in the early 1890s, displaying the influence and rooting of Shōyō's literary worldview in Meiji Japan and concomitant with them the spreading of the belief in the artistic nature of the novel.[65]

The vehement criticism of detective fiction in the *Kokumin no tomo* editorial, which may appear as an instance of historical blindness regarding the developmental link between the novel and the detective story, begins to make sense in light of this correlation between the rise of "Shōyō-esque clichés" and the popularity of Ruikō's detective stories. The detective, as a metaphorical double of the novelist within the storyworld, may have legitimated the novelist's 'objective' and 'moral' stance, but he also pointed to the need for such legitimation in the first place due to the inherent paradox of Shōyō's formulation of the novel that left the novelist with the potential to revert back to an immoral eavesdropper. Thus, the detective was a bandage over a wound that protects it from exposure and further damage but constantly serves as a reminder that there existed a wound beneath. As such, the intimate connection between the novel and the detective story had to be suppressed, just as the former was taking root as an art form, and conscious effort had to be made to present the latter instead as the enemy of and foil against the novel. Nonetheless, or precisely because of this, the detective story as the novel's Other would cast a dark shadow over the Japanese novel, exerting a profound effect on its developmental trajectory in modern Japan.

65. Nakayama, "'Bungakushi' to nashonaritī," 85–101.

TWO

Allegories of Detective Fiction: Kuroiwa Ruikō and the Refashioning of a Meiji Subject

On April 28, 1887, the *Tōkyō Nichinichi shinbun* carried the following news of seemingly frivolous nature, but its unimportance was quickly placed in question by the sheer number of newspapers carrying the same story:

> A few nights ago, a rickshaw driver hearing the clock of a nearby university strike midnight was about to head to his lodgings when a young lady who seemed to be from a respectable family came running from the direction of Nagatachō. Approaching the driver in a frantic manner, the lady, who the driver realized was barefoot, asked to be driven to a mansion in Surugadai. As the rickshaw headed toward her destination, it was stopped by a carriage around Hibiya where a well-dressed maid came out of the carriage to take the lady away.[1]

At first glance, this news appears to be a trivial story about a man who has had a mysterious experience, as his account ends with a statement that he feels he may have been fooled by a fox. However, many scholars including Maeda Ai attest that this story was understood by its readers

---

1. *Tōkyō Nichinichi shinbun*, April 28, 1887. According to Maeda Ai, the newspapers that reported the news in question were *Tōkyō Nichinichi shinbun*, *E'iri jiyū shinbun*, *Yamato shinbun*, and *E'iri chōya shinbun*. For details of this scandal including the full article that appeared in the *Tōkyō Nichinichi shinbun*, see Maeda, "Mishima Michitsune to Rokumeikan jidai."

as a scandalous story of political significance. As Maeda states, the ambiguous nature of this article, in which "the contour of the event is intentionally muddled or skewed to suggest the blunders of the government or the scandals of officials . . . [was] one of the last resorts devised by the Meiji newspaper journalists who were exposed to severe regulations such as the Libel Law [Zanbōritsu] and the Newspaper Ordinance that suppressed the freedom of press. In addition, the method of taking apart the name of officials one character by one character and inserting it here and there within the text was also employed often."[2]

Importantly, a comparable practice could be found in the political novels, a distinct and popular literary genre of the 1880s directly connected to the ideas of the Freedom and People's Rights movement. As Asukai Masamichi states, political novels—of which the first work is most often regarded to be *Jōkai haran* (A storm on the passionate seas; 1880) by Toda Kindō (1850–1890)—emerged when "the contentions of people's rights [movement] were inserted into the text in the form of 'allegory.'"[3] In other words, political novels were written or translated in such a way that readers could identify characters or groups within the fictional world as idealistic representations of real-life counterparts and, thus, transpose the turn of events within the fictional world as the projected but necessary outcome of the movement's struggles in reality.[4] Together with the newspaper reporting about scandals of government officials, such as the one discussed above, political novels promoted what I will call the allegorical writing and reading practices during this period, necessitated by Meiji social reality in which the 'truth' of a situation could not be frankly spoken due to severe publishing regulations or the 'truth' was an unfulfilled political ideal that had to be sought in an alternate universe.

Read within this allegorical interpretative framework that required a sort of 'detective' work by readers—to decipher the 'true' reality of po-

---

2. Maeda, "Mishima Michitsune to Rokumeikan jidai," 124–25. For other examples of this type of reporting, see Yamada Shunji, *Taishū shinbun ga tsukuru Meiji no "Nihon,"* 226–27.

3. Asukai, *Tennō to Nihon kindai seishinshi*, 87.

4. Asukai writes: "The position of the natural rights theory must take the position that people have rights by nature and the reason it has not surfaced is because it has not been noticed. If this is the case, then 'allegory' should be different from that of the Restoration period and should be reasoned by making clear the 'reality' that exists by nature, and this had to take the form of reinterpreting the past of Japanese history or the 'realities' of foreign countries" (ibid., 88).

litical significance hidden beneath seemingly trivial details—the *Tōkyō Nichinichi shinbun*'s news becomes a report of an attempted sexual assault on a woman by the Prime Minister and well-known lecher Itō Hirobumi (1841–1909) who had held a costume ball at his mansion on April 20. Despite the fact that the widely publicized event at Itō's mansion a week before seems unrelated to this report, it was easy, according to Maeda, to connect the place name Nagatachō, the location of the Prime Minister's residence, to Itō Hirobumi and the costume ball.[5] Moreover, it was possible from the place name Surugadai to hypothesize the identity of the woman in question: the wife of Count Toda, who was famed as "the beauty of Rokumeikan," lived in Surugadai.[6]

In such a way, the seemingly trivial article reveals itself as the scandal among all political scandals, taking up the favorite subject of the newspapers at the time, namely, the immorality and ineptitude behind the so-called Rokumeikan diplomacy. Named as such for the government building central to its implementation, Rokumeikan diplomacy manifested itself most visibly in the form of fancy balls held at the Rokumeikan building on a nightly basis where government officials and members of Japanese high society along with foreign dignitaries and their families danced the night away to Western music, wearing Western clothes. Through such balls, the Meiji government sought to provide a site of social intercourse where the Japanese could display the extent of their Westernization to promote a favorable renegotiation of the unequal treaties that Japan was forced to sign with Western powers in the late Edo and early Meiji periods.[7]

---

5. For an example of the reporting on the costume ball at Itō's mansion, see Maeda, "Mishima Michitsune to Rokumeikan jidai," 115–16.

6. Ibid., 116. This scandal is filled with many complicated factors that cannot be explored here, but suffice it to say that Count Toda made an unprecedented political climb during the next couple of months, ultimately becoming a minister plenipotentiary to Austria. In his examination of this scandal, Maeda hypothesizes a scandal within a scandal, suggesting that this story was leaked to Kuroiwa Ruikō, the editor in chief of the *E'iri jiyū shinbun* at the time, by Police Chief Mishima Michitsune (1835–1888). According to Maeda, Mishima, who was from the former Satsuma domain and was very close to his clan mate Kuroda Kiyotaka (1840–1900), sought to bring down Itō so that Kuroda could become the next prime minister. For details, see ibid.

7. For a detailed discussion of the unequal treaties, see Auslin, *Negotiating with Imperialism*.

While these balls may have had such a noble goal, it was natural that using taxpayer's money to host extravagant parties, which appeared to be nothing but a trivial mingling among the rich and the famous and a blind worship of all that was Western, led to an unfavorable reception among the general public. As the accounts of these balls by the French officer and novelist Pierre Loti (or Julien Viaud [1850–1923]) reveal, moreover, these balls did not have the intended effect of impressing the foreigners with the Western-ness of the Japanese people.[8] Consequently, various rumors and criticisms began to circulate regarding the balls and their participants. Most of these rumors involved the topic of adultery, whether involving the philanderer Itō Hirobumi or the wife of the Education Minister Mori Arinori (1847–1889), who was said to have bore a blue-eyed baby. One document that reveals the pervasiveness of these rumors was the so-called "Rokumeikan intō jidai ni okeru nijukkajō no kenpakusho" (Letter of petition with twenty articles regarding the lewd Rokumeikan age) by the politician Katsu Kaishū (1823–1899) that criticized the fancy balls as a breeding ground for rumors.[9]

Considered within the context of the scandal surrounding the costume ball held at Itō Hirobumi's mansion and other pervasive rumors of Rokumeikan balls in conjunction with the allegorical reading practice fostered by the political novels and the newspaper, it should be evident how timely and fraught with implications was Tsubouchi Shōyō's *Nisegane tsukai* (serialized from November 27 to December 23, 1887). A story of a detective whose investigations into a money counterfeiting case exposes, by mistake, a dark scheme hiding behind the façade of a costume ball, *Nisegane tsukai* appeared just as Rokumeikan diplomacy ended in utter failure when the Foreign Minister Inoue Kaoru (1835–1915) resigned in September after he had placed treaty renegotiations on indefinite hold. Inflamed at this turn of events, the activists of the Freedom and People's Rights movement who had been subdued by government suppression resurged, as they converged in Tokyo to petition the government for treaty revision, land tax revision, and freedom of speech and assembly in what came to be known as the "three major issues petition movement" (Sandai jiken kenpaku undō).

Naturally, the attacks on Rokumeikan diplomacy and its participants became harsher than ever. It was also natural, I would argue, that a story

---

8. See Pierre Loti, *Japoneries d'Automne* (1889) and *Madame Chrysanthème* (1887) for details.

9. For more of this petition, see Matsuyama, *Uwasa no enkinhō*, 83–84.

telling the existence of criminal intent behind the façade of a costume ball would be read within this flow despite it taking place in a foreign land. Seen in this light, the role of the detective presented in *Nisegane tsukai* takes a more specific form: the detective as one who seeks to determine the truth value of rumors surrounding the fancy balls of Rokumeikan diplomacy and, in so doing, exposes the criminal/immoral intent of the organizers, which has nothing to do with the reported or presumed intention of the fancy balls. Particularly fitting here is that Shōyō introduces the American detective Kurisu with a disclaimer that "there are no detectives in our country today that are like him" and thereby presents him as a figure of wish fulfillment who imparts necessary justice on the authorities themselves.[10] Given the negative connotation of the Japanese detectives in the first half of the 1880s as pawns of the unjust and immoral government to suppress the Freedom and People's Rights movement, as discussed in the Introduction, it was the substitution of a Westerner for a Japanese detective within such a social and literary environment—the total collapse of Rokumeikan diplomacy and the allegorical mode of literary production and consumption necessitated by the inner logic of the Freedom and People's Rights movement and the external threat of government censorship—that appeared necessary for the detective to emerge as fictional hero. In this sense, Shōyō's *Nisegane tsukai* was a pivotal work in the nascent stages of the detective fiction genre that reflected the conditions of its birth.

But what about the detective stories of the journalist and political activist Kuroiwa Ruikō who would popularize the genre in the late 1880s and the early 1890s? To what extent can we understand them to be a continuation of *Nisegane tsukai*? Critical to answering these questions is the timing of Ruikō's emergence as an adapter of Western detective stories. His first serialization *Hōtei no bijin* in January 1888 came just after the largest and most absolutist government suppression of political activists in the short history of the Freedom and People's Rights movement. In order to quench the "three major issues petition movement," the government issued the Public Order Ordinance on December 26, 1887 and banned 570 activists from the capital, effectively eliminating any political activity within Tokyo.[11] Ruikō's detective stories thus ap-

---

10. Tsubouchi, *Nisegane tsukai*, 664.

11. This ordinance prohibited assemblies and made possible for the government to banish anyone suspected of conspiring against the government or disturbing the peace out of the approximately twelve kilometer range of the Im-

peared after the 'death' of politics when the attacks on the Rokumeikan diplomacy had no choice but to subside without running their full course, forced to become buried in the minds of the people. As such, Ruikō's detective stories had to take on a different role than *Nisegane tsukai*'s that suited the post-Freedom and People's Rights age when a radical redistribution of political energies as collective recuperative process became necessary.

Through an examination of Ruikō's early adaptations—in particular, his *Yūzai muzai* (Guilty, not guilty; 1888)—as well as his original work *Muzan* (Merciless; 1889), this chapter considers how the detective fiction genre figured into such redistribution of political energies at the critical juncture in the sociopolitical landscape of Meiji Japan. As we shall see, Ruikō presented his detective stories—selected and adapted from American dime novel collections that flooded the Japanese market in the late 1880s—as successor to the political novel, evoking characteristic tropes of the latter all the while negotiating the resentment and frustrations of those involved in the Freedom and People's Rights movement. And he did so by utilizing the various literary and extra-literary strategies within the allegorical interpretative mode discussed above to refashion the politically minded readers as new Meiji subjects whose relationship to the detective was not one tinged with feelings of injustice and oppression but one defined by his role as fictional hero who supplied their private entertainment.

The Politics of the Falsely Accused

When Kuroiwa Ruikō serialized *Hōtei no bijin* in the early months of 1888, he was the editor-in-chief of the illustrated political newspaper *E'iri jiyū shinbun*, a *koshinbun* whose official goal was to inculcate the general public regarding the ideals of the already dissolved Liberal Party. Yet, like his next three stories, also published in 1888—*Daitōzoku* (The great thief; a translation of Émile Gaboriau's *File No. 113* [1867]), *Hito ka oni ka* (Man or devil?; a translation of Gaboriau's *The Widow Lerouge* [1866]), and *Tanin no zeni* (Other people's money; a translation of Ga-

perial Palace for up to three years. Requiring no investigation or trial for its enforcement, the Public Order Ordinance was not an abuse of the judicial system that was common during the early Meiji period but a total disregard of the judicial system. I have taken the number of activists expelled from the capital from Matsuo, *Kindai tennōsei kokka to minshū/Asia*, 165.

boriau's *Other People's Money* [1874])—*Hōtei no bijin* did not appear in the *E'iri jiyū shinbun* as we would expect but rather in another newspaper *Konnichi shinbun*, which had no political affiliation.[12]

Although this fact may suggest that Ruikō began the serialization of Western stories as a side project, there is no doubt that Ruikō's motivation behind his adaptations were wholly in line with his background as a political activist. As he makes explicit in the introduction to his third story *Hito ka oni ka*:

> This story called *Hito ka oni ka* that I will translate on this occasion involves the turn of events regarding a major false imprisonment without precedence which occurred in France. . . . The reason why I translate this story is to inform the detectives of society regarding the difficulties of their occupation, and to get the judges of society to understand that verdicts should not be decided without care. If I were to say this concisely, then [I translate this work] in order to show the value of human rights and to warn against the careless application of the law.[13]

With this warning for those involved with the law in Meiji society about the gravity of their occupations, Ruikō tells a seemingly typical detective story about a detective who solves a mysterious murder through the gathering and analyzing of evidence. However, Ruikō is careful to construct a specific interpretative framework—one that suits his sociopolitical purpose—by claiming in the introduction that "this story is not fiction [*shōsetsu*] but fact [*jijitsu*]."[14] The ending paragraphs of the main text cleverly reinforce this claim, as Ruikō—in an authorial intrusion—states that he became aware of the existence of the story he translated as *Hito ka oni ka* through an actual political pamphlet. Originally produced and distributed by the story's characters who have formed an organization calling for the end of capital punishment, or so Ruikō claims, the pamphlet was a result of the characters' involvement in the criminal case

---

12. Prolific almost beyond the point of imagination, Ruikō serialized around 100 fictional works during a span of about 20 years. Of these there are 28 long novels that can be considered detective stories, and most of these appear in the first six years of his writing career, beginning with *Hōtei no bijin* in January 1888. Interestingly, it was the English translations of French novels that seemed to have caught Ruikō's interest. While the originals for some of his works remain a speculation, among the 28 full-length detective stories, 15 are by Boisgobey and four are by Gaboriau (The figures are from Nakajima Kawatarō's *Nihon suiri shōsetsu shi*, vol. 1, 44).

13. Kuroiwa, *Hito ka oni ka*, 169.

14. Ibid.

of this story, which made them painfully aware of the ease with which the innocent can be found guilty within the court of law and wrongfully executed.[15]

Despite the ingenious artifice employed in conveying a message to the story's readers, such a concern for the accuracy of the judicial system expressed by Ruikō and characters alike in *Hito ka oni ka* was nothing new in the short history of Meiji Japan. The necessity for Japan to adopt a new judicial system similar to that of Western nations led to its radical reorganization during the 1880s, and consequently, various works were published to guide those in the judicial system through its Westernization process. For example, there was *Jōkyō shōko gohan roku* (Records of wrong judgments based on circumstantial evidence), a translation of an American document, which contained numerous examples of court cases whose defendant was judged guilty only to be found innocent after his or her execution.[16] Published with the support of the Department of Justice in June 1881, *Jōkyō shōko gohan roku* intended to warn those involved in the judicial process of the difficulties of trial within the new law system, namely, the Criminal Code (Keihō) and the Code of Criminal Procedure (Chizaihō) promulgated on July 17, 1880 and enforced from January 1, 1882.[17] As scholars have noted, moreover, the work quickly trickled down to intellectual circles, serving as one of the primary source books from which Meiji writers gained ideas for their detective stories. Indeed, not only did Ruikō recall in 1905 that this work was one of the reasons why he

---

15. Mark Silver provides a detailed analysis of this ending, which Ruikō changed completely in the process of adaptation (*Purloined Letters*, 74–77).

16. For excerpts and explanation of this work, see Itō Hideo, *Meiji no tantei shōsetsu*, 36–40.

17. Devised with the assistance of the French jurist Gustave Emile Boissonade (1825–1910), the Criminal Code introduced the principle of *nulla peona sine lege*, which delineated what acts were crimes, the sentences for these crimes, and the guarantee that one cannot be charged for acts which were not delineated as crimes in the law. Moreover, for the first time in Japanese law, the social class of the defendant did not affect the punishment for the crime. The Code of Criminal Procedure, in turn, outlined the process of criminal trial and instituted the practice of lawyers to represent the defendant in a criminal case. Following the lead of the Revised Law (Kaitei ritsuryō) of 1873 and the prohibition of torture in 1879, this code also stressed the importance of using evidence rather than torture, which was the primary investigative method during the Edo period. The Criminal Code and the Code of Criminal Procedure are now commonly referred together as *kyūkeihō* (the old criminal code) in contradistinction to the new criminal code that took effect in 1908.

began to serialize stories that warned the public of the difficulties of a trial system and the injustice of public officials, but it was also in this work that he found the base idea for his original detective story *Muzan*.[18]

Of course, it was natural that the interest in and anxiety over the new Western justice system would carry over into the public sphere in such a way, particularly with the alarming rise in crimes and growing visibility of the police in the 1880s.[19] Crime reporting—"the police-related topics, such as murder, robbery, arson, and double suicide"—became the staple of *koshinbun*, serving to make the public aware of the workings of the new justice system as well as the dangers of contemporary society.[20] Moreover, these reports often became the base story for *tsuzukimono*, the dominant narrative form of the early Meiji discussed in the previous chapter, and, in particular, the *dokufu-mono* that were extremely popular during the 1880s. Drawing on original news reports not only of the crime and the trial but also regarding the criminal's often dark past, these stories attempted to explain the criminal's background and, thus, his or her motivation behind the crime in an entertaining manner to capture the curiosity of its readers all the while informing them of the various issues relating to the justice system.[21]

---

18. Itō Hideo, *Kuroiwa Ruikō: tantei shōsetsu no ganso*, 65. Ruikō's statement was made in "Yo ga shinbun ni kokorozashita dōki" (The reason why I became involved with the newspaper), published in the February 1 issue of his newspaper *Yorozu chōhō*.

19. Between 1877 to 1885, the number of prisoners increased threefold, signaling the arrival of "the age of the prison" (Yasumaru, "'Kangoku' no tanjō," 300–301). Also, the number of criminals prosecuted was 75,857 in 1882, and this number increased to 105,844 in 1883 and hovered around 100,000 until 1890, when it jumped to 145,281 (these figures are from Serizawa, *Hō kara kaihō sareru kenryoku*, 23).

20. Tsuchiya, *Taishūshi no genryū*, 241. As many scholars have pointed out, there exists an intricate relationship between criminal reports in newspapers and detective fiction. For a discussion of this relationship, see Uchida Ryūzō, *Tantei shōsetsu no shakaigaku*, 4, 11–13.

21. As Kamei Hideo argues, the various versions of the story of Takahashi Oden, one of the most popular *dokufu-mono*, reveal the intricate relationship between the public's anxiety with the rapidly changing justice system and the construction of Oden into the figure of *dokufu*. For example, the kabuki writer Kawatake Mokuami (1816–1893) took interest in Oden's testimony in court and wrote the play *Toriawase Oden no kanabumi*, in which the primary focus was to educate the public regarding the new justice system. In this play, Mokuami "depict[s] Oden as a woman who did not understand the philosophy of the new laws, and

As was the case with many *dokufu-mono*, the trial—as the display site for the working of the new justice system in action—also became a favorite topic of newspapers and fictions alike, including translations of foreign stories dealing with the trial such as *Dokusatsu saiban* (The trial of poison murder) serialized in the *Yomiuri shinbun* in November 1885. In the latter half of the 1880s, the readers' interest in the trial would be further fueled by more politically oriented real-life events that swept the nation. The trial of the Normanton Incident of 1886, in which the British ship *Normanton* sank off the coast of Kishū (present day Wakayama Prefecture) killing all Japanese passengers while all but one member of the British crew survived, turned into a public scandal when the British crew were exonerated of failing to assist the Japanese passengers.[22] On the domestic side, the various trials of political activists in the Freedom and People's Rights movement, and especially the trial of the Osaka Incident, which took place from May to September 1887, became huge public events due to the radical nature of their crimes, including an attempted overthrow of the Korean government in the case of the Osaka Incident, and, consequently, the proceedings were reported by various newspapers and published in book form to the delight of the readers.[23]

As these examples should make clear, anxieties and interests regarding the new judicial system gave rise to various literary and discursive formations, which in turn helped lay the groundwork necessary for the emergence of detective fiction in Meiji Japan. And given such a geneal-

---

from this point of view, set[s] up Oden as a poisonous woman." In contrast, *Takahashi Oden yasha monogatari* by Kanagaki Robun (1829–1894), by far the most popular version of Oden's story, depicts Oden as a woman "who used the new laws as a shield to assert her rights." According to Kamei, it was because "the people at that time could not understand the exhaustive nature of her assertions regarding her rights" and "feared this thoroughness" that Oden became a poisonous woman (*Meiji bungaku shi*, 30). For Kamei's analysis of Oden's stories, see ibid., 17–34. Also for another discussion of Oden, see Marran, *Poison Woman*, 1–64.

22. For details of the Normanton Incident, see Morinaga, *Saiban jiyū minken jidai*, 198–204.

23. For details of the Osaka Incident, see ibid., 213–56 as well as Mertz, *Novel Japan*, 113–38. The reports in book form were filled with detailed observations on the workings of the court and insertions of a comedic nature, making them extremely popular reading material in the late 1880s. One easily accessible example of such records is *Kokujihan jiken kōhan bōchō hikki* (Records of hearings on the incident of the crimes against the state) published by Naniwa shinbunsha in September 1887.

ogy of development, it was natural that these literary and discursive formations also provided detective fiction with a rich source from which to draw its narrative and thematic ideas. Like any newly emergent literary formation, Ruikō's early stories were a hodgepodge of already existing literary and discursive forms of the 1880s and, as such, were implicated in a hegemonic struggle for narrative dominance and nominal uniformity, acting parasitic all the while waiting for the opportunity to promote their own identity.

For example, the previously discussed presentation of the story as factual news in *Hito ka oni ka* reveals Ruikō's utilization of two essential topics of *koshinbun*, namely, crime reports (including semi-factual stories based on these reports) and reports of events in foreign countries, which also became one of *koshinbun*'s main staples in 1884 with the start of the Sino-French War (1884–1885). Another example would be *Baikarō* (original text unknown; serialized from February 17 to April 10, 1889 in *E'iri jiyū shinbun*), which tells the story of the protagonist Baikarō, a young man from a wealthy family in Bordeaux, France, and his quest to solve the murder of his friend and to save a girl he loves from her evil half-sister. While the story does involve some elements that are characteristic of the detective fiction genre, such as gathering and analysis of evidence, it would be a reach to classify *Baikarō* as a detective story, considering that the investigation of the murder of Baikarō's friend is a secondary plot line that is resolved passively without an active involvement of a detective-like figure. Instead, the primary focus of the story seems to be in line with that of *dokufu-mono* in the portrayal of the evil half-sister Hatsune who attempts to murder both her half-sister and her father in order to marry Baikarō.

That Ruikō sought to utilize the previously existing genres for his own purposes is also clear from the way in which he promoted his stories. His second story *Daitōzoku* as well as *Hito ka oni ka* had the subtitle of "trial novel" (*saiban shōsetsu*), no doubt reflecting Ruikō's sociopolitical motivation behind adapting the stories and taking advantage of the growing interest in trials on the part of the reading public in the wake of major trials of national and international import. In fact, we would have to wait until the introduction to his fifth story *Yūzai muzai* (a translation of Gaboriau's *Within an Inch of His Life* [1873], serialized from September 9 to November 28, 1888 in *E'iri jiyū shinbun*) for Ruikō to use the term "detective novel" (*tantei shōsetsu*) to describe his adaptations. But this designation, too, would be short-lived, as Ruikō redefined and reclassified his adaptations more systematically in a commentary, which appeared in the *E'iri jiyū shinbun* on September 22, 1889 during his serialization of *Makkura* (Utter darkness; a translation of Anna Katharine Green's *The Leavenworth Case* [1878], serialized from August 9 to October 26, 1889) in the same newspaper. Ruikō writes:

> The detective story first presents the crime, next [its] inquiry, and finally the solution or the confession. . . . The criminal romance always presents the trial in between the inquiry and the solution [of the crime]. . . . The sensational novels are those by French [writers] Gaboriau and Boisgobey, and they do not require that there is an inquiry or a trial. . . . To put it plainly, the difference in perspective is what separates the three. The detective story has the detective as its protagonist. The criminal romance focuses on the judge and presents his clever decision-making. In the sensational novel, there might appear a judge but he is not the protagonist; there might appear a detective but he is not the protagonist; its protagonist is the falsely accused who is involved in the crime and investigated or tried and progresses through various situations.[24]

Through its specific mention of Gaboriau and Boisgobey, the authors whose stories Ruikō adapted most often, this commentary actively positions his adaptations as sensational novels rather than detective stories. But while the falsely accused—whether he/she is actually tried (Hoshikawa Takeyasu in *Yūzai muzai*), arrested (Komori Arinori in *Hito ka oni ka*), or merely kept under police surveillance (Ōsu Eriko in *Makkura*)—was no doubt a staple of Ruikō's early stories, to call the falsely accused the protagonist would be a reach in many cases, including *Hito ka oni ka* and *Makkura*, the primary focus of which rests on those who try to prove the innocence of Arinori and Eriko, respectively. Thus, Ruikō's classification of stories about crime into three categories functioned as a strategy to emphasize the falsely accused of his stories. In so doing, Ruikō sought to promote, I would argue, a certain vector in the reading of his stories that coincides with—and thus, makes more effective—the sociopolitical message expressed in *Hito ka oni ka*'s introduction, which warns the difficulties of trial and criticize the state of the judicial system in Meiji Japan, a message, despite the heterogeneous subject matter and focus of his early stories, that seemed to be a singular one for Ruikō.[25]

---

24. Kuroiwa, *E'iri jiyū shinbun*, September 19, 1889. Cited in Itō Hideo, *Kuroiwa Ruikō: tantei shōsetsu no ganso*, 89.

25. But Ruikō's classification of his adaptations as sensational novels did not last either, as he would come to recognize his adaptations as detective stories (*tantei-dan*) in the near future as he makes clear in his 1893 editorial "Tantei-dan ni tsuite." This editorial was quoted in length in the book's introduction.

And in emphasizing the falsely accused—and by extension the unjustly imprisoned—Ruikō did more than provide a framework through which to understand his stories within the context of social criticism. He also positioned his stories to feed off the dominant literary genre of the time, namely, the political novel, which, despite the collapse of the Freedom and People's Rights movement in the late 1880s, was at the height of its popularity perhaps as a fictional consolation for and an escape from the harsh reality facing the movement. Vividly portrayed in its representative works like *Jiyū no kachidoki* (Torch of freedom; Miyazaki Muryū's translation of Alexandre Dumas's *Taking the Bastille* [1853], serialized in *Jiyū shinbun* from August 12, 1882 to February 8, 1883), *Kishūshū* (Demons softly crying; Miyazaki Muryū's translation of S. M. Kravchinsky's *Underground Russia* [1882], serialized in *Jiyū no tomoshibi* from December 10, 1884 to April 3, 1885), and Suehiro Tetchō's original story *Setchūbai* (Plum blossoms in the snow; 1886), the falsely accused and the unjustly imprisoned was an established trope of the political novel, providing an allegorical substitute for its readers and comrades as political activists struggling in their fight against the government.

But if Ruikō's early stories shared the same trope as the political novels and were politically motivated, what was the difference between Ruikō's adaptations and the political novels? Particularly revealing in answering this question is *Yūzai muzai*. Telling a story of Baron Hoshikawa Takeyasu who is falsely accused of shooting Count Kuroda, *Yūzai muzai* would become one of Ruikō's most popular works along with his *Hito ka oni ka*, with which the story shares many important characteristics.[26] But unlike *Hito ka oni ka*, *Yūzai muzai* was the archetypal sensational novel ac-

---

26. According to Itō Hideo, the foremost scholar of Kuroiwa Ruikō, the two stories were the most popular fictions of its time: "This story [*Yūzai muzai*] seemed to have been very well received, for after the final 66th installment, Ruikō states: 'Because this translation has surprisingly been enjoyed by the readers, I have taken to heart this utmost fortune and started another translation.' And even in the Meiji 30s, this novel was cherished among Ruikō fans, and its reputation was comparable to the former *Hito ka oni ka*. As a result, these two novels were reprinted repeatedly from Ōkawaya, surpassing the popularity of the Robin Hood novels (*batchinbin shōsetsu*) of Murakami Namiroku and the sentimental stories dictated by San'yūtei Enchō, which were said to be the staples of lending libraries in Tokyo, and became the drawing card of Ruikō's early detective novels" (*Kuroiwa Ruikō: sono shōsetsu no subete*, 28). Also, for anecdotal evidence of Ruikō's popularity during the Meiji 30s, see Asaoka, "Meiji kashihon kashidashi daichō no naka no dokushatachi," especially 33–41.

cording to Ruikō's definition in the aforementioned commentary, for the story's primary focus rests on the falsely accused Takeyasu, the investigation to prove his innocence taking up more pages than the search for the real criminal. Significantly, *Yūzai muzai* was the first of his adaptations to be serialized in the *E'iri jiyū shinbun*, of which Ruikō was the editor-in-chief.[27] Affiliated with the already dissolved Liberal Party as previously mentioned, this newspaper still shared and reflected the beliefs of the party, which was the most radical of all mainstream political parties at the time. Thus, *Yūzai muzai* was the first serialization for a newspaper geared more toward a politically minded audience, and it makes perfect sense that the sociopolitical motivation behind the serialization of Western detective stories is particularly explicit in his introduction to *Yūzai muzai*. Ruikō writes:

> The main purpose [of this novel] lies in showing the difficulties of human trial and informing the readers about the injustice of those involved with the law who abuse the law without thought and determine lightly the guilt of people. What those involved with the law see as evidence is not necessarily true evidence, and because it is common for innocent people to be found guilty by those who easily believe the evidence, I would be most content if the readers of this novel would reflect and understand that law should not be applied carelessly and a person's guilt should not be judged carelessly.[28]

Reiterating the ease with which innocent people are found guilty in society that he previously discussed in *Hito ka oni ka*'s introduction, Ruikō connects this state of affairs to the careless belief in evidence by magistrates and judges of the government. In so doing, Ruikō highlights the difficulties of a Western justice system, which determines a person's guilt based upon evidence, precisely because what the officials believe to be evidence in many cases is actually not "true evidence."

But there existed a major difference between the judicial problem expressed in Ruikō's introduction to *Yūzai muzai* and the actual state of things in Meiji society, for Ruiko's introduction suggests a belief in the court system—its fairness in the determination of guilt—that was far from prevalent in Meiji society. While the Meiji government may have strove hard to Westernize the justice system in the first half of the Meiji

---

27. Hereafter, most of Ruikō's stories appeared in this newspaper until he joined the *Miyako shinbun*, the later incarnation of the *Konnichi shinbun*, toward the end of 1889.

28. Kuroiwa, "Hanrei," in *Yūzai muzai*. It originally appeared in the supplement to the *E'iri jiyū shinbun* on September 9, 1888.

period, Japan certainly did not become the land of the free overnight with the enforcement of laws such as the Criminal Code and the Code of Criminal Procedure. As Haruta Kunio observes, high officials of Meiji government involved in the construction of the Criminal Code "poured all their energy into emasculating the air of freedom of the French law" that was reflected in the French jurist Gustave Boissonade's draft of this law, all the while preserving the façade of a Western law system.[29]

For example, the Criminal Code included specific measures—such as crimes of contempt against officials (*kanri bujoku zai*) and crimes of disrespect (*fukeizai*)—devised for the suppression of the Freedom and People's Rights movement through 'lawful' means. In addition, regulations such as the Libel Law, the Newspaper Ordinance, and the Assembly Ordinance (Shūkai jōrei) were issued separately as the need arose for the same purpose. These regulations were especially powerful and difficult to evade because their application was left for the most part to the interpretation of judges, who, in turn, were often coerced by high officials regarding the outcome of a case, especially when the defendant was an activist in the Freedom and People's Rights movement.[30] As many historians attest, moreover, the practice of torture, although prohibited in 1879, was still the most often employed investigatory technique of the authorities.[31]

When laws are created to incarcerate a specific group of people and judges are coerced to function as executors of the government's will, the court cannot be a place to determine whether the law should be applied to the person in question. It becomes instead a place to invoke whatever laws necessary in order to send away this enemy of the state. In such an environment, there is no concern for making a mistake in the verdict: it is not that officials "easily believe the evidence" or that they "abuse the law without thought" as Ruikō claims; rather, they exploit the evidence and abuse the law *with* thought and intention. And it was precisely this state of injustice that was allegorically described in numerous political

29. Haruta, *Sabakareru hibi*, 16.

30. For details of the nature and examples of governmental coercion of judges, see ibid., 77–82.

31. For example, Morinaga Eizaburō, who has written extensively on trials during the Freedom and People's Rights movement, states matter-of-factly regarding the prohibition of torture in 1879 that it was only on paper and that "it goes without saying that torture would rule investigations in Japan long after this [prohibition]" (*Saiban jiyū minken jidai*, 5).

novels during the 1880s, in particular, in those previously mentioned works that vividly portrayed the falsely accused and the unjustly imprisoned. The activists of the Freedom and People's Rights movement had been suffering government suppression for over a decade. In many cases, activists were framed for crimes they did not commit or imprisoned for crimes, which to them, were not crimes. To suggest that the courts were fair, albeit careless and inept, in the determination of guilt of the activists was to present a delusion that did not jibe with reality, especially considering that Ruikō himself was imprisoned as a result of this system of suppression during the mid-1880s and that the Public Order Ordinance—the most absolutist measure of government suppression of the movement, which completely disregarded the judicial system—had just been issued.[32]

Of course, Ruikō could not help but articulate his criticism of the Meiji justice system in such terms, given that he would be arrested again if he were to express his real thoughts on the matter. But this does not mean that *Yūzai muzai*'s introduction by Ruikō was simply a passive concession to the government's publishing laws. On the contrary, it actively rewrites the history of political injustice as the immaturity of criminal investigations and judicial procedures; it replaces politics with epistemology. Ruikō's introduction functions to transform the favorite topic of the political novel—the unjustly accused and imprisoned—into the falsely accused who is a result of a judicial mishap. It wipes away the malicious intent of the government in the prosecution and false imprisonment of political activists. But at the same time, it does not do away with the victims of political injustice. Rather, it emphasizes the falsely accused as the protagonist and hero of *Yūzai muzai* and positions the falsely accused character of a French story within the Japanese history of injustice during the Freedom and People's Rights movement era. While replacing political injustice with epistemological failure, the introduction also promotes

---

32. On January 28, 1882, Ruikō wrote an article entitled "Kaitakushi kanri no shobun o ronzu" (Argument for the punishment of officials of Colonization Bureau). As a result he was charged with contempt of officials, although he was found innocent in the first trial. However, he was later recharged with the same crime. At the time of the second warrant to appear in court, Ruikō was extremely ill and had disappeared from the public scene for a year. As a result, the warrant apparently never reached Ruikō. His absence in court was taken as a sign of flight, and he was found guilty of the charge. When Ruikō returned to the public scene, his whereabouts were discovered, and he was sent to prison in Yokohama for 16 days (Itō Hideo, *Kuroiwa Ruikō: tantei shōsetsu no ganso*, 42).

the allegorical substitution—a substitution which was fostered by the political novels and by their allegorical mode of production and consumption—of the falsely accused in *Yūzai muzai* with the Meiji political activists who were victims of the government's injustice.

Yūzai muzai's introduction expressing the epistemological concerns of the judicial system was a part of the first steps to unite the nation that had been so divided in the past decade. It tried to make amends with the many political and moral injustices committed by the government against the political activists during the Freedom and People's Rights movement. In this sense, it signaled a coming of a new age beyond radical activism and violent protests, especially considering that *Yūzai muzai* also contains an introduction by Nakae Chōmin (1847–1901), one of the leading philosophers of the Freedom and People's Rights movement who like Ruikō had close ties to the Liberal Party, that expressed a similar criticism of the Meiji judicial system. Coming about a year after he was banned from Tokyo as the result of Public Order Ordinance, Chōmin's introduction, like Ruikō's, suggests that Ruikō's adaptations were a part of an attempt to reshape the political consciousness of the likes of *sōshi*, a newly emergent group of nationalistic youths whose political fervor during the "three major issues petition" movement prompted this ordinance. No doubt an integral part of their 'political' education, the *E'iri jiyū shinbun* was the venue where Ruikō and Chōmin could speak to the fervent *sōshi* who appeared not only boisterous but also dangerous and out of control even after December 1887 as Japan prepared to consolidate itself as a modern state with the promulgation of the Meiji Constitution planned for 1889 and the opening of the Diet for 1890.

Indeed, such criticism was not Ruikō's alone but had been brewing in public forums prior to his emergence, with the most vocal advocate being Tokutomi Sohō. In his "Shin Nihon no seinen" (The youth of new Japan), an essay published in 1887 of a lecture he gave in 1885 that propelled him onto the national scene, Sohō writes that "The so-called age of political parties has passed, and the age of education has arrived." The opening editorial in the first issue of *Kokumin no tomo* (February 1887), which Sohō founded to serve as the editor-in-chief, reiterates and expands on this sentiment, stating: "The aged of old Japan have left at last, and the boys [*shōnen*] of new Japan have arrived indeed. The Eastern phenomena have passed at last, and the Western phenomena have arrived indeed. The destructive age has passed at last, and a constructive age is to come indeed."[33] Marked by a strong desire to separate the present age from the past, these passages put to rest the "destructive" activities backed by "political parties" in the Freedom and People's Rights movement and call for the production of new subjects and citizens based on "Western education." Sohō and *Kokumin no tomo* continued to herald this paradigmatic shift in the sociopolitical landscape, as they called for the transformation of politically minded and violent *sōshi* into *seinen*, or new youth, characterized by their Western education, apolitical attitude, and entrepreneurship.

According to Sohō, such a task was not easy and must be carefully guided because the term *sōshi* did not simply designate the violent political activists of the latter half of the 1880s but also "the dangerous facet of 'student-youth' that existed on the flip side of [their] violent powers."[34] And carefully did Ruikō's detective stories guide this transformation of the Meiji subject. They did not disappoint, employing various strategies to ensure the success in this task, not the least of which was to emphasize them as stories of the falsely accused—as variations of political novels—via paratexts, including the introductions by Ruikō as well as Chōmin and Ruikō's classification of stories about crime discussed above. In so doing, they functioned as an active force in reorganizing the political energies of their readers that had been thwarted as a result of the collapse of the Freedom and People's Rights movement, in general, and of the absolutism of the Public Order Ordinance, in particular. And it was in this process that the detective emerged as a hero in Meiji Japan. By positing his primary task to be the exoneration of the falsely accused rather than the capturing of the criminal, Ruikō's stories transform the detective—once the enemy of the people who, in service of the government, violated their privacies and caused their false imprisonment—into the savior of the falsely accused who fights against the injustice of the government, proving, or rather reassuring, that such injustice can be overcome by an epistemological search for the truth. But the various paratexts discussed in this section provide only a frame and, as such, can only do so much. The reason that Ruikō's detective stories, and especially his *Yūzai muzai*, were effective in reorganizing the thwarted political energies in the post–Freedom and People's Rights era

33. Both passages cited in Kimura Naoe, *"Seinen" no tanjō*, 20–21.

34. Ibid., 46. For details on *Kokumin no tomo*'s criticism of *sōshi*, see ibid., 42–50.

was because the narrative structure of *Yūzai muzai* also revolved around this substitution of politics with epistemology.

Rumors, Secrets, and the Shōyō-esque World of Yūzai muzai

Although Ruikō may have placed the trial and the judicial system as a focal point of his stories for political reasons, *Yūzai muzai* goes further than criticize the credibility of the court system; rather, it seems to dismantle it altogether.[35] It is true that the innocent Takeyasu is found guilty of shooting Count Kuroda, bringing to the fore the inaccuracy of the trial system, and so the story seemingly reiterates the sociopolitical concerns expressed in Ruikō's introduction to the story. But the problem here is that neither the lawyers, defendant, nor witnesses show any respect for the truth that is supposedly at stake in a trial. In the trial scene of *Yūzai muzai*, the story's long-awaited climax, everything turns to rhetoric: lawyers Ōkawa and Makura in Takeyasu's services concoct a false story for him to tell the court because they have no evidence that would prove his innocence, and Count Kuroda, in order to avenge Takeyasu's infidelity with his wife, gives false testimony that Takeyasu was the one who had shot him. Interestingly, the readers are told that the description of the trial is an excerpt from a special newspaper report:

---

35. *Yūzai muzai* begins when Count Kuroda is shot at his mansion in Sawabe Town near Paris and Baron Hoshikawa Takeyasu, who lives in the next village, surfaces as a possible suspect. The officials, including the examining court judge Karumino, who are friends of Takeyasu are doubtful at first, but they arrest him upon discovering numerous incriminating evidence and upon Takeyasu's inability to provide an alibi. Notified of the arrest of her son, Takeyasu's mother hires the lawyer Ōkawa, but Takeyasu's refusal to disclose his whereabouts on the night of the crime hinders the investigation. Ultimately, Takeyasu reveals to his friend Makura that he has been the lover of Countess Kuroda for some time and that he was at Kuroda's mansion on the night of the crime to break off his affair with her. Just before the trial, Takeyasu escapes from his cell for a meeting with the Countess, where they accuse each other of shooting the Count. While they eventually realize that neither of them is the culprit, Count Kuroda overhears their conversation, and, realizing the infidelity of his wife, he, despite not seeing his attacker, vows to make sure that Takeyasu will be found responsible for the crime. True to his word, Count Kuroda testifies at the trial that Takeyasu was the man who had shot him, and Takeyasu, whose lawyers (Ōkawa and Makura) could not obtain any evidence to prove his innocence, is found guilty of the crime. The day after the trial, however, various evidence in Takeyasu's favor comes to light, and he is quickly exonerated of the crime.

according to the reporter, people believed Takeyasu's story and his innocence because of the circumstantial evidence that Ōkawa had gathered in order to support the story, but the court found the testimony of Count Kuroda against Takeyasu too convincing. In short, the verdict is decided based on the truth value of two lies, Takeyasu's and Count Kuroda's.

Instead of being a place where truth of the case is exposed, the trial then becomes a place where the truth value of circumstantial evidence and witness testimonies are destroyed: constructed evidence and false testimonies have just as much power as the 'real' ones that the magistrate Karumino had gathered in his preliminary investigations. Indeed, the newspaper report of the trial barely touches on the physical evidence and testimonies that Karumino had collected. While the text portrays Karumino as Takeyasu's friend who betrays him for political ambitions and as an unjust official who "abuse[s] the law without thought and determine[s] lightly the guilt of people," Karumino is the only person who is actually presenting evidence that he believes to be true. And the problem is not that Karumino draws incorrect inferences from collected evidence, for he correctly reasons in light of the evidence that Takeyasu was present at the scene of the crime around the time that the Count was shot and that Takeyasu had used his gun on the night of the crime. Rather, the problem seems to lie with Takeyasu, who refuses to admit these facts to Karumino, instilling in the latter's mind that Takeyasu has something to hide.

If the truth of the case is not determined through physical evidence and testimonies—the way it is supposed to be done under Western law—then how is it established in *Yūzai muzai*? The day after the trial, several pieces of evidence, most of which concern the relationship between Takeyasu and Countess Kuroda and the falsity of Count Kuroda's testimony, come to light to help exonerate Takeyasu. In theory, however, such information should not affect the case against Takeyasu. On the one hand, Count Kuroda's recanting of his testimony that Takeyasu was the one who had shot him simply returns the state of affairs to the end of the preliminary investigation when there was no doubt in many people's minds of Takeyasu's guilt, despite Count Kuroda's testimony that he had not seen his assailant. On the other hand, the revelation of the adulterous relationship between Takeyasu and Countess Kuroda, as well as their meeting at the Kuroda Mansion on the night of the attack, seems to worsen Takeyasu's situation by giving him a major motive for killing Count Kuroda and by placing him at the scene of the crime.

Of course, these possibilities for interpretation are not explored in the story because they become pointless when Tatarō, a helper at Kuroda's estate, confesses to shooting the Count. Ultimately, the investigation of Tatarō by the detective Tōda—which leads to the former's confession—is the only method through which the truth of the case is established.

Given the cautious attitude toward material and circumstantial evidence expressed in the introduction, *Yūzai muzai*'s reliance on the criminal's confession as the ultimate sign of his or her guilt seems natural. At the same time, it could be construed as a conservative attachment to a premodern judicial system, which operated under the assumption that "confession can always be obtained" or, to put it in another way, "institutionalized torture always brings out the truth."[36] But it is important to note here that Tatarō does not confess because he has been tortured or caught, nor does he confess to cleanse his conscience, as in the traditional sense of the term. Rather, his confession is an act of braggadocio expressed as a result of his inebriety. Tatarō's confession is a result of trickery, of the detective's befriending him—that is, deceiving him—and getting him drunk to a point where his inhibitions are wiped away.[37]

And here, we see the first instance of a connection between Ruikō's detective stories and the notion of the novel as espoused in Tsubouchi Shōyō's *Shōsetsu shinzui*. Getting a person drunk is one way to weaken the power of his/her reason, which would in turn lead to the weakening of reason's suppression of the *external* manifestations of *internal* thought and emotion. In this sense, the investigatory method of Detective Tōda, as commonplace and primitive as it seems, finds relevance in the world described by Shōyō's treatise whose fundamental dichotomy is that be-

---

36. Yasumaru, "'Kangoku' no tanjō," 281.

37. A similar reliance on the act of confession as well as the detective's use of trickery to induce a confession can also be seen in Ruikō's other detective stories. For example, in *Makkura*, the detective Wakimi stages a false conference where he first names Eriko as the criminal only to change his mind to name her sister Mariko as the criminal. What Wakimi is hoping to achieve by this one-man show is to read the reactions of the two real suspects of the case whom Wakimi had called to hear this conference in another room. According to Wakimi's analysis, the murder of Ōsu Senzō was committed by someone who is in love with either of his daughters, Eriko or Mariko. Thus, Wakimi surmises that if Eriko or Mariko is named as the criminal, the real criminal will speak up and confess his crime. Indeed, this is what happens. When Wakimi names Mariko as the criminal who will be charged with the murder of Ōsu Senzō, Koshie, the secretary to Ōsu Senzō, charges into the room and confesses his crime.

tween interior and exterior. Indeed, it is hard to deny that Ruikō's detective stories more than any other fictional narratives of Meiji Japan—including Shōyō's own fictions—took to heart the novelistic worldview espoused in Shōyō's *Shōsetsu shinzui*. For, whether bastardized or not, *Yūzai muzai* and Ruikō's adaptations are relentless, just as Shōyō was in his treatise, in their portrayal of the world as constituted by epistemological dichotomies and fragmented identities, and it makes perfect sense that the proliferation of Ruikō's detective stories in the late 1880s and early 1890s preceded the emergence of "Shōyō-esque clichés," as mentioned in the conclusion to Chapter 1, as evidence of the institutionalization of Shōyō's novelistic worldview.

Fittingly, such a worldview lies at the heart of one of the most striking features of *Yūzai muzai*: namely, the prominent role that rumors play in the narrative. Take for instance the introductory description of the marriage between Count and Countess Kuroda:

> Because at the time the Count was 47 years old and the Lady only 20, the people with mouths that do not know right from wrong started various rumors that the Lady was very ugly and could not marry anyone else so she promised to marry the old Count or that, because the Lady's father was poor, she considered his desperate living situation and became the wife of the Count. However, because the Lady was none other than the first daughter of the Tazawa Family, said to be one of the richest among French aristocracy, and because the Tazawa Family presented 150,000 yen as a gift upon her marriage, it didn't seem to be a case of considering the living situations. Moreover, the Lady whose name was Baishi was rumored to be a rare beauty. . . . Because it [such age difference in marriages] was few in example, people still whispered and rumored that there was a deep secret in this marriage, but this was certainly not the case for it appeared that the Count received Lady Baishi because he loved her, and Lady Baishi promised to serve her husband because she loved the Count. . . . And within four or five years, they had two daughters, and people came to revere her as the mirror of chastity.[38]

And here is the narrative description, this time of Tatarō's life:

> Tatarō was by nature an idiot without equal, not knowing east from west nor even his own name. . . . When he was 15 or 16, Countess Kuroda felt sorry for his condition and, paying a large amount of money, sent him to Doctor Seki Noboru of Sawabe Town. There he received as much treatment as possible, but there's no medicine for fools, or so they say, and even after one and a half year, there was not a slight bit of change. . . . Although he was born an idiot to this degree, what was strange was that sometimes he would say things fluently and listen to reason.

---

38. Kuroiwa, *Yūzai muzai*, 4–5. All subsequent reference to this source will appear in the text in parentheses.

Seeing this, some people rumored that Tatarō was not a real idiot and that he was pretending to be an idiot to gain people's sympathy (14–16).

Revolving almost entirely around rumors that the narrator has heard, these passages show the way in which rumors arise from people's observation of phenomena that deviates from the norm. It is the age difference between Count and Countess Kuroda that starts the rumors because such age difference is not normal in a marriage. It is Tatarō's occasional fluency and display of reason, which go against the normal understanding of "an idiot without equal" and, thus, produce rumors that he is actually faking his mental condition. Rumors, then, are not nonsense but a result of commonsense that understands deviations from the ordinary state of reality in terms of a depth in reality, that is, that there is something out of the ordinary hidden beneath the surface, which would explain the deviations. And it is precisely because people are always suspicious that others are hiding something—that they are not what they seem to be—that people resort to interpreting what lies behind the mask of an individual: people of *Yūzai muzai* believe in the existence of a rift between public and private identities.

But what about the dichotomy between external appearance and internal thought, which constitutes the other half of the worldview presented by Shōyō's *Shōsetsu shinzui*? Take for example the following passage, in which Ōkawa warns Takeyasu's mother as they exit the train station of Sawabe Town for the first time since Takeyasu's arrest:

However worried you may be, you must hide your worries and walk through the crowd with a calm expression on your face. If your eyes show a trace of tears, then the people in the crowd would no doubt say that even his mother believes Master Takeyasu to be a criminal. This Sawabe Town is a very small place, and one person's rumor immediately spreads all over town, so as long as you are steady, you will be able to dispel the rumors. There is nothing scarier in a trial than rumors because jurors determine guilt entirely based on rumors (54).

Indicating that the propensity of people to produce rumors figures prominently in the minds of the characters, this passage reveals Ōkawa's belief in the power of rumors to determine the outcome of a trial because the judicial system employs jurors from the general public who are easily manipulated. But more importantly for our purposes, Ōkawa argues here that tears on the eyes of Takeyasu's mother would signify to the observer that she believes her son to be guilty because people would deduce from her tears a corresponding internal state or thought, which in this case is her grief that her son has committed a heinous crime. In this sense, *Yūzai muzai* posits rumors as being produced according to the belief that external appearance or demeanor has a corresponding internal state or thought, although such a relationship between external appearance and internal emotion is presented here in negative terms, as a producer of misunderstanding and untruth, because tears as signifiers have multiple signifieds. The tears of Takeyasu's mother comes not from her belief in his guilt but from her concern for him despite her belief in his innocence; in effect, her tears come from her suspicion of the judicial system that she shares with Ōkawa.

Nonetheless, this sort of vulgar psychology or psychological reasoning abounds the pages of *Yūzai muzai* and provides the fundamental interpretative framework for the characters to understand each other.[39] For instance, the clerk to the magistrate Muchine, who accompanies Karumino to Takeyasu's mansion to make the latter's arrest, gives the following reason—one based on psychological reasoning—for why he believes Takeyasu to be innocent: "This crime couldn't have been committed by Master Takeyasu. If he was guilty, he wouldn't be able to suspect that something is going on and yet still maintain his composure" (35). Indeed, this sort of analysis, if we can call it that, can be found in most if not all of Ruikō's stories and reaches ridiculous proportions in *Majutsu no zoku* (Villain of magic; supposedly a translation of Harry Rockwood's *Donald Dyke* [1883], serialized in *E'iri jiyū shinbun* from January 16 to February 16, 1889) when its detective claims: "I can determine most villains just by looking at their face."[40]

Of course, if the criminals of detective fiction were "most villains" and could be determined through such a method, then there would be no story. It is precisely those who can give the appearance of being innocent while being guilty that are fit to play the criminal in a detective story. Ōkawa is well aware of this, as suggested by the following passage, in which he explains the reasons for his belief in the innocence of Takeyasu whom he has yet to meet:

> Though it isn't like I have a deep reason but when the magistrate [Karumino] first stepped into his room, Master Takeyasu thought it was a joke and said, "okay, enough, cut it out." Can someone who is guilty say such bold things? If he was guilty and still said these words, Master Takeyasu is a big hero. However, he

---

39. At the same time, the examples of psychological reasoning offer the readers of *Yūzai muzai* and Ruikō's adaptations with a code—one that Shōyō never attempted to produce—by which one can understand internal thoughts and emotion through external appearance and behavior.

40. Kuroiwa, *Majutsu no zoku*, 23.

couldn't defend himself at all after he realized that it wasn't a joke. A real criminal definitely would have thought of an excuse in advance to get himself out of the situation. Anyone who does not think of this is a big fool. So, if Master Takeyasu was the real criminal, then Master Takeyasu was first a big hero and within an hour, he became a big fool. Because one person cannot become a big hero then a big fool, this crime was not committed by Master Takeyasu but by someone else (62).

This passage makes clear Ōkawa's use of psychological reasoning ("Can someone who is guilty say such bold things?"), but he goes a step further than Muchine's analysis. Unlike Muchine, who believes it to be impossible that a guilty person can maintain his composure under pressure, Ōkawa believes this type of behavior to be characteristic of a master criminal ("big hero"). Rather, Ōkawa's argument for Takeyasu's innocence revolves around a contradiction in his character—that he appears as a master criminal one second and a "big fool" in another—which could be explained only if Takeyasu was indeed innocent but unable to justify his innocence for one reason or another.[41] While Ōkawa understands that the people of Sawabe Town believe in the interior/exterior correspondence, as suggested by his comments to Takeyasu's mother, he does not adhere to it, but believes instead in the unity of identity whose disruption can only be explained by missing information, namely, a secret harbored by an individual.[42]

And if such logic on the part of Ōkawa is so convincing in *Yūzai muzai*, it is because the harboring of a secret is not for Takeyasu alone. As the story would have it, all the characters involved in the crime—Tatarō,

---

41. A similar kind of reasoning founds the detective Chirakura's realization of Komori Arinori's innocence in *Hito ka oni ka*, although it was Chirakura who had urged Magistrate Taburo to arrest Arinori in the first place. Hearing from Taburo that Arinori has not confessed to the crime or made any attempt to prove his innocence, Chirakura states: "Oh dear! If that's the case, Arinori is not the criminal. The true criminal is elsewhere" (Kuroiwa, *Hito ka oni ka*, 299).

42. Indeed, the refusal to provide explanations that would exonerate himself or herself is one of the primary characteristics of the falsely accused in Ruikō's stories, and it is viewed by the detective as a sign of his or her innocence. The reasoning here is that a criminal would have thought of false explanations to argue his or her innocence because the inability to provide explanations such as an alibi would indicate his/her guilt. However, the detective would argue that to do something that would be an indication of his/her guilt (in this case, not give any explanations) is an indication that the accused is innocent precisely because no one would do something that would incriminate oneself.

the criminal; Count Kuroda, the victim; Takeyasu, the accused; and Countess Kuroda, an indirect victim as well as the accused in the eyes of Takeyasu and Ōkawa—have a secret that they are keeping from the people of their community. They are all not what they seem. While some people in Sawabe Town rumor that he is faking his condition, Tatarō has succeeded for the most part in presenting himself as an idiot. The same can be said for Count and Countess Kuroda, who, despite past rumors, have been hiding the truth concerning the marriage (that he 'bought' her with money).[43] Appropriately enough, the most important secret of *Yūzai muzai* is also the most 'secret'—without any rumors—as Takeyasu and Countess Kuroda have been extremely careful in hiding their affair from everyone, the latter being considered "the mirror of chastity" by many who live in Sawabe.

By hiding their secrets and faking their appearances, these characters have problematized the truth value of the correspondence between public and private identities, a problematization that characterizes the modern individual in Shōyō's literary theory (and the woman in his novels) but is directly linked to criminal responsibility in the world of Ruikō's adaptations exemplified by *Yūzai muzai*. While only Tatarō is a criminal in the court of law, all four characters in question are, thus, guilty of breaking the social law of correspondence between interior and exterior that is taken as granted by the members of the Sawabe community. It is no surprise then that Takeyasu's false story is believed by the court, although upon being recommended to lie to the court by Ōkawa, he states: "It is true that Mr. Ōkawa's lies are very well-constructed, but I can't tell them as if they were true, knowing in my heart that I am telling a lie. Even if I lie a little bit, my nature is such that my face immediately turns red, so I will be found out by the judge in a second" (229). He may still believe that he is a subject of the law of correspondence, but Takeyasu has already fallen from grace.

Fittingly within the framework of the detective story marked by the penetration into private lives, it is the event of the crime and the ensuing investigation that expose these secret harborers as violators of the

---

43. To the extent that there were rumors surrounding the marriage of Count and Countess Kuroda as well as Tatarō's mental condition, *Yūzai muzai* describes the process of discovering that rumors are not always empty hogwash. What starts this process, of course, is the catastrophic event of the crime, and what catalyzes it is the investigation that ensues, for it is precisely in a criminal investigation that the truth value of floating claims must be verified.

correspondence between interior and exterior. But such exposure is not only a result of the crime but also its cause. Tatarō's assault on the Count is a repayment for the kindness that Countess Kuroda has shown him. And the opportunity for such repayment arrives with the overhearing of a conversation between Countess Kuroda and Takeyasu that reveals their love affair. It is because Tatarō believes the words of Takeyasu ("If you were a free woman, I would take you as my wife" [182])—uttered not in honesty but as a way to end the affair without angering her—that Tatarō decides to kill Count Kuroda. Thus, it is the newly gained knowledge of another's secret that instigates the crime. Indeed, this is not only true in *Yūzai muzai* but also in Ruikō's other stories. In *Hito ka oni ka*, Minoru murders Oden upon discovering that she was involved in a plan to switch the baby born out of the adulterous affair between his mother Lady Sawada and Count Komori with the baby between Count Komori and his wife.[44] In *Makkura*, Koshie murders Ōsu Senzō, the father of Mariko, upon realizing that Mariko, with whom he is in love, has become involved with the British aristocrat Kurihara against her father's wishes and that her father has threatened to remove her from his will.

The exposure of a secret to a third party as the cause of a crime—this is the form of Ruikō's early stories. Moreover, the secrets are most often, if not always, aristocratic secrets involving and harbored by the members of the aristocratic class that are discovered by members of the non-aristocratic class. In this regard, *Hito ka oni ka* is exemplary, for the story involves a murder committed by the non-aristocrat Minoru that is instigated by a false hope that he in fact may be the rightful heir of the aristocratic Komori family. Even *Makkura*, which takes place in New York City and depicts a crime within the non-aristocratic Ōsu family, seems to fit into the mold to the extent that their lifestyle, wealth, and social status—all of which dissuade the hardworking secretary Koshie from pursuing Mariko as his wife—make them no different from the aristocratic families of *Yūzai muzai* and *Hito ka oni ka*, who reside in France. But what is the significance of this structure made possible by the over-

44. More specifically, Minoru discovers that Oden, who was asked to carry out this plan of baby-switching, did not carry out this plan at the request of Lady Sawada. Thus, the direct cause of Minoru's crime is the realization that Minoru can claim himself to be the son of Count Komori and his official wife—that is, the rightful heir of the Komori family—as long as Oden is dead so that she cannot testify otherwise.

whelming presence of aristocratic families at the heart of the crime that constitutes one of the primary textual characteristics of Ruikō's translations? What kind of role does it play in constructing the ideological message of the stories? And how does it affect the stories' reception by the Japanese readers? Surprisingly enough, if we were to take Ruikō's word, it means nothing, for the question of aristocracy is an insignificant side effect of his stories.

The Aristocratic Question and Allegories in Conflict

In his foreword to *Makkura*, Ruikō tells us by way of an anecdote how he came to adapt this work. One day, the president of the *E'iri jiyū shinbun* notifies Ruikō that the readers have given him the nickname Professor Count (*hakushaku hakase*). Ruikō does not understand the reason for this, but the president calls him a "simple" man with a smirk and leaves without answering. Ruikō then turns to his coworkers for the reason, but they only laugh at him. Finally, he learns that he has been dubbed Professor Count because among the numerous stories that he has adapted, "there is not one in which a character who is either a count or countess does not appear."[45] To this 'accusation' Ruikō responds:

> I prefer to translate French stories. Of the famous stories of France as well as England, there are hardly any that consist only of people without rank or title. Then is it the case that we should call all French and English writers Professor Count? And it is not without reason that aristocrats appear in the story, for in these countries, aristocrats basically make up the entire high society. Moreover, because aristocrats without exception come from wealthy families, they often find themselves in a situation that is fit to be made into a story, and because of their high social standing, they draw the attention of people. If I were to pick a story without aristocrats, there is no choice but to look for a story about the United States. However, American stories tend to be less extraordinary than those of France. This is the reason why I had to abandon the aristocrat-less stories of the United States and choose the aristocrat-filled stories of France.[46]

But hearing this response, one of his co-workers comments that Shōyō's *Nisegane tsukai* is an American story but an interesting one. Thus, Ruikō goes home to his library and digs out a copy of *The Leavenworth Case*, which is also by the author of *XYZ* Anna Katharine Green. Discovering that there are no aristocrats in the story, Ruikō translates a few chapters

45. Kuroiwa, *Makkura*, 1.
46. Ibid., 2.

and shows it to the president asking, "Am I still Professor Count?" But to this, the president smirks and calls him a "simple" man yet again.[47]

While there exists an aristocrat in *Makkura*—the British aristocrat Kurihara whose secret marriage to Mariko serves as a spark to her father's murder—this factual discrepancy is not what makes this episode interesting. It is rather Ruikō's vehement denial of any significance to the prominence of aristocratic characters in his stories: their prominence is merely a trivial side effect of translating French novels, so trivial that he was unaware of it and could not fathom why his readers would call him Professor Count. Yet also implicit in his apology is the suggestion that it is the presence of aristocratic characters, almost a necessity in European novels and lacking in American ones, that make the former more interesting for him than the latter. That is, while he believes the aristocratic prominence to be of no importance within the context of Meiji Japan, he believes otherwise within a European context where aristocrats, because of their wealth and social standing, are fitting subjects of storytelling. And of course, the choice he makes in order to deny his nickname—to tell of the murder of a millionaire who is equal to the best of aristocrats in all aspects but an official title—reveals indeed that the aristocratic element is crucial to his stories. But why then the vehement denial?

In presenting this episode, Ruikō is not really a "simple" man as the president of the *E'iri jiyū shinbun* claims. He is far from it. The episode that is included in the foreword to *Makkura* is not just an innocent anecdote that reveals the behind-the-scenes look at the newspaper/translation industry. Instead, it is a carefully thought-out story, most likely fiction, I would argue, that explicitly denies the importance of the aristocratic element in his stories all the while implying something else. His argument that aristocrats are fitting subjects for the production of interesting stories begins with the premise that "in these countries [France and England] the aristocrats basically make up the entire high society." But this premise holds true not only for France and England, as well as other European countries, but also in Japan, where such an aristocratic class made up "the entire high society" and was characterized by wealth and high social standing: the members of the newly formed peerage system who pretended to lead the life of European aristocrats.

---

47. Ibid., 3.

On July 7, 1884, the government issued the Peerage Ordinance (Kazoku rei), in short, "a law that allowed the cutting in of influential members with samurai antecedents [*shizoku*] into the peerage, that is, a law to make peers out of non-peers."[48] With this ordinance, numerous people were added to the peerage, which to this point only consisted of those of noble birth as defined during the Edo period. Devised primarily by Itō Hirobumi, this ordinance had in sight the establishment of the House of Peers in the Diet to be opened in 1890. The members of the peerage would be stripped of their right to vote or run for the House of Representatives, but they in turn gained the exclusive right to vote or run for the House of Peers. In this sense, the Peerage Ordinance sought to provide titles to those who were deemed fit to make up the House of Peers, which was a machinery concocted by the government to thwart radical republicanism in the Diet. That the majority of these 'qualified' individuals were from the old Chōshū or Satsuma clan only revealed the already well-known fact that this new system was another ploy to secure the political dominance of the Chōshū-Satsuma alliance within the government.[49]

In addition to their importance as political entities, the new peers had another more immediate task: namely, their participation in the social world of Rokumeikan, the venue through which the peers became known among the general public as we saw in the introduction to this chapter. And it is within this context that Ruikō's episode in *Makkura*'s foreword begins to make sense, as a defense to deny the possible allegorical reading of his stories, precisely because he understood that such a mode of reading was part of what made his stories popular. Of course, the readers' effecting of the allegorical mode of reading does not depend merely on the simple conflation of the terms ***kizoku*** (aristocracy) as used in Ruikō's texts and ***kazoku*** (peers) of Meiji society. While the former term operates as a marker that instigates as well as confirms the possibility of such a reading, it is ultimately the narrated events which must

48. Ōkubo, *Kazokusei no sōshutsu*, 9. For an English overview of the new peerage system, see Jansen, *Making of Modern Japan*, 391–92.

49. As Ōkubo argues, this did not mean that the peers were independent group of elites who looked out only for their own interests. Their task consisted of thwarting radical republicanism in the Diet, but their existence, as "guardians of the imperial house," meant that this protection was not only for the government but also, and primarily, for the emperor to have a voice in the Diet (*Kazokusei no sōshutsu*, 180–81).

hold up to the realities of context. The readers must be able to make sense of the secondary narrative produced as the result of a substitution of peers for aristocrats in terms of the Meiji realities. Thus, the question becomes: what kind of narrative events in Ruikō's texts allows for this substitution? And what kind of secondary narrative is produced as a result?

As we have seen, the dynamic of identification in *Yūzai muzai*—the falsely accused Baron Hoshikawa Takeyasu as its protagonist and hero is conflated with the political activists of the Freedom and People's Rights movement through paratextual materials—is reinforced by the focus of the majority of the text that lies not in the search for the 'true' assailant of Count Kuroda but in the reason that prevents Takeyasu from disclosing his side of the story to anyone. This reason, of course, is his infidelity with Countess Kuroda, the knowledge of which instigates Tatarō's assault on Count Kuroda. But while it is this assault that constitutes the crime-to-be-solved in *Yūzai muzai*, Takeyasu's infidelity was also a crime in Meiji Japan according to the 354th article of the Criminal Code, which designates an imprisonment of six months to two years for adultery.[50] It is clear that Ruikō was aware of the article and sought to emphasize this fact, for the criminal nature of Takeyaku's infidelity is made explicit in the text through an alteration made in the process of translation.

After hearing Takeyasu's story of his meeting with the Countess on the night of Count Kuroda's attack, the lawyer Makura asks Takeyasu: "That next morning when Karumino and others came to question you, what did you think?" (185). This translation is almost verbatim to the English text of *Within an Inch of His Life* that runs: "And the day after, when they came to arrest you, what was your first impression?" In the English version, the answer is a simple but ambiguous one: "I thought at once of

---

50. The article reads: "A woman with a husband who commits adultery is imprisoned for no less than six months and no more than two years. The same applies to the man with whom the adultery is performed. The guilt described in this article is argued after the lawful husband makes a complaint. However, if the lawful husband has permitted adultery previously, the complaint has no effect" (Ishii and Mizubayashi, *Hō to chitsujo*, 402). The misogynistic nature of this law is evident from the fact that this law makes no mention of husbands who commit adultery with an unwedded woman.

Valpinson [the name of the Count's estate]."[51] In the Japanese text, in contrast, the answer is longer and leaves no doubt regarding Takeyasu's thoughts: "I thought it to be a joke, but when I soon realized that it wasn't, I thought that the Countess had confessed everything to the Count, and so they came to question me on the charge of adultery" (185). In such a way, the Japanese text frames Takeyasu's affair with Countess Kuroda within the moral/lawful context of Meiji society, and, in so doing, presents Takeyasu as a criminal who is aware of the criminality of his involvement with the Countess.

It is this theme of adultery, I would argue, that served as one provocation to effect the allegorical reading of Takeyasu as a member of peerage in the immediate post-Rokumeikan and post–Freedom and People's Rights age. Topics involving the sexual immorality of the upper class, such as adultery (*Yūzai muzai*), illicit love affairs (*Makkura*), and even the swapping of an illegitimate child (*Hito ka oni ka*), were precisely the subjects of various rumors and scandalous news surrounding the peers and the Rokumeikan balls in which they participated. And this equation was made stronger, I would argue—despite sexual immorality certainly not being a vice restricted to those at the high echelons of Meiji society as leaders of Freedom and People's Rights movement were guilty in this regard as well—by the relationship between the peers and the ideology of *risshin shusse* that had been driving the ambitious youths of Meiji Japan to go out into the world to seek success.

As Maeda Ai has discussed, this ideology finds its origin in the bestsellers of early Meiji, Nakamura Masanao's *Saigoku risshi-hen* (Success stories of the West; 1870-1871; a translation of Samuel Smile's *Self-help*) and Fukuzawa Yukichi's *Gakumon no susume* (Encouragement of learning; 1872–1876), both of which espoused the notion of human equality and the universal potential to succeed in life through learning. But while works such as Kikutei Kōsui's *Sanpū hiu: sero nikki* (Walks of life diaries; 1884) reproduced the social ideals of *risshin shusse* ideology in fictional format, it was rather the failures to achieve these ideals that became the subject of many fictional narratives. Maeda writes:

> The youths who gathered in cities with their backpacks whose passions for *risshin shusse* were incited by *Sero nikki*—the world that they should encounter was described in [*Tōsei*] *shosei katagi*, *Ukigumo*, and *Maihime*. Let us leave aside Ko-

51. Gaboriau, *Within an Inch of His Life*, 308. Although the edition cited here is not that which Ruikō used, it contains the same text as the edition to which he most likely referred: the Seaside Library version published in 1883 by Munro.

machida Sanji, but it goes without saying that Utsumi Bunzō and Ōta Toyotarō suffered heavy defeat or were forced a bitter failure, externally by the system of bureaucracy or by vulgar society and internally by their own introverted personalities. What's more, behind Utsumi Bunzō and Ōta Toyotarō lay accumulated the tragedies of those youths who had become mixed up in the ebb of the Freedom and People's Rights movement and had lost sight of their goals in life. The design plan of *risshin shusse* presented by *Sero nikki* was exposed by the realities around Meiji 20 and would fade rapidly.[52]

As this passage argues, around 1887 (Meiji 20), it was becoming clear to the Meiji intellectuals and youths that *risshin shusse* ideology was collapsing, that it was no longer tenable within the realities of Meiji society. And it was during this period that the peers pranced around in their Western dresses at their Rokumeikan fancy balls, peers who in a perverted way were the emblems of the possibilities of *risshin shusse* ideology precisely because the selection of new peers—according to the Peerage Ordinance in 1885—was not based on family heritage but rather on their contributions to the nation. Whether consciously or not, the new peerage system functioned as a part of the *risshin shusse* ideology that produced the 'illusion' of social mobility. But this illusion was already beginning to fade a couple of years after the Peerage Ordinance, and what was left was a façade that revealed itself as such.

Despite being incorporated into the peerage system because of their important contribution to the nation and, thus, symbolizing success of the highest honor, the new peers who were invariably high-ranking government officials were not the beacons nor exemplars of Westernization, civilization, and enlightenment they claimed to be representing. And the proof was the scandalous articles in the newspapers that revealed them as immoral persons who were no better, if not worse, than the ordinary Japanese. After all, as many Meiji intellectuals should have been aware, what many of the new peers did to achieve their rank and 'success' was to commit violent crimes, sometimes even assassinations, against the Tokugawa shogunate in the waning moments of the Edo period and against the political activists of the Freedom and People's Rights movement. In this sense, it might appear that Ruikō's detective stories, in revealing the dark secrets of aristocrats-as-peers and proving that they are not as high and noble as advertised, had a similar task to the scandal reporting during the Rokumeikan age. If this were indeed the case, however, fiction would merely be a support of already existing

52. Maeda, "Meiji risshin shusse shugi no keifu," 143.

phenomena in reality. But as a closer look into the text of *Yūzai muzai* makes clear, Ruikō's detective stories, while evoking these newspaper reports, operated in a very different manner from them.

Takeyasu is an adulterer and, as such, a criminal. But what happens to him in *Yūzai muzai*? Count Kuroda—who could have brought adultery charges against Takeyasu—dies, leaving a will stating that the infidelity of his wife should be kept a secret. And the younger daughter of the Kurodas, who Countess Kuroda claims is her child with Takeyasu, also dies from an illness from which she had been suffering. With all obstacles out of his way, Takeyasu marries his fiancée Lady Nishiki, his involvement with her having prompted his breakup with Countess Kuroda in the first place. The sins of Takeyasu are not atoned but merely wiped away through the discretions of the authorities and the detectives. It is only Tatarō—the poor fool—who is punished in the story. To the extent that Tatarō commits the crime with the intention of making possible the marriage between Countess Kuroda and Takeyasu, that is, of making *lawful* their *criminal* affair, Tatarō functions as a martyr to whom the guilt of Takeyasu is transferred. Tatarō's crime makes the happy end for Takeyasu possible.

It is this narrative structure found not only in *Yūzai muzai* but many of Ruikō's other works—the exposure of a criminal secret that is wiped away through the criminal act of a third party—that produces a conspiratorial relationship between the detective, the authorities, and the readers as those in the know.[53] They are the only ones who realize the truth of the case. The fact that Takeyasu's trial is presented to the readers in the form of a newspaper report underscores this point: the fictional public who read the aforementioned report would have no idea of the truth that motivates the testimonies of Takeyasu and Count Kuroda.

---

53. For example, in *Hito ka oni ka*, the secret does not lie with Arinori, the falsely accused, but with his father Count Komori, who had switched the baby between him and his wife (or so he thinks) with the baby he had with his mistress. To prevent his wife from realizing this switch, Count Komori forbids his wife from having any contact with the baby, resulting in her madness and death. This secret is exposed to the authorities during the criminal investigation, but it does not become public because Minoru commits suicide in return for money to establish a foundation of the falsely accused (the establishment of a foundation is an addition that Ruikō made in the process of adaptation). Importantly, Minoru receives a large sum of money from Count Komori in exchange for his silence regarding Komori's criminal secret, a silence that Minoru guarantees by his own suicide.

To the fictional public, Takeyasu's criminal secret—the cause of the assault on Count Kuroda—remains just that, a secret, and the readers who have followed the story through a behind-the-scene perspective that only the novelistic gaze can provide are actively situated in opposition to this fictional public. In fact, the newspaper reporting of the trial makes explicit emphasis of the divide between the fictional public and the real readers and of the privileged position of the latter in having access to the secret that the former does not know yet cannot help suspecting: "Takeyasu and Count Kuroda stared at each other as if to curse severely with their eyes, and this arose the suspicion that there is a great secret hidden [between them] that might be seen through by the judge" (300).

What's more, the medium-specific characteristic of *Yūzai muzai* as a newspaper serialization produces a similar opposition between knowing and unknowing within the actual reading public. At first glance, a detective story of significant length, such as *Yūzai muzai*, seems like a perfect fit for the newspaper. Having to divide itself into small daily portions, serialized detective fiction forces its readers to wait for their clues, and this wait contributes to making readers into devout fans and, thus, newspaper subscribers: wanting to know what will happen next, the readers keep reading the newspaper everyday.[54] Yet, this characteristic also has the opposite effect on readership. Because each clue matters and the story's end is only satisfying as an untangling of the intricate web of suspicions and the resulting resolution of suspense produced through the course of the narrative, the serialized detective story precludes new readers who may have heard rave reviews of the story from joining it midpoint: readers who do so will literally have no clue about what is going on. Thus, a serialized detective story offers its enjoyment and satisfaction to exclusive readers who had the good fortune of joining the story from the beginning.

In these ways, *Yūzai muzai* sets up its readers on the imaginary level as those in the know on two different but interrelated levels. On the one hand, it creates an exclusive club of readers (newspaper subscribers) whose enjoyment of the story partially derives from their privileged posi-

54. The wait that the readers of serialized detective fiction must experience in consuming the story allows for ingenious ways to promote it among the reading public. For example, Ruikō held a contest where readers sent in their guesses on the identity of the criminal during the serialization of *Makkura*. Such a contest would obviously be impossible in a single-book detective story.

tion within the reading public, both fictional and actual. On the other hand, it consciously aligns its readers not on the side of the general public, but on the side of authority whose position within the story world—as those who know the whole of the story just like the readers—prompts and supports such alignment.

And as holders of exclusive information, readers judge the story of *Yūzai muzai*, in which the criminal secret of the falsely accused aristocrat is forgiven and no social or public consequences result from it in the text. By positioning the readers in such a manner, *Yūzai muzai* succeeds in reproducing the critical narrative structure at the level of story-events—the exposure of a criminal secret that is wiped away through the criminal act of a third party—on the level of the readers' reception. In other words, the sense of moral condemnation that the readers may have had for the aristocratic Takeyasu as an immoral adulterer allegorical of the Meiji peers is neutralized through the story's ending, in exchange for the privilege of being on the side of the know. For, to punish Takeyasu would mean public (obviously, on the fictional level) exposure of his dark secret and, thus, the loss of the exclusive status that the text has constructed for its readers. Within this mode of allegorical reading, then, the fictional public uproar that might arise if the adultery between Takeyasu and Countess Kuroda were exposed is replaced by the private enjoyment of the real reader. Through their individuation as private readers whose enjoyment derives from the contrast between their position of knowledge and the ignorant (both fictional and actual) public, the readers fall to the side of the authority, sharing their knowledge of the truth behind the case as depoliticized entities.

And assisting in this process of forgiveness by and depoliticization of the reader is the *other* allegorical reading promoted through various paratextual materials. Given the theme of the falsely accused outlined in *Yūzai muzai*'s introductions, the readers know that Takeyasu is innocent when he is arrested in the early chapters. To the extent that the introductions promote the identification of Takeyasu as the falsely accused hero of the Freedom and People's Rights movement, as we saw earlier, it is with him that readers' sympathies lie. The readers' interests also lie with Takeyasu because his secret—the reason for not defending himself despite his innocence—is what keeps the pages turning in the first half of the story. But when the secret is revealed, Takeyasu, while innocent of the crime with which he has been charged, proves himself indeed to be a criminal. It is at this moment, I would argue, that the other allegorical reading—the aristocrats-as-peers reading—takes effect, and the quality of being an aristocrat rather than a falsely accused becomes the dominant characterization of Takeyasu. But almost simultaneously with Takeyasu's confession, there begins the search for the real criminal of the assault on Count Kuroda, redirecting readers' interest toward the more proper detective story framework of the whodunit. This interest finds its resolution when the story exposes Tatarō as the true culprit in the assault of Count Kuroda, and this is when Takeyasu's innocence becomes most symbolic. That is, Tatarō's confession of the crime functions as a foil, emphasizing Takeyasu's innocence in the assault on Count Kuroda such that even his past crime—his affair with Countess Kuroda—is forgiven, if not forgotten, in the process.

The two allegorical readings of *Yūzai muzai*—one promoted and the other suppressed by paratextual materials—operate in their opposition to weave a text that fosters the production of a 'national' subject fit for the post–Freedom and People's Right movement age, an apolitical figure whose allegiance to the nation was based on his identity as a private reader who, as an individuated subject, conspired with the government to share the truth that the general public did not know. In promoting the creation of a new reading public through the depoliticization of his readers, Ruikō's detective stories were a continuation of Tsubouchi Shōyō's literary project. Whereas my examination of Shōyō's project in the previous chapter focused on its moral characteristic, his notion of the novel articulated in his *Shōsetsu shinzui* was also a political one, providing a fundamental criticism of the political novel to redirect the frustrated energies of political activists. For, in emphasizing the novel's proper object of depiction as human feelings and private lives—not of heroes or villains but of ordinary people with both virtues and vices—*Shōsetsu shinzui* argued that what was important and meaningful did not have to be found in the public or political realm of action but also lay hidden beneath the surface and behind closed doors in the ordinary world of everyday life.

Just as Ruikō's stories were responsible for the institutionalization of Shōyō's novelistic worldview of epistemological dichotomies and fragmentary identities, however, *Shōsetsu shinzui* had to wait for the proliferation of Ruikō's detective stories to complete its political project. Indeed, the novel as a newly emergent genre seems to have had no immediate effect on the production and consumption of political novels, which, as previously mentioned, became more popular as the Freedom and People's Rights movement waned in the late 1880s. According to Yanagida Izumi, the number of political novels published, which had hovered around 30 works a year, suddenly jumped to around 100 works in 1887 and peaked at around 120 works in 1888. It was only in 1889, when Ruikō's detective stories had become popularized, that the number of political novels published dramatically decreased.[55] In this sense, it was not Shōyō's *Shōsetsu shinzui* but Ruikō's detective stories that served to quench the popularity of the political novel and, by extension, the political energies and dreams that were the backbone of its consumption.

As argued above, the key to Ruikō's success had much to do with the ingenious manner by which he approached the political project that he shared with Shōyō. Unlike Shōyō, who presented the novel squarely against the political novel, Ruikō presented his detective stories, first and foremost, as political novels and promoted their consumption within the allegorical interpretative mode characteristic of this literary genre. That is, he duped his readers, redirecting and reorganizing the qualities characteristic of the political activists of the Freedom and People's Rights movement and of *sōshi*, who were their successors, with those more suitable for a 'national' subject: political indignation and frustration expressed as public uproars with private enjoyment of individual readers fueled by an epistemological desire for truth as well as a vulgar interest in the scandalous. And it was in this process of the production of a 'national' subject that the detective emerged as a hero who not only exonerated the falsely accused–as–political activist but also exposed the dark secrets of the aristocrat-as-peer. But as his original detective story *Muzan* makes clear, it was not so easy to temper the frustrated political energies of former activists and produce a subject fit for the new age of authoritarian Meiji state, for, as suggested by the disclaimer with which Ruikō introduces the detective in *Muzan*—"there is no profession in this world that

---

55. These publication numbers are from a list of political novels compiled by Yanagida. According to this list, the number of political novels published in 1889 was around 50 works, decreasing to around 30 works in 1890. The list's shortcomings relating to the question of generic boundaries aside, we could make the argument that 1889–1890 marked the end of politics in Meiji Japan with the promulgation of the constitution and the opening of the Diet, which, in turn, led to the decline in the number of political novels published. I would say, however, that the frustrated political energies of the activists were not diffused so easily by the historical events themselves—especially given the gap that existed between the activists' vision of the constitution and the Diet and their actual manifestations—but required active ideological manipulation, in which Ruikō's detective stories played a key part. For further detail, see appendix to Yanagida, *Seiji shōsetsu kenkyū*.

is this detestable and this honorable"—the detective would remain a figure of deep ambivalence in Meiji Japan.[56]

Logic and Prejudice of Muzan

On September 10, 1889, Ruikō published *Muzan*, his only original work of detective fiction of significant length.[57] Consisting of three parts—suspicion, conjecture, and resolution—*Muzan* deviated from the usual style of his adaptations and focused on the analytical aspects of crime solving. Importantly, this tripartite structure corresponded to Ruikō's definition of the detective story articulated within the previously cited commentary that classified stories about crime into the detective story, criminal romance, and the sensational novel. Given the timing of their publication, with the commentary appearing just nine days after the publication of *Muzan*, it is clear that Ruikō sought to differentiate *Muzan* from his adaptations and to present it as a true work of detective fiction, an attempt that appears have been successful, at least historically.[58] For example, Edogawa Ranpo emphasizes *Muzan*'s import beyond the history of Japanese detective fiction, positioning it as a pioneering work in the genre's international development as one of the earliest examples of analytical detective fiction in the short story format that *would later* be established by Arthur Conan Doyle and R. Austin Freeman (1862–1943).[59]

Reflecting such paratextual strategy and critical reception, the story's central focus is the young detective Ōtomo's analysis of the case, which

---

56. Kuroiwa, *Muzan*, 16.

57. *Muzan* appeared in the first installment of a story collection series *Shōsetsu sō* by the publishing house Shōsetsukan, which also published the book versions of Ruikō's *Hito ka oni ka* and *Majutsu no zoku*.

58. The publication notice of *Muzan*, which appeared in the *E'iri jiyū shinbun* on September 13, 1889, claims that this work is "the beginning of detective fiction in Japan." Also, the same claim is made in the introduction by Umenoya Kaoru to the book version of *Muzan* published in February 1890.

59. Ranpo writes: "Considering that Meiji 22 is 1889 and the first story of Conan Doyle *A Study in Scarlet* is 1887 and his first collection of short stories *Adventures of Sherlock Holmes* is 1892, Ruikō published a pure detective story in the short story format in the vein of Conan Doyle or Freeman three years before the Holmes stories when it was still the golden age of long detective stories internationally. . . . This is an important aspect that cannot be forgotten by those who write the history of Japanese detective fiction" ("Ruikō no sōsaku *Muzan* ni tsuite," first appeared in *Shin tantei shōsetsu* [July 1947], reprinted in *Hitori no Bashō no mondai*, 17).

begins with his discovery of the strands of curly hair on the victim. Examining these strands of hair under a microscope, he ascertains that the curl is not natural but rather made through repetitive weaving. With the knowledge that hairs have a characteristic of being smooth to the pull in one way but not in another, Ōtomo discovers that one of the hairs is aligned in the opposite direction. In light of this finding, he reasons that the strands of hair must have come from someone who uses false hair to increase the volume of his/her hair. Because the wounds on the victim were made from the back, Ōtomo further reasons that the victim was running away from the criminal. And because it is difficult to think that a man will run away from a woman, he argues that the criminal must be a man, despite the fact that the use of false hair is a feminine practice. What kind of a man uses false hair and weaves his hair in such a way to create the kind of curl found on the strands of hair in question? Ōtomo tells the police captain Ogisawa:

> This way of curling must be from a Chinese man. You know the head of Chinese men? They separate it [hair] in three and weave it into a string. . . . And there are no men aside from Chinese men who add false hair. Not only do they use false hairs, if that is not enough they add strings. The false hair and this condition of curling—if this is not from a Chinese man, I will resign my job.[60]

In this way, Ōtomo narrows the suspects, but his analysis continues. From his observation of the contours of the head wound, which was the direct cause of death, he argues that the wound was made by a spinning top and, thus, the criminal must have a young child. Moreover, he discovers that the natural hair found on the victim was actually dyed gray hair. Reasoning that a person who would commit such a violent crime requiring strength cannot be an old man, he concludes that the murderer must be a person who dyes his hair because he has "gray hair unfit for his age" (38). Ultimately, Ōtomo constructs the following profile of the criminal: a Chinese man who dyes his gray hair but is not old and has a child who plays with tops. It is through this meticulous process of observation and reasoning (however flawed they may be to the readers of the twenty-first century) that he arrives at the identity of the criminal whom he has never heard of or met. Through Ōtomo's analysis, then, *Muzan* reveals the power of the scientific—that is, Western—methods of investigation to

---

60. Kuroiwa, *Muzan*, 35. All subsequent references to this source will appear in the text in parentheses.

identify criminals and to control criminal activities that disrupt the order of Japanese society.[61]

But despite such a narrative structure that would receive the aforementioned praises of Ranpo, this is not to say that Ruikō reproduces completely the ideological 'essence' of Western analytical detective fiction in Meiji Japan through his *Muzan*, as highlighted by Uchida Ryūzō. On the one hand, Uchida points out the existence of two contrasting detectives in *Muzan*—a "great detective" who employs "logical and scientific reasoning" and a "mediocre detective" who bases his investigations on "experience"—and, noting that this duality exists as Dupin and the prefect Monsieur G------ in Poe's Dupin trilogy, states that *Muzan* "follows the form of the classical detective story started by Poe in which reasoning and analysis are superior to crude empiricism."[62] On the other hand, Uchida views the fact that the "great" detective of *Muzan* is a police detective as a sign of the story's limitation resulting from the 'un-modernness' of Meiji society, for the likes of Dupin and Holmes are private citizens belonging on the side of the public. Uchida states:

> Whether the detective attaches himself on the side of state powers or civil society is an important issue, but in this work [*Muzan*] there is not yet a consciousness of a clear distinction regarding the position of the subject who enforces justice. The absence of this consciousness to distinguish, in one way, relates to the extent of modern nature (*kindai-sei*) of Japanese society at this time, and can be said to be due to the way in which Ruikō expresses this condition."[63]

As this passage indicates, Uchida's focus lies in the analysis of *Muzan* as an imitator of a Western literary form whose level of consciousness regarding the significances of its characteristics—whether the detective is a private citizen or belongs to the police, in this case—reveals the extent

---

61. Takahashi Osamu states: "The mystery brought about by a 'Chinese' in [Tsukiji] is solved by a 'Japanese' detective who has acquired Western logic and knowledge and is heralded as 'the Lecoq of the East.' That is, it repositions [*chaos*] on the side of order (*nomos*). The repositioning of *chaos* within a Western order from such an opposition between *chaos* and *nomos*—that is, 'a story that dissolves *chaos* within *nomos*'—can be thought of as the ideology that underpins western style detective stories" ("'Tantei shōsetsu' ga inpei suru mono," 31–32).

62. Uchida Ryūzō, *Tantei shōsetsu no shakaigaku*, 8. The contrasting investigatory methods of the two detectives are not only observed by critics like Uchida; indeed, they are emphasized in the text, for example, through a following aside by Ōtomo: "If he [Tanimada] is going to investigate [*tantei sureba*] through experience, experience, and experience, I will investigate with science and logic" (26).

63. Uchida Ryūzō, *Tantei shōsetsu no shakaigaku*, 10–11.

of Japan's modernization. And because *Muzan* was the only 'classical detective story' by Ruikō or any other writer in Meiji Japan, it seems natural to understand this work, as Uchida does, as an isolated experiment advanced for its time and, thus, a work lacking in contemporaneity, a condition brought on by the fact that it is a superficial imitation of a foreign model and not a cultural artifact that reflects the concerns and problems of a modern society.

But here I would argue the opposite. The status of the detectives as belonging to the police is not a failure to imitate a Western model but a necessity arising out of the sociopolitical conditions of the late 1880s that interpellated the detective story as a fitting framework to negotiate the paradigmatic shift taking place during the period in question. In other words, what is truly significant about *Muzan* is not the success with which Ruikō manages to reproduce the ideological 'essence' of Western analytical detective fiction in Meiji Japan. Rather, it is the fact that *although* Ruikō appears to be doing just this, he does something completely different, as discerned in the rather surprising narrative developments of *Muzan* that force a radical reinterpretation on the part of the readers in making sense of this story.

Considering the story's focus on the analytical methods of Ōtomo, it is amazing that it is not Ōtomo but Tanimada, the old veteran and empiricist 'fool,' who captures the leading witness Okon whose testimony reveals the entirety of the criminal case. Okon, a woman who works in one of the gambling houses of Tsukiji, was suspected by Tanimada of being involved in the murder. That this suspicion itself is highly suspect is obvious to Ōtomo as well as to the readers given the simplicity of Tanimada's reasoning: according to his memory, Okon, with whom Tanimada became acquainted during his past undercover stint in Tsukiji, has curly hair similar to those found on the victim.[64] But regardless of the quality of his reasoning, Okon was involved in the murder, albeit not criminally and not in the way Tanimada had imagined, and it is her capture and confession which lead to the revelation of her former husband Chin Shinei as the murderer. That is, while Ōtomo's analytical method exposes the irrationality of Tanimada's method, the former does not prove the ineffectiveness of the latter. How is this possible? And what is the significance

---

64. Rightfully, then, Ōtomo has this to say to the police captain regarding Tanimada's investigation: "Tanimada thought this to be curly hair and thought of Okon. That is his mistake. If his suspicions are right, then it is a fluke" (31).

of this strange narrative structure of *Muzan* that seems to go against Ruikō's own positioning of this work?

Upon arriving at the crime scene, Tanimada observes the numerous wounds on the victim and quickly comes to the hypothesis that the victim was killed by multiple assailants. But since such a way of killing would create lots of noise and there has been no report of such commotion, Tanimada argues that the crime must have occurred in a place where such commotion is commonplace. Ōtomo, however, is full of doubt regarding this conclusion, not believing in the existence of a place where a fight is so common that the neighbors would not report it to the police. To this Tanimada suggests the gambling houses, but Ōtomo does not believe that such places exist in Tokyo either. He states: "There is no way that a gambling house like that exists in this world of civilization and enlightenment [*kaimei sekai*]" (21). Here Ōtomo is a naïve believer in the power of the law who cannot distinguish between what should be and what is. With the enforcement of the Criminal Code in 1882, gambling became illegal in Japan, and gamblers became the target of severe government prosecution around 1884 when it became clear to the authorities that there was a strong connection between groups of gamblers and radical members of the Liberal Party responsible for various violent acts against the government.[65] In this context, Ōtomo's view of 1889 Japan as a society of "civilization and enlightenment" suggests his presumption of the government's success in eliminating gamblers and gambling houses through its laws and, thus, his failure to question the government's ability to accomplish what it set out to accomplish.

But Tanimada's hypotheses regarding the murder case put into question not only the effectiveness of the government but also its very authority. According to Tanimada, gambling houses do exist in Tsukiji, a foreign settlement consisting mainly of Chinese denizens where Japanese laws are not applicable because of the extraterritoriality clause in the unequal treaties.[66] To this bit of news, Ōtomo responds in a manner tinged with nationalistic undertones: "So in Tsukiji, the Chinese are taking advantage of the fact that Japanese law doesn't apply there to do disre-

---

65. A government detective's report in June 1884 makes this connection explicit. For details, see Yasumaru, "'Kangoku' no tanjō," especially 305–9.

66. Edward Seidensticker states: "Tsukiji was never popular with Europeans and Americans, except the missionaries among them. The foreign population wavered around a hundred, and increasingly it was Chinese" (*Low City, High City*, 36).

spectful things like that" (22). As a naïve rookie detective who denies the existence of an unlawful and chaotic space where a murderous commotion would not be reported by its denizens, Ōtomo accepts Tanimada's propositions only when he realizes that this space exists within the foreign settlements beyond the reach of Japanese law.

Through Tanimada's hypotheses and Ōtomo's response to them, then, *Muzan* constructs a binary opposition between the 'enlightened' and vigilant Japanese citizens who would no doubt report any commotion to the police and the criminally "disrespectful" Chinese who not only abuse the extraterritoriality clause of the unequal treaties to dabble in 'unenlightened' activities like gambling but who also prey on Japanese citizens—like the victim—goading them into doing the same and thereby exposing them to criminal danger. And this binary opposition extends to the respective spaces in which they live: Tokyo as a space of law and order and Tsukiji as a crime nest located outside it. But precisely because Tsukiji, while separate from the rest of Tokyo in terms of the law, exists geographically within the city, Tsukiji and its Chinese denizens are presented by the text as threats to the development of Japan as a nation of "civilization and enlightenment." The story's ending assigns Tanimada, despite his faulty analysis, to the role of the mediator between a mysterious crime and its truths and confirms these binary oppositions and the underlying equation of racial/national prejudice that constitute them: Tsukiji = the Chinese = crime.

By giving such a role to Tanimada, *Muzan* not only questions the need for a detective like Ōtomo who employs the analytical method but also problematizes the analytical nature of his method by bringing attention to the fact that it, too, bases itself on such racial/national stereotypes. This can be seen in his analysis of the hair found on the victim in the previously cited passage—"this way of curling must be from a Chinese man . . . there are no men aside from Chinese men who add false hair"—and is reiterated in the way that he ultimately discovers the criminal's identity. After he learns that the criminal also dyes his hair, Ōtomo simply asks a Chinese seller of ink if he knows anyone who sells or uses hair dye. That this seller immediately directs Ōtomo to Chin Shinei in Tsukiji reflects, as does Tanimada's capture of Okon, the ease with which the Chinese criminals of Tsukiji can be identified and controlled by Japanese authorities.[67] Thus, Ōtomo's analysis confirms the

---

67. The highly prejudicial attitude toward the Chinese in this text—and, by extension, Ruikō, who would reveal his jingoistic tendencies during the Sino-

equation of racial/national prejudice on which Tanimada's speculations are based, positing it as the *reality* that founds the world of *Muzan* as a whole.

But the identification of the criminal by Tanimada and Ōtomo alike does more than provide a seemingly reassuring message regarding the ability for Japanese authorities to fight crime. By locating the source of the crime outside the purview of Japanese authorities—that is, the Chinese living in Tsukiji—*Muzan* leaves the internal order of Japanese society and its continued progress toward civilization and enlightenment briefly disrupted but fundamentally unscathed, despite the violent murder that initiates the story. At the bottom of this mechanism is the extraterritoriality clause of the unequal treaties that underscores the disruption of social order brought on by the crime as the result of a problem whose causes are not only external but also political in origin.[68] This emphasis, in turn, produces a slippage in *Muzan* where the crime becomes an aftereffect of the criminality brought on by the absence of law, a slippage of the problem-to-be-solved from the crime case to its political cause that is particularly resonant in *Muzan* because it manifests itself in the figure of Ōtomo as the protagonist of the story.

Upon discovering the identity of the criminal but prior to disclosing his analysis to the police chief and to the readers, Ōtomo suggests the magnitude of his findings and their political implications. He states:

> This isn't an ordinary crime. Because the criminal is at an unexpected place, the day I reveal his name, it will cause a flutter; it will move public opinion. If people have public speeches because of this, like the time of treaty negotiations, I will most likely be their orator; I will be like Ōi Kentarō. I can return to my hometown with success accomplished (30).

Japanese War (1894–1895)—can be inferred from the name that he gives to the criminal of *Muzan* Chin Shinei. Although such a name can be found among the Chinese population, the combination of the surname Chin, one of the most common surnames, with Shinei, which in phonetic Japanese is the imperative form of the verb "to die," reveals a racial slur that was most likely understood as such by the readers of *Muzan*.

68. The presentation of the crime's cause as existing externally to the society of the detective and the readers is a common practice among the detective stories of Poe and Conan Doyle, which locate the source of the crime—the origin of the criminal and/or the motive of the criminal—in the non-Western countries and colonies. But as I argue below, *Muzan* develops this characteristic along a different trajectory.

In this passage, Ōtomo reveals himself as a subject whose investigations into the murder case bring out his political aspirations. Believing that the murder case involves the killing of a Japanese citizen by a Chinese national, Ōtomo fantasizes an international scandal involving the issue of extraterritoriality and of the unequal treaties that force this condition on the Japanese authorities. Importantly, his fantasy develops within the framework of the Freedom and People's Rights movement as he compares the 'impending' scandal to the public uproar during the treaty negotiations of 1887, identifying himself with Ōi Kentarō (1843–1922), one of the most prominent figures of the movement.[69] That is, the police detective Ōtomo views the likes of boisterous *sōshi*, who were responsible for the public uproar during the treaty negotiations, not as past enemies of the state who disrupted the order of Japanese society, but as heroes of the past whom he hopes to emulate. In so doing, *Muzan* suggests that the reorganization of frustrated political energies, as the goal of Ruikō's adaptions of Western detective stories, has not been fully successful, ready to rear its ugly head if given the chance. For, in *Muzan*, the detective whose task *should* be the restoration of order disrupted by the event of the crime reveals himself as a patriot who seeks to use the crime as an opportunity to disrupt social order by creating public uproar and political dissension.[70]

---

69. Historically speaking, such a view on the part of Ōtomo suggests the success of the government to incorporate, rather than to punish, the political activists of the Freedom and People's Rights movement into the national program. On the most visible level, this process took the form of the incorporation of the movement's leaders into the cabinet and the peerage system. For example, Ōkuma Shigenobu (1838–1922), the founder and leader of Rikken kaishintō (the Constitutional Reform Party) and Gotō Shōjirō (1838–1897), a member of the Liberal Party and the leader of the nationwide political movement that took place in the late 1880s, became peers and members of the Kuroda cabinet in the late 1880s. In conjunction with the promulgation of the Meiji Constitution on February 11, 1889, moreover, prisoners of political crimes were pardoned and released. Among the more famous of these prisoners included Kōno Hironaka (1849–1923) who was serving time for his 'involvement' in the Fukushima Incident, Hoshi Tōru (1850–1901) who was a leading member of the Liberal Party, and, fittingly enough, Ōi Kentaro who had been imprisoned for his involvement in the Osaka Incident.

70. The fact that this political fantasy becomes his primary interest behind the solving of the murder case can be easily discerned by Ōtomo's repeated emphasis of the political magnitude of the case in his comments to the police captain Ogisawa: "If it was just a murder then it is just a crime, but if [the criminal]

But as the story would have it, such aspirations are shattered, and the possibility of an international scandal becomes foreclosed when the detectives learn at the end of the story that the victim—presumed to be Japanese—was actually Chin Shinei's brother (and Okon's lover), and, thus, Chinese. Coming to light through Okon's confession, the mistake in the assumption of the victim's national identity stems from the simple fact that Chin's brother was dressed and had a haircut like a Japanese person. To the extent that the murder involved two Chinese brothers who shared the same woman, the discovery of the victim's national identity negates the nationalistic outrage on the part of Ōtomo—and, by extension, on the part of the readers—that a Japanese citizen was killed by a Chinese national whose criminality had been harbored by the extraterritoriality clause of the unequal treaties.

At the same time, however, it brings out another fear: just by imitating a Japanese on the most superficial level, any Chinese person—who, according to the world of *Muzan*, is most likely to be criminal in nature—has the power to blend in with the Japanese, and in so doing, 'pollute' the lawfulness of Japanese society. And here Walter Benjamin's observation once again seems relevant, albeit tangentially: "The original social content of the detective story was the obliteration of the individual's traces in the big-city crowd."[71] In *Muzan*, of course, the obliteration is not of the individual but of national identity. And in the detective story that Benjamin discusses, it is precisely the task of the detective to counter this "obliteration of the individual's traces" in the *actual* world and to resurrect the individual and its traces in "the big-city crowd" on the level of the *imaginary*. In contrast, *Muzan* works not in individual details but in racial/national stereotypes, but to the extent that they make a mistake in their assessment of the victim's national identity, the detectives of *Muzan* fail the task of the detective that Benjamin describes.

In the end, *Muzan* problematizes the assuring message—that Chinese stereotypes allow for easy arrests of Chinese criminals—through the discovery of the victim's national identity that suggests the ease with which such stereotypes can be shed. While the 'solving' of the crime in *Muzan* may assuage the fear of the 'criminal' Chinese to spread outside the foreign settlements, the story also incites the exact same fear by pointing out the limitations of the investigatory methods of Ōtomo and

---

is Chinese, it might become a problem between countries" (35); "If the newspapers got a hold of this, it will create a public uproar" (43).

71. Benjamin, "The Paris of the Second Empire in Baudelaire," 43.

Tanimada alike. Rather than proposing an investigatory method whose reproduction will ensure order—albeit at the level of the imaginary—in the everyday lives of the story's readers, *Muzan* posits a social condition and the coming of an age in which such an investigatory method based on racial/national stereotypes will no longer be valid. The social condition is the mixing of Japanese and Chinese citizens; the age is when the boundaries of superficial national identity have become blurred.

In so doing, *Muzan* reinforces the popular fear regarding the issue of cohabitation (*naichi zakkyo*; literally, mixed residence in the interior) that was growing during the late 1880s in conjunction with the government's renegotiations of the unequal treaties headed by the Foreign Minister Inoue Kaoru. One of the stipulations in the renegotiations was that, in return for the partial restoration of Japan's rights to prosecute and tax foreigners, Japan would abolish the system of foreign settlements and open itself up to foreigners. But this stipulation prompted various oppositions in and out of the government. As Sakamoto Takao notes, behind these oppositions existed "the anxiety triggered by the laws of then fashionable social Darwinism that if the inland were opened, foreigners would dominate the Japanese in various social spheres."[72] While the indefinite postponement of the renegotiations on July 29, 1887 and Inoue's resignation on September 17, 1887 assured that cohabitation would not take place, at least for the time being, this issue would continue to plague Japan well into the 1890s.

In *Muzan*, the fear is not of the Westerners as a 'superior race' that would dominate Japan if given the chance. Rather, the fear is of the Chinese as criminals who will 'pollute' the order of Japanese society and threaten Japan's progress toward "civilization and enlightenment." By revealing the ease with which the differentiation between a Japanese and a Chinese can be made problematic, *Muzan* fuels this fear and makes it particularly poignant precisely because such differentiation depends on national identity rather than racial identity: in the most superficial terms of *Muzan*, a Japanese and a Chinese can look alike. But fueling this fear also does something else. It reorganizes the hierarchy between Japan and Western nations—a hierarchy that weighed heavily on Meiji officials and intellectuals alike—as a hierarchy between Japan and China, in which the latter is posited as the uncivilized and unenlightened nation from which the former must set itself apart. In short, the fear of the Chinese

72. Sakamoto, *Meiji kokka no kensetsu*, 316.

reinforces a hierarchical relationship in which Japan and its citizens can understand themselves as occupying a superior position. And it is through the figure of the detective Ōtomo who utilizes Western methods of investigation that *Muzan* secures this Japanese superiority: although a Japanese and a Chinese may look alike, a Japanese thinks like a Westerner.

ᴥ

In November 1892, Kuroiwa Ruikō left the *Miyako shinbun* to establish his own newspaper *Yorozu chōhō*. By this time, he had amassed a vast number of fans who craved their daily dose of detective fiction, as vividly illustrated by the following figure: by December 1892, only a month after the establishment of *Yorozu chōhō*, the *Miyako shinbun*'s readership had dwindled from 27,000 to 7,000 while the *Yorozu chōhō* already boasted a circulation of 35,000.[73] But significantly, the *Yorozu chōhō* would not become known for its detective stories but another project whose precedents played a fundamental role in their emergence. With the reporting of the House of Sōma scandal in July 1893, the *Yorozu chōhō* established itself as the leader of yellow journalism and, through the decade and into the new millennium, it continued to uncover various scandals of the upper class, political parties, and religious organizations.[74] And complementing the *Yorozu chōhō*'s project was Ruikō's turn away from detective stories to family romance and tales of adventure whose moral world of values could serve as the criteria by which the subjects of scandal reports were to be judged.

Indeed, given the historically specific function of the genre, it seems natural that the golden age of detective fiction was short lived.[75] While

---

73. The figures are from Itō Hideo, *Kuroiwa Ruikō: tantei shōsetsu no ganso*, 135.

74. The House of Sōma scandal involved the rightful heir of a family of the peerage who had been imprisoned in his own house by the members of his own family because of his mental illness. For an overview of the scandals covered in *Yorozu chōhō*, including the House of Sōma scandal, see Oku, *Sukyandaru no Meiji*.

75. The detective fiction boom would continue until around 1895 thanks to those who tried to cash in on the popularity of detective stories fashioned by Ruikō. The *Miyako shinbun* responded to the rapid drop in sales caused by Ruikō's departure by serializing what they called "real-life detective stories" (*tantei jitsuwa*, stories based loosely on real-life events) beginning in March 1893. As mentioned in the Introduction, moreover, the literary group Ken'yūsha began publication of the "detective novel" series in January 1893.

Ruikō's translated detective stories would continue to be popular reading materials, I would argue that their political function had become largely inoperative by the early 1890s. As much a story of the exposure of dark secrets of the upper class as the story of the discovery of the criminal, Ruikō's adaptations functioned to redirect the unresolved political energies of the Freedom and People's Rights movement, which had quickly deteriorated in the late 1880s. On the one hand, the specific structure of Ruikō's detective stories suggested that the members of the upper class, the victors within *risshin shusse* ideology, were just as immoral, if not more so, as those whose sociopolitical ambitions and dreams were shattered by the harsh realities of Meiji society. On the other hand, by embedding such a structure within the detective fiction form in which all the tensions developed within the narrative are forcibly resolved in the discovery of the criminal, Ruikō's stories sought to temper the readers' responses to the immorality of the upper class in the story-world *as well as* in the real world and turn frustrated political activists into entertained private readers.

In this sense, Ruikō's detective stories ultimately were an ingenious mechanism of misdirection to weather the period of crisis in the late 1880s just as Japan was consolidating itself as a modern nation. And as misdirection, they never succeeded in resolving the fundamental problem created by the collapse of the Freedom and People's Rights movement, namely, the future of Meiji youths left without ways to be productive citizens in an apolitical society. But this is not to say that Ruikō was oblivious of such issues, as his keen awareness of this problem is made clear in *Muzan* through its protagonist Ōtomo. To the extent that the acquisition of Western learning was one of the primary pursuits of the Japanese intellectuals in the Meiji period, Ōtomo is a successful figure of such a pursuit and a model for Meiji students whose goals were to do the same. But at the same time, his turn toward nationalistic politics in the course of his investigations reveals Ōtomo to contain elements of unresolved political energies that could erupt at any moment if given the chance.

As suggested by the lack of *Muzan*'s successors, it would be a difficult task to mediate the ideological fusion between the detective, the student, and the political activist within the sociohistorical realities of Japan at the turn of the twentieth century and to present a successful example of incorporating the Meiji educated class into the national program as productive citizens. Indeed, as we shall see in the following chapters, the Japanese novel as the flip side of the detective story developed in the opposite direction—the interpellation and identification of the educated with the criminal rather than with the detective—as if in search of a new ideological mechanism through which the detective can emerge. And fittingly enough, this search finds its foundation in the example of an eruption of frustrated political energies that results in a double murder of an old pawnbroker and her sister in Fyodor Dostoevsky's masterpiece *Crime and Punishment* whose Japanese translation appeared in the same month that Ruikō established his *Yorozu chōhō*.

THREE

Of Crimes and Punishments: The Tribulations of Meiji Students in the Writings of Japanese Naturalism

Often touted as the first modern novel of Japan, Futabatei Shimei's *Ukigumo* already suggests the fundamentally different inflection of the development of the Japanese novel to its Western counterpart. Its protagonist Bunzō—characterized by his "Western learning" and "boarding house" existence, the two critical traits of the student as described in the opening passage of Tsubouchi Shōyō's *Tōsei shosei katagi*—seems to have had a bright future.[1] But we do not even get a glimpse of this future fulfilled, for *Ukigumo* begins with the destruction of one future hope, his success in a government post, to tell the chain of events leading to the destruction of another, his marriage to Osei. And importantly, in narrating this tragic fate of a Japanese intellectual, *Ukigumo* squarely places his characteristic Western learning at the center of his failures,

---

1. Tsubouchi, *Tōsei shosei katagi*, 223. This is not to say that *Tōsei shosei katagi* simply provides a positive view of the future for Meiji students, for, as Atsuko Ueda has argued, it depicted the students of private schools dreaming of success when "an irreversible hierarchy was being instituted between state and private schools. The future of private-school students was grim: if government were to succeed in its endeavor, they would have no hope of taking part in politics at the center" (*Concealment of Politics, Politics of Concealment*, 119).

thereby providing a scathing criticism of *risshin shusse* ideology that drove the ambitious Meiji youths in the preceding decade.

Not only does *Ukigumo* present Bunzō's idealistic and stubborn belief in reason and logic as determiners of what is right and wrong—that is, Western learning as a code of praxis as opposed to nominal credential—as the reason for his dismissal from his post, but it also reveals the tendencies for such reason and logic to quickly deteriorate into something different altogether. In the course of the story, Bunzō's reason-based reflection (or so he thinks) regarding Osei turns into rhetoric of fantasy that enables him to disavow the realities of his relationship to her, producing one delusion after another so that he can reclaim his self-worth in the world from the confines of his second-floor room to which he has become withdrawn.[2] And to the extent that the seemingly large-scale nature of dismissals that serve as the backdrop of the story must have evoked in the Meiji readers the major restructuring of the bureaucratic system in 1885, *Ukigumo* reframes and represents such a *sociopolitical* cause that lies, for the most part, beyond one's control in *individual* terms of his relationship to Western learning.[3] In this sense, *Ukigumo* posited the Meiji student as a subject of blame who needed rescuing and, through this sacrifice, maintained the façade that the possibilities for *risshin shusse* were still alive and well, despite the primary avenues for advancement—the bureaucrat and the political activist—no longer being viable choices for most by the late 1880s.

But if such were the case, then it was logical that a need would arise for a positive model within *risshin shusse* ideology, which the detective story was happy to provide through its hero, the detective, whose knowledge of Western logic and science assisted in the capture of a criminal and thereby posited him as a productive citizen within the framework of the nation. Indeed, this characteristic of the detective and his function is emphasized in Ruikō's *Muzan*, published just a month after the last installment of *Ukigumo* appeared in the journal *Miyako no hana* (The flower of the capital) in August 1889. Through its detective Ōtomo, *Mu-*

2. As Komori Yōichi observes: "at the source of the production of Bunzō's delusions was precisely the 'reflection' and 'examination' based on 'facts' according to 'reason and learning'" (*Kōzō to shite no katari*, 145).

3. Futabatei seems to suggest a sociopolitical cause behind Bunzō's dismissal that stems from his family lineage when the text reveals that Bunzō is from Shizuoka, a stronghold of *bakufu* sympathizers, and that his father served for the old *bakufu*. However, this suggestion never finds further support in the text.

zan posits the second-floor room of his lodgings—which would become an important trope of modern Japanese literature thanks to *Ukigumo*, as Maeda Ai has argued—not as an antisocial space of delusion and disavowal but as a productive space of analysis and investigation.[4] In so doing, *Muzan* counters *Ukigumo*, presenting Ōtomo in direct opposition to Bunzō.

Like Bunzō, *Muzan*'s Ōtomo, characterized by his student-like appearance and described as an educated man who reads Western novels and is versed in Western science and logic, is a man of contemplation. But unlike Bunzō, whose Western learning proves useless in getting at the truth in question (the feelings of Osei), Ōtomo's knowledge of Western science and logic is revealed as a powerful tool in arriving at the truth of the murder case. Analyzing evidence and formulating hypotheses, he concludes the time spent in his room with his praise of the Western ways: "The power of science and logic is amazing. By examining only three pieces of hair on the second floor of [my] lodgings, I was able to produce this many clues."[5] Furthermore, *Muzan* seems to present Ōtomo's 'rise' to a police detective as a dream come true. Unlike Bunzō who became a government official out of monetary necessity and contemporary custom, Ōtomo does not see himself as someone who has been forced to join the police squad. Ōtomo is a police detective not because he could not become a government official or a politician; rather, his being a detective is presented as a conscious choice: "I am a person who was kicked out of school because [playing] detective was my hobby."[6] In Ōtomo, we seem to find the dream of making work out of one's hobby.

But, as we saw in the last chapter, *Muzan* ultimately is an ambivalent text that also suggests the difficulty for such a hero to maintain his symbolic power as an apolitical and productive utilization of Western education when Ōtomo's political ambitions that were no doubt thwarted by the collapse of the Freedom and People's Rights movement in the late 1880s reemerge as a chauvinistic cry for renewed political action in the course of his investigations. And if such ambivalence surrounding the detective intimated the need for further ideological operation connecting him with apolitical productivity within the framework of Meiji Japan, then such developments were made difficult by the emergence of a new archetype of the student, which would leave an unforgettable impression

---

4. For details, see Maeda, "Nikai no geshuku."
5. Kuroiwa, *Muzan*, 29.
6. Ibid., 26.

on Meiji intellectuals. This figure was Raskolnikov, the protagonist of Fyodor Dostoevsky's *Crime and Punishment*, the translation of which appeared in Japan in the early 1890s. A troubled student who turns to crime after his hopes of rising in the world through education had been shattered, Raskolnikov foreshadowed the dark future awaiting those who aspired to rise in the world through education in 1890s Japan and beyond and the potential dangers they may pose for the society at large.

The Meiji reception of *Crime and Punishment* and how the literary works of modern Japan negotiated the dangers intimated by the Russian masterpiece are the subjects of this chapter. As I argue, although varying in their connection to the Russian work in terms of direct influence, key works within the development of modern Japanese literature utilized similar narrative structures to that of *Crime and Punishment*—the focus on the criminal secret harbored by an individual, the revelation of this secret, and the resulting banishment from society—to explore the dark fate awaiting the educated youths in the world that did not operate according to ideals and principles. And nowhere was this more evident than in Shimazaki Tōson's *Hakai* and Tayama Katai's *Futon*, the groundbreaking works of Japanese Naturalism, which emerged as the dominant literary trend after the Russo-Japanese War. Although standard literary histories have seen a rift separating these two works due to the difference in the social significance of their subject matter, I argue that they are intimately connected in their attempt to engage critically with the fundamental problematics of *Crime and Punishment* for Meiji Japan, as they narrated the tribulations of its youths within the ideology of *risshin shusse* who, because of their marginalizing marks, are ultimately interpellated as criminals by the people and communities that surround them.[7]

---

7. Tomi Suzuki succinctly summarizes the traditional understanding of Japanese Naturalism as follows: "The standard literary histories divide Japanese Naturalism into two stages: 'early Naturalism' (*zenki shizenshugi*), which emerged around 1900 under the direct but undigested influence of Émile Zola, and 'late Naturalism' (*kōki shizenshugi*), a more domesticated form of naturalism represented by such writers as Tōson, Katai, Masamune Hakuchō, and Tokuda Shūsei. Early Naturalism is generally thought to be a superficial adaptation of Zolaism, whereas late Naturalism, whose direction *Futon* is thought to have irreversibly determined, is characterized as a factual description of the author's private life, without the wider social dimension found in European naturalism" (*Narrating the Self*, 79).

Raskolnikov in Meiji Japan

In November 1892, the same month that Kuroiwa Ruikō established his newspaper *Yorozu chōhō*, Uchida Roan published the first installment of *Tsumi to batsu*, the translation of *Crime and Punishment* (covering up to Part 2, Chapter 3 of Fredrick Whishaw's English translation of *Crime and Punishment*, the source of Roan's translation). The second installment (covering up to the end of Part 3) would be published in February 1893, leaving just about half of the novel untranslated when Roan abandoned the project supposedly due to poor sales, a surprising turn of events in hindsight given the sociocultural environment at the time.[8] Despite focusing on the actions and thoughts of the criminal instead of the detective, *Tsumi to batsu* undoubtedly possessed many characteristic elements of the detective fiction genre, which was enjoying its golden age thanks to Ruikō, and seemed destined to be consumed within this trend, as Irokawa Daikichi among others has suggested.[9]

As Takahashi Osamu has argued, moreover, Roan seemed to have helped such a mode of consumption, whether consciously or not, by "actively devising elements that would be construed as a 'detective novel,'" such as translating the phrase "prying eyes" in the English base text of the Russian work "it was gloomy enough to hide him from prying eyes" as "the hawk eyes of a detective" when Raskolnikov goes to the pawnbroker's apartment to consider the possibilities that his crime would be detected.[10] The psychological battle between Raskolnikov and the police detective Porfiry in the nineteenth chapter (next to last chapter that was published) also presented *Tsumi to batsu* as a successor to Ruikō's detective stories to the extent that Porfiry's first attempt at incriminating Raskolnikov—by asking him whether he saw painters when he visited the pawnbroker two days before her murder when the painters were only working on the day of the murder—constituted the exact kind of trickery

8. Akiyama Yūzō states that Roan's translation only sold about 400 copies (*Hon'yaku no chihei*, 78).

9. Irokawa states that "works like *Crime and Punishment* were appreciated simply as detective stories" during the 1890s (*The Culture of the Meiji Period*, 73). Takahashi Osamu argues that reviews by Yoda Gakkai and Iwamoto Yoshiharu, contained in the second installment of *Tsumi to batsu*, suggest their reading of *Tsumi to batsu* within the context of "crime fiction." For details, see Takahashi, "'Tantei shōsetsu' ga inpei suru mono," 37.

10. Takahashi, "'Tantei shōsetsu' ga inpei suru mono," 41. The original text is the English translation by Fredrick Whishaw.

that Ruikō's detectives often employed. Raskolnikov is not as easily duped as Ruikō's criminals, however, instantly discovering "the trap hidden within Porfiry's question" and thereby foreshadowing the psychological battles that would have continued between the two if Roan had not abandoned the translation.[11]

Even more peculiar when considering Roan's abandonment of the translation is the overwhelmingly positive critical response that the work received immediately upon its appearance. Indeed, the second installment of *Tsumi to batsu* contains a compilation of 18 reviews totaling 49 pages that were written after the publication of its first installment in various venues by the key figures of Meiji intellectual circles, including Tsubouchi Shōyō, Aeba Kōson, Iwamoto Yoshiharu (1863–1942), Morita Shiken (1861–1897), and Kitamura Tōkoku (1868–1894). While obviously differing from each other in significant ways, the reviews shared their positive reception, filled with phrases such as "a masterpiece," "a must-read among all the recent novels," and "the best of the psychological novels," the last of which suggests the work's appeal to those who shared Shōyō's understanding of the novel given the story's detailed depiction of Raskolnikov's internal conflict. Many of the reviewers also expressed a strong, albeit ambivalent, impression felt upon reading Roan's translation. For example, Shōyō states that on the night that he began reading this work, he had "an unpleasant dream," which he later discovered was related to a "pessimistic feeling." Similarly, Kōson, the translator of Poe's "The Murders in the Rue Morgue" and "The Black Cat," states that he "grew a feeling of fear as if he was sitting alone in a dark empty room and felt the eyes of a person from behind" and was "filled with a feeling of an unspeakable unpleasantness as if [he] had taken on half of the crime and punishment of the protagonist" with whom he identified.[12]

In addition to their profound impressions of the story, the reviews shared their characterizations of Raskolnikov as a student (*gakusei*, *shosei*, or *daigakusei*). Of course, this is not surprising considering that *Crime and Punishment*, in short, is a story about a university student who has fallen on hard times and the dreadful crime he commits as a result. It is surprising, however, that not a single reviewer of *Tsumi to batsu* makes an explicit mention of *Ukigumo*'s Bunzō—a Meiji exemplar of a student

---

11. Uchida Roan, *Tsumi to batsu*, in *Meiji hon'yaku bungakushū*, 263. All subsequent references to this source will appear in the text in parentheses.

12. "Zenkan hihyō," in Uchida Roan, *Tsumi to batsu*, vol. 2, 4, 19, 3, 1, and 2–3, respectively.

down on his luck—especially given their shared characteristic of being a contemplative subject prone to fantasy and alienated from society. As described in detail from the first pages of *Tsumi to batsu*, Raskolnikov is a man suffering from "a nervous depression similar to hypochondria" and "completely divorced from society, shutting himself up in his room, and loathed unbearably to come face to face not only with the landlady of his lodging but also with anyone" (141). It is true that, Raskolnikov, unlike Bunzō, seems to be aware of his own condition, but the downward spiral of a contemplative subject is no different in the latter from the former. When Raskolnikov finally leaves his room, he reflects: "I just theorize too much. That's why I don't do anything. Or rather, it is because I don't do anything that I theorize. From day to night, I lie in the corner of the room and think hard" (142). And when his thoughts turn to his plan (the murder of the pawnbroker, although the text does not specify): "No, I am just consoling myself by kindling such fantasies" (142).

But despite the reviews not making an explicit connection between the two works, this is not to say that no one sought to get to the bottom of his unease at reading *Tsumi to batsu* and its relationship to Raskolnikov's similarities to the likes of Bunzō. In his two reviews of the Russian work, the poet and critic Kitamura Tōkoku provides a detailed analysis of Raskolnikov's character and the motives behind his crime, and it is in Tōkoku's arguments—especially those found in the second review which appeared in *Jogaku zasshi* (Journal for women's education) in January 1893—that we discover the ideological significance of Roan's translation within the intellectual circles of 1890s Japan. Written in part as a response to the Chinese studies scholar and critic Yoda Gakkai (1833–1909), Tōkoku's second review states that *Tsumi to batsu* is not a work that "entertains the vulgar like the detective novels of Ruikō" and rejects Gakkai's criticism that "to develop a murderous intent of the wealthy old lady just because he becomes angered at her avarice is extremely superficial as an motive for murder."[13] Tōkoku writes:

> If a stubborn man cannot obey the sanctions of society and the powers of nature, and for this reason he is turned away by people and cast away by society, coming to mock activity and enterprise, think of human beings as inane, think of things like class order as annoying, believe love and sincerity to be meaningless, suspect people indiscriminately, bear a great grudge against the heavens; and ultimately

---

13. "Zenkan hihyō," in Uchida Roan, *Tsumi to batsu*, vol. 2, 40, 43; Kitamura, *Kitamura Tōkoku shū*, 110, 108 .

the peace of his spirit is broken, and he does something he should not do and commit a crime whose evil is beyond his own knowing—should such crime, a murder for example, be considered meaningless and without cause? Should a book that dissects psychologically and describes in detail the process of how this crime was established be dismissed as superficial and shallow?[14]

In this long passage in which he outlines the steps through which Raskolnikov came to commit the heinous crime, Tōkoku suggests the social nature of Raskolnikov's motivations by describing how a crime is connected to the individual's alienation from society.[15] Unable or unwilling to "obey the sanctions of society and the powers of nature," Raskolnikov becomes excluded from society, which consists of people who adhere to these rules, and, to justify his disobedience, turns to discredit the social and 'natural' values that found society such as activity, enterprise, social order, love, and sincerity. It is through this course of alienation that we get to the direct cause of the crime whose "evil is beyond his own knowing," namely, that "the peace of his spirit is broken"—a cause that suggests Tōkoku's understanding of Raskolnikov's crime to be a result of a mental breakdown or *shinkei suijaku*, a term that was quickly gaining currency in 1890s Japan and from which Tōkoku himself was said to suffer.[16]

Importantly, the key in establishing such line of argument is the intimate connection between the causes behind the murder and Raskol-

---

14. "Zenkan hihyō," in Uchida Roan, *Tsumi to batsu*, vol. 2, 41; Kitamura, *Kitamura Tōkoku shū*, 109.

15. Indeed, the issue of the social origins of crime was one of the recurring topics among the reviewers of Roan's translation. For example, Iwamoto Yoshiharu writes that "the sins of humans come from the social system" ("Zenkan hihyō," in Uchida Roan, *Tsumi to batsu*, vol. 2, 10). Also a review that first appeared in the journal *Katei zasshi* states the goal of *Tsumi to batsu* to be "to reveal the crimes of society and to discuss the relationship between crime and punishment" ("Zenkan hihyō," in Uchida Roan, *Tsumi to batsu*, vol. 2, 19).

16. According to Watarai Yoshiichi, the first appearance of the term *shinkei suijaku* can be found in *Ensei ihō meibutsu kō* (On the reputed medicine of the far west) by the scholar of Dutch studies Udagawa Shinsai (1769–1834) in 1822. However, this condition, as well as the concept of mental disease in general, became well known in Japan only in the late 1880s when *Waei gorin shūsei* (Japanese-English dictionary) by the American James Curtis Hepburn (1815–1911) included the entry for *shinkei byō* (disease of the nerves) in 1886. Shortly thereafter, various media, including newspaper articles, advertisements, and fiction, began using the terms *shinkei byō* and *shinkei suijaku*. For details, see Watarai, *Meiji no seishin isetsu*, 31–33, 63–65.

nikov's background as a student. Arguing that "a murder does not necessarily occur from a visible cause," Tōkoku instead describes "the thrust" of the Russian work as showing "how a horrifying magical power lurks in the ultimate darkness of society, and how a wrongdoing that even those without learning and reason would hesitate to devise is plotted inside the mind of [a person] with learning and reason."[17] In drawing this conclusion of the critical connection between education and crime, then, Tōkoku evokes Raskolnikov's notion of the "exceptional" man, which he expounds in his discussion with the detective Porfiry. Upon the detective's inquiry regarding an essay he published in a journal on the relationship between crime and social environment, Raskolnikov tells Porfiry: "The exceptional has a right—of course, it is not from a legal point of view but from the point of view of individual belief—to violate [the law] in executing his ideas to the extent that his conscience allows" (259). In such a way, Raskolnikov argues for the existence of two moralities, one for the "unexceptional" based on the laws of society and another for the "exceptional," exemplified by Napoleon, whose actions are based on individual ethics.

Raskolnikov's articulation of the "exceptional" man occurs in the nineteenth chapter contained in the second installment of *Tsumi to batsu*, which was published after Tōkoku had written his two reviews. Because of this fact, it is questionable that Tōkoku knew of such belief held by Raskolnikov at the time, although there are many passages leading up to the murder that foreshadow his notion of the "exceptional" man.[18] But whether Tōkoku knew of this notion through other means prior to his writing of the two reviews or not, what is clear is that lurking behind

---

17. "Zenkan hihyō," in Uchida Roan, *Tsumi to batsu*, vol. 2, 42; Kitamura, *Kitamura Tōkoku shū*, 109. In his first review of *Tsumi to batsu*, which appeared in *Jogaku zasshi* in December 1892, Tōkoku also explicitly links education with a propensity for mental illness, or, more specifically, hypochondria, from which Raskolnikov is said to suffer. Tōkoku writes: "What kind of illness is a hypochondrium? Is this an illness suffered only by those who are physically weak? Cannot a healthy person also suffer from this illness? The uneducated do not suffer from this [illness]; on the contrary, learning brings about this illness. The unlearned do not suffer from this; and there are many with knowledge who suffer from this. The grudge toward life is one of the biggest elements of this illness" (ibid., 25; 107).

18. According to an anecdote, there existed three copies of the English version of *Crime and Punishment* at Maruzen bookstore at the time, which were purchased by Tsubouchi Shōyō, Morita Shiken, and Uchida Roan. It is believed that the first two never read the purchased copies (Kimura Ki, *Maruzen gaishi*, 199).

Tōkoku's reviews was a similar notion of his own, which occupied a central place in his philosophy in the early 1890s and finds its most explicit articulation in the essay "Ensei shika to josei" (Disillusioned poets and women) that appeared in *Jogaku zasshi* in February 1892.

A widely influential essay, which begins with the phrase "Love is the secret key to life," "Ensei shika to josei" articulates Tōkoku's idealistic, albeit narcissistic, notion of love that is crystallized in the statement "Love is an unerring mirror that reflects the true 'self' once one sacrifices oneself."[19] But more important for our present discussion is the conflict between "real world" and "imaginary world" facing the individual in life that buttresses this understanding of love. Tōkoku writes:

> It cannot be avoided that there comes a time when that imaginary world, or the world of innocence, stares at and becomes conflicted with the real world. . . . The imaginary world can only be maintained by the ignorance of the disharmony of society; thus, it is inevitable that once it touches the piercing of the real world, it will be doomed. . . . At this time, the defeated general of the imaginary world, dispirited and disheartened, will look to satisfy himself by gaining something. Being the reserves of the real world, things such as labor and duty are always taking aim at the imaginary world. . . . What then is that which helps and satisfies him [the defeated general of the imaginary world]? It is love.[20]

Arguing for love as that which fills the gap created in the defeat of the imaginary world by the real world, Tōkoku presents life as a conflict between these two worlds in which the real world necessarily wins and forces a compromise on the individual. Yet, according to Tōkoku who would echo the same phrase in his analysis of the downward spiral of Raskolnikov's alienation from society less than a year later, the "disillusioned" is comprised precisely of those who cannot make this compromise: "in the first place, the disillusioned are those who cannot obey the rules of society; those who do not take society as their homes."[21]

The connection between Tōkoku's notion of the "disillusioned" and his analysis of Raskolnikov grows even stronger in the essay when he turns to the details of the conflict between individual and society. He writes: "It is during youth when knowledge and experience become hostile toward each other and imagination and thoughts on reality come to war that a feeling of suspicion and hostility toward the real world

19. Kitamura Tōkoku, "Ensei shika to josei," in *Kitamura Tōkoku shū*, 64.
20. Ibid., 65.
21. Ibid., 67.

arises."[22] Corresponding almost verbatim once again to his understanding of Raskolnikov's condition, this description makes clear the deep divide between the imaginary world of the thinking subject and the real world of the experiencing subject. To the extent that the imaginary world consists of "knowledge," moreover, it is clear that one's education and learning have much to do with this world. On the one hand, education and learning provide individuals with knowledge in various forms and function to promote reflection: they are sustenance for the growth of the imaginary world. On the other hand, they bring about its doom, for "the imaginary world can only be maintained by the ignorance of the disharmonies of society." And with learning, individuals not only become more observant of society's problems but also come to hold ideas of what society should be like, ideas such as Raskolnikov's notion of the "exceptional" man that come into conflict with the realities of the society in which they exist. Through such a conflict arising from comparison between the 'should' and the 'is,' the real world becomes a place filled with "disharmonies" for the subject.

And here lurks the historically tragic significance of *Crime and Punishment* in Russia and *Tsumi to batsu* in Japan, two later developing countries that were feverishly trying to catch up with more powerful Western nations. Central to this catching up process—institutionalized under the rubric of *bunmei kaika* in Japan—was the education of the young on the technologies and values of advanced Western societies, which, in turn, provided powerful models for comparison that revealed their own societies as backward and full of contradictions. In this sense, the educated youths of these countries—Bunzō and Raskolnikov, who are fluent enough in English and German respectively to be able to work as translators as their last resorts—were most prone to what might be called the specter of comparison whose haunting would lead them to become disillusioned with their own societies.[23]

---

22. Ibid., 66

23. The power hierarchy between Russia and Germany is illustrated by the following example in *Crime and Punishment*: despite the novel's negative portrayal of Germans, Raskolnikov is offered a translation job by his friend Razhumikin that pays three rubles for one page of German translation, whereas the watch of Raskolnikov's father nets only one and half ruble at the pawnbroker. Also, Futabatei's *Ukigumo* contains a scene in which Bunzō translates a British political tract (Futabatei, *Ukigumo*, 121, 143).

Furthermore, Russia and Japan share another fate. To the extent that societies are filled with "disharmonies," their peaceful maintenance requires a certain level of resignation on the part of its people to question the rights and wrongs of society's rules. Of course, this is not to say that society's rules should not be questioned. In a democratic society, such questioning should take the form of political action. But Russia and Japan were two nations whose citizens are excluded for the most part from the political process, the former of which Tōkoku makes sure to highlight in his first review of *Tsumi to batsu* as a country where "there exists an iron fence between the aristocracy and the ordinary people" before tying Raskolnikov's crime to his education.[24] The political energies thwarted by the oppressive government re-manifest as criminal action when social issues, which should be resolved through political action, are taken into an individual's own hands in the name of justice as revealed by Raskolnikov's belief in the "exceptional" man: the "exceptional" man becomes an educated man's subjective justification of his helpless alienation from society that robs its participants of possibilities for political action.

In *Ukigumo*, Bunzō's alienation from society was described as a result of his Western learning and rationalism, which deteriorated from functioning as an ethical standard for his actions to a tool to disavow reality by producing delusions. Ruikō's *Muzan* sought to provide a more positive view of Western learning and rationalism through the figure of the detective Ōtomo whose use of Western science and logic leads to the identification of the criminal in a murder case. And buttressing this presentation of Western learning were Ruikō's wildly popular adaptations of Western detective stories that portrayed the detective as a hero who served for the good of society. Roan's *Tsumi to batsu*, however, counters the positive presentation of Western learning at a time when Ruikō's popularity was at its peak by portraying a much darker fate of the educated class through the intimate connection it makes between the student and the criminal. Despite the fact that it was a translation, the pertinence of this work to the realities of Meiji intellectuals was undeniable. If Bunzō's encounter with the contradictions of society made him into a man of contemplation and inactivity, then Raskolnikov shows that when such a man comes out of his shell, the result may be criminally violent. And it was all because they had studied, read, and thought too much. Like *Ukigumo*, the Russian work suggested the possible 'madness' awaiting those youths whose road

24. "Zenkan hihyō," in Uchida Roan, *Tsumi to batsu*, vol. 2, 25; Kitamura, *Kitamura Tōkoku shū*, 107.

to social advancement had become foreclosed and how such 'madness'—self-quarantined in his second-floor room in Bunzō's case—could explode in the form of a heinous crime against society.

And what made the unsettling message of *Tsumi to batsu* even more powerful in the first half of the 1890s were the paradigmatic changes in the theoretical understanding of crime and the criminal during this period, which would culminate in the promulgation of the New Criminal Law (Shin-keihō) in 1907. Establishing itself when criminal cases were growing more rampant than ever, the new school of criminologists, including Tomii Masaakira (1858–1935), Koga Renzō (1858–1942), and Hozumi Nobushige (1855–1926), viewed the criminal law, first and foremost, as "a necessary tool for the maintenance of public order of a nation," attacking the prior focus on the notion of universal morality and the law as a means of just punishment.[25] In so doing, the new criminologists turned their attention to the criminal and society where the internal workings of the criminal provided the theoretical bridge between the two. As Serizawa Kazuya states in his discussion of this shift: "the threat to society exists not in the criminal act itself but in the nature of those who committed the crime and in the dangerous nature of that subjectivity [and] the danger that the possessor of that subjectivity might bring to society in the future."[26] No doubt in the same line of thought as Shōyō's theory of the novel in their emphasis on the private thoughts of the criminal as object of detection and examination rather than on the public act of the crime, the arguments of the new school criminology suggest the timely or rather untimely nature of *Tsumi to batsu*'s publication. In other words, at a time when the psychology and the inner workings of criminals were becoming a major issue, *Tsumi to batsu* discussed the fundamentally logical and inherent potential of the criminality of fallen/disillusioned/alienated intellectuals, especially those with Western education. As such, *Tsumi to batsu* had to be repressed, with its translation abandoned after two installments despite the fact that the foreword to the second installment already included an announcement of the third installment.

As suggested by the major literary and cultural trends of the 1890s, moreover, the process of repression went well beyond Roan's translation, for these trends were characterized by a turn away from the exploration of the student/intellectual within the framework of social problematics,

---

25. From Tomii's work *Keihō-ron kō*, which was published in 1889. Cited in Serizawa, *"Hō" kara kaihō sareru kenryoku*, 25.

26. Ibid., 32–33.

taking up instead issues of the high and low. On the one hand, yellow journalism became a cultural phenomenon, led by Ruikō's *Yorozu chōhō*, which had emerged as the top selling newspaper in Tokyo only three years after its establishment, and soon the likes of the *Niroku shinpō* (est. 1893) followed suit and adopted the ways of the *Yorozu chōhō*. These newspapers relentlessly exposed the wrongdoings of the upper class, exemplified by the *Yorozu chōhō*'s hit series "Chikushō no jitsurei" (The actual examples of keeping a mistress), which began on July 7, 1898. Deploying reporters to spy on the rich and the famous, this column exposed the adulterous affairs of the upper class, including those by Itō Hirobumi and Mori Ōgai (1862–1922). The topic of infidelity provided the *Yorozu chōhō*'s readers (male readers, at least) who had no hopes of social mobility or political involvement with a structure of projection and disapproval crucial to the emergence of yellow journalism as entertainment: they were able to project their fantasies of having a mistress onto the subjects of scandals all the while disapproving infidelity as an immoral and unenlightened act to gain a sense of moral superiority toward these subjects who existed 'above the clouds.'[27]

On the other hand, reportage writings exemplified by Matsubara Iwagorō's *Saiankoku no Tokyo* (The darkest Tokyo; November 1893) and Yokoyama Gennosuke's *Nihon no kasō shakai* (The lower societies of Japan; April 1899) depicted the harsh realities of the lower classes as an emergent problem in Meiji society. Such focus on the lower classes became the trend of literary production, moreover, as the latter half of the

---

27. In his discussion of the rise of yellow journalism in Meiji Japan, Matsuyama Iwao states: "The reason people desire gossip articles of the famous is because of jealously and envy toward them. That these feelings were fomenting within society explicitly did not mean that status and class became equal. Rather, a hierarchy became clear, and whether through wealth or social status, a handful of elite class began to dominate, and below them grew a group who did not have either. And this is precisely why people began to talk, sometimes out of spite, of scandals regarding the elites" (*Uwasa no enkinhō*, 88). Although this analysis of scandal journalism is insightful, we should keep in mind that this phenomenon is not a reflection of an unequal society in general. Rather, scandal journalism is one of the distinct characteristics of a modern nation that has human equality and the abolition of a class system as its major premises. It is precisely because there emerges distinct classes of the haves and the have-nots—despite the fact that the major premises of a modern nation should allow for social mobility—that scandal journalism blossoms.

1890s would often be referred to as "the age of misery [*hisan*] novels."[28] While many of these works examined social problems and contradictions and, in this sense, shared their interest with *Crime and Punishment*, their protagonists were characterized by their "non-everydayness," including their belonging to the social group now referred to as *hisabetsu burakumin* (hereafter abbreviated *burakumin*) whose differentiation from the Meiji intellectuals was guaranteed from the start.[29]

No doubt, these literary and cultural trends functioned in other important ways that go beyond the scope of this book. But at the same time, they operated within the rhetoric of disavowal, serving to repress collectively the dangers that *Crime and Punishment* brought to the social legitimacy of the educated who stood outside the main system of authority in Meiji Japan. The rest of this chapter considers the literary responses to this problematics of the modern intellectual and his/her relationship to the ideology of *risshin shusse* at the heart of this problematics through the examination of the pivotal works of Japanese Naturalism, Shimazaki Tōson's *Hakai* and Tayama Katai's *Futon*.

Hakai *and the Criminalization of the Victim*

Narrated in the third person with the elementary school teacher Segawa Ushimatsu as its protagonist, Shimazaki Tōson's *Hakai* describes Ushimatsu's inner turmoil about his discriminated *burakumin* origins and its eventual exposure, which takes the form of his confession to his students and of his subsequent move from Iiyama, Nagano, to Texas. Even from this most basic synopsis, the influence of *Crime and Punishment* on *Hakai* should be easy to spot for those who have read the Russian work (although such must have been few at the time of *Hakai*'s publication given that Roan's *Tsumi to batsu* did not sell many copies). The progression from inner turmoil to confession to banishment finds its counterpart in Raskolnikov's agony over the murder he has committed, his confession at the town marketplace, and his banishment to Siberia. And just as Raskolnikov was accompanied by Sonia, the daughter of the drunk Marmeladov, on his banishment to Siberia, Ushimatsu, too, will

---

28. Nakamaru, "Kindai shōsetsu no tenkai," 135.

29. Ibid., 136. *Hisabetsu burakumin* is a modern term that refers to a group of people derogatorily called *eta* and *hinin* (among others terms) who were forced to exist outside the class system during the Edo period but were officially liberated in 1871. The term *hisabetsu* (discriminated) denotes the prejudice with which they are treated in Japanese society in the past and the present.

be accompanied by the sympathetic Oshiho, whose father Keinoshin is a drunk.[30]

No doubt, Tōson's relationship with Kitamura Tōkoku—his mentor who committed suicide on May 16, 1894 at the age of 25 after a long bout with depression—must have exercised much influence on his reception of the Russian work. Indeed, Tōson's autobiographical work *Haru* (Spring; 1908), published two years after *Hakai*, includes a scene in which Aoki, modeled after Tōkoku, compares himself to Raskolnikov:

> It's in *Tsumi to batsu* that Uchida-san translated. There is a scene when that protagonist, when asked by a woman at the lodging what he was doing not going out to make money, states that he is doing some thinking. I am shocked to hear that there is already someone who has said something like that. Doing some thinking—that is exactly what I am doing.[31]

Uttered in a private conversation with his wife without the presence of Kishimoto (modeled after Tōson himself), Aoki's comments suggest Tōson's active strategy to incorporate the Russian work and its protagonist into creating the myth of his mentor-friend, a strategy buttressed by Tōson's understanding of the murderer Raskolnikov as a tragic and sympathetic figure. But this is not to say that Tōson's reception of *Crime and Punishment* was simply through his mentor Tōkoku, for there is clear evidence that Tōson engaged critically in his own way to deal with the quiet yet profound impact of Roan's *Tsumi to batsu* through *Hakai*. In his letters to other writers, including Ueda Bin (1874–1916) and Tayama Katai, it is well documented that Tōson not only read Roan's *Tsumi to batsu* but also sought out and completed reading the English translation of *Crime and*

---

30. We should note that the narrative motifs of *Hakai* also closely resemble those of Shimizu Shikin's short story "Imin gakuen" (School for émigrés; 1899). But at the same time, as discussed below, the resemblance between *Hakai* and *Crime and Punishment* struck *Hakai*'s contemporaries and recent scholars alike. My interest here does not lie in establishing a direct line of influence between *Hakai* and *Crime and Punishment* but rather in discussing their shared narrative and conceptual structures and of the differences within these similarities as they relate to the problematics of Meiji intellectuals. For an English translation of "Imin gakuen," see "School for Emigrés," trans. by Rebecca Jennison, in Copeland and Ortabasi, *The Modern Murasaki*, 240–66. For an example of the discussion of the connection between *Hakai* and *Crime and Punishment*, see Walker, *The Japanese Novel of the Meiji Period and the Ideal of Individualism*, 183–86.

31. Shimazaki, *Haru*, 97.

Punishment just before he began working on *Hakai*.[32] In a commentary sent to the *Yomiuri shinbun* less than a month after his publication of *Hakai*, moreover, Tōson praised the "works of Tolstoy and Dostoevsky" as "new tragedies" that mix "emotion" and "intelligence," suggesting that his *Hakai* was the Japanese attempt to do the same.[33]

Given the narrative resemblances not to mention Tōson's self-promotion, it was not surprising that, within months of *Hakai*'s publication, there appeared two commentaries that specifically discussed the influence of *Crime and Punishment* on *Hakai*. The novelist Morita Sōhei (1881–1949) praised *Hakai* as "a work that begins a new era" and viewed the Russian work only as a facilitator to Tōson's project, not making much of the similarities ("[similarities] are just that if one reads this, then it reminds one of that").[34] In contrast, the literary critic Hasegawa Tenkei (1876–1940) stated that the power of the Russian work comes from murder as a "universal and great moral problem" and criticizes that *Hakai* "simply made the fact of being *eta* into a book." For Tenkei, "*eta*" only connects "the concepts of evil, ugliness, immorality" with "prejudice," which, while it still exists in Japan, is "recognized as prejudice" that is a problem in "rural" areas, and it is this locality that is "one reason that this work does not bring out an infinite feeling of sorrow" that is characteristic of *Crime and Punishment*.[35]

Although Tenkei may be guilty of casually dismissing the prejudices against *burakumin* at the time, he does bring out the fundamental discrepancy around which the subsequent debate on the relationship between the two works will revolve: Ushimatsu as *burakumin* is a victim of social prejudice and injustice who, unlike Raskolnikov, has not violated any laws let alone murder, and his guilt derives from the unjust prejudices of society rather than from the immorality of his own actions. In this sense, there is a slippage in *Hakai*, which makes clear that the text is not a mere imitation of the Russian work but a conscious reworking of it to suit the conditions of early twentieth-century Japan. And the slippage, instead of resulting in the failure to reproduce the "universal and great moral problem" found in *Crime and Punishment*, shifts the focus of

---

32. See Kawabata, Hakai *no yomikata*, 162–63. Also mentioned in Walker, *The Japanese Novel of the Meiji Period and the Ideal of Individualism*, 183–84.

33. "Ryokuin zōwa," *Yomiuri shinbun*, April 9, 1906. Cited in Kawabata, Hakai *no yomikata*, 164.

34. Cited in Kawabata, Hakai *no yomikata*, 164.

35. Hasegawa, "Handō no genshō," 160.

Ushimatsu's dilemma of whether to hide or confess his origins from one of inner moral struggle to that of inner political struggle whose alternatives are exemplified by the two critical figures of the story, namely, his father and the politician Inoko Rentarō.

On the one hand, Ushimatsu's father is a herdsman living quietly in the mountains who warned Ushimatsu that "the secret—the only hope and only way—for a child of *eta* to go out into society and establish oneself is to hide his origins."[36] On the other hand, Inoko Rentarō is an outspoken political activist who has built his philosophy and career upon the fact—that is, the confession—that he is of *burakumin* origins. Through Rentarō's works, which Ushimatsu ardently reads, Ushimatsu comes to hold the belief that "as same human beings, there is no reason that [*burakumin*] should be viewed with such contempt" (49). In this way, *Hakai* presents Ushimatsu's dilemma as one torn between his adherence to his father's "commandment" and his becoming a political subject in line with Rentarō's belief in the ideals of human rights and equality.

For much of the narrative, *Hakai* seems to build readers' anticipation for Ushimatsu's development from the former to the latter, even despite the fact that Ushimatsu's desire to confess lacks the political thrust of Rentarō's teachings because it is only directed to Rentarō who would no doubt keep his secret from society at large. Ushimatsu never succeeds in confessing to Rentarō, however, for he is eventually murdered by *sōshi* on the payroll of the politician Takayanagi whom Rentarō exposed as having married a girl of *burakumin* origins for money. But this tragedy, in turn, makes Ushimatsu realize the true importance of confessing his origins to the entire society:

> At that time, Ushimatsu for the first time realized it. He had tried to hide it [his origins] so hard that he had been wearing down the natural characteristics that he was born with. Because of it, he could not for a moment forget the self. Thinking back, his life up to now was a life of falsehood. He was deceiving himself. Why think and worry? It would be better to just confess to society like a man that he was *eta*. Rentarō's death had made Ushimatsu realize this (306).

Enmeshed in rhetoric of authenticity, this passage suggests Ushimatsu's moment of epiphany in a fashion that is highly characteristic of *Hakai*'s narrative strategy, which provides detailed depiction of his inner turmoil. The thoughts and emotions of Ushimatsu are presented to the readers

---

36. Shimazaki, *Hakai*, 47. All subsequent references to this source will appear in the text in parentheses.

in such a way that they seem to collapse with the viewpoint of the third-person narrator and the border between external and internal reality becomes blurred, thereby actively promoting the reader's identification with the story's protagonist.[37] And if such identification is achieved, it is no doubt done so with the anticipation of Ushimatsu's rise as a political subject who may follow in the footsteps of Rentarō.

Yet, when the time comes for Ushimatsu to confess, the message of rebirth contained in the above passage and the moment of triumph anticipated by the readers become negated by the way in which he does so to his students. In his confession, he does not assert the equality of human beings nor does he criticize the society that enforces prejudices against those of *burakumin* origins. Instead, he apologizes for hiding his origins, stating: "Truly, I am *eta*; I am *chōri* [another pejorative term for *burakumin*]; I am an unclean human being" (321). To conclude his confession, moreover, Ushimatsu gets on his knees and begs forgiveness, "as if he thought that he still hadn't apologized enough" (321). Although his decision to confess may have been prompted by the realization of social injustice against those of *burakumin* origins, Ushimatsu confesses not as a means of protest against social injustice but to apologize for hiding his "unclean" origins: despite being a victim and not a criminal, Ushimatsu nonetheless confesses as a criminal might. In so doing, he seems to acquiesce to the social prejudices surrounding *burakumin*, sucking the life out of the political energy that has been developing in the course of the narrative, an acquiescence that struck many of *Hakai*'s contemporary readers as unnatural and, thus, one of the biggest problem spots of the story.[38]

---

37. Regarding *Hakai*'s narration, Itō Ujitaka writes that "the overall tone of *Hakai* lacks the sense of distance from the object [of depiction]" and "despite it being a third-person narrated novel, *Hakai* is a work in which the narrator roars and wails with the protagonist" (*Kokuhaku no bungaku*, 71).

38. In the collection of reviews that appeared in the May issue of *Waseda bungaku* in 1907, five out of the seven reviewers question Ushimatsu's confession. For example, Ōtsuka Kusuoko questions "whether Ushimatsu himself had to say that he was sorry by putting his head on the wooden floor" and views the confession as "a bit strange"; Yanagita Kunio also states that "the way [Ushimatsu] confessed feels odd"; and Shimamura Hōgetsu points out the confession scene as one of the "poor" spots of the story and wonders if "the excessive self-abasement about his being *eta* does not hurt the sympathy [toward Ushimatsu]" ("*Hakai* gappyō," *Waseda bungaku*, May 1906. Reprinted in Yoshida Seiichi et al., *Kindai bungaku hyōron taikei*, vol. 3, 408, 410, and 417). Fittingly, the confession scene is also at the

But this 'problem' is not a problem at all. Rather, it constitutes a fundamental part of the slippage previously mentioned in relation to Tenkei's criticism of *Hakai* that enabled Tōson to enact a political criticism of a different nature. While the way Ushimatsu confesses may strip *Hakai*'s possibility as a story of the rebirth of Ushimatsu as a discriminated individual, there is also no denying that such a method of confession produces a powerful political message at the level of the text. Ushimatsu's confession reveals that he judges himself according to the social prejudices surrounding his origins and identifies with the piercing gaze, social and unlocalizable, which has been haunting him throughout the narrative. And the key here is that such prejudices went directly against the official law of the Meiji government whose so-called Emancipation Edict (Kaihō rei) of 1871 "disposed of the designation of *eta*, *hinin*, and others" and proclaimed that persons previously of these classes "shall be the same as commoners in terms of rank and occupation."[39] In other words, it is the social prejudices, rather than the official policies of the Meiji government, that produce Ushimatsu as a subject, and such a result functions to reveal the powerlessness of Meiji government to produce citizens according to its own vision through its policies.

The tragic fate of Ushimatsu (and Rentarō) marks the contradiction between the ideals of Meiji government expressed through its laws and the realities of their sphere of influence and exposes the falsity of the government's official promise of a classless society.[40] And the contradiction manifests itself even more vividly in *Hakai* precisely because Ushimatsu, thanks to his father who "did not forget to send Ushimatsu who was eight to an elementary school" (50), does exactly what he was prompted to do through the ideology of *risshin shusse* by working hard at school and trying to rise in the world through education as propounded by such Meiji bestsellers as Fukuzawa Yukichi's *Gakumon no susume*. That *Hakai* takes place at a public school also functions to underscore

---

heart of the critical consideration of *Crime and Punishment*'s influence on *Hakai*, with the dominant criticism often taking the form of a permutation of Kataoka Ryōichi's statement: because Tōson "modeled [*Hakai*] after the frame and scenery of *Crime and Punishment* too much . . . this work, which should have been [about] a dignified proclamation of new life, became peculiar at its most important moment" (cited in Kawabata, Hakai *no yomikata*, 165).

39. Reprinted in Hirota, *Sabetsu no shosō*, 78.

40. The criticism of Meiji government regarding its promise of classless society is reiterated by the episode of Heita, also of *burakumin* origins, who is teased by his classmates during the celebration of the Meiji emperor's birthday.

the point, for, despite the remaining prejudices of the people, the school system should have been a safe haven for people like Ushimatsu to the extent that the school system is under the direct jurisdiction of the government, which issued the Emancipation Edict. But if Ushimatsu's confession scene functions as a moment of radical political criticism of the Meiji government and its ideologies in such a manner, then it is also important to recognize that this criticism is countered by another more conservative message that emerges within the detective fiction framework that is embedded in the text.

In *Nihon kindai bungaku to "sabetsu"* (Modern Japanese literature and "discrimination"), Watanabe Naomi notes the rise from the 1890s in the number of fictional works depicting *burakumin* (including the aforementioned "misery novels") and points out that their primary characteristic lies in the recognizable attributes—whether extraordinary physical features or extreme wealth—which mark their protagonists and distinguish these characters from the ordinary Japanese. Watanabe sees this textual characteristic as a "clear inversion" of the fact that their "foreign blood line," which is the hypothetical reason of the difference of *burakumin* from the ordinary Japanese, is "something that cannot be seen by the eye."[41] When considered within this narrative lineage, *Hakai*'s biggest characteristic, as Watanabe argues, becomes Tōson's elimination of any recognizable 'mark' from its marginalized protagonists. While their names Segawa *Ushi*-matsu and *Ino*-ko Rentarō contain the characters for animals (bull and boar, respectively) and set them apart from others, this 'mark' is literally nominal and, thus, functions to highlight the substance-less nature of the prejudice against *burakumin*, especially considering that this nominal difference exists only for the readers to discern, as no characters make this observation within the text.

This is not to say, however, that the characters of *Hakai* share such critical understanding of the prejudice. In fact, they are no different from the *burakumin* literature of the 1890s, believing that those of *burakumin* origins are easily distinguishable from others via physical characteristics. Even Ginnosuke, the closest friend and biggest supporter of Ushimatsu, upon hearing the rumors of Ushimatsu being *burakumin*, states:

---

41. Watanabe Naomi, *Nihon kindai bungaku to "sabetsu,"* 24. Michael Bourdaghs also argues this point within in the framework of disease (*The Dawn that Never Comes*, 57).

Does that Segawa Ushimatsu have features that are *eta*-like . . . I, too, have seen many new commoners [*shin heimin*, another derogatory term for *burakumin* that appeared after the Emancipation Edict]. From that skin color, they are different from ordinary humans. Indeed, it's obvious from the facial features whether one is a new commoner or not. And, because they are ostracized from society, their disposition is very jaundiced. See, there is no way that a manly steadfast youth will be borne out of the new commoners. How can the likes of them take interest in education? (275–76).

Despite being wholly different in significance, such views on *burakumin* cannot help calling to mind the detective stories of Kuroiwa Ruikō from the second chapter. On the one hand, we have the confident detective of *Majutsu no zoku* who claims that he "can determine most villains just by looking at their face."[42] On the other hand, we have *Muzan* whose ultra-nationalistic message is the danger of foreign criminality that may spread within Japanese society if the system of cohabitation (*naichi zakkyo*) is enacted precisely because other Asian nationals—the Chinese in this case—have no inherent recognizable features that set themselves apart from Japanese citizens. On this point, in fact, the connection to the rhetoric of fictional narratives depicting the 'newly emancipated' commoner seems particularly vivid. One result of the promulgation of the Emancipation Edict in 1871 was the liberation of *burakumin* from the specific occupations to which they were tied in the Edo period. Although this measure often did more harm than good on the level of reality—many were unable to find jobs due to resilient prejudice—it enabled the 'newly emancipated' to travel freely in Japan. In this sense, the Meiji-period liberation of *burakumin* posed the same prejudicial concerns expressed in *Muzan*, that is, a foreign element circulating within society without being recognized as such. But it is not that *Hakai*, like *Muzan*, simply presents the possibility that a certain group may be unrecognizable from others, whether it is to argue the dangers of such a situation or the substance-less nature of the prejudice against such a group in the first place. Rather, there is a process of re-marking taking place in *Hakai* by something other than physical features employed to distinguish the marginalized characters in the *burakumin* fictions from the 1890s.

Hakai tells a story of how Ushimatsu's disreputable origins become exposed. And while the narrative events and strategies prior to the confession scene may force the readers to experience it as problematic, there

42. Kuroiwa, *Majutsu no zoku*, 23.

is also no doubt that the text prepares for the specific mode of Ushimatsu's confession—that is, as a repentant criminal—in the course of the narrative. At the most surface level of plot, the story begins when Ōhinata, also a *burakumin* and Ushimatsu's fellow lodger, is evicted from their lodging after his origins become exposed, and Ushimatsu quickly moves from the lodging to the temple Rengeji with fears that his origins too will become known. Already in the first chapter, then, the exposure of his disreputable origins and resulting banishment that are to happen to Ushimatsu are foreshadowed through the fate of Ōhinata. And a similar process of preparation takes place on the level of narration whose detailed depiction of Ushimatsu's internal turmoil is characteristic of this text but not uniform in following the actions, thoughts, and emotions of Ushimatsu exclusively, for the story, from the very beginning, includes scenes that occur without Ushimatsu. Such scenes are limited in number, no doubt, but precisely because such is the case (and because they are systematically laid out and developed), it is easy to discern the strategic intent of their inclusion, namely, to frame Ushimatsu as an object of detection and exposure.

Already in the second chapter (out of 23 chapters), we encounter a perfect example in the conversation between the school principal and the inspector from the district board of education. In this conversation, the principal complains how his control of the school is being compromised because of Ushimatsu's attitude. The inspector, in reply, suggests that the principal may want to find a way to get rid of Ushimatsu, for example, by transferring him to another school. The principal is hesitant, however, because of Ushimatsu's popularity among the students and states that for such to happen, "there needs to be some kind of pretext" (57). Importantly, this line of conversation naturally leads to why Ushimatsu is the way he is, and the principal brings up the "thoughts of Inoko Rentarō or thereabouts" to which the inspector responds, "Oh, that *eta*" (57). Of course, the principal does not suspect Ushimatsu's origins at this point, but the link between Ushimatsu's behavior and Rentarō's philosophies are enough to suggest to the readers who already know of Ushimatsu's secret of the story's dynamic where a casual connection between Ushimatsu and Rentarō develops into the exposure of Ushimatsu as "*eta*," thereby providing the principal with a perfect pretext to get rid of Ushimatsu and establish his kingdom at a country elementary school. Indeed, Tōson makes sure to promote this cat-and-mouse game—unknown to Ushimatsu but recognized by the readers who are provided with information beyond that held by the protagonist—by having the unsuspecting Ushimatsu walk into this conversation upon which conspiring parties feign ignorance of their dubious plans.

In the course of the narrative, similar scenes will be repeated, each time with the principal coming closer to his wish of discovering the "pretext" to rid of Ushimatsu. On the one hand, these scenes give reality to Ushimatsu's fear of having his origins exposed through the presentation of a specific subject who is motivated to get rid of Ushimatsu's presence at the school. Thus, these scenes promote the understanding of Ushimatsu as a victim of persecution who deserves sympathy, an understanding augmented by the text's negative portrayal of the principal as a conniving villain who is characterized by his "vulgar considerations" typical of a provincial bureaucrat (54). On the other hand, these scenes, in deviating from the characteristic narrative perspective of *Hakai* that closely depicts Ushimatsu's thoughts and feelings, offer the critical distance necessary to grasp him not as a subject of suffering and persecution but as an object of detection and exposure: because the readers know that Ushimatsu does have a secret to hide, the depictions of a persecuting gaze function to promote the readers' anticipation of when and how Ushimatsu will be exposed.[43] As Chida Hiroyuki states regarding these scenes: "Although these dialogues that could be said to be unnecessary if the purpose is to depict Ushimatsu's anguish are a maneuver to mark the principal and Bunpei as villains who persecute Ushimatsu, they at the same time naturally cannot help but foster in the readers' interior interest and anxiety regarding when Ushimatsu's heritage will be exposed [and foster the readers'] interest towards Ushimatsu that is similar to reading a popular crime novel."[44]

These scenes forming around the principal without the presence of Ushimatsu actively evoke the framework of detective fiction with the principal as the subject of detecting and Ushimatsu as the object of detection. When the principal's gaze to persecute Ushimatsu is aligned with the vulgar interest of the readers who anticipate his impending exposure, Ushimatsu as victim is criminalized, and his origins become a

---

43. Interestingly, the only extended scene in which Ushimatsu is not present aside from those involving the principal occurs between Ushimatsu's aunt and Rentarō who came to visit Ushimatsu in his hometown during his father's funeral. Here, too, it is significant that Rentarō is there as a detective, to collect evidence against the politician Takayanagi, who is running against Ichimura, whom Rentarō supports.

44. Chida, "'Yomu' koto no sabetsu," 80–81.

'crime' he must hide. If social prejudices produce Ushimatsu as a 'criminal' within the story world, then these scenes produce Ushimatsu as a 'criminal' at the level of the text in the minds of the readers. For Chida, the interest of the readers necessary to produce Ushimatsu as a 'criminal' within the framework of a detective story is directly related to the prejudice against *burakumin*: "The readers, by being consumed by the illusion that they have completely shared the suffering of *burakumin* Ushimatsu, forget the vulgarity of their own reading process that is interested in when Ushimatsu's secret will be exposed and maintain [the illusion] without clearly realizing the prejudice that exists within the self."[45]

I agree with Chida regarding the predominantly unconscious nature of the reader's understanding of Ushimatsu as a criminal during the reading process, but I am not sure if such scenes construct the "discursive structure" of *Hakai* characterized by its "promotion of prejudicial consciousness."[46] As the unnaturalness that strikes readers (both contemporary to *Hakai* and not) upon reading *Hakai*'s denouement suggests, the over-the-top quality of the confession has the function of making the readers question why Ushimatsu, who is a victim of social prejudice, must confess as if he were a criminal.[47] By doing so, the readers realize the vulgarity of their own interests that had been anticipating Ushimatsu's exposure precisely because the manner in which Ushimatsu is produced as a subject through his internalization of the social prejudice against him parallels the positioning of Ushimatsu as an object of anticipation for exposure that promotes the understanding of Ushimatsu as criminal—at least, structurally speaking—in the reading process.

But while Ushimatsu's confession scene might be a moment of self-realization on the part of the readers regarding the vulgarity of their interest in him, it is also a moment of forgetting in the sense that the natural focus given to the issue of his origins—both by the text and by readers—mask another narrative strand developed through the story of the principal. That is, the readers forget that the beginning of the principal's machinations to rid Ushimatsu from the school—the conversation with the inspector from the district school board that we discussed above—had nothing to do with Ushimatsu's origins. Rather, the princi-

---

45. Ibid., 81.

46. Ibid., 79.

47. For reactions by contemporary reviewers on the confession scene, see footnote 38 above.

pal's desire to rid of Ushimatsu stems from his 'disrespectful' attitude, and, more specifically, the comments he made upon learning that the principal has been awarded a gold medal for his contribution to education. According to the principal, Ushimatsu is said to have commented: "It is a big mistake for an educator to believe that he has captured the head of a demon just because he has received a gold medal" (56).

It is this anti-authority attitude that sets Ushimatsu apart from others within the world of *Hakai* but places him in the literary lineage of *Ukigumo*'s Bunzō, who is fired from his job for insubordination because he operates upon his belief based on his Western education (rationality) and not upon the power relations within which he exists. And the textual introduction of the principal seems to reiterate this connection through his belief—"education is rules. The order of the inspector of the district board of education is the order of a superior officer" (52)—that expresses his adherence to militaristic vertical hierarchy. According to the principal, however, Ushimatsu is not a man who honors such a hierarchy, acting instead upon what he believes. But what forms the basis of Ushimatsu's beliefs? As we saw, the principal is quick to point out: "most likely, it is the thoughts of Inoko Rentarō."

In such a way, Ushimatsu's resistance to authority is connected to the thoughts of "that *eta*" Rentarō, but, at the same time, there is no connection made between Rentarō's thoughts and the 'questionable' origins of his followers. The text makes sure to emphasize this point through the principal's lumping together of Ushimatsu with Ginnosuke in his complaint to the inspector: "It is frustrating for me to do anything when Mr. Segawa and Mr. Tsuchiya hang about in that way. . . . If Mr. Katsuno [the nephew of the inspector] was the head teacher, then it would be a great peace of mind for me" (56). Moreover, the principal is quick to point out that he clearly sees the anti-authority attitudes as a trend of the times by comparing his own beliefs with those held by the rebellious youths of today like Ushimatsu and Ginnosuke: "Considering this day and age, it might be us who are a bit behind. But it is not necessarily the case that the new is always better" (56).

Importantly, the principal's view of Ushimatsu does not seem to change when he learns of Ushimatsu's secret, as illustrated at the end of the story when he has a discussion with the member of the town council regarding Ushimatsu. As if to evoke the first introduction of the principal, Tōson uses the phrase "according to the principal" to portray his internal thoughts, which only occurs on these two instances in the text. Here are his thoughts regarding his involvement in the case of Ushimatsu:

> It is not that I am removing a foreign element with malice. I am someone who is said to be an educator of the old school and am completely of a different generation from the likes of Ushimatsu and Ginnosuke. . . . There is nothing scarier than the new generation. . . . I want to hold on to the same position and honor forever. I don't want to surrender by removing my helmet to the students of the next generation. . . . Unlike Bunpei, Ushimatsu and Ginnosuke do not accept my wishes. Every time there is a teacher's meeting, our opinions clash. . . . That the students admire such inexperienced people more than me bothers me in the first place. It's not that I am removing a foreign element with malice, but from the perspective of the unity of the school, this, too, cannot be helped (312–13).

This internal monologue, which significantly does not include a single mention of Ushimatsu's origins, displays the principal's surprising clarity regarding his motives behind supporting the removal of Ushimatsu. Rather than justifying Ushimatsu's removal from the perspective of an a priori necessity—his "unclean" blood—which would eliminate the need for the principal to acquiesce his selfish motives, the principal readily admits to himself of his selfish desire to hold on to his position of power. And even despite the revelation of Ushimatsu's origins, which set him apart from others of the new generation, the principal, as was the case at the beginning of the story, lumps Ushimatsu with Ginnosuke. For the principal, who in the end has not much to do with the actual exposure or banishment of Ushimatsu, Ushimatsu's secret seems to matter only to the extent that it would enable him to get rid of Ushimatsu without making it seem like the principal had forced him out.

But the same cannot be said of Ushimatsu's colleague Katsuno Bunpei who provides a stark contrast to the principal and serves as the subject who comes to represent the social prejudices against Ushimatsu as *burakumin*. Significantly, Bunpei was hesitant in becoming part of the principal's machinations to rid Ushimatsu from the school, but everything changes upon learning the secret of his origins from the politician Takayanagi. From this point onward, Bunpei actively spreads rumors around school and town, ultimately confronting Ushimatsu to prove the rumor's veracity. In a scene at the teacher's lounge after Rentarō's death, Bunpei engages Ushimatsu in a conversation to question why Ushimatsu "became interested in studying the things that teacher [Rentarō] wrote," offering his own hypothesis before Ushimatsu can speak: "When you think about life's problems, you take note of the suffering of Inoko *sensei*. Isn't this because there is something about which you are suffering as well?" (281). In this way, Bunpei, in contradistinction to the principal, argues Ushimatsu's fondness for Rentarō's works—which he criticizes as that of a "daydreamer" and a "madman," going as far as stating that "there is no way that anyone of value would come out of an inferior race like that" (283)—as evidence of Ushimatsu's origins that he shares with Rentarō. And at the conclusion of the scene, the text highlights Bunpei's prejudice, as Bunpei stares at Ushimatsu with hatred ("'What did you say? You, *eta*,' his [Bunpei's] eyes said with anger"), after which Bunpei tells another teacher: "Did you hear the conversation just now? Didn't you? Mr. Segawa has confessed his secret on his own" (285).

In the course of *Hakai*, there is a passing of the torch from the principal to Bunpei as the story's primary villain who seeks to persecute Ushimatsu, coupled with a shift in the primary motivation for doing so. If the principal was motivated by self-interest and ambition because of Ushimatsu's anti-establishment tendencies, then Bunpei seems motivated by his pure hatred for *burakumin* in general. Moreover, the fact that Bunpei—akin to the worldly Noboru of *Ukigumo*—is of the same generation as Ushimatsu presents him as a counterexample to the principal's argument that the insubordinate nature of Ushimatsu is generational. And as Bunpei would have it, what separates Ushimatsu and him is Ushimatsu's adherence to the teachings of Rentarō, the source of anti-establishment thought, and the reason behind his adherence, his *burakumin* status. If, as Suga Hidemi informed by Watanabe's aforementioned analysis states, *Hakai* is "a story that makes the Other who lacks stigma conspicuous as an other once more," then I would argue that this process of marking involves the textual construction of the direct connection between Ushimatsu's anti-establishment tendencies originating in Rentarō's teachings and Ushimatsu's familial heritage that he shares with Rentarō.[48]

In this line of argument, moreover, Ushimatsu's confession, which lacks a shred of defiance that set him apart from others in the eyes of the principal and became evidence of his origins in the eyes of Bunpei, posits itself as a moment of his rebirth, as he recants his anti-establishment tendencies to adopt establishment viewpoints on what he should do (and how he should confess). And the same could be said for Ushimatsu's self-imposed banishment to Texas. Although Rentarō's death may have led Ushimatsu to realize that he should "confess to society" of his origins, Ushimatsu does not even give momentary thought to following in Rentarō's footsteps to fight against the injustices of society. Instead, Ushimatsu chooses to go to Texas with Ōhinata, whose eviction from his

48. Suga, *"Teikoku" no bungaku*, 34.

lodgings began the story of *Hakai*. Significantly, it is Rentarō's colleague Ichimura, the politician and a proponent for the rights of the lower classes, who brings to Ushimatsu this proposal and Ginnosuke who "fervently agrees" with the plan (337). Indeed, Ichimura suggests that Ushimatsu continue to seek achievement through education, even if he must go to Texas to do so, stating that "depending on the mindset, he might be able to study considerably" (337). Thus, Ushimatsu embarks on his journey to continue pursuing "learning for learning's sake," which Rentarō abandoned in favor of becoming a political figure and an advocate of the lower classes (50). Through his confession and banishment, Ushimatsu betrays his mentor and severs ties with his anti-establishment politics that got him in trouble in the first place to continue his pursuit of an official ideal—*risshin shusse*, about which we will have more to say in the next section—promoted by the Meiji society that had already broken its promise to him.

Of Failures and Martyrs in Futon *and* Hakai

In his commentaries on the masterpieces of the Meiji period in the April 1907 issue of *Bunshō sekai* (The world of texts), Tayama Katai, who, as mentioned in the last section, corresponded with Shimazaki Tōson about *Crime and Punishment*, reminisces about a famous author's comment regarding Roan's *Tsumi to batsu* upon its appearance: "What? A masterpiece? You can say that it's a masterpiece, but it's nothing but a detective story with good form."[49] While such a comment implies the naiveté and superficiality of reading as exercised by the Meiji intellectuals in the 1890s, it must be taken with a grain of salt as historical evidence, for it no doubt functioned simultaneously as a strategy to affirm that such is no longer the case in 1907, the intellectuals as readers having become enlightened in their appreciation of Western literature. And if Tōson had invoked the name Dostoevsky immediately following the publication of his groundbreaking work *Hakai*, then Katai's comments on *Crime and Punishment* precedes his groundbreaking work *Futon* by a few months, suggesting that this work was the result or a sign of such enlightenment. Indeed, Katai's *Futon*, despite its frequent consideration as a major departure from Tōson's *Hakai* within traditional literary histories, exhibits important structural similarities with *Hakai* that reflect their shared interest in the Russian masterpiece.

---

49. Cited in Takahashi, "'Tantei shōsetsu' ga inpei suru mono," 42.

Telling the tenuous relationship between the novelist Takenaka Tokio and his female pupil Yokoyama Yoshiko that revolves primarily around the former's ponderings of the latter's feelings for him, *Futon* on the surface not only lacks the seriousness of *Hakai*'s sociopolitical subject matter but also deviates from the narrative perspective of Tōson's work. *Futon*'s protagonist is Tokio rather than Yoshiko whose feelings for him posit themselves as objects of his analysis from the first pages of the story when he wonders whether she loved him as a man or a teacher. And by positing Yoshiko, his love interest, as a mystery-to-be-solved, it is clear that *Futon* presents Tokio in the lineage of Japanese intellectuals exemplified by *Ukigumo*'s Bunzō who understand their love interest in such a manner. But try as he might, Yoshiko—in particular, her face—confronts him as an "enigma" ("There was certainly something very mysterious contained in that powdered face of hers"), preventing him from understanding her internal thoughts and emotions by means of external appearance and thereby asserting her status, in turn, as a modern individual within the Shōyō-esque paradigm characterized by the non-correspondence of interior and exterior.[50]

Learning that Yoshiko has found a boyfriend, the young minister-to-be Tanaka, Tokio's focus shifts from her face that may hide her true feelings for him to her letters that may contain clues to suggest the physical nature of Yoshiko's relationship with Tanaka. In this shift, Tokio's interest in understanding Yoshiko takes on a more investigatory feel, especially considering that Tokio not only analyzes letters written to him but those written to her by Tanaka as he goes "furtively through her writing-case and the drawers of her desk" (156; 64), in what Indra Levy calls the "virtually pornographic invasion of Yoshiko's privacy."[51] To the extent that Tokio in committing such an "invasion" attempts to "placat[e] his conscience with the pretext of supervision," Tokio represents the reversal of operations enacted by Tsubouchi Shōyō's *Nisegane tsukai*, in

50. The passage in parentheses is from Tayama, *Futon*, in *Tayama Katai shū*, 135. I have used the English translation from Tayama Katai, *The Quilt and Other Stories*, 46. All subsequent references to these sources will appear in the text in parentheses, with the page numbers from the Japanese edition followed by those from English translation. The term "enigma" is used by Indra Levy in her insightful discussion of *Futon*: "What enabled *Futon* to marshal sympathy from a readership that had been largely dismissive of Katai's maidenitis was its unprecedented representation of modern female interiority as enigma" (*Sirens on the Western Shore*, 172).

51. Levy, *Sirens on the Western Shore*, 182.

which the vulgar invasion of privacy by the detective fueled by his curiosity is legitimated by the need for "supervision" necessary to keep crimes in check.

If *Futon* describes Tokio's development from a psychologist to a spy as the two poles of the detective in the course of its narrative, then what remains constant is his psychic world that is defined by his "fallacious identification" with characters from Western novels such as those by Hauptmann, Turgenev, and Maupassant.[52] And within this psychic dynamic, which gets played out at critical junctures of the narrative, Yoshiko seems to bear only a secondary status as Tokio's object of desire, for her function is first and foremost as a facilitator of Tokio's identification with the Western protagonists through her occupying of the position of the heroines. In this sense, Yoshiko might be called a supplementary object of identification who actively sutures "an unbridgeable gap" Tokio feels "between himself and the 'modern' younger generation" precisely because Yoshiko appeals to him as a modern woman who has, at least in the eyes of Tokio, successfully overcome the gap between a Japanese woman of the actual world and the Western heroines of the fictional world.[53]

---

52. On the topic of "fallacious identification," Tomi Suzuki writes: "Whenever he feels lonely or depressed, he recalls the fate of the tragic characters in the novels of Hauptmann, Turgenev, and Maupassant. Although Tokio himself believes that he is deeply alienated, the manner in which he superimposes his 'agony' on that of his favorite literary heroes makes him appear to be a complacent narcissist enraptured with his own 'tragic' and literary image" (*Narrating the Self*, 85). In fact, the text reveals that Tokio not only recalls the tragic characters with whom he identifies but actively seeks them through reading Western novels. For example, after meeting Tanaka for the first time, Tokio asks himself whether he can act as a protector of her relationship with Tanaka and questions the value of wife and children. This scene ends with the sentence, "De Maupassant's 'As Strong as Death' lay open on the desk," indicating that Tokio is presently reading a novel which tells a story similar to his situation (165; 71).

53. Tomi Suzuki, *Narrating the Self*, 73. The teacher/student relationship within which Tokio encounters Yoshiko has much to do with enhancing her value as his supplementary object of identification. Not only is she able to provide the necessary narrative movement in their daily interactions for him to situate himself in subject positions similar to those found in Western novels, but also by teaching her about "Ibsen's Nora and Turgenev's Elena" and "the women in Russia and Germany," he can mold her into these literary images that he views as representing the ideal modern woman (133; 44).

But to the extent that this system of identification is facilitated by the tension that Tokio feels in his relationship with Yoshiko, Tokio seems to endanger it by desperately seeking out the truth about the relationship between Yoshiko and Tanaka. In a sense, of course, Tokio's search for truth is just the opposite: an opportunity to be relieved, at least for an instant, that Yoshiko is not physically involved with Tanaka. Thus, Tokio is more of a reader of detective fiction than a detective, engrossing himself in the signs provided to him on a page in search for clues that will reveal the truth of the case but hoping that such revelation will be suspended so that he can maintain the pleasure of searching and anticipating. Fittingly, the absence of the letter—her inability to provide Tokio with a text full of signs as potential clues for Tokio's reading pleasure—that is brought to light through Yoshiko's claim to have burned the letters during a confrontation with Tokio and her father ultimately becomes the damning evidence of her physical involvement with Tanaka.[54] Also fittingly, Yoshiko, rather than admitting her guilt on the spot, confesses her sin to Tokio in a letter, which she begins by calling herself a "fallen schoolgirl" (*daraku jogakusei*), a phrase that was becoming a cultural phenomenon around the time of *Futon*'s publication.[55]

In such a way, Yoshiko confesses her secret that she had been hiding from Tokio only to be banished from Tokyo as punishment and, thereby, presents herself as a fitting successor to *Hakai*'s Ushimatsu. From secret, to confession, and then to banishment, this course of narrative development found in *Crime and Punishment* and *Hakai* also underlies *Futon*. And the connection between *Hakai* and *Futon*—and the two to *Crime and Punishment*—grows even stronger when we consider that banishment for Yoshiko means her removal from the path to become a writer, the profession that she had been pursuing. In other words, when we understand *Futon* as a story that tells of the failure that arises in the process of rising in the world and of establishing oneself in society, it becomes clear that Yoshiko and Ushimatsu share their relationship to the ideology of *risshin*

54. On the anger Tokio expresses in this scene, Levy writes: "Ostensibly, the cause for his rage is the belated realization that Yoshiko has been deceiving him, that she must have already 'had relations' with Tanaka. But it is also possible that his rage is sparked by the burning of the letters themselves: now he has been deprived of the primary object of his fetish, Yoshiko as text" (Levy, *Sirens on the Western Shore*, 183).

55. For an overview regarding the cultural context of the phrase "fallen schoolgirl," see Nagai, *Shizenshugi no retorikku*, 252–76.

shusse that was becoming ever more difficult each day to fulfill in Meiji Japan.

As we saw in the previous section, Ushimatsu ultimately chooses to pursue learning in Texas rather than to follow in Rentarō's footsteps. While this choice may strike the readers of today as rather unrealistic, going to the United States, as Earl Kinmonth has discussed, was "much in vogue" in Japan around the turn of the century as "the most extreme choice available to those seeking higher education."[56] The leading proponent of this choice was Katayama Sen (1859–1933) who wrote the immensely popular *Gakusei to-Bei annai* (Student guide for going to America) in 1901 and published his own magazine called *To-Bei* (Going to America). In these works, Katayama described the United States as "a country where self-help really worked the way it should, the way the biographies all said it did," stating that the "best-qualified" candidates to become "self-supporting students" were "the sons of poor peasants" who had the "necessary perseverance to stand up under the hardships that came with study in America."[57] Given such presentation of the United States as the land where everyone, as long as they worked hard, had the same opportunities to succeed regardless of their race, nationality, or gender, it makes sense that Ōhinata and Ushimatsu who were banished from Japan because of their *burakumin* origins choose to move to Texas.[58]

---

56. Kinmonth, *The Self-Made Man in Meiji Japanese Thought*, 188.

57. Ibid., 188, 191. Although idealistic in his vision, Katayama was not utopian in the sense that he also spoke of hardships and racial discrimination that Japanese students will surely face in the United States.

58. In his discussion of the history of *burakumin*, Suga discusses *Shakai gai no shakai: eta hinin* (Society outside society) by the anthropologist Yanase Keisuke published in 1901, which argues that, while the members of this social group should attempt to become national citizens through education, the best course of action for the members of this discriminated group may lie in immigration to another country. In Suga's words, Yanase recognizes that, despite the Emancipation Edict, those of *burakumin* origins are discriminated as the Other, and only when they go abroad as immigrants do they become "a national citizen" as "the subject of the Great Imperial Japan," that is, immigration functions "to make into 'national subjects' those which cannot be 'national subjects' on the inside by expelling them to the outside" (Suga, *"Teikoku" no bungaku*, 49). But it is also important to note that the United States was rapidly fading around the time of *Hakai*'s publication as a potential destination of Japanese immigration, for, under "the spector [*sic*] of a 'Yellow Peril,'" there was "effective exclusion [of new Japanese immigrants in the United States] in the form of the so-called

Of course, that such extreme measures would gain currency suggests the harsh realities facing the Meiji students and revealed "the generalization of the desire for personal advancement through education" across all socioeconomic classes and, at the same time, "the narrowing of opportunities within Japan."[59] Importantly, these conditions were brought about in part because of governmental policies in the 1890s that actively sought to position the graduates of middle schools as the future constituents of the Japanese middle class and resulted in the rapid expansion of the middle-school system after the Sino-Japanese War (1894–1895). The number of middle-school students nationwide, which was around 15,000 in 1885, had increased to 61,000 by 1898, and to over 100,000 in 1904.[60] Yet, despite this increase in the number of middle school students, the government did not increase the number of students admitted to its higher schools (*kōtō gakkō*). The result was increased competition to enter these higher schools, which would basically guarantee the students an elite status in society: 67 percent of higher-school applicants were admitted in 1895, but this rate decreased to 34 percent in 1901 and to as low as 20 percent in 1908.[61]

By the latter half of the 1890s, more and more students were able to dream of a future success gained through education, but such success was becoming less and less achievable in reality, many experiencing the bitter taste of failure and loss of their dreams actively promoted by the government. Fittingly, then, riding the wave of economic growth as result of the Sino-Japanese War, business, as we will discuss in more detail in the next chapter in our discussion of Natsume Sōseki's *Wagahai wa neko de aru* (I am a cat; 1905–1906), became understood in the 1890s as an alternate mode of rising in the world that catered to the educated but, at the same time, did not require a degree from an elite institution. And it seems natural, given the harsh conditions facing those who aspire to learn, that literature was not only the medium through which stories of rising in the world were described but would also become an institution through which success was achieved. In other words, fiction writing

---

Gentlemen's Agreement (*Nichibei shinshi kyōyaku*)" by 1907 (Kinmonth, *The Self-Made Man in Meiji Japanese Thought*, 193).

59. Kinmonth, *The Self-Made Man in Meiji Japanese Thought*, 188.

60. These figures are from Kōno, *Tōki to shite no bungaku*, 97.

61. These figures are from Kinmonth, *The Self-Made Man in Meiji Japanese Thought*, 187.

began to be promoted around the turn of the century as a viable path for someone who aspired to succeed in the world.

Kōno Kensuke has described in detail how literature as an institution emerged in Meiji Japan, arguing the critical role played by newspapers and journals that promoted the institutions of reader correspondence, which was popular from the early Meiji, and, more specifically, of the novel-writing contests that emerged in the mid-1890s. Here again, Kuroiwa Ruikō and his *Yorozu chōhō* take center stage as the forerunners of a cultural phenomenon, as the *Yorozu chōhō* began hosting a weekly novel-writing contest in January 1897.[62] Other newspapers and journals, such as *Ōsaka Mainichi shinbun* and *Shinshōsetsu* (The new novel), quickly followed the *Yorozu chōhō*'s lead and established novel-writing contests of their own, fostering what Kōno calls "the age of novel-writing contests" around the turn of the century.[63]

Importantly for our present discussion, "the age of novel-writing contests" and struggling middle-school students were intimately connected through various educational magazines, such as *Chūgaku sekai* (World of middle school; est. 1898), that specifically targeted these students and consisted largely of their correspondence. Although the main issues of *Chūgaku sekai* reflected the middle-school curriculum and, as such, did not include novel-writing, the supplementary issues that began to be published on a quarterly basis in 1899 took up the subject of novel writing and established its own novel-writing contest, with Tayama Katai becoming the sole judge of the contest in the winter issue of 1899. As judge, Katai went beyond making simple comments about the winning entry, actively criticizing contemporary literary trends and discussing his own views of literature. This was especially the case when he returned as judge in 1905 after a hiatus of the magazine's supplementary issues caused by the Russo-Japanese War, as he began his first review of the winning entry after his return with the sentence "I am a believer of Naturalism" and

---

62. Kōno, *Tōki to shite no bungaku*, 44. The first winner announced on January 31 was chosen from 95 submissions and awarded ten yen, and, in February, the prize money was expanded to award five yen to second-prize winners and three yen to third-prize winners. The contest continued until 1924 and amassed over 1,700 winners. Takagi Takeo's *Shinbun shōsetsushi nenpyō* contains a list of the winners in this contest (331–77).

63. Kōno, *Tōki to shite no bungaku*, 30. On May 6, 1897, the *Yorozu chōhō* wrote that "the flourishing of awarding prizes is a new phenomenon of the literary world" (cited in ibid., 58).

went on to discuss its foundations.[64] In such a manner, Katai utilized the educational angle of the novel-writing contest—seen as supplementing middle-school education and, as such, vital to the construction of the cultured members of the middle class—to promote novel writing and help shape the course of literary production and reception among his middle-school readers.

Whether middle-school student or not, the novel-writing contest boom around the turn of the century no doubt produced aspiring writers nationwide. Through these contests, the profession of novelist became the goal within an alternative mode of *risshin shusse* ideology that differed from those based on education yet built itself on the education that students had received.[65] In many ways, in fact, the novel-writing contest symbolized the essence of ability-based *risshin shusse* ideology: anyone could enter the contest; the winner was decided based on the quality of the writing and not based on the applicant's origins, sex, or age; and the winner gained instant fame and fortune through the publication of his or her story and the awarding of a monetary prize.[66]

It is within this context of the development of novel writing as a mode of rising in the world that *Futon*'s Yoshiko asserts her historical

---

64. Cited in ibid., 103. Katai had actually moved to *Shōnen sekai* (Boys' world), an affiliate magazine of *Chūgaku sekai*, in the summer of 1901 before returning to *Chūgaku sekai* in 1905. His influence on the literary-minded readers would increase when he became the editor-in-chief of the newly established literary journal *Bunshō sekai*, which was established in March 1906 and became the central venue for the Japanese Naturalist movement.

65. Citing the scene from Mori Ōgai's *Seinen* (Youth; 1910–1911), in which a character reads the literary column of the newspaper, Komori Yōichi states: "An age had arrived when a provincial reader of the newspaper's literature column could mistake his going to Tokyo in the hopes of becoming a contributor to the column as being something similar to the past belief that going to Tokyo to study would lead to *risshin shusse*" ("Bungaku no jidai," 3).

66. Of course, this was the novel-writing contest in its ideal state, when no behind-the-scene dealings compromised the contests. Kōno hypothesizes that "in reality the novel-writing contests may not have been a system of discovering writers completely open to the general reading public, but rather a place to step up or an occasion to make some extra money for up-and-coming writers who were already pupils to famous writers or working as reporters or editors" (*Tōki to shite no bungaku*, 148). Although this is a question that needs to be examined further, the important point for our present discussion is not the credibility of these contests but their effect on the reading public.

value, as made clear by the way in which *Futon* describes the first contact between Yoshiko and Tokio:

> It was at that time that he had received an absolutely idolizing letter from a girl named Yokoyama Yoshiko, a great admirer of his works from Niimimachi in Bitchū, and a pupil at the Kobe Girls' Academy. Under the name of Takenaka Kojō he wrote novels of elegant style, and was not unknown in the world, so he quite frequently received letters from various devotees and admirers in the provinces. He didn't concern himself overmuch even with letters asking him to correct the sender's texts, or asking permission for the sender to become his pupil. And so, even when he received this girl's letter, his curiosity hadn't especially prompted him to reply. But after receiving three such enthusiastic letters from this same person, even Tokio had to take notice. . . . Her [Yoshiko's] one great hope, she said, was to become his pupil and devote her whole life to literature (128; 39).

As the passage states, Tokio often receives letters from his "devotees" and "admirers," who ask either for his suggestions on writing or to become his pupil, and, as such, Yoshiko's desire to become Tokio's pupil—and to ultimately become a novelist—is revealed not as a special case but a common phenomenon. Just as Ushimatsu was part of a group that aspired to establish themselves through education, *Futon* presents Yoshiko as belonging to a group of youths from the provinces who dream of becoming writers.

Granted, unlike Ushimatsu, who was shackled to the education system because of his socioeconomic situation, Yoshiko comes from a wealthy and respected family, and, in this regard, her decision to move to Tokyo and study literature has nothing to do with the economic restrictions placed on her. As Tokio's response to Yoshiko's letters reveals, however, Yoshiko also bears a 'mark' that she cannot escape: "He explained in detail in the letter the imprudence of a woman getting involved in literature, the need for a woman to fulfill her biological role of motherhood, the risk involved in a girl becoming a writer, and then added a few insulting phrases" (128–29; 39). Intended as a rejection of Yoshiko's solicitation to become his pupil, Tokio's response focuses on the fact that she is a woman, and in suggesting to her that she should "fulfill her biological role of motherhood," he echoes the ideology of *ryōsai kenbo* (good wife, wise mother) that began to be promoted actively within Meiji society around the turn of the century.

Central to the spreading of this ideology was the girl's school system that saw a major reorganization when the Upper Girls' School Act (Kōtō jogakkō rei) was issued in 1899 to establish a secondary-school system consisting of four years of education after elementary school.[67] As the following words of its designer Kabayama Sukenori (1837-1922) reveal, this act did not have much to do with education as a path to women's independence in society or equality with men:

> A healthy middle society cannot be nurtured by the education of boys alone. Only after serving the house together with a good wife and a wise mother can [they] promote the welfare of society. . . . [The upper girls' school] should equip [girls] to become a good wife and wise mother. Thus, it is necessary for them not only to cultivate a graceful and refined character along with a moderate and chaste nature but also to gain knowledge of learning and arts necessary for a life of the middle class.[68]

As this passage makes clear, the act was devised to complement the revised middle-school system that sought to foster the establishment of a middle class in Japan. At least on the level of ideology, such acts excluded women from the path to social success regardless of their education, for the primary purpose of women's education was to make them into good wives and wise mothers whose service to the nation was confined within the family unit outside the public realm of society.

But novel writing posited itself as one possible avenue—and a widely publicized one at that—within which women could imagine an existence outside of this ideology to succeed based on one's talents in a society ruled by the opposite sex. And such imaginings were possible not only because the fashionable novel-writing contests theoretically offered a venue where the sex of the participants did not matter, but also because there were numerous female writers who had made their mark on society, such as Miyake Kaho (1868–1943), Higuchi Ichiyō (1872–1896), and Yosano Akiko (1878–1942), whether in prose or in poetry. In this sense, just like Ushimatsu, whose choice of being a teacher was a fitting one at least theoretically given his origins and economic condition, Yoshiko's decision to become a novelist, too, is intimately connected to a profession where her 'mark' would not be a detriment.

---

67. As suggested by the establishment of various women's journals such as *Jogaku zasshi*, women's education was one of the hot topics for debate during the 1880s. However, the rate of school attendance for girls steadily decreased in the late 1880s to the early 1890s, and it was only after the Sino-Japanese War that the issue of women's education resurfaced in various newspapers and journals. For more details, see Fukaya, *Ryōsai kenbo shugi no kyōiku*, 116.

68. Cited in ibid., 155.

Just as *Hakai* asserted on the fictional level how difficult it was for Ushimatsu and Rentarō to escape their 'marks' whatever the actual state of reality may have been, however, *Futon* also tells of how escaping her 'mark' is a difficult if not impossible task, as Yoshiko's stay in Tokyo clearly shows.[69] Her modern dress and hairstyle and her casual fraternization with male friends are not only sources of concern and vexation for Tokio's wife and his wife's sister but also catch the eyes of a patrolman—a representative of the authorial gaze—who mistakes her for a prostitute.[70] To Tokio, she appears firstly as an object of desire and his interest in her for much of the story involves getting to the bottom of the truth behind her relationship with Tanaka. In this sense, it seems natural that *Futon* ends the way it does. Not only is Yoshiko's confession that she has had a sexual encounter with Tanaka considered a sin by Tokio precisely because she is a woman, but her confession also completes her branding as a sexualized body, which has no place in the world of *risshin shusse*. Ultimately, the text frames and defines her within the confines of *ryōsai kenbo* to judge her as a failure within this ideology from which she sought to escape in the first place.

---

69. This is not to say that the difficulties of these characters accurately reflect the historical reality of Meiji society. For example, as many scholars have noted, a person of *burakumin* origins who served as the model for Rentarō did not die as Rentarō did but ultimately became a principal of a school. While this example should not be taken as a sign that there existed no prejudices toward *burakumin* in Japan at the time of *Hakai*'s publication, I would argue that there is a conscious literary effort on the part of Tōson to present the fate of Ushimatsu and Rentarō in such terms regardless of the specific reality of Meiji society as it relates to *burakumin* as a social group. And I would also argue that the same can be said for Katai's literary concern in *Futon* as it relates to Yoshiko's tragic fate as a woman, for, as Rebecca Copeland has illustrated, there were available models of success, both in real life and in the fictional world, for the educated women in Meiji society. For details, see Copeland, *Lost Leaves*.

70. That the patrolman mistakes Yoshiko as a prostitute is not explicit in the text but is suggested in the following words of Tokio's sister-in-law: "There's nothing really bad about her, and she's bright and intelligent and a rare sort of person, but if she does have a fault then it's this habit of hers of walking nonchalantly around at night with her men friends. . . . And then I hear how, at the police-box on the corner, they felt it suspicious that she was always hanging around with these men and how a plainclothes detective had been stationed outside the house" (149; 57).

In *Hakai* and *Futon*, youths who aspire to establish themselves in society are forced to abandon their chosen paths to success, not because of their abilities as teachers or writers, but because of their secrets that become exposed despite their best efforts to hide them from others, an exposure that takes the form of a confession in a manner similar to that of a criminal admitting guilt. Yet, in both stories, the secret that becomes exposed should have no bearing on what happens to Ushimatsu and Yoshiko. Ushimatsu's *burakumin* origins should not have anything to do with his job as a teacher after the dissolution of the class system. And in the case of *Futon*, Tokio's response to Yoshiko's confession, "with things as they are now, it's only right for you to go back home" (187; 89), is more illogical than contradictory, and the illogicality of the situation—that is, the male-centered logic—is clearly indicated by the fact that Tanaka, who comes after Yoshiko and whose future as a writer does not seem as bright as Yoshiko's, is allowed to remain while Yoshiko goes back to her hometown with her father.

As we saw in the first section of this chapter, Raskolnikov's turn to crime had much to do with his expulsion from the world of social mobility through education, especially within the interpretative framework of 1890s Japan, which had already foreshadowed the coming of Raskolnikov in the figure of Bunzō whose dismissal from his governmental post sends him spiraling down a road to delusion and madness. The historical developments of 1890s Japan must have augmented the potential dangers facing Meiji students in becoming another Bunzō or Raskolnikov, as the path to success through education became harder and harder to navigate yet the desire to do so was being actively fueled through the expansion of the middle-school system, which enabled many more students to at least stand at the start line. But whereas Raskolnikov commits the crime because he fails to rise in the world, Ushimatsu and Yoshiko fail to rise because of their crimes. Thus, we have a reversal of cause and effect, the primary mechanism by which the two representative works of Japanese Naturalism sought to tackle and neutralize the dangers that were suggested by a Russian work of fiction and were becoming clearer by the day in the realities of Meiji society. If *Crime and Punishment* suggested the potential for intellectuals as a whole to turn criminal in a later-developing country like Russia and Japan where contradictions between social ideals and realities were particularly vivid, then *Hakai* and *Futon* function to connect the failures of Ushimatsu and Yoshiko to their 'criminal' secrets—made so by the prejudices of society—to affirm their tragic existence and experience, in turn, as marginal in nature.

But in their execution of this ideological operation, the two works move in different ways. Through its presentation of the contrasting fates of Ushimatsu and Ginnosuke that function to emphasize the non-connection between failure and ability, *Hakai* asserts Ushimatsu's marginality beyond one established through the connection made in the text between his origins and his failure. For Ushimatsu, who believes that "if he had volunteered [for the higher teacher's college], he would have already been selected," there is no sense of competition or doubts of his ability to obtain a higher education (185).[71] It is only the perceived social prejudices against his origins that shackle Ushimatsu to his current position. In contrast, Ginnosuke who is not shackled by any limitations quickly obtains a job in the Agricultural Branch of the Tokyo Imperial University upon becoming disillusioned with Iiyama's elementary school and thereby highlights the *external* limitations placed on Ushimatsu that thwarts his advancement.

In this sense, Ushimatsu, despite being the "son of a poor peasant," would not have been a likely candidate to go abroad to the extent that Katayama's works were geared primarily toward those who could not succeed in the Japanese school system because of their abilities. Ushimatsu leaves because he is forced out through prejudice and not failure. Thus, if *Hakai* evoked the contradiction between the ideology of *risshin shusse* and the real difficulties Meiji students faced in achieving its goals—

71. The phrase appears within the most vividly described passage of Ushimatsu's desire for advancement after he learns that Ginnosuke will be leaving the elementary school for the Agricultural Branch of the Tokyo Imperial University: "The passion that yearns for achievement and fame violently stimulated Ushimatsu's heart as he read his friend's letter. Truly, the reason that Ushimatsu entered the teacher's college, like that of many other students, was to gain a way to support oneself. . . . Certainly, Ushimatsu was not satisfied with the current position. But besides a special case like Ginnosuke's, there was no way other than to go to the higher teacher's college [*kōtō shihan*] for a schoolteacher to advance. If not, then, there's the long ten years of service. During that mandatory period, one had to be bound and work. If he had volunteered [for the higher teacher's college], he would have already been selected. That was the sad thing about *eta*. For some reason, he did not want to go that way. According to Ushimatsu, even if he graduated the higher teacher's college and became a teacher at a middle school or a teacher's college, what would he do if he encountered a situation like Rentarō's? Wherever he might go, he won't be able to relax. Rather than that, [it would be better] to hide patiently in the country like Iiyama and wait for the end of mandatory service. [It would be better] to study meanwhile and prepare the groundwork to go out in another direction" (184–85).

as the sociopolitical source of the intellectual's criminality as suggested by *Crime and Punishment*—then it does so in order to marginalize this contradiction through the figure of Ushimatsu. For, by actively tying his failure within this ideology to his discriminated origins, *Hakai* posits this contradiction as that between the ideal of classless society specific to the liberation of *burakumin* and the persistent social prejudices of Meiji society despite such official liberation, that is, in terms that have nothing to do with the average aspirers within the *risshin shusse* ideology. In so doing, *Hakai* rewrites the realities of ability-based failure with a fiction of prejudice-based banishment within which Ushimatsu functions as a martyr for the ordinary Meiji students in the 1890s and beyond who must face the realities of their internal lack of ability brought on by the sociopolitical conditions of the society in which they exist.

In contrast, *Futon* does not deal explicitly with the ability-based failure side of the equation beyond the tying of Yoshiko's banishment to her sex and not to her abilities as a writer. Rather, *Futon* goes a step further within the context of our discussions through its presentation of a figure of success within the path to success chosen by Yoshiko. That is, if Yoshiko represents failure to become a writer, then naturally Tokio as a writer is a figure of success whose abilities and status are sought by those who also desire to become writers, as we previously saw. But what is striking when considering Tokio as a figure of success is his modest life. Indeed, the portrait of Tokio that we get in the first pages of the story is that of a struggling writer:

> It was in one of those many factories that he went to work every afternoon, in a large Western-style room upstairs with a single large table standing in the middle and a Western-style bookcase, full of all sorts of geographical works, at its side. He was helping, on a part-time basis, with the editing of some geographical works for a certain publishing house. A man of letters editing geographical works. . . . What with his rather tardy literary career, his despair at only having produced odds and ends without an opportunity for putting all he had into a work, the painful abuse he received every month from the young men's magazines, his own awareness of what he ought to do some day—it was inevitable he should feel upset. . . . Every day, then, he would go mechanically along the same route, in through the same big gate, along the same narrow passage with its mixture of vibrating noise from the rotary press and smelly sweat from the factory-hands. He would casually greet the employees in the office, climb laboriously up the long and narrow steps, and finally enter that room. The east and south sides were open to the sun, and in the afternoon, when the sun was at its strongest, it grew unbearably hot in there. To add to it all the office-boy was lazy and didn't clean, so the table was covered with an unpleasant layer of white dust (125–26; 36–37)

Editing geographical works most likely to make ends meet, Tokio views his literary career as a tardy and frustrating one: he cannot produce a work in which he has given it his all, and, as for the works he produces, he receives poor reviews. As the lengthy description of his working environment reveals, moreover, his life is portrayed as being no different from that of a regular office worker, characterized by routine and monotony. Yet, the fact of the matter is that he has a pupil in Yoshiko and that he "quite frequently received letters from various devotees and admirers in the provinces," asking him to "correct the sender's texts, or asking permission for the sender to become his pupil."

The early chapters of *Futon* provide a contrasting portrayal of Tokio as a struggling writer and an office worker versus a writer and a teacher who is admired by many aspiring youths. At first glance, such a portrayal seems to deter from the allure of the profession of a novelist. How can Tokio's modest life inspire others to follow in his footsteps? If it fails to inspire, then does the portrayal of Tokio's life in these terms function to warn of the harsh realities of the writing profession and to encourage the aspiring novelists to seek other means of living? Does *Futon* serve to shut the door on the road to success through fiction writing? While answers to these questions must ultimately lie with individual readers, the proliferation of stories about novelists from around the time of *Futon*'s publication, as Hibi Yoshitaka demonstrates, suggests that *Futon* had a profound impact not only on literary production but also on literary consumption, addressing and promoting the desires of its readers to identify with struggling novelists.[72]

Indeed, I would argue that it was precisely the modest portrayal of Tokio's life as a writer which had the profound effect on the contemporary readers of *Futon* because such a portrayal functioned to position Tokio on the side of the ordinary man, offering a figure of success that fundamentally differed from those appearing in and criticized by the most popular newspapers of the late Meiji period such as *Yorozu chōhō* and *Niroku shinpō*. And the effectiveness of such a presentation was no

---

72. For details, see Hibi, *'Jiko hyōshō' no bungakushi*. As Hibi argues, there was a surge in the number of works between the publication of *Futon* in September 1907 and the end of 1908 that can be read within the context of the authors' actual lives, which, for Hibi, demonstrates the impact of *Futon* whose newness was to be found in the fact that it tells a story surrounding Katai's actual life. But I would argue that the impact of *Futon* lay more in its portrayal of a struggling writer as hero, whether this hero had the real-life author as model or not.

doubt augmented by the fact that *Futon* operated within the framework of yellow journalism in the nature of its central conflict, which the introduction to the collection of criticisms on *Futon* published in the October issue of the literary journal *Waseda bungaku* in 1907 describes in the following manner: "He [Tokio] by nature had a strong self-awareness and could not indulge himself in anything and stands at the contradiction between sexual desire on the one hand and morality on the other and experiences extreme anguish."[73] That is, in pitting sexual desire against morality, *Futon* took up the favorite theme of yellow journalism, namely, the illicit affairs of successful figures, whether it was the Prime Minister Itō Hirobumi or the writer Mori Ōgai.

Yet, despite evoking the framework of yellow journalism, *Futon* differs fundamentally from this medium, for, as Nakamura Mitsuo dismissively but accurately describes, *Futon* is about a "failed affair," and as such is a story about a non-scandal, at least as it relates to Tokio.[74] In this sense, *Futon* is a story about a man who chose not to commit a common but immoral scandal despite numerous opportunities. And if scandals exposed in various newspapers functioned to alleviate the jealousy and anger felt by the ordinary citizens toward the members of the upper class as the successors within the *risshin shusse* ideology, then *Futon* positions Tokio on the side of the ordinary man who, despite, or precisely because of, his modest life, is superior to the 'truly successful' in terms of his morality. In the figure of Tokio, the writer is elevated into a hero of the common people by exemplifying the understanding of the ordinary man that was implied by Ruikō's detective stories and by scandal journalism.

Furthermore, the emergence of such a figure is supported by another characteristic of *Futon* that differs fundamentally from *Hakai*. In *Hakai*, Ushimatsu's fate symbolizes the failure of the official Meiji promise to the extent that being of *burakumin* origins should have no bearing at all according to the government. In *Futon*, in contrast, Yoshiko becomes judged by the Meiji ideology of *ryōsai kenbo* supported and propounded by the state to produce young girls as complements to the middle-school-educated boys who would become the pillar of the nation by forming the middle class, a class that must be formed through the inevitable failure of social advancement via education as the official state ladder of success.

---

73. "*Futon* gappyō," in Yoshida Seiichi et al., *Kindai bungaku hyōron taikei*, vol. 3, 417.

74. Nakamura, "Tayama Katai ron," 277.

Whereas *Hakai* criticized the Meiji government through the criminalization of a victim in Ushimatsu, *Futon* criticizes Yoshiko as criminal by invoking state ideology.

In this context, Tokio's choice to relentlessly pursue the truth of Yoshiko's affair takes on another significance. As we saw, Tokio's search for truth goes against his psychic system of "fallacious identification" with Western characters, which is fundamental to his identity. By making Yoshiko confess and thereby banishing her not only from Tokyo but also from his psychic life (at least as an active and immediate part of it), Tokio 'chooses' to embody the gaze of state authority and ideology rather than to continue reproducing his fantastic relationship with the West. In other words, *Futon* posits Tokio as an ordinary man of morals who takes on the role of the detective, going as far as to sacrifice his intimate, fundamental ties to Western influence, in order to complete his 'official' duty to enforce state ideology. And considering that primary objects of his identification—as Western influence—are Russian characters, the timing of *Futon* seems quite suggestive. *Futon* appeared in the immediate aftermath of Japan's victory over Russia in the Russo-Japanese War, which signaled, at least on the surface, that Japan had arrived onto the international scene and that the Japanese had caught up with the Western powers.[75] As such, it was a fitting time for Japan to shed its connection to the West and assert its own nationalistic identity. Of course, as we shall see in the coming chapters, it was not so easy to get rid of Western influence, as suggested by the fact that the notion of chastity that Tokio uses to punish Yoshiko within the framework of *ryōsai kenbo* derived itself from the notion of platonic love and virginity as ideals of distinctively Western origin.

75. The superficial nature of Japan's victory over Russia can already be discerned from the stipulations of the Treaty of Portsmouth, which did not grant Japan the 'typical' spoils received by the victor, most notably, monetary reparation and territorial transfer. The frustrations and anger over the stipulations of the treaty immediately led to political protests in Japan, erupting in the Hibiya Riots in September 1905 during which protestors burned a majority of the police boxes in Tokyo.

FOUR

Mysteries of the Modern Subject: The Detective and the Detective Fiction Framework in the Writings of Natsume Sōseki

In January 1903, Natsume Sōseki, who would soon start on the path to becoming the most famous writer of modern Japan, returned to his native country after a 26-month stay in England ordered by the Ministry of Education. Well documented by himself and by numerous scholars as a very unhappy sojourn, his life in London was not only economically demanding due to his meager stipend but also intellectually and culturally unfulfilling, leaving him with "a dislike for England and even for English literature."[1] Furthermore, his mental health, which was already in question prior to his trip, worsened abroad, and there arose rumors that he had suffered a nervous breakdown. The source of such rumors was a student who had visited Sōseki's lodgings in London. Inquiring about Sōseki to his landlady—who, according to Sōseki, constantly spied on him—the student discovered that Sōseki often shut himself up in his room and cried in the dark. The student reported his findings to the Ministry of Education whereupon news quickly spread among the pub-

1. Keene, *Dawn to the West*, 310.

lic that Sōseki had gone mad, and his acquaintances in Tokyo often approached his unwitting wife about the health of her husband.[2]

Many Sōseki scholars have pointed out this biographical experience—rumors about his mental health triggered by the spying landlady and student—as one of the primary reasons for Sōseki's hatred of detectives. Indeed, Sōseki, more than any other writer in the modern Japanese literary canon, argued the evils and immorality of the detective as a profession.[3] But whatever his reasons may have been, he put his hatred of the detective to good use, employing the detective as a powerful metaphor with which to reflect upon the various phenomena of Japanese modernity and modernization, including the development of literature, as exemplified by his essay "Bungei no tetsugaku-teki kiso" (The philosophical foundations of literary arts), originally given as a lecture and later serialized in *Tōkyō Asahi shinbun* from May 4 to June 4, 1907.

Arguing that the foundations of literature consist of the four ideals of beauty, truth, love/morality, and solemnity, this essay criticizes the state of contemporary literature for its unbalanced emphasis on the search for truth. And in making his point, Sōseki quickly turns to a vehement attack of the detective as a profession whose "essence is to search for the truth in the most vulgar sense," going as far as stating that the detective cannot "pass as a human being" and is only "important as a machine." It is only after this 'rant' that he turns to the topic at hand:

> It is extremely rude to compare the contemporary literati to the detective, but if a writer is proud to openly publish works that only profess truth and do not care what happens to the other ideals, then he must be a person with a defect, perhaps not as an individual, but certainly as a writer. We must say that he is unhealthy.

While Sōseki only names foreign writers like Maupassant and Zola to be "just as vulgar as a detective," it is easily understandable that his criticism extended to Japanese writers, especially considering that, around

---

2. For more details on this anecdote, see Natsume Kyōko's *Natsume no omoide*, 123–29. According to this memoir, Sōseki is said to have said the following about his landlady and her sister: "The landlady and her sister are very kind to me, but they say bad things about me behind my back. . . . They keep an eye on me as if they were detectives. How detestable they are!" (126).

3. For example, Uchida Ryūzō writes: "In the beginning of the twentieth century, there was none other than Natsume Sōseki who reacted more sensitively and bore more ill will toward the mysterious existence of the 'detective'" (*Tantei shōsetsu no shakaigaku*, 21).

1907, a literary movement heavily influenced by the works of these French writers—Japanese Naturalism whose 'obsession' for truth was examined in the previous chapter—was gaining momentum in Japan.[4]

Yet, as already seen in his first work *Wagahai wa neko de aru* (hereafter referred to as *Neko*) in which the cat, though critical of the detective, cannot help being detective-like, Sōseki's relationship to the detective was always characterized by ambivalence.[5] By examining his later works *Higan sugi made* (Until after the equinox; 1912) and *Kokoro* (1914) in conjunction with *Neko*, this chapter considers this ambivalence surrounding the figure of the detective that also manifests itself in Sōseki's repeated equating of the detective with the criminal, which, in turn, problematizes the polarizing subjective positions offered by the detective story. In so doing, I argue that the detective and the detective fiction framework were not only targets through which Sōseki criticized modern society but also sites within which he sought solutions to the ills such society brought to its subjects, however maddening such a search became. And here, Sōseki's project posits itself as the flip side of Japanese Naturalism by taking up the issue of *risshin shusse*: if the latter sought to deal with those who were failing within this ideological system through the presentation of marginalized martyrs—that is, by circumvention through substitution—then Sōseki got at the heart of the matter by his relentless portrayal of those who should be elites of their society given their educational and socioeconomic backgrounds but nonetheless—or rather, precisely because such backgrounds lead to their predilection for being detective-like—fail to be productive citizens in society.

---

4. Natsume Sōseki, "Bungei no tetsugaku-teki kiso," in *Sōseki zenshū*, vol. 11, 76–77.

5. On this point, Ara Masahito states: "The most curious thing [about *Neko*] is that the cat effectively plays the role of the detective that Sōseki detested most. The mystery of this unconventional story probably lies in the fact that the cat is the sublimated figure of the detective. Solving this mystery will no doubt lead to a better understanding of the fundamental nature of *Wagahai wa neko de aru*" (*Natsume Sōseki*, 136). Uchida Ryūzō makes a similar observation: "this novel, on the one hand, is a criticism against the existential form of the detective, and, on the other hand, is founded on the detective-like perspective and actions performed by the cat" (*Tantei shōsetsu no shakaigaku*, 29).

Spying Cat, Narrating Cat

Originally written to conclude in one installment but continued for ten more because of its popularity in the literary journal *Hototogisu* (Cuckoo; est. 1897), *Neko* takes the form of a series of vignettes that describe the everyday lives of Kushami, a school teacher, and his friends and former students who gather at his home. Made clear by the title—also the story's opening sentence—from the very beginning, the story's first-person narrator is a cat who proclaims himself to be a writer of *shaseibun*.[6] As Sōseki would later articulate, *shaseibun* (which can be translated as sketch writings) was a form of writing that Sōseki set against the novel. Its primary characteristics were the lack of plot ("What is plot? Does the world have a plot? It is no use to create a plot within something that doesn't have plot") and the distant yet sympathetic and humorous attitude toward the object of depiction, which Sōseki describes as that of "an adult looking at a child" and of "parents facing their children."[7]

True to his word, the cat's narrative, consisting of numerous anecdotes and infused with humor, seems to fulfill these characteristics of *shaseibun*, no doubt assisted by the absurd premise of the cat as narrator that makes possible a viewpoint outside the social and moral confines of the human world from which to criticize and relativize human habits and customs in a comical way. Yet, despite the cat's self-conscious presentation of the text as *shaseibun* and the unplanned nature of *Neko*'s serialization, there does exist a consistent thread that runs through the work's eleven chapters, namely, the supposed courtship between Kushami's former student Kangetsu and the daughter of the neighborhood entrepreneur Kaneda. Fittingly enough, this courtship finds its resolution in the final chapter when Kangetsu tells Kushami's salon that he has actually married a girl from his hometown during a recent trip there. In light of this information, Kushami suggests to Kangetsu that he should inform the Kanedas of the marriage, but Kangetsu rejects this suggestion, stating that the Kanedas would surely know of this fact already thanks to their "detectives," who have been snooping around the Kushami household to

---

6. *Shaseibun* was a form of writing originally developed by Sōseki's friend Masaoka Shiki (1867–1902) and Shiki's disciple and the editor of *Hototogisu* Takahama Kyoshi (1874–1959). *Shaseibun* grew out of Shiki's efforts in the field of *tanka* and *haiku* to provide objective descriptions of subject matter.

7. Natsume Sōseki, "Shaseibun," in *Sōseki zenshū*, vol. 11, 22–23.

get information on Kangetsu.[8] Kushami agrees with Kangetsu, but this use of the word "detective" sets Kushami off into a rant regarding the detective:

A pickpocket is someone who picks people's pockets on the occasion of their carelessness; a detective is someone who fishes the thoughts and feelings on the occasion of their carelessness. A thief is someone who takes off the shutters and steals people's belongings without their knowledge; a detective is someone who makes people slip their tongue and reads their hearts without their knowledge. A robber is someone who stabs a knife into a tatami-mat and grabs people's money by force; a detective is someone who talks threatening words excessively and forces people's wills. So the creature called detective is a kindred of pickpockets, thieves, and robbers and cannot be placed windward to a person (501).

After this rant by Kushami, his friend Dokusen asks an out-of-the-blue question: "Speaking of detectives, how is it that the people of the twentieth century have a general tendency to become detective-like?" (502). Kushami's friends give their curt, smart answers, but Kushami takes this question as an occasion to rant further. He states:

According to my interpretation, the reason for the detective-like tendency of the people today is definitely because the individual's self-awareness is too strong. . . . By the self-awareness of people today, I mean that people are too aware of the existence of a distinct gap in terms of the interests between oneself and others. And this self-awareness becomes acute day by day with the advancement of civilization so in the end, you will not be able to make any little move naturally. . . . On this account, the people of today are detective-like, thief-like. The detective is a profession that tries to do well just for oneself by doing things behind people's backs, so, of course, [it] can only be done [by someone] with a strong self-awareness. Because the worry of being caught and being discovered never leaves a thief, he too is forced to have a strong self-awareness. The people of today are always thinking about what is to one's advantage/profit and one's disadvantage/loss whether they are sleeping or awake, they too cannot help but have strong self-awareness like the detective and the thief. Looking and sneaking around restlessly day and night without a moment of relief until they enter the grave—this is the hearts of people today and the curse of civilization (502–4).

In these long monologues, Kushami equates the detective with criminals, seeing them as two sides of the same coin in their need for "self-awareness," which results from their desire to access something that they are not entitled to from others. It is not the murderer—the favorite criminal of detective fiction—but a pickpocket, thief, and robber

8. Natsume Sōseki, *Wagahai wa neko de aru*, in *Sōseki zenshū*, vol. 1, 501. All subsequent references to this source will appear in the text in parentheses.

who are compared to the detective. That is, Kushami compares the detective to 'professions' whose essential characteristic is the unlawful usurpation of private property via a transgression of the boundary between public and private realms in order to describe the immoral and despicable nature of the detective who pickpockets, steals, and robs the private thoughts of individuals against their will. In so doing, Kushami's rant clearly places Sōseki's criticism of the detective within Tsubouchi Shōyō's novelistic worldview in which the novelist becomes a privileged mediator between the individual's external actions/behaviors and internal thoughts/emotions whose correspondence has become severed in the modern age.

This criticism of the detective finds further elaboration in the second passage when Kushami discusses the reason why modern individuals have a heightened sense of self-awareness. For him, the heightened sense of self-awareness is a result of the awareness that there exists "a distinct gap in terms of the interests between oneself and others," an awareness that increases "day by day with the advancement of civilization" and leads to a modern condition where no one can go "without a moment of relief." Modern individuals turn detective thanks to their constant analysis of the Other to assess what is advantageous to the self or not, which, in turn, is necessitated by the framework of social evolution where one person's success may mean another's failure. The primary form of social competition in Meiji Japan, social advancement through education, no doubt fostered such "self-awareness," as government policies in the 1890s actively promoted the escalation of competition, as we discussed in the previous chapter. Indeed, the members of Kushami's salon, despite their witty but mostly substance-less chatter that suggests their "moment of relief," are precisely the victors within the social ladder of success through education that makes individuals self-aware. Yet, they are not presented as such in *Neko*, and in their stead, the textual representation of self-interest and self-awareness takes the specific form of the Kanedas, whose mention prompted Kushami's rant in the first place.

Fittingly, then, it is the cat's encounter with Kaneda's wife when she visits Kushami's house uninvited in the third chapter that prompts the cat to use the word "detective" for the first time (117). In her conversation with Kushami, Kaneda's wife shamelessly reveals that she has asked his neighbors to spy on his relationship with Kangetsu, whom she hopes to have as her daughter's husband, a desire admitted as being based wholly on self-interest: although Kangetsu is not rich, the Kanedas would like the status that he might bring to the family, and, thus, their stipulation for the marriage is that he obtain his doctorate degree and thereby reach the pinnacle of the educational ladder of success in Meiji society.[9] In *Neko*, the Kanedas function as the epitome of the twentieth-century individual as schemers who are always thinking about advantages and disadvantages, profits and losses. And this is hardly surprising precisely because heightened self-awareness in monetary terms, as Kushami suggests, was not a unique characteristic of the Kanedas but a common one among the people of Kushami's time, when the belief in social success through education was quickly diminishing. In other words, the Kanedas whose name contains the character 'money,' literally symbolizes such way of thinking about profit and loss that had become a sociohistorical phenomenon in the first decades of the twentieth century characterized by the catchword *seikō* (success).

As Earl Kinmonth has argued, concomitant with the official attempt in the 1890s to expand the middle class through the expansion of the middle school system, which in turn made advancement within the educational system extremely competitive, was a radical shift in the way people thought about success. He writes:

> Far more important than the stimulus given to militaristic or expansionistic visions of advancement was the contribution the war made to the growth of the economy and the subsequent definition of advancement in monetary terms. In the short run the war gave rise to a speculative boom of considerable intensity. *Kokumin no tomo* lamented that energy generated by the war, rather than being turned to science, religion, or academia, had ended up in speculation and get-rich-quick schemes. People's heads were full of stock prices. . . . Whereas the past had seen a surplus of youths dreaming of politics, the postwar era saw them shouting "Gold! Gold!" and "Make Money! Make Money!" or so the editorial claimed. . . . the economic growth stimulated by the war had in turn stimulated a new interest in business among even relatively well-educated youths who would previously have only considered government affiliation worthy of their efforts.[10]

---

9. In this instance, then, the word "detective" (*tantei*) is used as a verb rather than as a noun (variation of the form *tantei suru*). Although this practice was already common in the 1880s and there was and still is the propensity within the Japanese language to create a verb by simply attaching the verb-ending *suru* (to do) to the noun, the use of the word *tantei* as a verb, a use that is impossible in English ("detective" does not equal "detect"), detaches the word from the profession of the detective, enabling it to describe actions of ordinary persons.

10. Kinmonth, *The Self-Made Man in Meiji Japanese Thought*, 154, 157.

As Kinmonth describes in this passage, the newly and rapidly developing capitalistic system in the aftermath of the Sino-Japanese War provided the "relatively well-educated youth" for whom success through education was becoming harder and harder to achieve with an alternative mode of rising in the world. But while such a mode of success became widely spread among various economic classes and social groups by the turn of the century, the real possibilities of succeeding in society within this mode of rising in the world, too, were short-lived as Japan experienced "a severe depression with substantial unemployment" during the first years of the new millennium, leaving only the dreams of striking it rich intact.[11]

It was within such a sociohistorical reality that the Kanedas, as figures of success in a new mode of rising in the world, pranced around the neighborhood with a haughty air, demanding obedience and commanding respect from their neighbors. Kaneda was a successful embodiment of a dream in a society where such a dream had already become very difficult to achieve. It is also within such an atmosphere that Kushami's characterization of the twentieth-century individual as always worrying about profits and losses must be understood. The twentieth-century individual is detective-like, always aware of one's actions, to the extent that he is a participant in the social Darwinian struggle for money as success. For Kushami, however, such an attempt at entrepreneurship as lawful accumulation of private property is no different from stealing as unlawful usurpation of private property. And Kangetsu, his star student around whom the discourse on the detective in *Neko* revolves, rejects the most traditional (underhanded) route to material success by refusing to marry into wealth.

But while the members of Kushami's salon may be immune to such self-awareness bred through competition, the same cannot be said for the cat, whose encounter with Kaneda's scheming wife prompts him not

11. Ibid., 162. Importantly, it was only when the market became harsh and money-making difficult that journals like *Jitsugyō no Nihon* (Business Japan) and *Seikō* (Success) gained popularity and general-interest magazines like *Taiyō* (The sun) and *Chūō kōron* established columns on success and money-making. As such, it was natural that the underlying framework of these journals and columns was one of a social Darwinian struggle where coming out on top in a competition required not a straightforward approach but 'secrets' to acquiring wealth. In a sense, these journals offered ways to succeed economically in a dire condition. In another sense, they promoted people to hang on to a dream when the dream was quickly becoming a fantasy.

only to use the word "detective" but also to spy on the Kanedas—that is, to act like a detective—and to become conscious of the detective-like nature of his previous and present actions. From the fourth chapter on, the cat repeatedly uses the word "detective" as a verb to describe his own actions, whether they involve spying on the Kanedas or simply following Kushami around the house. Together with this use of the word "detective" is the use of the word *jiken* (affair, incident, case) to describe the mundane events surrounding Kushami's life. The prevalence of the word *jiken*, which is used to designate criminal cases in Japanese, suggests the cat's conscious framing of his narrative within the discourse of the detective and of criminal investigations.

Even before such a shift in the cat's narration, there is no denying that the early chapters of *Neko* present the cat as a natural detective. Not only is he better suited than humans to play the role of the detective because of his stealthy and nimble nature, as he himself points out, but he can also easily circulate within the private lives of people precisely because the cat does not appear to them as the Other whose presence requires a heightened sense of "self-awareness." For the cat, there is no such thing as a transgression of someone's private sphere, because his presence, even when recognized, does not disturb the privacy of the space, as characters go on with their actions and conversations as if he did not exist. Moreover, the cat seems to enjoy prying into the private details of others, as already made clear in the first chapter, when he reads Kushami's diary—a private object understood to contain the internal thoughts of a person—to divulge his thoughts, such as his envy for a geisha wife, that "should not be uttered by a teacher" (19).

This is not to say, however, that the cat is fully comfortable with his detective-like actions or nature. He also shares the hatred for the detective—at least in theory—expressed by Kushami and his friends at various points in the narrative, stating that "there is no profession in this world that is more vulgar than a detective and a loan shark" and thereby foreshadowing the connection Kushami will make between the detective and private property in the final chapter of the story (134–35). In fact, the cat's narrative is filled, even before the above statement, with his repeated attempts to justify the contradiction between this hatred of the detective and the awareness of his own actions as detective-like. For example, after learning that Kaneda's wife has devised a plan to spy on Kushami and Kangetsu, the cat decides to go to the Kanedas to spy on them in turn for Kangetsu's sake. But upon realizing that he will not be able to pass on the information to Kangetsu because he cannot communicate with human beings, his justification of selfless duty quickly turns into that of narcissistic pleasure and self-edification as he states: "It is pleasant in itself to accomplish something that others cannot do" (119).

Ultimately, the cat's justification evolves into one of defiance, as he rejects the idea of private property and privacy—critical to the criticism of the detective in *Neko*—as contractual constructs of human society that have nothing to do with him. For him, the repeated visits to Kaneda's mansion are an assertion of his right to roam wherever and observe whatever he pleases, and it cannot be helped if in asserting his inherent right, "the circumstances at Kaneda's house naturally reflect in my eyes that don't want to see and leave an impression in my brain that doesn't want to remember" (136). In such a way, the cat turns his aforementioned abilities as a natural detective into an excuse or justification for his conscious attempt to spy on the Kanedas and presents himself as a supra-moral figure who should not be condemned—at least in theory—for his detective-like acts.

But what about writing about such acts? As a narrated self, the cat may be a physical entity free from human rules and morality, but, as a narrator, the cat is a linguistic entity who can communicate with his human readers. Ironically, the cat's explanation of his supra-moral status based on his lack of ties to human society must take the form of human language, the use of which undermines the premise on which he justifies his detective-like actions. Given the progression (or regression) of the cat as a user of language in the course of *Neko*, moreover, we could make the argument that the story tells how a cat comes to terms with his inherently detective-like nature to become a perfect detective. In the course of the narrative, the cat, who could not shed his subjective involvement with the objects of his investigations as the narrated self in the early pages of the story—unnecessary information for a detective's report—gradually disappears from the text, replaced by the narrating cat as gaze and perspective.[12] By the final chapter, when the prolonged conversation on the

12. The cat's development into a perfect detective can also be seen in the supra-human abilities that he obtains in the course of the narrative, namely, the ability to access information that exists outside the reach of a first-person narrator's limited viewpoint—that is, the inner thoughts of Kushami and others. Despite stating that "There is nothing more difficult to understand than the psychology of human beings. I have no idea whether this master is now upset, merry, or seeking comfort in the way of the philosopher's work" (32) in the aforementioned scene when he reads Kushami's diary, the cat has no such trou-

detective takes place at Kushami's house, the narrated cat is nowhere to be seen, and the narrating cat is no different from a third-person narrator who 'faithfully' records the conversation that is taking place. And if the cat's inherent detective-like nature was brought to the fore of his consciousness with the introduction of Kaneda's wife, who willingly admits her hiring of spies to report about the ongoing affairs of the Kushami household as they relate to Kangetsu, then the cat's narrative posits itself as precisely that which she was seeking from her spies, making the cat out to be the ultimate detective that the Kanedas have (not) hired to spy on Kushami and Kangetsu.[13] Fittingly, the cat dies and his narrative ends when the Kanedas no longer need a detective to spy on Kangetsu as a result of his marriage to a girl from his hometown.[14]

As we saw in the first chapter of this study, Shōyō's introduction of the detective was intricately tied to his need for the moral legitimation of his notion of the novel. To the extent that the primary focus of Shōyō's novel was the private lives of individuals, the author/narrator of the modern novel was already implicated as an eavesdropper and a voyeur. Unlike the real-life detectives of the 1880s who were no different from an eavesdropper/voyeur, Shōyō's detective was an idealized figure of distinctively foreign origin who exposed the wrongdoings of society that would have gone unnoticed otherwise. In short, Shōyō appealed to the social benefits of the detective in order to legitimate the author/narrator of the modern novel. In *Neko*, however, the detective is not an idealized figure of justice and morality. He is real and ubiquitous, synonymous with the eavesdrop-

---

ble by the ninth chapter when he states: "I am a cat. There may be those who are questioning why I despite being a cat can record with precision my master's innermost thoughts in such a way, but for a cat, such things are nothing. I am versed in the art of mind reading. You don't have to ask an unnecessary thing like when I learned such a thing. In any case, I am versed in it" (384).

13. The irony of the situation is reflected in the fact that various characters in *Neko* including the cat refer to the hired spies of the Kanedas as dogs, as linguistic antonym to the cat, and the Kanedas as pet owners (*kainushi*). That is, if the dog is associated with servility and obedience and the cat with curiosity, then *Neko* tells the process of how the cat's curiosity ends up making him into an obedient dog of the Kanedas.

14. The cat dies when he gets drunk on beer and falls into a large pail. Unlike his previous crisis, when he choked on a rice cake in the second chapter, no one comes to rescue him. While it is true that his drowning takes place at night after people at Kushami's house have gone to sleep, it is also symbolic of the fact that the cat has become invisible to the people of the story world.

per and spy. This is not to say, though, that Sōseki did not share Shōyō's concern regarding the fundamental nature—that is, the fundamental immorality—of the author/narrator and of novel writing. If Shōyō sought to disentangle the connection between the author/narrator and the eavesdropper through the introduction of the detective as an idealized figure of justice and morality, then Sōseki reveals the absurdity and impossibility of such a figure through the talking/writing cat, whose story provides an allegory of how difficult it is to not become a detective as a narrator.

That Sōseki considered the figure of the detective as a necessary starting point to his literary project is evident from his repeated return to this topic in his other early works, including "Shumi no iden" (The heredity of taste; January 1906), *Botchan* (The young master; April 1906), and *Kusamakura* (Pillow of grass; September 1906). For example, the narrator-protagonist of "Shumi no iden," in a similar manner to the cat, states: "It is an extremely absurd phenomenon that I, who have always thought to myself and proclaimed to others that there is no business more inferior than a detective, would come to treat things with a purely detective-like attitude."[15] And in *Kusamakura*, its artist-protagonist—who claims that "ordinary novels are all invented by detectives"—foreshadows the criticism of the novel articulated in "Bungaku no tetsugakuteki kiso" when he states: "[I]t will become vulgar if I, like an ordinary novelist, investigate the root of their [people of the village] arbitrary behavior, delve into [their] mental operations, and examine conflicts of human affairs. . . . To the people that I will meet now, I will try to watch them from far above with detachment and not to let the electricity of human feelings arise in any party."[16]

As these examples show, the detective was an ubiquitous figure in Sōseki's early works. But such an articulation of the detective disappears completely, at least on the surface level of the text, around the time Sōseki joined the *Tōkyō Asahi shinbun* to become a full-time writer in April 1907. According to the index volume of *Sōseki zenshū*, in fact, the word *tantei*, which appeared repeatedly in his early works, does not appear at all in his fictional writings after *Nowaki* (Autumn wind; January 1907), the last fictional work Sōseki wrote before joining the newspaper.[17] But this is not to say that Sōseki abandoned his exploration of the fundamental issues embodied by the figure of the detective, for his literary

15. Natsume Sōseki, "Shumi no iden," in *Sōseki zenshū*, vol. 2, 216
16. Natsume Sōseki, *Kusamakura*, in *Sōseki zenshū*, vol. 2, 489, 396.
17. Natsume Sōseki, *Sōseki zenshū*, vol. 17, 478.

works after *Nowaki* continued to tell how modern society inevitably turns one into a detective without using the term. And when Sōseki brings back the detective in *Higan sugi made*, he does so with a vengeance, tackling the problem of the detective head on to examine the intimate connection—ignored by Sōseki in *Neko*—between the detective and the modern Japanese intellectual characterized by his penchant for curiosity and reflection.

The Rhetoric of the Secret

On New Year's Day, 1912, Natsume Sōseki began the serialization of *Higan sugi made* in *Tōkyo Asahi shinbun* after a year-and-a-half hiatus from fiction writing caused primarily by the aggravation of a stomach ulcer from which he had been suffering. As such, it is understandable that his introduction to the story expresses a resolve that grew out of this hiatus, as Sōseki writes that "there is a certain feeling that it would be inexcusable if I didn't write something interesting . . . [and] didn't repay my colleagues who treated me with generous spirit regarding my health."[18] And if Sōseki returned from a long hiatus determined to write an interesting story, then the choice he makes for the story's subject matter—the detective—is significant within the understanding of his literary oeuvre, for it reiterates his deep-seated predilection to gravitate to the detective as the most suitable metaphor to discuss the problematics of modern Japanese society and its individual, the two issues with which he was primarily concerned.

Revisiting the paradoxical ambivalence toward the detective found in *Neko*, *Higan sugi made* tells the story of Tagawa Keitarō, a young man who aspires to do things that "a detective of the metropolitan police department" might do, but, at the same time, feels that he cannot (43). As he describes to his friend Sunaga, who would become Keitarō's primary object of investigation in the course of the story:

> Primarily a detective is something like a diver of society who dives from the surface of the world into its depths, so there are not many professions like it that grasp the mysteries of people. And because his job is to simply observe the dark aspects of others and does not require him to be endangered by becoming corrupted himself, it is even more convenient. However, because his objective, from the beginning, is to expose the wrongdoings [of people], it is a profession

---

18. Natsume Sōseki, *Higan sugi made*, in *Sōseki zenshū*, vol. 5, 6. All subsequent references to this source will appear in the text in parentheses.

that is founded upon the preconceived idea of ensnaring people. I cannot do something as bad as that to people. I just want to be a researcher of people, or, rather, I just want to gaze with a sense of wonder at the way in which the abnormal mechanisms of people operate in the darkness of the night (44).

As this passage reveals, Keitarō's hesitancy to become a detective stems from moral reasons: rather than "expose the wrongdoings" of people as an active agent, Keitarō instead wants to "gaze" at their most private and extraordinary moments as a passive observer—an eavesdropper and a voyeur—who in his eyes is less morally offensive than a crime-fighting detective. Such a view of the detective, to the extent that it lacks a sense of social justice, presents itself as diametrically opposed to those put forth in Shōyō's *Nisegane tsukai* and Ruikō's *Muzan*, in which the social function of the detective as the executor of justice morally justifies the personally questionable potential of the detective as a violator of privacy.[19]

Whether logically sound or not, Keitarō's asocial understanding of the detective seems appropriate considering that his interest in being a detective is introduced as constituted by his primary characteristic, namely, his romanticism, which began to rear its head when he was introduced to Robert Louis Stevenson's *New Arabian Nights* (1882) in high school. Indeed, the specific influence of Stevenson's text can be seen in the otherworldliness and exoticism of Keitarō's fantasies, which include a plan to open a "rubber plant farm in Singapore" (18). To draw from our discussions from the previous chapter, such exoticism sets *Higan sugi made* against Tōson's *Hakai*, exposing the elitist naiveté of the former's protagonist: if Ushimatsu is banished against his will to a foreign land to work on a farm, then Keitarō views that land—whether the rubber plant forests of Singapore or Manchuria, where his fellow lodger Morimoto fled, leaving unpaid rent—as objects of romantic musing and yearning.

At the same time, it is also true that Keitarō's romanticism points to a problem similar to that of Ushimatsu: namely, the difficulty of finding

19. As Karatani Kōjin has argued, such a view of the detective completely detached from a sense of social justice exposes Keitarō as someone who is "more indifferent to morality than a criminal" (*Sōseki ron shūsei*, 308). In this sense, Keitarō can be compared to the cat in *Neko*. Fittingly, like the cat who transforms into a narrative perspective towards the end of *Neko*, Keitarō gradually shifts from an active agent to a passive observer who disappears from the text.

success in Japan. While Keitarō, unlike Ushimatsu, is an elite member of Japanese society as a graduate of the university (presumably Tokyo Imperial University), he does not see himself as a figure of real success:

> He had no awareness up to today that he had advanced forward on his own powers. Whether it was his studies, sports, or whatever, he had never managed to take them on seriously and see them through to the end. The only thing he had done as far as he could was that he graduated from the university. Even that, they dragged him out although he did not put forth the effort and was inclined to just be lazy, so, in return for there not being a feeling of stagnation, there also wasn't a sense of relief as if one had finally dug through a well (75).

No doubt, such a feeling of drifting through life has much to do with his upbringing in a well-to-do family that enabled him to grow up without experiencing the financial constraints and hardships of average citizens. But it is also brought on by the humbling 'view' from the pinnacle of this 'mountain' of social advancement through education, for Keitarō is left without a suitable job after obtaining a university degree, leading him, in turn, to contemplate a speculative venture abroad.

In this context, although the first half of the story until Keitarō finally gets to play detective at Taguchi's orders has often been criticized for being gratuitous, the slowness of narrative development was perhaps Sōseki's point.[20] That is, Keitarō's repeated failure even to get to meet with the successful businessman Taguchi, being stood up and insulted in the process, suggests Keitarō's desperation to find a job and his awareness that the best way to do so is to use not his education but his connection with Sunaga to get in with his entrepreneurial uncle. And just when he seems to have received his perfect job from Taguchi of playing detective—that is, the fusion of his romantic dreams and real-world aspirations—it turns out that he is made to play the fool instead by spying on a dinner date between Taguchi's daughter Chiyoko and her uncle Matsumoto for Taguchi's entertainment. Through this turn of events, the first half of *Higan sugi made* offers a radical criticism of the value of education and presents Keitarō's romanticism and his love of the detective as the flip side to his desperation in the harsh realities of 1910s Japan. In the end, as Keitarō is fully aware, he does exactly what his delinquent

---

20. In his analysis of *Higan sugi made*, Maeda Ai criticizes the first half as "elaborate to the point of being slightly verbose." He also presents as general opinion that the first half was "an unnecessary service for the newspaper readers forced upon Sōseki after his illness" ("Kashō no machi," 215, 201).

neighbor Morimoto said any university graduate would do, choosing reality and status over romantic adventure.[21]

But Keitarō's detective work does not end here, as he thereafter delves into "the complex situation" between Sunaga and Chiyoko, his cousin whom his mother had asked her father (Taguchi) to make Sunaga's wife upon her birth (201).[22] The following exemplifies Sunaga's tumultuous relationship—psychologically speaking—with Chiyoko, which, in turn, reveals Sunaga as a modern Japanese intellectual in the lineage of *Ukigumo*'s Bunzō and *Futon*'s Tokio, whose penchant for analysis posits the woman as mystery-to-be-solved:

> On occasion, she seemed as if I was the only one she loved in this world. . . . But as I contemplated whether I should take resolute action, she would escape from my grasp in an instant, and she would take on the face of someone who was no different from a complete stranger. . . . Sometimes, my heart would become cloudy with the slightest suspicion that she controlled this with her own will, approaching me and then becoming distant on purpose. Not only that. There were many examples when I felt the fruitless frustration after I had interpreted her words and actions as one meaning only to immediately reinterpret the same words and actions as having a complete opposite meaning and, in the end, not knowing which one was correct (266–67).

As made clear by this passage, which takes place after the introduction of Takagi (an extrovert in contrast to Sunaga who emerges, at least in the eyes of Sunaga, as Chiyoko's future husband), Chiyoko's words and actions lead Sunaga to analysis but such analysis only leads to multiple interpretations. Not only that, such analysis often ends up in self-doubt and the presentation of himself as a mystery: "I am of the type who is

---

21. Matsumoto tells Keitarō: "There are many interesting things in this world aside from hurricanes, and you seem to be trying hard to encounter such interesting things, but it's no good once you have graduated the university. When push comes to shove, you will recall your status. . . . In this day and age, there isn't a whimsical person who would seriously go as far as giving up one's status to wander" (31). Also, Keitarō later tells Sunaga: "I thought that education was a privilege but actually it is one type of constraint" (43).

22. The following comment Keitarō makes upon his decision to delve into the story of Sunaga and Chiyoko reveals his vulgar curiosity as well as his audacity and arrogance regarding his right to such action that resemble the cat's argument of why he is not a detective: "Of course, it was nothing but simple curiosity. He clearly recognized it as such. But he also recognized that if it was against Sunaga, then satisfying this curiosity would not be considered offensive. Not only that, he believed that he had the right to satisfy this curiosity" (201–2).

often suspicious of others but at the same time must be suspicious of the self that is suspicious" (243). Indeed, Sunaga goes as far as to claim that he does not even know whether he loves Chiyoko, as his own reactions to Chiyoko often surprise him. This happens twice in the story, first when he is shocked by her marriage announcement that turns out to be a lie (225–27) and second after he returns from Kamakura alone and contemplates the relationship between Chiyoko and Takagi and 'encounters' his own jealousy (281–82).

If one result of over-analysis is the turning inward of the gaze that leads one to question oneself, then the other is the lack of action exemplified once again by Bunzō of *Ukigumo*, who escapes into his second-floor room for endless contemplation. While Sunaga is undoubtedly his successor, he, unlike Bunzō, is well aware of the result of his overactive intellect—"my head was made to suppress my heart" (274)—which he takes to be a common characteristic of the educated, as he tells his friend why he would make a poor character in a novel: "those who are advanced in thought are always thinking and don't have the courage to act in a grand manner" (271). This comment leads to an interesting anecdote, in which Sunaga's friend lends him a novel in German translation titled *Der Gedanke*, by the Russian writer Leonid Andreyev (1871–1919), that tells of an intellectual who strategically fakes his insanity in order to kill his friend (who had married the woman he loves) without being charged in the murder.[23]

No doubt more extreme and contrived in its protagonist's plan and execution, *Der Gedanke* nonetheless shares many similarities with *Crime*

23. Sunaga calls the story an example of a "protagonist who possesses both extraordinary intellect and terrifyingly and fiercely daring action" (271). The work *Der Gedanke* depicts a man whose love is not welcomed by a woman, who instead marries his friend, and who therefore decides to murder his friend in as "complicated a manner" as possible (272). He chooses to portray himself as a crazy person by pretending to have psychological breakdowns in front of people. And when the rumors of his mental health had spread, he kills his friend in front of his wife in the pretense of another breakdown so that he is not charged with murder. The man succeeds in his task, but, of course, he is sent away to a psychiatric ward. The catch is that by the end of the story, the reader is not sure if the man is a sane man of superior intellect and action or simply a lunatic. In a sense, the craziness of his actions—the murder as well as the various steps he goes through in order to accomplish this task—makes it impossible to affirm as extraordinary the intellect with which he plans his move, and the story becomes one about a monster that can be created when reason aligns with passion.

and Punishment in their exploration of the madness that awaits those whose intellect loses direction, whether through socioeconomic hardships or a broken heart. And by having Sunaga claim that he envies the protagonist of *Der Gedanke* and by having him daydream about killing Takagi, the text seems to suggest the powerful effects that such literatures continued to exercise on the psychic life of modern Japanese subjects. But to the extent that the portrayal of such subjects was fundamentally as men of inaction in Japan, from *Ukigumo*'s Bunzō to *Futon*'s Tokio, Sōseki seems to reiterate the fundamentally non-radical nature of the modern Japanese subject who embraces Western education and literature not as models for action but as sources for fantasy, which, in turn, foster the inward directing of the subject's gaze. If a Russian work (*Crime and Punishment*) suggested the dangerous potential of intellectuals to turn criminal and was suppressed within Meiji literary history as a result, then Sōseki through his introduction of another Russian work (*Der Gedanke*) suggests the powerless nature of Japanese intellectuals to be like their Russian counterparts, whose frustrations with external reality explodes violently in the form of a crime.

Indeed, Sōseki underscores this point through the figure of Matsumoto, who is singular in his place among Sōseki's characters for his self-proclamation as "*kōtō yūmin*" (162), for, although many of Sōseki's characters have been described as such, this instance marks the only explicit use of the term in his literary oeuvre. But more importantly in the context of our present discussion, the term translated perhaps as an 'upper-class vagabond' was becoming prevalent in public forums to denote a social problem just when Sōseki was preparing and serializing *Higan sugi made*. As Nagashima Yūko argues, two fears buttressed the problematization of *kōtō yūmin* as a social phenomenon in the early 1910s: 1) "the increase in unemployment, which directly expressed the dead-end conditions of the post-Russo-Japanese War economy and would lead to the production of the 'educated poor'" and 2) "the inclination toward socialist activities by the educated who are unemployed within the climate of the suppression of socialists that strengthened after the Great Treason Incident [Taigyaku jiken], which occurred in May of the previous year."[24] As these

24. Nagashima Yūko, "'Kōtō yūmin' o megutte," 221. In the Great Treason Incident, various leftist intellectuals and activists were arrested by the government under the suspicion of planning the assassination of the emperor, among other atrocities. The trials of these suspects, most of whom labeled anarchists and communists, were undisclosed to the public, bringing criticism from within

fears suggest, the discussion of *kōtō yūmin* involved the real possibilities of the educated as a vulnerable and dangerous group who may be susceptible to radical action in the form of socialist politics, whether because of poverty, lack of social status, or boredom. Finally after twenty years from the translation of Dostoevsky's *Crime and Punishment* by Uchida Roan, Raskolnikov—whose political dangers were actively managed on the imaginary level through works such as Tōson's *Hakai* and Katai's *Futon*—resurfaces as the embodiment of a social problem that warrants extensive discussion both on the part of the government and the media.

Yet, despite such negative connotations surrounding the term at the time, Matsumoto as *kōtō yūmin* is anything but a dangerous misfit. Unlike Taguchi, who must suspect everyone and thereby present himself in line with Kushami's definition of the detective, Matsumoto is characterized by his undetective-like nature that enables him "to not worry about offending others" (162).[25] Such belief, as Nagashima argues, stems from his abandonment of sincere engagement with others by constructing "a buffer zone between the self and the Other," and his laissez-faire attitude is "made possible by receiving the 'thoughts of society' into oneself as they are" without protest, thanks in part to his wealth that allows him to be disengaged from society.[26] Matsumoto is, thus, an apolitical conformist rather than an anti-establishment element that the government states is the primary tendency of *kōtō yūmin*. In this sense, Matsumoto could be said to symbolize the resignation of an intellectual in "the Age of Winter" (*fuyu no jidai*), as the 1910s would be called for its lack of political activities in the aftermath of the Great Treason Incident: through the absolutist response to this incident, the government made clear that there was no room in Meiji society for disgruntled intellectuals to turn radically political and that any attempt to do so would be nipped in the bud.

If Matsumoto's self-proclamation as *kōtō yūmin* draws its symbolic significance from the specific sociopolitical conditions of Meiji society de-

---

the country as well as from without, and 24 people, including the well-known journalist and writer Kōtoku Shūsui (1871–1911), were sentenced to death.

25. Described by Matsumoto as someone who "can't relax" and "suspects" everyone because he is "always thinking whether this person is of any use or that person can be used without worry" (174–75), Taguchi is presented as someone who resembles Kushami's view of the Kanedas and of the modern individual who is driven by self-interest and characterized by suspicion of others.

26. Nagashima Yūko, "'Kōtō yūmin' o megutte," 222.

scribed above, then Matsumoto in his interview with Keitarō attempts, in turn, to frame the tribulations of Sunaga within the larger movement of modernization through his mention of a lecture that "dissected the civilization of modern-day Japan" (308).[27] Offering reasons why "we who are influenced by this civilization will necessarily fall prey to nervous prostration unless our thoughts and actions become superficial," the scholar-speaker of this lecture states that, although people "like to know the truth of things when they do not know," people often regret coming to know the truth once they know (308). Matsumoto tells Keitarō that upon hearing this, he thought of Sunaga: "At that point, I thought about Ichizō, and as I contemplated that, while we Japanese who must learn of such harsh truths are very pitiful, a youth like Ichizō who is terrified as he tries to find out his personal secret and tries again despite being terrified is even more miserable, I wept tears of sympathy inside for him" (308). In such a way, Matsumoto contextualizes Sunaga's secret that he is about to reveal by presenting him as a symbolic representative of those living in "modern-day Japan" headed for "nervous prostration."

But interestingly, despite such contextualization, the secret that Matsumoto reveals is one that smells of feudal times: Sunaga is an illegitimate child between his father and a housemaid. The topic of adultery is one that has surfaced and resurfaced in the course of modern Japan, whether in literary or public discourse. As we saw in the second chapter, the detective stories of Kuroiwa Ruikō often employed past adultery and its exposure to a third-party as the cause of the crime and thereby criticized the act as dangerous for society. And Ruikō would make his criticism of adultery more direct in the 1890s as he used his scandal reporting in the *Yorozu chōhō* as a way to inculcate readers on the evils of adultery as an immoral as well as an anti-modern act. In this context, adultery between the head of the household and a housemaid was as feudalistic as they come, evoking not only the violation of monogamy as a Western/Christian value but also the stereotypical abuse of master-servant relationship fundamental to feudal societies.

Indeed, Sōseki seems to emphasize Sunaga's family as remnants of a past era, for Sunaga's household, the site of this adultery and secret, is symbolically positioned within the feudalistic space of Edo tradition via the manipulation of geographical structure and organization within

---

27. In a self-referential moment, Sōseki inserts clips from his lecture "Gendai Nihon no kaika" (The civilization of modern-day Japan), which he presented in Wakayama on August 1911 during his hiatus from novel writing.

the story world. As Maeda Ai has argued, the locations of the houses of the primary characters of the story—Keitarō, Taguchi, Matsumoto, and Sunaga—form a triangle with Sunaga's household at the center of the triangle. Such positioning makes sense symbolically given the plot of the story in which Sunaga and his secret become the narrative kernel that connects Keitarō with Taguchi and Matsumoto. Moreover, while the other three households—occupied by the emblems of modern society: the social climber, the entrepreneur, and *kōtō yūmin*—are connected via "a web of new era transportation in the form of the tram," Sunaga's house is located in "the back alley aligned with houses" and has "a boarded fence with wall spikes and rough contours" that reminds one of "the old foundations of the city that still leaves the vestige of Edo."[28]

In this way, Sōseki presents Sunaga, on the one hand, as an exemplar of the modern individual's tendency to turn detective and, on the other hand, posits the reason for such tendency in the secret of a feudalistic household. Yet, despite this seemingly contradictory presentation of Sunaga, I would argue that, as Matsumoto observes, Sunaga functions as an allegorical figure who represents the ultimate fate of the modern Japanese intellectual whose seriousness toward discovering the truth sets him apart from the likes of Taguchi, Matsumoto, and Keitarō, who avoid "nervous prostration" through their "superficial" "thoughts and actions." And here, it is not simply that Sunaga's search for truth is one of knowing; rather, Sōseki seems to suggest that it is our dark pasts—represented in this novel with the vestige of Edo that is Sunaga's household—that fundamentally constitute us as individuals. To the extent that Sōseki's understanding of Japan's modernization is an externally forced change rather than an internal progression, the subject, despite the fact that the likes of Taguchi, Matsumoto, and Keitarō might act as if they have internalized such a change, is left to deal with this un-modern/Edo core of their being in a world full of modern façades.[29]

And it is precisely this haunting of the present by the past that gets played out in *Higan sugi made* within the detective fiction framework, wherein the significance of random signs on the page become clear after the revelation of the truth-as-secret. Some are more obvious, already pointing to the secret and functioning as evidence of how Sunaga's recollection of his personal past proliferates suspicion in him, which in turn

---

28. Maeda, "Kashō no machi," 203.

29. For details on Sōseki's understanding of Japan's modernization, see Natsume Sōseki, "Gendai Nihon no kaika," in *Sōseki zenshū*, vol. 11.

primes and feeds his over-analytical mind. For example, Sunaga tells of how Sunaga's father on his deathbed told Sunaga, "If you are unruly like now, mother won't care for you" (206). And upon his death, the mother seems to rebut the father's worries, stating: "Don't worry. Even if father dies, I will take good care of you as I did before" (207). Sunaga states that, at the time, he found these words strange, but as time passed, strangeness turned into suspicion: "I cannot explain it even if I asked myself why I had to take their words, which did not need to have any special meaning, as evidence for my deep suspicion" (207). In this manner, the text actively promotes the reader's interest by constructing a narrative dynamic where Sunaga's casual mentioning of what he thought was unusual or what seemed out of the ordinary become clues to discern the reason for Sunaga's "suspicion." Another such example occurs a bit later in Sunaga's story when he tells Keitarō that he used to have a sister who died very young before the death of their father. Casually told as an anecdote ("I will tell you here since I just remembered it" [209]), the story contains an additional bit of the out-of-the-ordinary, namely, that Sunaga's younger sister called him "Ichizō-chan" rather than 'onii-chan,' or elder brother (210).

Of course, these out-of-the-ordinary bits of information make perfect sense given the secret of Sunaga's birth, whether his parents' comments that suggest the less-than-certain relationship between mother and son or the sister's use of "Ichizō-chan" that reflects his outsider position as an illegitimate child within the Sunaga household before her death. But the revelation of Sunaga's secret goes well beyond providing the reader with answers to the out-of-the-ordinary behavior of his family members toward him of which he is already conscious. It also provides a powerful frame of reference from which to interpret the actions, emotions, and behaviors of Sunaga himself, revealing the secret's influence at the very core of the subject, including unconscious desire. For example, during his story in which he recounts of an episode when his mother and Chiyoko get their hair done, Sunaga reveals his fondness for the traditional Shimada hairstyle. While this episode is presented anecdotally with his admission that he "enjoys watching women put up their hair," Matsumoto's story later in the novel provides a new framework with which to consider its significance: one of the only facts that is known about Sunaga's real mother is that she wore her hair in Shimada style (287, 313).

Similarly, the anecdote of Sunaga's sister provides another example of how a past trauma comes back to haunt the subject in the present, revealing itself within this framework as the missing piece in understanding the significance of a story that Chiyoko tells Keitarō of the death of Matsumoto's youngest daughter Yoiko. The episode tells how Yoiko's mother forgot to bring a key required for Yoiko's cremation and how it turned out that Sunaga, who was "listening with coldness to the dialogue between the two [Yoiko's mother and Chiyoko] from behind" regarding the missing key, had it all along (195). Discovering this, Chiyoko calls Sunaga an "unsympathetic person," and the following exchange of words ensues:

> "I'm not unsympathetic. Since I don't have a child, I don't understand the love between parent and child."
>
> "My, how can you say such a careless thing in front of Auntie? So what about me then? When did I have a child?"
>
> "I don't know whether you have or not. But you are a woman so you might have a more beautiful heart than a man" (195–96).

This scene, which can be seen as evidence of the tenuous relationship between Sunaga and Chiyoko, takes on a different significance in light of the revelation of his secret and childhood memories. And it is not simply that his "unsympathetic" attitude stems from the fact that he, unlike Chiyoko, did not have a relationship with his real blood parents instead of the fact that he, like Chiyoko, has never had a child, as Sunaga claims here.

Rather, Sunaga's past raises the possibility that Yoiko's death, occurring at an age similar to the death of Sunaga's sister, provides an occasion for him to recall the death of his own sister. Considering that Sunaga's mother finally conceived the girl after much trouble, the sister's death is a traumatic moment when Sunaga could have realized that he and his sister were different in the eyes of their 'mother.' Or it could be that Sunaga had become an outsider in the household after the birth of the sister (as suggested by her calling him by his name), but his previously held insider status was restored with his sister's death since it once again made him the only child bearing the Sunaga name.[30] In this sense, the sister is a usurper of Sunaga's 'rightful' place within the Sunaga fam-

30. I say 'previously held insider status' here because Sunaga's mother asking to have Chiyoko as Sunaga's wife upon her birth suggests the mother's acceptance of Sunaga as the heir of the household. But, of course, this was at a time when the sister was not born and the mother believed that she could not have a child. As such, it is easily imaginable how the mother's attitude toward Sunaga may have changed upon the birth of her own child.

ily and, as such, a possible target of hatred and jealousy, and the sister's funeral could have been the moment when Sunaga realized the selfish nature of adults, as his mother, left once again without a child of her own, reaccepted him as her son. If Yoiko's funeral and cremation bring back this memory, then it makes sense that Sunaga would be "unsympathetic" and "careless" to Matsumoto's wife, who may have functioned as a surrogate of Sunaga's mother.[31]

And the central conflict of the novel—the relationship between Sunaga and Chiyoko—is fittingly bound by the same dynamic of the past controlling the present. As previously mentioned, Sunaga's mother upon the birth of Chiyoko made the Taguchis promise that she be made Sunaga's wife. In light of the revelation of Sunaga's secret, the reasoning behind this move on the part of his 'mother' is obvious, at least, to Sunaga and Matsumoto, as Matsumoto quickly confirms ("Yes, that's exactly right. There is no other reason") when Sunaga states: "So the reason that mother says to take Chiyoko as a wife is because, from the perspective of bloodline, she wants me to have a relative as a wife" (313). From this perspective, the relationship between Sunaga and Chiyoko is truly doomed. If he asks her to marry him, then it would be an affirmation of his outside status. If he does not marry her, then it would make him into an outsider. This double bind caused by the secret makes it impossible for him to act, and I would argue further that his intellectualism and penchant for analysis constitutes not so much an attempt to discover a solution but a response to relish in and submit to this double bind, which has foreclosed the possibilities of 'correctly' analyzing a desirable course of action.

In these ways, the revelation of Sunaga's secret by Matsumoto opens up various reinterpretations of the already read portions of the text and suggests the darkness lurking behind the most casual of anecdotes.[32]

---

31. Many scholars have pointed out that Sōseki's daughter died during his hiatus from fiction writing and see Chiyoko's story, which does not seem to have much connection to Sunaga's or Matsumoto's stories, as Sōseki fulfilling his desire to write about his daughter. While this may certainly be the case, my argument is that Chiyoko's story has intimate connection to the rest of the work and is, thus, a vital part of a whole.

32. But we should note that in this reinterpretation process, the biggest mystery of *Higan sugi made* surfaces, a mystery that involves the previously discussed observations made by Sunaga as a child on the out-of-the-ordinary comments made by his family members, which, in turn, raise his suspicions and foreshadow his illegitimate birth. Sunaga tells these observations to Keitarō, but impor-

And it is not Keitarō, the self-appointed detective of the story, but the reader who must take on the task of the detective to make connections between clues-as-effect and secret-as-cause, discerning, for example, the significance of the Shimada style hair. Importantly, such connections, when the reader makes it, are not necessarily true. It could be the case that Sunaga likes the Shimada style for a completely different reason than one relating to his biological mother. But the point seems to be that such a possibility becomes foreclosed upon encountering Matsumoto's story of Sunaga's traumatic past, for the narrative dynamic of a foreshadowed secret followed by its revelation forces the reader to submit to the interpretative framework of the secret being the end-all, making the reader believe that such connections shed light on the deepest inner workings of the subject.

Given the careful manner in which Sōseki constructs this interpretative framework—embedding, hiding, showing various clues within the text—it is rather surprising, then, that Sōseki is so casual in rejecting this framework as nothing spectacular. Matsumoto's tale, which reveals Sunaga's secret, is followed by a short conclusion that summarizes what Keitarō did in not-so-flattering terms and, in the final paragraph of the novel, the third-person narrator underlines this point, stating: "But ultimately he [Keitarō] could not place himself inside it" (334). This comment is interesting precisely because the interpretative framework constructed around Sunaga's secret seems to suggest that Keitarō has really gotten to the bottom of things. While it is true that Keitarō, as the text states, has remained a passive 'listener' throughout the story, the reader

---

tantly—as Matsumoto's story that follows Sunaga's within the novel reveals—Matsumoto tells Sunaga of his illegitimate birth before he graduated from the university. In other words, while the reader has not been made aware of Sunaga's secret, Sunaga himself already knew of his secret when he told Keitarō his story, filled with questions that are explained away by the knowledge of the secret. Thus, Sunaga in telling the story seems to dangle his feelings of suspicion without providing the answer, or rather, seems to feign ignorance on the reasons for such suspicions. Why does Sunaga provide clues that point to his secret but not the answer, which he knows? Has Sunaga repressed this knowledge that he obtained from Matsumoto? Or is Sunaga, who has joked to his uncle that Keitarō likes playing the detective, purposefully presenting his own story as a mystery for Keitarō to solve? While the text does not seem to provide evidence to suggest whether any of these possibilities have merit, this enigma is narratologically necessary to ensure that the revelation of Sunaga's secret produces maximum effect in the reader.

cannot help being surprised at how much of the story Keitarō was able to obtain through his 'detective' work, especially considering the personal nature of the stories describing the most private and traumatic moments of people's lives.[33] But the third-person narrator's dismissal of Keitarō's effort starts to make sense once we encounter Sōseki's *Kokoro*, in which its first-person narrator's involvement with the life of an older friend suggests what it really means to place oneself "inside" to get to the bottom of things.

Narrating Guilt, Narrating Betrayal

Serialized in *Tōkyō Asahi shinbun* from April 20 to August 11, 1914, Natsume Sōseki's most famous work *Kokoro* revisits the main theme of *Higan sugi made*—secrets from the past and their constitutive effect on the individual—through the exploration of "Sensei" (teacher), an educated recluse who lives with his wife in self-enforced banishment from society. As his testament, written to the narrator just before his suicide, clearly indicates, Sensei shares with *Higan sugi made*'s Sunaga his detective-like character that requires him to endlessly analyze the intentions of others via their actions and behavior. For example, Sensei recalls that, when he first moved in with "Okusan" (madam) and "Ojōsan" (young miss), he, "like a cat, watched the movements of others in the house . . . behaving like a pickpocket who doesn't steal."[34] This condition becomes worse with the introduction of his friend K to the household, as he becomes suspicious of the motivation behind each and every action by Okusan, Ojōsan, and K, especially as it relates to Ojōsan as the object of desire

---

33. Importantly, the text shows no coaxing or pleading on the part of Keitarō, especially when it comes to Matsumoto's story, which is not framed by a dialogue between Keitarō and Matsumoto that should have preceded the story. To the extent that Matsumoto is divulging Sunaga's secret, the content of which could certainly be considered slanderous if it were to become public, a narrative framing that might elucidate Matsumoto's reasons for telling what he tells seems most necessary. And in this sense, one could argue that *Higan sugi made* does not describe Keitarō's greatest talent, which is to get other people to open up to him. This aspect of the 'detective' will become crucial not only in Sōseki's *Kokoro* but also in the Akechi Kogorō stories of Edogawa Ranpo discussed later.

34. Natsume Sōseki, *Kokoro*, in *Sōseki zenshū*, vol. 6, 178; Natsume Sōseki, *Kokoro*, trans. Edwin McClellan, 150. All subsequent references to these sources will appear in the text in parentheses, with the Japanese original followed by the English translation.

for both himself and K.[35] In this way, Sensei whose suspicious nature is founded on his belief that "a person's 'words and actions' (external self) and 'heart' (internal self) should correspond"[36] presents himself as a quintessential subject trapped within the epistemological paradigm set forth by Tsubouchi Shōyō's *Shōsetsu shinzui*. Despite the difficulties if not impossibility of deciphering what lies beyond the observable, Sensei is unable to refrain from operating as if a person's external appearance and behavior sincerely expressed his or her internal emotion or thought.

The similarities between Sensei and Sunaga extend beyond their character to its cause as well. Like Sunaga, Sensei's detective-like character stems from his past experience of a radical shift in the attitude of family members toward him. For Sunaga, this was the attitude of his mother, who, as we discussed in the previous section, most likely flip-flopped in her treatment of her unrelated son. For Sensei, this is the attitude of his uncle and uncle's family, who were like a nuclear family to him after the death of his parents but became extremely cold to him once he rejected the uncle's proposal to take the uncle's daughter as his wife. Ultimately, it is revealed that the uncle had robbed Sensei of his rightful inheritance, and the uncle's proposal for Sensei to take the daughter as his wife a last ploy to hide this fact. Whether lurking in the unconscious as it was the case for Sunaga or festering in the conscious as it is the case for Sensei, both stories show how the conniving attitudes of adults based on self-interest make it difficult for individuals to trust others.

And in the case of *Kokoro*, an adult whose actions are motivated by self-interest and, thus, warrant suspicion, includes Sensei himself, whose self-centered treatment of K revealed that he was no different from his uncle. As such, *Kokoro* combines Sōseki's views on the detective as expounded in *Neko* and *Higan sugi made*: while *Neko* explained the detective-like characteristic of the modern individual as a reflection of his self-interest, *Higan sugi made* described it as his reaction to the self-interest of others, brought on by his education that fostered analysis and treat-

35. Indeed, Sensei's decision to invite K into the household despite Okusan's warning not to do so suggests his need to place himself in a situation where his suspicions would be aroused, enabling him to continue his detective-like ways in a household where such predisposition had seemingly become unnecessary. To this extent, Sensei's decision reveals the web of doubt and suspicion within which he finds himself as a mode of existence fundamental to his identity.

36. Ishihara, *Hanten suru Sōseki*, 162.

ment of others as objects of knowledge. Through Sensei's betrayal of K, *Kokoro* mediates between reflection and reaction, suggesting how acting like a detective as a result of suspicion toward others leads the subject himself to adopt a self-interested mentality. Sensei's story thus functions as a cautionary tale of the tragic consequences brought on by adopting a detective-like way of life, from self-interest to betrayal and from guilty introspection to distrust of others.

But if such is the message of Sensei's story, then it is only a part of the whole, for *Kokoro* begins as an account of the student-narrator that revolves around his desire to find out why an older intellectual Sensei, whom he met on a Kamakura beach, is the way he is. Even though the newspaper serialization had the title "Sensei no isho" (Sensei's testament), revealing that Sensei will be dead by the story's end, we only encounter this testament, involving his betrayal of K, in the last section (albeit the longest of three sections) of the story. Thus, as Komori Yōichi makes clear in his groundbreaking essay "'Kokoro' o seisei suru 'hāto'" (The "heart" that creates "kokoro"), it is only through examining the narrative dynamic between these two texts—the student-narrator's account and Sensei's testament—that we can come to understand Sōseki's story.

For Komori, this narrative dynamic is characterized by one of contrast between the narrator's treatment of Sensei and Sensei's treatment of K: whereas the latter is characterized by an attitude that "can only observe the Other with 'cold eyes' and relate to him in an 'analytical' way," the former "supports the warm and human-like relationship between Sensei and [the narrator himself]" and, as such, the narrator does not treat Sensei as an object of knowledge but instead searches consciously for a way to treat him as a subject in his own right.[37] For example, the narrator claims with "pride" that he "did not visit Sensei with the purpose of studying him" nor was he "curious in an impersonal and analytical way" and this was the reason why they "were able to become so close to each other" for "he [Sensei] was in constant dread of being coldly analyzed" (20–21; 13–14).[38]

---

37. Komori, *Kōzō to shite no katari*, 421. The article is re-titled "*Kokoro* ni okeru hanten suru 'shuki'" in the book version.

38. As supporting evidence of this treatment, Komori discusses the way in which they met at the beach for the first time: "Sensei and 'I' separate from the masses, and two of them finally exchange words when they are alone as they take the pose of floating belly-up on the waves of the wide blue sea. It is not the attitude of seeing and being seen, but they meet as transmitters of the body's

Importantly, this attitude that sets his relationship to Sensei apart from that of Sensei and K already finds support in the opening paragraph of *Kokoro*:

> I always called him "Sensei." I shall therefore refer to him simply as "Sensei," and not by his real name. It is not because I consider it more discreet, but it is because I find it more natural that I do so. Whenever the memory of him comes back to me now, I find that I think of him as "Sensei" still. And with pen in hand, I cannot bring myself to write of him in any other way (5; 1).

Employing the term of respect to address the person whose story he is about to tell, the narrator suggests through phrases such as "natural" and "cannot bring myself to write of him in any other way" that his narration to follow flows from his heart without guile or artifice. And precisely because the narrator as a narrating subject within the story world has already encountered Sensei's testament, the opening passage becomes emblematic of his narrative strategy to consciously distinguish his treatment of Sensei as the subject of his story and Sensei's treatment of K described in Sensei's testament. Not explicitly stated in the McClellan translation is the last sentence of this paragraph in the Japanese text, which reads: "I cannot bring myself to use such a cold thing as an initial" (5). As Komori notes, it is this phrase that directly contrasts with Sensei's introduction of K in his testament, which reads: "I shall here call my friend 'K'" (194; 164).[39]

But while such examples in *Kokoro* may present themselves as evidence for the non-analytical nature of the narrator's attitude toward Sensei, it is also true that they are reconstructions written by the narrator after the fact of Sensei's death and, as such, can be construed as a conscious effort on the part of the narrator to erase the traces of his analytical treatment of Sensei. Indeed, it is from such a perspective that Komori rearticulates his above argument in "'Watashi' to iu 'tasha'-sei—*Kokoro* o meguru ōto kuritikku" (Otherness called "I"—self-critique surrounding *Kokoro*). Noting the way the narrator relentlessly follows Sensei after noticing him on the Kamukura beach, not only by staring at him but even swimming after him (also picking up his glasses as soon as he drops it as if to say that the narrator had him under "surveillance all

---

resonance, giving themselves up to the waves as they direct their gaze to the blue sky. . . . The 'I' who met Sensei in such a manner does not observe or analyze the other. He just intuits with feeling and senses" (ibid., 425).

39. Ibid., 418.

along"), Komori characterizes Sensei's initial understanding of the narrator as "the silent Other who continues to observe himself like a detective of the Metropolitan Police that comes up in *Higan sugi made*."[40] The narrator's first visit to Sensei's house in Tokyo also reeks of the detective from this perspective. Rather than having Sensei be present at home, Sōseki makes sure to have Sensei not be present, prompting the narrator to track down Sensei at K's grave—the ultimate symbol of Sensei's secret—through the information he obtained from Sensei's wife. Sensei cannot contain his shock at seeing the narrator: "How in the world. . . . ? Did you follow me? How. . . ?" (15; 9).[41]

In the context of my present argument, the strength of Komori's provocative analysis lies in its ability to explain the fundamental contradiction of the narrator's story, namely, the coexistence of the narrator's claim of his un-detective-like treatment of Sensei and the characteristics of his story that suggest the fundamentally detective-like nature of their relationship. Noting Sensei's less-than-enthusiastic reactions to the narrator described above, Komori argues that "the narrator must have harbored anxiety of the possibility that it was his existence that was threatening Sensei."[42] And if such was the case, then everything changes with the arrival of Sensei's testament because "by reading the theme of the 'letter' that the reason for [Sensei's] anxiety and dark shadow all stems from K's suicide, he [the narrator] releases himself from the sense of incongruity felt before Sensei's death."[43] Calling him "the capable Holmes who hunts down the criminal called 'Sensei' and leads him to his confession," Komori concludes that the narrator, "in order to obtain the answer that would negatively affirm the question of whether he is disliked [by Sensei] . . . pushed his opponent to the point of death."[44]

---

40. Komori, "'Watashi' to iu 'tasha'-sei," 15–16. And when the narrator finally accomplishes to be on speaking terms with Sensei, he turns Sensei's question of how long he will be staying in Kamakura and asks Sensei the same question instead "as if a detective in interrogation" (ibid., 17).

41. As Komori argues, this scene introduces Sensei's wife as an informant who tells the narrator where Sensei is, and, in so doing, suggests the conspiratorial relationship that develops between the narrator and wife in the course of the narrative. For details, see ibid., 18–20.

42. Ibid., 21.

43. Ibid.

44. Ibid. This is not to say that the narrator is absolved of all guilt. As Komori argues, the narrator cannot help but feel culpable, at least partially, for Sensei's suicide, for the narrator "ignored" Sensei's telegram requesting to see him, which

But complicating this reading is the evidence of the narrator's detective-like nature that does not lay hidden beneath the surface level of the text to be unearthed, for the narrator seems conscious of the possibility that his treatment of Sensei was detective-like and actively employs strategies to preempt such criticisms as those raised by Komori. Whether describing Sensei as having a "strangely unapproachable quality" (18; 12) or wondering the meaning behind his comments—"What struck me then as being odd was his latest remark: '. . . we should be the happiest of couples.' Why 'should be'?" (30; 21)—the narrator highlights his impression of Sensei as someone who confronts him first and foremost as an enigma. Importantly, we are led to believe that exacerbating this impression is Sensei himself, who continuously showers the narrator with suggestive statements without providing any concrete answers or details, a prime example being his comment regarding his wife: "If I were the sort of person she thinks I am, I would not suffer so" (28; 19). And given Sensei's discomfort and unwillingness in discussing his life despite the narrator's best efforts, it seems natural that the narrator's understanding of Sensei as a self-promoted enigma becomes rearticulated within the framework of an interrogation where Sensei appears as "some kind of criminal, instead of the Sensei that [he] had come to respect" when the narrator expresses his desire to learn of Sensei's life "to the extent of digging up [his] past" (86; 68).

Echoing such a characterization of Sensei as an enabler who prompts the narrator into inquiring about his life all the while deferring the revelation of a traumatic secret lurking in his past, the narrator's own narrative also seems to tempt the reader by foreshadowing Sensei's demise and the content of the testament that will reveal all. The narrator writes:

> Whatever my thoughts regarding Sensei's reserve might have been, they were, of course, only speculations. And there was always, at the back of my speculations, the assumption that their marriage had been the flowering of a beautiful romance.
>
> My assumption was not proved entirely wrong. But I was imagining only a small part of the truth that lay behind their love story. I could not know that there had been in Sensei's life a frightening tragedy, inseparable from his love for his wife. Nor did his own wife know how wretched this tragedy had made him. To this day she does not know. Sensei died keeping his secret from her. Before he could destroy his wife's happiness, he destroyed himself (34; 24–25).

"could have been Sensei's final flash of flame to put his stakes on the possibility of life" (ibid., 24).

Through such passages, the narrator highlights the divide between the narrated self and the narrating self and posits this divide as one between a speculating subject who reacts to Sensei's strange behavior and suggestive comments and a knowing subject who actively connects these behaviors and comments to Sensei's secret past.[45] In so doing, the narrator reproduces his interactions with Sensei on the level of narrative in a manner similar to that found in *Higan sugi made*, by adopting the narrative strategy of the detective story that suspends the revelation of a secret as the mystery-to-be-solved until the very end, all the while promoting suspicion and speculation of its nature on the part of the reader.

To return once more to Komori's argument on the narrator's anxiety of Sensei's feelings towards him, such a mechanism functions to ensure that the final revelation of the secret will bring with it maximum explanatory force regarding Sensei's personality and behavior, including that toward the narrator, and thereby clear the narrator of his suspicion that Sensei saw him as a threatening Other. But convincing the reader that Sensei was constituted through and through by his traumatic past, which affected his behavior toward others and ultimately led to his suicide, does not simply serve the narrator's own purposes, because this also seems to be the point of Sensei's testament. Thus, we are able to understand the narrator's narrative strategy as being based not on self-interest but on the desire to enhance the power of Sensei's message contained in his testament, namely, to pass down most effectively Sensei's teaching of how a subject driven by self-interest and characterized by his detective-like ways is doomed to self-destruction in the modern world.

In this manner, the narrator's story confronts us as a fundamentally conflicted text that pulls the reader toward the opposite ends of the interpretative pole at every turn. In a sense, such a characteristic seems logical as a natural continuation of Komori's argument: that the narrator is a subject of deep ambivalence who cannot figure out the truth of his own motivations—as driven by his loyalty and respect for Sensei or by his self-interest and curiosity—in his interactions with Sensei. While the narrator may have been Keitarō of *Higan sugi made* as a narrated self, boldly and shamelessly delving into the private life of his friend, he is left to ponder Sensei's suicide and thereby becomes Sunaga, whose analysis of Chiyoko never yields answers but only multiple and contradictory hypotheses. Such ambivalence, then, also speaks to the motiva-

---

45. Ken Ito makes a similar observation regarding the effect of the narrator's extensive use of foreshadowing ("Writing Time in Sōseki's *Kokoro*," 3–21).

tion behind the narrator's publication of the story as a desperate appeal to the reader to turn detective and investigate his culpability in the 'crime' that he may have committed, which, in turn, provides reasons for his contradictory text. To the extent that the narrator seeks to resolve his sense of guilt by appealing to the reader, he must not only state how his treatment of Sensei was not detective-like but also present situations and exchanges that gave him the sense that Sensei may have thought of his treatment as detective-like. Ultimately, the narrator needs the reader to agree with him that, despite such and such situations with Sensei and such and such reactions by Sensei, these were in the end just ill effects of Sensei's traumatic and secret past.[46]

But in appealing to the reader for judgment, the narrator cannot stop feeding his fundamental guilt regarding his relationship with Sensei at the source of deep ambivalence, for the narrator, in publishing this story, seems to violate the only request that Sensei had made to him in the testament, which Sensei makes clear in the conclusion to his testament:

> I want both the good and bad things in my past to serve as an example to others. But my wife is the one exception—I do not want her to know about any of this. My first wish is that her memory of me should be kept as unsullied as possible. So long as my wife is alive, I want you to keep everything I have told you a secret—even after I myself am dead (288; 248).

In writing a story for the world to see, the narrator seems to do precisely what Sensei asked him not to do, for the story's publication will no doubt mean the revelation of Sensei's past secret to his wife. Of course, there exists a situation in which the narrator's writing of Sensei is not a betrayal. This situation is that Sensei's wife is already dead at the time of the narrator's writing of the story. But as many have pointed out, the evidence in *Kokoro* suggests otherwise, with the primary clue that Sensei's wife is still alive at the time of the narrator's writing being the phrase within the previously cited passage, which foreshadows the "frightening tragedy" lurking in Sensei's past, namely, the phrase, "To

---

46. In doing so, the narrator must be honest, for he must feel that he was judged for the crime he suspects he may have committed and to lie would do no good for his own conscience in dispelling his guilt over Sensei's suicide. At the same time, this is not to say that the narrator cannot employ techniques—such as presentation of Sensei as an enigma as well as his own foreshadowing of Sensei's death and past—that function not only to convince the reader but also himself.

this day she does not know [Sensei's secret]."[47] As such, in writing the narrative that is *Kokoro*, the narrator seems to betray the dying wish of a man whom he called Sensei and thereby perpetuate the lineage of betrayals that began with the betrayal of Sensei by his uncle and spread to Sensei's betrayal of K.

But if betrayal fuels his fundamental guilt, then the narrator makes sure to insist on its importance within the framework of Sensei's teachings: rather than hiding evidence that would mark his narrative as an act of betrayal, the narrator highlights it by 'placing' Sensei's commandment not to tell his story to his wife at the end of the testament, and, in so doing, actively constructs a contrast with the opening paragraph of the story that begins with the narrator's addressing of the general public. In this sense, the betrayal functions as a final 'confirmation' of the difference between the narrator's treatment of Sensei and Sensei's treatment of K, a difference whose operating mechanism is already put into place in the first paragraph of the story. And the betrayal becomes necessary precisely because Sensei, while having taken steps to overcome his mistrust of others by confessing his story to the narrator, still reveals in his final request his fundamental inability to share his secret with the person who deserves to hear it most, namely, his wife, who has wondered for years why Sensei seems so unhappy and whether this may be her fault. No doubt, Sensei's suicide will accelerate her suspicions whose downward spiral can only be stopped by his secret's guardian, the narrator. By divulging Sensei's life story, the narrator releases the wife from turning detective on her past, analyzing her interactions with Sensei to determine her culpability in Sensei's demise. Whereas Sensei considers his wife a helpless object—"pure, spotless thing"—that should not be stained with a traumatic past, the narrator treats her like a subject who deserves to know (277; 237).[48] In this sense, the narrator's betrayal of Sensei's dying wish is a betrayal that is necessary for the narrator to take Sensei's teach-

47. Among the literary scholars noting this phrase as evidence that Sensei's wife is still alive when the narrator tells his story, Miyoshi Yukio provides a detailed analysis of its implication. For details, see Miyoshi, "Watoson wa haishinsha ka," 7–21.

48. Sensei states: "That I refused to tell her the truth was not due to selfish calculation on my part. I simply did not wish to taint her whole life with the memory of something that was ugly. I thought that it would be an unforgivable crime to let fall even the tiniest drop of ink on a pure, spotless thing" (277; 237). As this passage makes clear, Sensei views his wife as a helpless object that has no ability to 'cleanse' itself of the 'ink' that is the past.

ings to heart and to overcome the shortcomings of a modern individual, exemplified by Sensei, who sees others as objects of observation and knowledge rather than as subjects for dialogue and interaction.

Befitting its fundamentally contradictory nature, however, the narrator's text makes certain to bury within it subtle hints as contrary evidence that suggest the above interpretation as a noble façade to mask the self-interest lurking behind the text. Throughout the course of the narrative, Sensei repeatedly recommends that the narrator take care of the issue of inheritance before his ailing father dies. Of course, this recommendation has much to do with Sensei's own past, which he recounts in his testament, regarding the betrayal of his relatives upon his father's death. Yet, despite Sensei's recommendation, the narrator never settles the matter of inheritance with his father or with his elder brother, who would be the rightful heir to his father's inheritance. And considering that the narrator leaves his father's deathbed to return to Tokyo to see Sensei—an ultimate betrayal of familial obligations—it is easily conceivable that the narrator's allowance, which he had been receiving as a university student, be stopped after his father's death and that he receive none of the inheritance.[49] In this context, the narrator's writing of his life with Sensei reveals itself as being based on his decision to pursue writing as a profession by which to make a living to the extent that he has no free time or money to pursue writing as a hobby. In other words, the narrator uses Sensei's story as a stepping-stone for his professional and economical success as a writer, utilizing the detective story framework to appeal to the vulgar curiosity of the reader and provide an entertaining and engrossing tale.

As the above discussion reiterates, the narrator's narrative is characterized first and foremost by its schizophrenia, which I have hereto interpreted as caused by the narrator's deep ambivalence and fundamental uncertainty about his own motivations behind his treatment of Sensei as well as his publication of his story. But at the same time, there is another side to the narrator's schizophrenic narrative filled with contradicting evidence: in short, rather than being an appeal for judgment by a conflicted narrator, schizophrenia itself constitutes a fundamental part of

---

49. In a way, the need for the narrator to have to write Sensei's story is a result of his position as the second-born son. And this fact is significant to the extent that Sensei is a first-born son whose father is also the first-born son. That is, an argument could be made that the uncle's usurping of Sensei's inheritance has much to do with the uncle's attempt to get his 'share' of the family inheritance.

the narrator's strategy in telling the story of *Kokoro*. In other words, his narrative is torn between the presentation of himself as Sunaga, which I discussed above, and the making of the reader into Sunaga, as I have been made to become in my examination of the narrator's story, by actively fueling the proliferation of suspicion and doubt on the part of the reader regarding the text and its deeper motivations lurking underneath the surface.

Indeed, the latter attempt is critical to the narrator's project precisely because it enables the narrator to place himself in the subject position that Sensei feared most, that is, "to be coldly analyzed." Seen in this light, the narrator's story asserts itself as an attempt to understand Sensei better, not as an object separate from himself—a relationship that characterizes the detective-like treatment of others—but through doing his best to become the Other and to experience what the Other has experienced, a feat made possible through the investigation and punishment by the reader as detective. Ultimately, it is in his submission to the detective fiction paradigm that we find the narrator's paradoxical attempt to get outside the powerful influence that this paradigm exerts on those who live in the modern age.

And this attempt serves to underscore a key difference between Sensei and the narrator, perhaps a true indication that the narrator had taken Sensei's teaching—not the message contained in the testament but the message produced through the act of confessing—to heart. For there is no question that Sensei's project involves not a submission to the detective but a preemptive rejection of it, which Sōseki seems to highlight by having Sensei connect his decision to commit suicide to critical historical events of Meiji Japan. These, of course, were the deaths of the Meiji emperor on July 29, 1912 and of General Nogi by way of *junshi* (following one's lord to the grave) on September 13, 1912, the first day of the three-day funeral ceremony for the Meiji emperor, that have contrasting significance within Sōseki's literary project.[50]

On the one hand, the emperor was an emblem of sacredness and privacy in Meiji Japan, protected by the government through such measures as the crime of disrespect (*fukeizai*), which prohibited any attempt

50. Sensei describes his sentiment upon hearing the news of the emperor's death as follows: "I felt as though the spirit of the Meiji era had begun with the Emperor and had ended with him. I was overcome with the feeling that I and the others, who had been brought up in that era, were now left behind to live as anachronisms" (285; 245).

to introduce the emperor within unofficial discourse.[51] Upon his falling ill in the early months of 1912, however, the Imperial Household Agency (Kunaishō), which was in charge of making official statements regarding the emperor, began to make public his physical and mental condition, and such information filled the pages of the newspapers. The publicized information was extremely private in nature, going as far as to describe the condition of his excrements, and, in this sense, they were "blasphemy of [the emperor's] sacredness and extremely 'disrespectful.'"[52] To put it in the terms of our present discussion, the desire to be a detective and the inevitability of becoming one despite one's best efforts in the modern age that were problematized in Sōseki's works find their ultimate conclusion in the death of the Meiji emperor, for in his illness, the emperor—the emblem of sacredness and privacy—came to be treated as an object of knowledge by the Japanese people.

On the other hand, Nogi's death was sudden and of his own choosing, including the decision to disseminate information through his will that functioned to explain rather than describe—as was the case of the emperor—his demise. *Kokoro* presents Nogi's death and will as having a huge effect on Sensei who, despite his denial of fully understanding the reasons behind Nogi's suicide, seems to have achieved a deep level of identification with him. Given Sensei's past, such identification seems natural: just as Nogi had lived with the thought of his failure—a betrayal of the trust that the Meiji emperor had placed in him during the Seinan War (1877)—and waited for the "proper time to die," Sensei too had lived with the burden of his betrayal of K for many years.[53] Although differing in length

---

51. As the third clause of the Meiji constitution states, the emperor and the imperial family were "sacred" and not to be "violated" in any way.

52. Watanabe Naomi, *Fukei bungaku ron josetsu*, 85. It is this violation of sacredness that is vividly, albeit implicitly, described in *Kokoro*: not only does the narrator's father, who is suffering from the same disease as the emperor, compare himself to the emperor, but the narrator also describes in detail the deterioration of his father, including information regarding his bowel movements (134–35; 110–11). As Watanabe argues, such description of the deterioration of the narrator's father functioned as an "extension" of the "disrespect" with which the government announced the emperor's illness (*Fukei bungaku ron josetsu*, 88).

53. Lifton, Katō, and Reich, *Six Lives, Six Deaths*, 57–58. In this regard, it also makes sense that many literary critics have understood Sensei's suicide, which seeks "to recompense for the 'death' of his best friend [K] with his own death," as "an imitation of the 'death' of General Nogi who died for the Meiji emperor" (Watanabe Naomi, *Fukei bungaku ron josetsu*, 83).

and nature, with Sensei's being much more detailed and damaging to his own public image compared to Nogi's one-liner citing the loss of "regimental colors in the battle of 1877" as the reason for his suicide, their testaments explicitly connect their deaths to suffering that stems from a past event caused by their own failures and weaknesses.[54] For Nogi, this framework of a traumatic past festering in the eternal present finally relieved as a result of *junshi* had a decisive role in determining his legacy within Japanese society after his death. While *junshi* was an anachronistic concept that had been outlawed from the early Edo period, Nogi's suicide, which simultaneously "expiated his guilt and substantiated his samurai character," resonated with the discourses of *bushidō* (the way of the warrior that served as one of the dominant ideologies in the Edo period) that were resurging in the late Meiji period.[55] As a result, despite the ambivalent reactions in the press and among intellectuals, Nogi's suicide "immortalized his popular heroic myth," and it was "Nogi—not the emperor—who became the embodiment of the Meiji period in popular culture" through this act.[56]

Especially to those, like Sōseki, who knew the details of Nogi's career, this turn of events must have revealed the power that the framework of a traumatic past haunting the eternal present had in controlling the interpretation of one's life. As James Fujii describes, Nogi's career involved more important failures than the one named in his testament, for he was "a man who had been dismissed from his post as governor of occupied Taiwan for administrative ineptitude," and "a general whose outdated strategies and intransigence caused the senseless slaughter of nearly 58,000 of his own men at the battle of Port Arthur, won only after he was

54. The first clause of Nogi's suicide note runs as follows: "On this occasion of the passing of Emperor Meiji, I am filled with remorse and have decided to commit suicide. I am aware of the gravity of this crime. Nonetheless, since I lost the regimental colors in the battle of 1877, I have searched in vain for an opportunity to die. To this day I have been treated with unmerited kindness, receiving abundant imperial favors. Gradually I have become old and weak; my time has disappeared and I can no longer serve my lord. Feeling extremely distressed by his death, I have resolved to end my life" (cited in Lifton, Katō, and Reich, *Six Lives, Six Deaths*, 31).

55. Ibid., 58.

56. The first citation is from ibid. The second is from Gluck, *Japan's Modern Myths*, 224.

replaced by another commanding officer."[57] But one could make the argument that Nogi's short testament framed his life in such a powerful manner that his life became defined by it—as he claimed was the case—rather than by myriad events throughout the course of his life that become buried and forgotten, in turn. By actively choosing death and by leaving a narrative that explains this choice, Nogi provided others with a framework by which to make sense of his life, a framework whose truthfulness was insured by sincerity of death.

And the same could be said for Sensei, although Sensei even goes a step further than Nogi. Rather than simply providing a master narrative, Sensei transplants his master narrative into the detective fiction paradigm of cause and effect where a past traumatic event serves as the ultimate cause that will explain his life as an effect, ensuring the interpretation of his life within this paradigm by tempting the narrator to turn detective.[58] By ultimately and willingly providing the narrator with the secret which *seems* to answer all—not to mention making the narrator feel guilty about his role in the suicide—Sensei promotes a specific interpretation of his life and forecloses the proliferation of discourse surrounding his life and the reasons why he is the way he is. But this is not to say that the 'charade' is for others alone. As his inner struggles and his willingness to submit himself to the detective fiction paradigm clearly suggest, the testament is also written for himself. Just as the narrator needs to hear Sensei's secret that functions to explain all his peculiarities and quirks, Sensei needs writing as external expression of his interiority to dictate the interpretation of his own life that has become a mystery to him, for a submission to such an *illusory* framework of cause and effect where an event in the past provides an explanation of the

57. Fujii, *Complicit Fictions*, 135. Despite such negative portrayals, this is not to say that Nogi was simply an utter failure as a general and an educator who did nothing to deserve public admiration. For example: "In contrast to other military leaders, such as Tōgō and Kodama, Nogi demonstrated great concern for war invalids and for the families of dead soldiers. He argued persistently for the presentation of 'honorable titles' to all dead soldiers and personally contributed to the government's Institute for Invalid Soldiers. Nogi visited families of dead soldiers to express sympathy and, indeed, empathy at their losses" (Lifton, Katō, and Reich, *Six Lives, Six Deaths*, 53).

58. This model of cause and effect goes beyond Sensei's mentality to explain the more physical aspects of Sensei's life. For example, Sensei explains, however jokingly, the reason that he and his wife do not have a child as being "divine punishment" (25; 17).

present state of affairs precludes him from pursuing other possible reasons for his shortcomings relating to two persons he holds most dear: his mistreatment of his wife and his inability to be a productive subject of the emperor.

In his earliest work of fiction *Neko*, Sōseki utilized the metaphor of the detective to criticize the modern individual caught in a web of self-interest, exposing the narrator's affinity to the detective in the process. It is the relationship between this dual connection—between the modern individual and the detective and between the narrator and the detective—that is examined in detail in his later works, *Higan sugi made* and *Kokoro*, through a pair of contrasting figures: Sunaga and Keitarō, and Sensei and the narrator. Suspicious and analytical, Sunaga and Sensei are presented as quintessential subjects within Shōyō's epistemological paradigm as they search for true intentions of each and every external action of others, guided by their belief that external actions and behaviors are manifestations of interior thoughts and emotions, despite the fact or precisely because they have been betrayed by others as a result of misunderstanding their true intentions. As these stories make sure to impress upon their readers, Sunaga and Sensei are constituted by their past experiences that revealed others—and the self—as driven by self-interest and therefore wearing a façade and being untrustworthy.

But while being a development of progressively detailed meditation on the detective-like nature of the modern individual, these stories exhibit a trajectory that also strikes us as peculiar. Ironically for Sōseki whose criticism of the detective in early works including *Neko* revolved around the attack on the subject who tries to penetrate the private lives of others in order to know the 'true' other, his project ends with *Higan sugi made* and *Kokoro*, which certainly seem more ambivalent on their treatment of the detective. *Higan sugi made* revolved around the detective fiction framework generated through Keitarō's desire to know the truth of Sunaga's story and adopted by the reader, who is forced to participate in the framework by the various 'clues' that the narration seems to embed within the text without making explicit sense of them. And if *Higan sugi made* ultimately seems to dismiss such framing through the 'evaluation' of the third-person narrator, *Kokoro* seems to affirm it as necessary, however illusory it may be, for the modern intellectual. For, unlike Sunaga who remains the object of knowledge within the detective fiction framework—held as such by Keitarō, the reader, and himself—Sensei utilizes the framework for his own purpose to make sense of his life in the modern world, full of doubt and myriad interpretations.

Also ironically for Sōseki, who began his criticism of the detective in *Neko* with a consideration of the sociohistorical causes that prompts the individual to turn detective in the modern world, his project ends with the submission to the detective whose rhetoric places the utmost importance on one's past and, in so doing, deemphasizes the social and the modern that provide alternative interpretations on the present state of affairs. And here, the way in which the student-narrator of *Kokoro* first takes interest in Sensei is quite suggestive. The narrator's interest in Sensei is piqued by Sensei's mingling as equals with a Westerner at a Kamakura beach, and, thus, the narrator's pursuit of Sensei can be seen as an effort to learn the ways of Westernization. Of course, the narrator instead finds Sensei, whom he believed to be a leader in the quintessential national program of Westernization as being *kōtō yūmin*, an antinational phenomenon that was just beginning to receive press. But such repression of the social could only offer momentary solace, considering the relationship between Japan and the West that was at the core of the modern Japanese intellectual. As the next chapter illustrates, it was the disavowal of the social and the modern and the concomitant delusions of the subject that would become the chosen themes of subsequent experimentations by modern Japanese writers through their engagement with the detective and his story.

FIVE

Rhetoric of Disavowal: "Secrets and Liberation" and the Specters of the West

The founding issue of the magazine *Shinseinen* (New youth) published in January 1920 contains a poem by Shiratori Shōgo (1890–1973), a member of the Populist Group (Minshū-ha) of poetry that espoused the liberal sociopolitical ideals of the so-called Taishō Democracy. Entitled "Atarashiki seinen ni gekisuru uta" (A song of encouragement for the new youths), the poem was a fitting one to commemorate the start of a magazine that would become the emblem of urban youth culture in part through its promotion of the detective fiction genre in the 1920s.[1] Fitting also of Shiratori's political stance, the poem was idealistic and polemic in its language, using such phrases as "Oh, League of Nations, democracy, for eternal justice and for happiness of all human kind" and "The international second restoration waits now for the power of new youths."[2] Dreaming of a world united by its pursuit of justice and human happiness made possible by the spread of democracy, Shiratori's poem crystallizes the representative characteristics of the discourses of Taishō Democracy—idealism, humanism, internationalism, and cosmopolitanism—and

1. The relationship between *Shinseinen* and the detective fiction genre will be discussed in detail in the next chapter.

2. Shiratori, "Atarashiki seinen ni gekisuru uta," 4–5.

incorporates them as the necessary elements of the movement's most important and concrete goal: universal male suffrage.[3]

This goal would be accomplished in March 1925, but historical realities, at least in hindsight, made the representative ideals of Taishō Democracy seem barely tenable from its early stages, leaving us to wonder the extent to which Japanese intellectuals actually believed in the realistic possibilities of the movement's idealistic vision of the world. As made clear by "the intensification of anti-Japanese movement and racial discrimination" in the United States, anti-Japanese sentiment was growing among Western powers, making it difficult to envision Japan's participation in the world as one of its important members.[4] Such sentiments were also growing among Japan's neighbors that it had sought hard to incorporate into its empire, as exemplified by the widespread protests in Korea against Japan's colonial rule in 1919. These protests provided the Japanese government with the occasion to shatter the ideals of internationalism harbored by its intellectuals and to impress on them and the world the undeniably imperialistic nature of Japan's relationship with its Asian neighbors, as 7,509 protesters were killed in the ensuing military suppression.[5] And at home, the despotic tendencies of the Japanese government should have been evident from its response to the 1910 Great Treason Incident, in which various leftist activists arrested under the suspicion of planning the assassination of the emperor, among other atrocities, were executed without a public trial. In the summer of 1918, moreover, the so-called Rice Riots erupted all over the country as a result of high rice prices, and, despite their primarily nonpolitical nature, foreshadowed the rise of socialist and labor movements in the early 1920s.

It was in such a sociopolitical landscape of the 1910s, a turbulent period of transition when the dreams expressed by the discourses of Taishō Democracy were seemingly on the verge of collapse in the face of

---

3. That many scholars have referenced this poem in their discussions of the literature of 1920s Japan suggests its symbolic significance for the understanding of this historical period. For example, Suzuki Sadami cites this poem in his seminal work on Shōwa literature, *"Shōwa bungaku" no tame ni*, 25–27, as does Kawasaki Kenko in "*Shinseinen* no tanjō to sono jidai," 4.

4. Kawasaki, "*Shinseinen* no tanjō to sono jidai," 6.

5. Figures cited in Eguchi, *Futatsu no taisen*, 64. For the details of extreme violence exercised by the Japanese military during the suppression of these protests, see ibid., 64–66.

historical realities, that the general interest magazine *Chūō kōron* published an issue titled "Himitsu to kaihō" (Secrets and liberation; July 1918). The issue's focus was broad and extensive, ranging from essays dealing with the topic of secrecy from a wide variety of perspectives to eight fictional works organized under the heading of "new artistic detective novels" and "plays and novels taking up the topic of secrets" by Tanizaki Jun'ichirō, Satō Haruo, Akutagawa Ryūnosuke, Satomi Ton (1888–1983), Nakamura Kichizō (1877–1941), Kume Masao (1891–1952), Tayama Katai, and Masamune Hakuchō (1879–1962). As these names make clear, the contributors to the fiction section of the issue were prominent and up-and-coming members of the Japanese literati and suggested the seriousness with which the editors of the magazine sought to tackle the issue of "secrets" and "liberation" as well as "detective novels."

When considering the "Himitsu to kaihō" issue from the perspective of detective fiction, however, we see that the issue actually contains very little of what could pass as detective fiction. Of the four stories organized under the "new artistic detective novels," none contains a detective as protagonist. As for the essays, the primary focus is the issue of secrets, with the word "detective" (*tantei*) not appearing in the title of a single essay. As such, the combination of the topic of "secrets" and "liberation" with "detective novels" strikes us as a curious one. The task of the detective is to seek and reveal the secrets of others (criminals), but the result is normally not one of liberation. Rather, the combination of secrets and liberation suggests a missing link that would connect the two more aptly, namely, a confessional story in which the subject reveals his or her secret in an act of confession and gains liberation from guilt through this act. In fact, the next issue of *Chūō kōron* contained essays such as Nakamura Seiko's "Kokuhaku shōsetsu no ryūkō" (The trend of confessional novels) and Honma Kumeo's "Kokuhaku bungaku to jiko hihyō" (Confessional literature and self-criticism), suggesting that the decision to organize the four stories under the heading of "new artistic detective novels" was a conscious choice on the part of the editors to provide a bridge between detective stories and "confessional novels," which were in vogue at the time.

It is therefore fitting, but also surprising because of the extent, that many of the stories contained in the "Himitsu to kaihō" issue exhibit similar narrative structure to that of Natsume Sōseki's *Kokoro*. Published four years prior and exemplifying what might be called the "confessional novel" as a work that addresses the issue of "secrets" and "liberation" as well as engaging critically with the detective story genre as we saw in the last chapter, *Kokoro* was no doubt on the minds of the writers when they wrote their stories for the "Himitsu to kaihō" issue. More specifically, as Iida Yūko in her *Karera no monogatari* (Their stories) illustrates by drawing on René Girard's seminal work *Deceit, Desire, and the Novel*, the fictional works in the "Himitsu to kaihō" issue mimic the triangular structure of desire underlying the last section "Sensei's Testament" of *Kokoro* between male characters of close resemblance (Sensei and K) as rivals for their object of desire (Ojōsan).[6]

Beginning with the reconsideration of the triangular relationship of desire, this chapter examines three works in the "Himitsu to kaihō" issue, namely, Akutagawa's "Kaika no satsujin" (Murder in the age of enlightenment), Tanizaki's "Futari no geijutsuka no hanashi" (The story of two artists), and Satō's "Shimon" (The fingerprint). Although these stories no doubt share important characteristics with Sōseki's *Kokoro*, they also deviate from it in significant ways, precisely because they reexamine Sōseki's meditation on the course of Japan's modernization process and the trials and tribulations of the modern intellectual. Central to this reexamination process is the rewriting of the modern Japanese subject in terms not only of crime but also of authority, highlighted by the detective fiction rubric under which these stories were published and circulated. In so doing, these works explore the modern intellectual's predilection for crime within the specific sociohistorical context of modern Japan and its relationship to the West, an exploration that operated within the framework of disavowal—of actively denying self-consciousness of the truth—befitting 1910s Japan, fraught with contradictions between ideal and reality.

Crime and Love in Akutagawa Ryūnosuke's Story of Enlightenment

In a letter to a friend dated June 19, 1918, Akutagawa says this of the story that he was writing for the "Himitsu to kaihō" issue of *Chūō kōron*: "Because I promised to write a detective story for *Chūō kōron*, I am grudgingly writing an odd piece. It's no good that I feel helpless because I feel like I am prostituting [my] talents. And despite writing it as a de-

6. For details on Girard's discussion of the triangular relationship of desire, see Girard, *Deceit, Desire, and the Novel*. For Iida's discussion of the triangular relationships found in the stories of "Himitsu to kaihō," see Iida, *Karera no monogatari*, 202–28.

tective story, it seems like it will not be a detective story."[7] Indicating the magazine's explicit request for a detective story as well as suggesting Akutagawa's lowly opinion of the genre's literary value, this letter also reveals how, despite his intention to write detective fiction, Akutagawa was unable to do so. Indeed, the story he produced, "Kaika no satsujin," contains no detective, although it does contain a murder. But while Akutagawa may have felt as if he was "prostituting" his literary talents, his inability to produce a "detective story"—an inability that would be shared by many 'detective story' writers in the 1920s and 1930s—displays the seriousness with which he engaged in the work as a literary endeavor of significance that had profound implications in determining the trajectory of his literary project. "Kaika no satsujin" would become the founding work of the so-called *kaika-mono* or stories of enlightenment, in which Akutagawa explored the world of early Meiji to reflect upon the period's legacy in the Taishō period.[8]

From its employment of the epistolary style to a written confession of a secret by a person who has committed suicide, "Kaika no satsujin" shares many characteristics with Sōseki's *Kokoro*.[9] As Iida Yūko argues, moreover, the primary narrative structure driving the story is a triangular one organized around a love affair between the subject, his object of

7. Akutagawa, *Akutagawa Ryūnosuke zenshū*, vol. 18, 221.

8. For an overview of the critical reception of Akutagawa's *kaika-mono*, see Andō, *Akutagawa Ryūnosuke*, 127–28. For a comparative work on Akutagawa's *kaika-mono*, see Matsumoto Tsunehiko, "Kaika no futari," 121–42; and Asano, "Kaika e no manazashi," 42–48.

9. "Kaika no satsujin" takes the form of Doctor Kitabatake's testament that begins with his confession of love for Akiko, the wife of Viscount Honda. As the story goes, Kitabatake becomes enamored with her as a teenager, but before he could confess his love and ask her hand in marriage, he is sent to London to study medicine at the age of 21. Upon returning from his three-year stint there with thoughts of Akiko on his mind, he learns that she had married a banker named Mitsumura Kyōhei. Kitabatake is dejected by this news, but when he learns of Kyōhei's deplorable character, he decides to kill Kyōhei. Using his knowledge of medicine and, thus, poison, Kitabatake murders Kyōhei, making his death appear like a brain hemorrhage. After Kyōhei's death, Akiko and Honda rekindle their relationship, which they had prior to her marriage to Kyōhei, and quickly decide to get married. This turn of events is no surprise to Kitabatake, who had learned of their past relationship during the planning stages of Kyōhei's murder, but, as their relationship progresses, Kitabatake is struck with a desire to kill Honda. Haunted by this desire, Kitabatake ultimately decides to commit suicide, leaving his testament for Honda and Akiko.

desire, and his rival. No doubt Akutagawa was conscious of these similarities, and precisely because of such awareness, the differences within the similarities are of particular interest in order to understand "Kaika no satsujin" as a way for Akutagawa to develop the issues raised by *Kokoro*. For example, unlike in the case of Sensei, the victor who had succeeded in 'attaining' the object of his desire, Doctor Kitabatake, the writer of the testament, is the loser who has failed to wed his childhood love interest Akiko who, in turn, marries his friend Viscount Honda, and his testament addressed to these newlyweds, thus, is not a confession stemming from the guilt of a victor due to the way in which he achieved such a result. "Kaika no satsujin" also does not simply depict two friends' competition for the same woman, for there is added to the mix a third man, the banker Mitsumura Kyōhei (Akiko's first husband), creating a doubling of Girard's triangular structure of desire.

And unlike Sensei's suicide, Kitabatake's is presented as a preventive one, having more to do with the crime he fears he will commit than the crime he has committed. Indeed, regarding the murder of Kyōhei—the actual crime committed—Kitabatake shows no sense of guilt, as he believes and makes the case that he is fully justified. Recounting his impressions of Kyōhei on their first meeting at a social event, Kitabatake notes his instantaneous disgust for Kyōhei, shuddering at his deplorable character as he "sang loudly a trendy song so obscene that it was unbearable to listen, as he embraced an older geisha on his right and was accompanied by an apprentice geisha on his left."[10] Notwithstanding the visceral nature of his feelings towards Kyōhei, Kitabatake is quick to deny any possibility of personal interest at stake by invoking a moral framework for his hatred: "The motive for murder from the start of inception was absolutely not a simple feeling of jealousy but rather a moral fury to punish wrongdoings and remove injustice" (221). To support this claim, Kitabatake describes how he enlisted the help of his journalist friends to dig up "the footprints of his [Kyōhei's] lewd and immoral actions," citing in particular a rumor relayed to him by Narushima Ryūhoku of how Kyōhei violated "the virginity of an apprentice geisha, leading to her death" (221).[11]

---

10. Akutagawa, "Kaika no satsujin," *Akutagawa Ryūnosuke zenshū*, vol. 3, 221. All subsequent references to this source will appear in the text in parentheses.

11. Narushima Ryūhoku (1837–1884) was a Meiji writer famous for his knowledge of the pleasure quarters, which were the subject of his work *Ryūkyō shinshi* (New chronicles of Yanagibashi; 1859–1871).

Kitabatake also makes certain to show how such a moral framework is not a work of revisionist history by prefacing the above line of argument with a citation from his diary—a method repeatedly employed in his testament—from the date of his first meeting with Kyōhei, in which he vows to "rescue my sister Akiko from this lecher with my own hands" (221). As reflected in the use of the word "sister," the diary entry goes on to explain how Kitabatake had abandoned Akiko as an object of his desire upon hearing the news of her marriage to Kyōhei thanks to his newfound belief in the Christian God, which occurred during his stay abroad. And it is a new fact discovered after Kitabatake's decision to murder Kyōhei that reinforces the humanistic and moral framework for doing so: namely, that Akiko and Honda had promised to marry each other but "pressured by Kyōhei's power of gold, could not help but break the promise in the end" (222). This posits Kyōhei as someone who bought Akiko with money (fitting considering that he is a banker) and suggests that Akiko is a victim of her family's economic circumstances. It also implies that, even despite Kyōhei's 'disappearance,' Kitabatake will not be able to win Akiko's love and, thus, cannot have a personal stake in Kyōhei's death, for Kitabatake's murder of Kyōhei benefits not himself but Akiko and Honda. This is a point which Kitabatake reiterates by drawing once again from his diary entry: "Thinking that my dear Viscount and Akiko would enter a happy life in time as a result of my murdering that giant of a beastly heart [Kyōhei], I could not prevent a smile from appearing on my lips" (223).

Importantly, Kitabatake, in making this point, emphasizes the purity of the relationship between Honda and Akiko that goes beyond the social contract of marriage. He states: "It seems that he [Honda] and Akiko had not simply made a promise to get married but also truly had the feelings of mutual love [*sōai*]" (222). Kyōhei's boorish character, exemplified by his deplorable treatment of women as sexual objects who can be bought, is pitted against the pure love between Honda and Akiko, which models itself after the ideology of *ren'ai* (love), even before the word gained currency in late 1880s Japan.[12] Honda and Akiko are pre-

12. Tomi Suzuki states: "*Ren'ai*, which is now so naturalized that almost no one is aware of its historical origin, was a neologism adopted in the late 1880's to translate the English 'love' and the French 'amour.' In contrast to the traditional word *koi*, *ren'ai* signified the newly imported notion of love, understood to mean a more spiritual, deeper, and more highly valued mutual affection between man and woman" (*Narrating the Self*, 74).

sented as forerunners in the way of 'modern' love, Kyōhei as the anti-modern, feudalistic element of Japanese society which must be exorcised, and Kitabatake as the enlightened man of Western education and means who will take it upon himself that this 'modern' love will bear fruit in Meiji Japan through the removal of Kyōhei.

But this moral framework begins to crumble after Kyōhei's murder when Kitabatake begins to become aware of the "strange desire" to murder Honda, a process that results in his gradual breakdown as a conscious subject cognizant of his own actions (224). When he discovers himself reaching for the poison bottle (which he used to kill Kyōhei) upon Honda's complaint of a stomachache one evening, Kitabatake is shocked and must ask himself: "For what purpose am I carrying this medicine? Is it coincidence? I truly hope that it is a coincidence" (226). And a month later when he has dinner with Akiko and Honda, it is no longer a question of unawareness of his actions, as his desire has become an object that exists separate from himself: "I did not forget for a second about the poison at the bottom of my pocket. It was as if my heart contained a monster that was incomprehensible even to myself" (226). Kitabatake presents the destruction of his moral framework as an othering of the self, and, in his understanding of the self as mystery, he evokes *Kokoro*'s Sensei who calls himself "mysterious" (*fukashigi*) in his testament.[13]

Ultimately, Kitabatake chooses suicide as a way to exorcise this "monster," explaining the logic behind his decision as follows:

> Where would I find the reason for killing Mitsumura Kyōhei if I killed Viscount Honda in order to save myself? And do I find the egoism that I am not conscious of lurking inside as the reason for murdering him? If so, my character, my conscience, my morality, and my contention would all disappear. . . . I kill myself because I believe that I will be victorious over spiritual bankruptcy (227).

---

13. Given this depiction of the breakdown of the subject aware of his own actions, Akutagawa's "Kaika no satsujin" presents itself as a successor not only to Sōseki's *Kokoro* but also to Shiga Naoya's "Han no hanzai" (Han's crime; October 1913), which tells the story of Han, the knife thrower, who kills his wife during a knife-throwing exhibition but is himself uncertain whether the death was accidental or premeditated. That Akutagawa was deeply interested in the problematics of the self-conscious subject posed in "Han no hanzai" can be seen in the fact that he would revisit the topic in more detail in "Giwaku" (Suspicion), which appeared in *Chūō kōron* in July 1919.

Describing his moral dilemma as one in which "egoism" is pitted against "character" and "morality," this passage shows how Kitabatake's "moral fury" that was the basis for his murder of Kyōhei becomes problematized through his desire also to kill Honda, a friend with whom he can find no moral high ground. In short, his desire to kill Honda suggests that Kyōhei's murder may have been motivated by jealousy, an admission that Kitabatake would rather reject through suicide than make.

Through this turn of events, "Kaika no satsujin" presents itself as being diametrically opposed to Sōseki's *Kokoro*, despite the undeniable similarity in the defiant and proud tone of Sensei's and Kitabatake's final words that suggest the high esteem with which they view their act, not of suicide necessarily, but of sincere confession. Sensei's testament is an act of coming to terms with his egoism, the self-interest that led to his 'betrayal' of K by asking Okusan for Ojōsan's hand in marriage without K's knowledge. Kitabatake's is an act of denying his egoism, preempting the possibility that egoism had anything to do with his actions in the first place. The act of suicide forecloses the possibility of a final proof—in the form of the murder of Honda—to the egoism underlying his actions by stopping the transformation or reversion of the moral triangle between hero (Kitabatake), villain (Kyōhei), and victim (Akiko) into the love triangle between subject, rival, and their object of desire. "Kaika no satsujin" shows the power of external action (suicide) to overcome internal desire (jealousy); it presents a mechanism of active disavowal of egoism and of the rejection of self-consciousness.[14]

"Kaika no satsujin" offers a permutation to the relationship between morality, self-interest, and love in the age of enlightenment examined in *Kokoro*, a relationship whose importance for Akutagawa can be discerned by the fact that he would quickly revisit it in his next *kaika-mono*,

---

14. Of course, one could argue that Kitabatake is already implicated in his egoism/jealousy to the extent that he had thoughts of murdering Honda, but the point seems to be that Kitabatake's suicide functions as an action exorcising such thoughts. It is also possible to argue that Kitabatake's attempt to reject internal egoism itself is egotistical, as Oketani Hideaki does in his essay on the relationship between Sōseki's *Kokoro* and Akutagawa's *kaika-mono*. He writes: "This suicide smells of hypocrisy. To commit suicide because admitting the latent egoism leads to one's spiritual bankruptcy suggests a deluding of oneself in order to push through one's claims [*tatemae*] and cannot help giving off the impression that that after all is also another type of egoism" ("Akutagawa to Sōseki," 30).

"Kaika no otto" (Husband of enlightenment; February 1919).[15] Such preoccupation seems fitting considering that this relationship pitted character against personal desire, a conceptual opposition that echoed the ideological transition from Meiji to Taishō, and enabled Akutagawa to reflect on the legacy of the Meiji project from this perspective.[16] By describing the Japanese subject's unwavering adherence to the Western ideal of love, to the extent that he would not only commit murder but kill himself, "Kaika no satsujin" suggests at once the power with which Western ideas grasped Meiji intellectuals, prompting the blind worship of these ideas as universal truths, and the caricature-like nature of the extremes to which they went in trying to adopt these ideas in the name of *bunmei kaika*. In so doing, "Kaika no satsujin" inscribes within the relationship between morality, self-interest, and love the indelible marks of Japan's encounter with the West that were not fully revealed in Sōseki's fictions on the fragmentation of the Japanese intellectual in the modern age. And in this regard, "Kaika no satsujin" offers more than Kitabatake's inner world of moral struggle as a site of such inscription, for a similar sort of inscription can also be found in the turn of events within the story world that founds Kitabatake's dilemma in the first place.

In "Kaika no satsujin," Kitabatake is prevented from acting as a rival for Akiko's love against Kyōhei (or Honda) to create a *Kokoro*-like love triangle because he is not in the country when all the parties involved

---

15. "Kaika no otto" tells the story of Miura, a seeker of and believer in true love, who finally finds a girl he loves and marries. But soon, he discovers that his wife is having an affair, but to the surprise of his friend, the narrator, Miura affirms their relationship. He states: "You remember that I espoused 'a marriage of love,' don't you? That assertion was not to satisfy my own self-interest. It was a result of putting love above everything. . . . So I was of the belief that if there existed a love that was more pure than the one between my wife and me, I was prepared to readily become a sacrifice for them who were childhood friends. Unless I did so, my assertion to put love above everything would die out in reality" (Akutagawa, *Akutagawa Ryūnosuke zenshū*, vol. 4, 198). In this way, Miura presents himself as a successor to Kitabatake, who puts aside his "egoism" for the sake of love as an ideal, although unlike Kitabatake Miura himself is the obstacle to the fulfillment of true love that stands in the way of his wife and her cousin. But it is also this predicament—of being a victim of adultery—that enables Miura to elevate himself morally and prove his belief in true love by actively forfeiting his participation in *Kokoro*'s triangular relationship of desire.

16. Harry Harootunian provides a succinct overview of this transition in "A Sense of an Ending and the Problem of Taishō," 3–28.

come of age. When Kitabatake returns from his stint abroad, Kyōhei has already defeated Honda in their quest to wed Akiko: the triangle of love and betrayal exemplified by Sensei, K, and Ojōsan has already happened without the involvement of the subject, for Kitabatake arrives at the battle too late. Significantly, his stint abroad is not of his own accord but by the orders of his father, who wanted him to obtain the proper training and education necessary for taking over the family business of medicine. Already enamored with Akiko before leaving for London, Kitabatake would have had the opportunity to court her if he were allowed to stay in Japan. But his familial obligations take him away from the opportunity to fulfill his personal desire, placing Kitabatake in a situation where he can only act as an executioner of "moral fury," that is, as an agent of morality who stands outside the realm of personal desire and subjective goals.

Furthermore, Kitabatake's studies abroad represent more than his fulfillment of familial obligations; they are also a perfect reproduction of the ideology of *bunmei kaika*, the primary goals of which were to study and adopt Western values and knowledge: in particular, those related to science and technology. Kitabatake sacrifices his future with Akiko not only for the good of his family but also for the good of the nation as a Japanese pioneer of Western medicine. Indeed, the text makes sure to emphasize the intricate relationship between the West and Kitabatake's personal sacrifice made for modernizing the nation, which explodes as his murder of the un-modern Kyōhei. Kitabatake's studies abroad provide him with the means—poison based on his knowledge of Western medicine—as well as the ideology—his 'misguided' idea of humanity stemming in part from becoming a Christian while in England—necessary to execute Kyōhei's murder.[17]

Through the story of Kitabatake, "Kaika no satsujin" presents an allegory of the Meiji project, but the allegory does not end with him, for the story's narrative frame, characteristic of Akutagawa's stories during this period, produces another tale of inner struggle. Granted, the narrative

---

17. In this sense, "Kaika no satsujin" describes an extreme result of self-sacrifice for the good of the nation, and, in so doing, reiterates the cultural shift from Meiji to Taishō described by Harry Harootunian in the following manner: "Meiji civilization summoned purpose and goal—self-sacrifice and nationalism (*fukoku-kyōhei* and *bussan* [*sic*] *kōgyō*)—where as Taishō culture, as it was conceived, evoked new associations related to the nuances of consumers' life, to individualism, culturalism (*bunkashugi*), and cosmopolitanism" (ibid., 15).

frame is not an elaborate one in the original "Himitsu to kaihō" version, taking the form of a postscript after the end of Kitabatake's testament that reads: "Postscript: When this testament was written, the peerage system had not been established. The use of the word Viscount here follows the title of Honda's later years."[18] Akutagawa made the narrative framework more explicit, however, when the story was reprinted in the short-story collection *Kairaishi* (Puppeteer; January 1919). In the new version, which is also the version included in Akutagawa's collection of complete works, the postscript becomes incorporated into the story's early paragraphs where the narrator-editor introduces Kitabatake's testament to the readers. In so doing, the editor explicitly confirms the fact that he has recently obtained Kitabatake's testament from Viscount Honda, highlighting the temporal gap that exists between the testament written in the age of enlightenment and the Taishō present when the testament is made public.

The narrative frame, then, generates a specific historical context through which the readers can interpret Kitabtake's testament, enabling them to relativize his disturbing story as a relic of the past. But the frame offers more than a critical perspective, for lurking behind Kitabatake's story is the story of Honda, who has lived with the knowledge of the truth behind his friend's suicide for the last 30 years. Significantly, the text leaves ambiguous whether Akiko ever saw the testament, and it is easily conceivable that Honda hid the testament from her given its content. Perhaps it is because she has died that Honda is finally releasing the testament to 'liberate' him from the 'secret' that has bound him all these years like Sensei. But this is not to say that the dynamic of secret and exposure is the same in "Kaika no satsujin" and *Kokoro*. In the latter, the person who committed the 'crime' and the bearer of the secret of that 'crime' are the same. In the former, they are different: crime and punishment are not directly connected but arbitrarily conferred. Honda did nothing wrong, yet he is burdened with Kitabatake's crime through the latter's confession. Thus, while the length that Honda had withheld Kitabatake's secret from the public may suggest his likeness to *Kokoro*'s Sensei, it is rather the narrator of *Kokoro* that Honda resembles to the extent that both are recipients of a will that puts them in a double bind of whether or not to go public with the story.

---

18. Cited in notes to "Kaika no satsujin," *Akutagawa Ryūnosuke zenshū*, vol. 3, 422.

On the one hand, if Honda went public with this information, it would certainly mean a scandal that would taint his marriage to Akiko. Also, going public would mean making his best friend Kitabatake, who made their marriage possible, a criminal in the name of the law. On the other hand, if Honda does not go public with this information—which is his course of action, at least, until he gives the testament to the editor—then Kitabatake makes him into a criminal. Unlike in the case of Sensei as well as the narrator of *Kokoro*, the knowledge Honda holds is not only a dark past that has stained his marriage to Akiko but also a crime committed against the state to the extent that he is not providing authorities with information he knows about a murder. And it is here that the other significance of the frame—aside from alerting the readers of a presence of an editor who 'exists' in the present—becomes evident. Honda is a central contributor to the Meiji state, for which he was awarded with the title of Viscount, but he has turned his eyes away from Kitabatake's murder of Kyōhei who, despite his 'immoral' existence, was a successful banker and thus a productive member of Meiji society like Honda.

In such a way, Kitabatake transfers the guilt of his crime onto Honda through his testament, a cruel decision that suggests his sense of resentment regarding the sacrifice he made to the nation, which, in turn, foreclosed the possibility of the fulfillment of his personal desires. If the Western ideal of love provided the moral justification for a violation of Meiji law in the form of murder for Kitabatake, then Honda, too, is forced to live the deeply conflicted life brought about by selecting the Western ideal of love over state interests, as a conspirator in this crime committed against a productive member of Japanese society. In short, Kitabatake and Honda are fragmented subjects torn between a Western ideal and a Japanese law. To the extent that "Kaika no satsujin" constitutes a public exposure not only of Kitabatake's testament but also of Honda's secret, the story reveals itself as an attempt to come to terms with the fundamental fragmentation and contradiction existing at the heart of the Meiji subject and the state in the new age of Taishō, suggesting that Kitabatake's story is not a relic of the past but something that needs to be negotiated in the present. As we shall see in the ensuing sections, a similar negotiation takes place in the stories of Tanizaki Jun'ichirō and Satō Haruo in the "Himitsu to kaihō" issue of *Chūō kōron*, revealing their shared concern over the issue of what could be called fragmentary allegiances at the heart of the modern Japanese intellectual.

The Double and the Allegories of Modern Japanese Experience

"Kaika no satsujin" tells the story of a disavowal of egoism to maintain an ideal. As such, it pits personal interest against an ideal—precisely the reason why the ideal is considered universal and, therefore, applicable to every individual—creating an opposition between the two. By actively rejecting one through the other, the subject fails to see the intimate connection between the two and thereby denies self-reflection and self-understanding. But given the new environment of the Taishō period which was characterized by "new individualism" and involved "the important transition from 'inner conscience' to the defense of 'private interest,'" it was fitting that a story would be written that suggested how self-interest and universal ideal do not necessarily have to go against each other.[19] This story was Tanizaki's "Futari no geijutsuka no hanashi" (later re-titled "Kin to gin"; hereafter referred to as "Futari no geijutsuka"[20]), telling the story of the well-to-do artist Ōkawa and his decadent rival Aono, in which the former attempts to kill the latter.[21]

"Futari no geijutsuka" shares with Akutagawa's "Kaika no satsujin" the triangular structure and the role of an ideal within it, although Ōkawa's logic is diametrically opposed to that of Kitabatake. The following passage in which Ōkawa explains (to himself) his decision to kill Aono illustrates the similarities as well as the differences between the two stories:

> Aono dies or I die, there are no other possibilities. If I die, Aono's art will grow. If Aono dies, my art will be saved. Although killing Aono might be immoral, isn't killing one's own art more immoral? I want to be faithful to myself before being faithful to others. If my art is saved, I will be able to live an eternity. If the will to live an eternity is the most precious among human values, it would be okay to bear any sacrifices to carry on that will. Only by having the passion and courage to carry on, I can finally become a genius. If that becomes the case, then God will

---

19. Harootunian, "A Sense of an Ending and the Problem of Taishō," 12, 17.

20. A portion of this story had appeared two months before the "Himitsu to kaihō" issue in the literary journal *Kokuchō* as "Kin to gin." The title was later changed from "Futari no geijutsuka no hanashi" to "Kin to gin" once again.

21. "Futari no geijutsuka no hanashi" tells of two artists: Aono and Ōkawa. The latter funds the former because he believes in and is jealous of his talents. For an upcoming exhibition, they both employ a woman named Eiko as a model. Ōkawa, fearful of what Aono might produce, sneaks into Aono's studio to examine Aono's painting. Realizing not only how superior Aono is as an artist but also how similar they are in their artistic ideals, Ōkawa decides to murder Aono. Carefully planning his crime, Ōkawa ultimately attacks Aono, leaving the latter brain damaged and mute.

> not abandon me. Even if people won't know how serious and solemn a motive my crime was committed under, God will allow it. In the past, was there even one person who had murdered a person with a more solemn motive as mine? Someone who was more faithful to one's own art? Even only by that motive, I have the right to be a genius. . . . Yes, how can one murder a person for art if he didn't have the right to be a genius? A thing like this happened because I am a genius. To kill Aono is to exercise the privilege permitted only to a genius.[22]

As this passage makes clear, Ōkawa's logic revolves around the notion of art as an ideal—not unlike the notion of love for Kitabatake—which, as the highest ideal in life existing above the law, functions to justify murder. But unlike Kitabatake, who justifies his murder as serving a greater good by emphasizing the victim's deplorable character, Ōkawa's focus rests on himself and on his own qualifications to commit murder. Calling his motive for killing Aono a "serious" and "solemn" one, Ōkawa turns his own argument upside down at the end of the passage by claiming that his desire to murder Aono for the sake of art qualifies him as a "genius" who is, in turn, qualified to commit murder. In "Futari no geijutsuka," self-interest—rather than being a despicable personal desire to be rejected—is justified through the ideal of art as a mode of self-expression: egoism and ideal serve to reinforce each other.

And unlike Kitabatake, whose focus is to disavow the notion of jealousy as the emotional manifestation of self-interest at all costs—even his life—Ōkawa readily admits his jealousy for Aono's talents, although he understands the jealousy as fundamentally existential in nature. He states, as a part of his decision making process to murder Aono:

> My animosity toward him comes not only from simple jealousy but also from the uneasy awareness that another person who is the exact same type of artist as myself exists in this world. He lives in the world of imagination I live in. He produces the things that I try to produce. When I see his paintings, I discover the home [*kyōdo*] that my soul is hurrying to reach someday (425–26).[23]

---

22. Tanizaki, "Kin to gin," *Tanizaki Jun'ichirō zenshū*, vol. 5, 427. All subsequent references to this source will appear in the text in parentheses.

23. Also: "I am starting to feel as if I were Aono's shadow. Indeed, if there exist two artists here who are trying to express beauty that is exactly the same, it follows that one out of the two doesn't need to exist. To the extent that a thing called art is something that expresses the existence of the self, two persons must try to eliminate each other. The moment I recognized this, I began to take a jaundiced view of the self" (424).

The problem with Ōkawa is that he believes he and Aono are fundamentally the same in their artistic sensibilities. To the extent that he believes art to be an expression of the self, this is not something that should happen. How can the Other be the Same? Embedded within this notion of originality, moreover, is the sense of belatedness—of being a repetition of another—that Ōkawa feels, intimated by the phrase "When I see his paintings, I discover the home that my soul is hurrying to reach someday." Fittingly, then, he continues on to conclude the above line of argument: "In the end, the threat that I feel is the same threat felt by William Wilson who suffered from his own doppelgänger" (426). Ōkawa sees Aono as his doppelgänger, citing the famous short story by Edgar Allan Poe, which was translated by Tanizaki's younger brother Seiji in 1913 and had a major impact within Taishō literary circles.[24] Like Poe's famous double, Ōkawa and Aono exist on the opposite sides of the morality spectrum, but, unlike in Poe's story in which the bad half kills the good, "Futari no geijutsuka" tells the story of how the good half tries to kill the bad.[25]

From the various works of this period, it is clear that the subject of the doppelgänger was of much interest to Japanese writers, including Satō Haruo, whose "Shimon" will be the subject of the next section. This fact is fitting, considering that, as Ichiyanagi Hirotaka writes, the doppelgänger is "an excellent representation of a soul that has been ripped apart by age and society that continues to run the road to modernization at an intense speed."[26] Indeed, the mid-1910s were precisely the height of rapid modernization in the form of industrialization and urbanization stemming from Japan's new role as an exporter of war goods during World War I. But while the rise in stories about doubles no doubt has much to do with the ubiquitous processes of modernization, Tanizaki's "Futari no geijutsuka" as well as Akutagawa's short story "Futatsu no tegami" (Two letters; September 1917) reveals the culturally specific nature and in-

---

24. For details on the reception of Poe in Japan, see Sadoya, *Nihon kindai bungaku no seiritsu*, 727–824.

25. Tanizaki returns to this motif of the struggle between good and bad in his "A to B no hanashi" (A story of A and B; August 1921), in which the 'good' writer decides to take on the pains of the 'bad' writer by publishing his own works as those of the 'bad' writer.

26. Ichiyanagi, "Samayoeru dopperugengā," 122.

flection of the Japanese writers' experimentation with the topic of the doppelgänger.[27]

Similar to "Kaika no satsujin" in its employment of the epistolary style, "Futatsu no tegami," which was published about a year before "Kaika no satsujin" and is one of the earliest examples of a story describing the subject's confrontation with his double, presents two letters written to the police chief by a man named Sasaki. In the first letter, Sasaki, after recounting his experiences of seeing his and his wife's doppelgänger on various occasions, pleads to the police chief to deal with his neighbors, who accuse his wife of being an adulterer. In the second letter, he admonishes the police chief for not taking any action despite his first letter and reports that his wife has gone missing, possibly kidnapped. Framing these letters is the narrator-editor (who somehow obtained the letters like the narrator of "Kaika no satsujin") who cuts the second letter short, concluding his presentation of Sasaki's story in the following manner: "From that point, philosophical-like things that do not make much sense are written at length. That is unnecessary so I have decided to omit them here."[28]

Through this postscript (another instance of Akutagawa's use of the framing technique), then, the narrator-editor makes clear that he judges "the text presented by Sasaki to possess coherence only within himself and has no power of persuasion to the outside world" and rejects Sasaki's letters as the ramblings of a madman.[29] For the narrator-editor, there is no reality to Sasaki's experiences with the doppelgänger, except as evidence that Sasaki is a man who cannot handle the harsh realities of his wife's adultery. Sasaki's encounters with his and his wife's doubles result from witnessing the instances of adultery where he projects his desire to be his wife's lover onto the adulterer, thereby recognizing the adulterer as himself. The doppelgängers, thus, provide Sasaki with the mechanism to disavow the visual and traumatic reality of adultery and, by extension, the triangular relationship between subject, his object of desire, and rival as victor that Akutagawa would later revisit in "Kaika no satsujin."

---

27. In his work on doubles in modern Japanese literature, which will be discussed a bit later on in this chapter, Watanabe Masahiko labels the Taishō period "the age of doubles" (*Kindai bungaku no bunshinzō*, 70).

28. Akutagawa, "Futatsu no tegami," *Akutagawa Ryūnosuke zenshū*, vol. 2, 247.

29. Ichiyanagi, "Samayoeru dopperugengā," 120–21.

As powerful as the postscript is in framing the readers' interpretation of Sasaki's letters, it is also worth noting that the letters themselves provide evidence of his madness. A professor of English and ethics, Sasaki begins his letter by discussing the existence of doppelgängers in this world, citing many Western examples he has garnered from various sources.[30] After these examples, Sasaki tells the story of his first encounter with his double, which takes place when he goes to the orchestra with his wife. During intermission, he leaves her to go to the bathroom, and, upon returning, sees standing next to her his double, who quickly disappears upon her seeing him in turn. Sasaki concludes the episode in the following manner: "From that night on, I began to be stricken with one type of anxiety. That is because, as the examples previously provided show, the appearance of the doppelgänger often foreshadows the death of the person concerned."[31]

Indicating his fear of dying from the moment of his first encounter with the double, this passage intimates Sasaki's madness through his mention of the Western examples of the doppelgänger that provide the basis of his psychological reaction. For, the passage reveals that Sasaki has knowledge of the phenomenon, perhaps information he may have encountered through his occupation as a professor of English and ethics, *prior* to his first encounter with his double. Knowledge precedes experience, revealing the interpretation of the latter by the former as a hallucination produced by the second-hand knowledge of the doppelgänger in the first place. And in this reversal of knowledge and experience, of knowledge producing experience, we can discern the sense of belatedness—the shadow of the Western influence—haunting the Japanese modern experience. Western knowledge literally splits the subject (Sasaki) into fragments, 'enabling' him to see his double to disavow the triangular relationship in which he is the victim.

In this way, "Futatsu no tegami" explores the relationships between the sense of belatedness and the mechanism of disavowal and between Japan and the West that are implicated in the phenomenon of the double. As we saw in the previous section, Akutagawa would revisit these relationships, while not dealing explicitly with the doppelgänger, in his "Kaika no satsujin" through the figure of Kitabatake, whose crime has

30. Akutagawa obtained the examples from the "Döppelganger" [*sic*] chapter of Catherine Crowe's *The Night Side of Nature: Or, Ghosts and Ghost Seers*. Cited in Ibid., 122.

31. Akutagawa, "Futatsu no tegami," *Akutagawa Ryūnosuke zenshū*, vol. 2, 237.

much to do with losing his chance to court his love Akiko because of his studies in England. And Tanizaki's "Futari no geijutsuka," too, explores these relationships beyond what we have already discussed, although at first glance, what remains seems more superficial than Akutagawa's, limited to playful insertions of Western signifiers in the form of material objects and literary references into the tale of Ōkawa's crime. For example, Ōkawa decides to wear a "black wool suit" that he had purchased when he was "returning from the United States" to serve as a tuxedo when dining on the ship as a way to ensure that he not be identified by his clothes on the night of the crime (443). In considering the feasibility of murdering Aoki, moreover, Ōkawa specifically cites Sherlock Holmes and Auguste Dupin and thereby reveals himself as a reader of Western detective fiction. Yet, despite such insertions, these signifiers do not really become involved in the crux of the story. The question of Ōkawa's disguise in the form of American formalwear never enters the investigation of the assault on Aono. Nor does Ōkawa utilize the specific details of the detective's method that he may have learned from reading the classical detective stories by Conan Doyle and Poe.

But as trivial as they might seem, these Western signifiers have a major function within the dynamics of disavowal and belatedness in Tanizaki's work. For, by clearly invoking the West as a part of Ōkawa's life, these signifiers superficially hide and thereby actively flag how it is precisely the recognition of Western influence that Ōkawa is working so hard to disavow. As we have seen, the primary source of Ōkawa's murderous desire stems from the sense of belatedness that he keenly feels towards Aono, and Ōkawa, unlike Kitabatake, does not seem to be in denial of his own motivations, readily admitting and accepting (and perhaps relishing in) the personal interest that is at stake in his decision to kill his rival. At the same time, however, Ōkawa is operating within a mechanism of disavowal to the extent that he is blind to the paradoxical nature of his understanding of art as an ideal, which provides him with the rhetoric of justification to murder Aono. That is, while Ōkawa emphasizes the strangeness that someone like Aono who shares his artistic vision exists in this world, it is wholly understandable if not obvious that such a person could easily exist in Taishō society considering the overwhelming influence of Western values and concepts within the development of art in post-Restoration Japan as a whole. But this is not to deny the possibility of artistic originality in modern Japan, which would be another debate all together. Rather, in addition to the critical discursive trends of 1910s Japan, which will be discussed shortly, the text of

"Futari no geijutsuka" prompts the understanding of Ōkawa as someone characterized by his blindness to and disavowal of Western influence through a narrative strategy that presents Ōkawa's existential struggles as a parody of sorts.

That Tanizaki was consciously casting such blindness in ironic light can be discerned by the story's resemblance to *Crime and Punishment* that reveals the influence of Western literature in the production of this story, which, in turn, takes up the topic of the desperate search for artistic originality in Taishō Japan. Indeed, it is not only Tanizaki's story but also Akutagawa's "Kaika no satsujin" that display the Russian work's influence in the major theme of the story: the dangers of a rift that is created when a foreign ideal that is understood as absolute and universal in later-developing countries like Russia and Japan faces off against real social conditions. The thought processes of the protagonists of these stories, in believing that there exists morality beyond the law of the land, strongly evoke Raskolnikov's notion of the Übermensch, or the exceptional man.[32] But in Tanizaki's story, the connection goes beyond this larger theme, especially after Ōkawa decides to kill Aono when the connection becomes conspicuously direct.

As mentioned above, Ōkawa, in considering the feasibility of murdering Aono, cites the famous protagonists of Western detective stories, Sherlock Holmes and Auguste Dupin. More specifically, Ōkawa cites the detectives to ponder the reasons why crimes are detected, to which he ultimately concludes that the primary reason lies in the carelessness of the criminal. For Ōkawa, the question that detective fiction replies in the affirmative—"in the strict sense, does each and every single move of a human being necessarily leave some kind of trace in this world?" (429)—is answered in the negative. No doubt, the line of questioning through which Ōkawa comes to his conclusion that individual traces can be eliminated is highly disappointing, involving, for example, asking himself whether his action can be known by a detective if he simply stood up, walked to the mirror, looked at himself in the mirror, and then sat down again. But at the same time, it is undeniable that this line of thinking is identical to that of Raskolnikov when he plans the murder of the pawn lady in Chapter 6 of the Russian masterpiece: "At first—long before indeed—he [Raskolnikov] had been much occupied with

32. Nakajima Reiko also makes this point in "'Zenka mono,' 'Kin to gin,' 'A to B no hanashi' ni tsuite," 81.

one question; why almost all crimes are so badly concealed and so easily detected, and why almost all criminals leave such obvious traces?"[33]

At the moment when evidence of Western influence is strongest—that is, when Ōkawa's logic most resembles that of Raskolnikov—Tanizaki introduces unrelated signifiers of Western origin—Sherlock Holmes and Auguste Dupin—only to reject their influence by letting Ōkawa conclude that, unlike in Western detective stories, every act is not detectable. The text pretends as if Ōkawa is operating within the framework of the classic detective stories when his logic, in fact, is firmly entrenched in that of *Crime and Punishment*, and, in so doing, the text misdirects and suppresses the influence of *Crime and Punishment* on the production of this story. Yet, such misdirection and suppression can only be superficial to the extent that the reader will discern the 'hidden' Western influence, especially considering that the mid-1910s enjoyed a boom in the translation of Dostoevsky's works, in general, and his *Crime and Punishment*, in particular.

Starting with Etō Tōden's translation of *Crime and Punishment* under the title *Fuan* in 1909, the Russian work underwent numerous translations during this period, including the Russian scholar Nakamura Hakuyō's version in 1914.[34] Hakuyō's version would be reprinted in September 1918, just two months after the publication of "Himitsu to kaihō," as a part of *Dosutoefusukii zenshū* (The complete works of Dostoevsky) from *Shinchōsha*. Given such a literary environment, Tanizaki's juxtaposition of the protagonists of Western detective stories with *Crime and Punishment* and the suppression of the latter from the surface level of the text not only speak to his playful use of intertextuality but also cast Ōkawa's criminal logic in an ironic light. In other words, through the textual suppression of the influence that *Crime and Punishment* had on the production of this story, Tanizaki, consciously and actively, parodies Ōkawa's confidence in the possibility of the notion of artistic originality in Taishō Japan—where Western cultural influences abound whether in the field of literature or art, including the story in which Ōkawa is the protagonist—as characterized by a certain disavowal and blindness.

---

33. Dostoevsky, *Crime and Punishment*, 65.

34. Other translations of *Crime and Punishment* included versions by the monk Kyōgoku Itsuzō as well as by the writer Ikuta Chōkō and the poet Ikuta Shungetsu (co-translation) in 1915. *Crime and Punishment* was also made into a screenplay by Tsubouchi Shikō, the nephew of Tsubouchi Shōyō, in the same year. For details, see Sakakibara, "Dosutoefusukii hon'yaku sakuhin nenpyō."

And, of course, such a text would have produced a parodic effect precisely because Ōkawa's way of thinking—albeit a less radical and criminal one—revolving around his belief in artistic originality was nothing original. As various literary and social discourses of the period reveal, the discursive environment of the 1910s was characterized by exaltation of Western notions of originality and individuality, which resulted from the rejection of various -isms that had organized the Japanese intellectual sphere. On this point, Iida Yūko writes: "At the base of [the] hatred of '-isms' lies the assertion of individuality as the unification of diverse elements not able to be represented by one '-ism.' 'Originality' at the level of the individual that is different from the level of '-isms' becomes worshiped."[35] The intimate coupling between criticism of "-isms" and assertion of individuality/originality makes perfect sense, for to adhere to an "-ism" suggests the subject being influenced by an external source and is diametrically opposed to the notion of originality.[36]

But the rejection of "-isms" also requires the existence of and adherence to universal values to the extent that individual action requires criteria by which it is to be judged and made meaningful. Thus, while various "-isms" are criticized as constraining individual expression, universal values or rather tag words such as "art," "beauty," "self," and "world"—what Hasumi Shigehiko has called "'Taishō-esque' nature of abstraction"—become ubiquitous, as exemplified in the rhetoric of the Shirakaba group that was active during the 1910s.[37] As Tomi Suzuki writes of Mushanokōji Saneatsu (1885–1976), the leader of the Shirakaba group, and of the group in general:

> For Mushanokōji and the Shirakaba group, there were no Japanese: there existed only Humanity [*ningen*], or Mankind [*jinrui*], together with such universals as Love, Art, Nature, Justice, Beauty, and Life. . . . This absolute acceptance of Western discourse, the uncritical universalism and internationalism, and the notion of cultivating the individual self reflected the general intellectual atmosphere of the 1910s—a time when the sense of national crisis had dissipated in

---

35. Iida, *Karera no monogatari*, 219.

36. Iida writes: "What the unification of binary oppositions and the rejection of -isms signify is, at once, a rejection of already-existing frameworks that produce meaning and, above all, a strong resistance to the restrictions of the subject through such frameworks that are set outside the subject" (ibid., 222).

37. Hasumi, "'Taishō-teki' gensetsu to hihyō," 132.

the aftermath of the Russo-Japanese War but when political activity was tightly controlled by the government.[38]

As Suzuki makes clear, the rhetoric of the Shirakaba group was fraught with contradictions, for lying behind the rhetoric of universal values were events such as the Great Treason Incident and the annexation of Korea in 1910 that made clear the absolutist and imperialistic vector of modern Japan. In this context, the overtly liberal and humanistic rhetoric of the Shirakaba group, which would be echoed by Shiratori Shōgo's poem in the inaugural issue of *Shinseinen*, reveals itself as overcompensation for and an active disavowal of the harsh political and international realities of this period.

"Futari no geijutsuka" tells a story in which obsessive adherence to the universal value of originality and art leads one to an excessive reaction—murder—but, at the same time, it makes sure to mark itself with signs of Western influence that problematizes the notion of originality in the first place. In so doing, it presents itself as a parody of the discursive environment of 1910s Japan as well as an allegory of artistic originality in a later-developing nation like Japan that had been heavily influenced by Western artistic values.[39] It suggests that in order to speak about the self and originality in Japan is to suppress and disavow the Western influence and what it has done to the possibility of originality in modern Japan. That is, the question of artistic originality only arises when Ōkawa successfully disavows the Western influence that he and Aono share. Or to put it in another way, Ōkawa's obsession with Aono, by focusing on the similarities of their art as an *existential* question, enables him to be blind to the larger picture that would reveal a *social* problematic lurking behind their similarities.

---

38. Tomi Suzuki, *Narrating the Self*, 53. Suzuki also writes of the group: "Pursuing the self through art was a common goal of the Shirakaba (White Birch) group. . . . Influenced by such humanitarian philosophers and writers as Tolstoy and Maeterlinck, the Shirakaba group espoused an idealistic humanism rooted in the belief that the pursuit of the self was the goal of the highest value. . . . 'self,' 'individuality,' and 'personality' were key terms for the group" (ibid., 94).

39. Such influence, rather than being an issue of whether or not an artwork is derivative of Western art (a difficult theoretical problem on its own), clearly reveals itself in the consciousness of modern Japanese intellectuals, as exemplified by works such as Natsume Sōseki's "Gendai Nihon no kaika," which presents the developments of modern Japan as externally forced rather than internally developed.

But if Tanizaki's work operates primarily as a parody and an allegory, then what are we to make of Ōkawa's success as an artist after incapacitating Aono? And how do we interpret the story's ending, where not Ōkawa but the mute Aono is ecstatic in his coma-induced fantasy world? It seems that blindness and disavowal are all we have, especially when we consider Aono's, rather than Ōkawa's, story, for Aono, who is presented as someone to whom issue of artistic originality is not relevant, also operates fundamentally within the rhetoric of disavowal, namely, masochism. For, as Gilles Deleuze has discussed, the masochist "does not believe in negating or destroying the world nor in idealizing it: what he does is to disavow and thus to suspend it, in order to secure an ideal which is itself suspended in fantasy."[40] Within this understanding of masochism, Aono's art proves itself to be a means to an end—a tangible manifestation of his fantasies in the real world he seeks to disavow—and his state of incapacitation a godsend that enables him to maintain the state of disavowal and, thus, his fantasy indefinitely without such an external crutch.

Stories about disavowal, Akutagawa's "Kaika no satsujin" and Tanizaki's "Futari no geijutsuka" are diametrically opposed to the framework of the detective story to expose the truth of the case.[41] If detective fiction emerges when the public internalizes the panoptic authority of the state, as scholars have noted, then these stories dubbed as "new artistic detective novels" by placing Western ideals over the law of the land,

---

40. Deleuze, *Coldness and Cruelty*, 32–33. According to Deleuze, reality for the masochist is a world of the law, established by the father as a bearer of the phallus, and the realm of fantasy is the world of the mother who, through the subject's disavowal and suspension of her lack, represents the possibility of an ideal that the father outlaws by perpetuating the fear of castration. Thus, the fundamental operational framework of masochism is the "twofold disavowal, a positive, idealizing disavowal of the mother (who is identified with the law) and an invalidating disavowal of the father (who is expelled from the symbolic order)" (ibid., 68).

41. Indeed, not only do both stories deny the presence of the detective, easily committing a perfect crime, but they consciously mock the authority of the state. Kitabatake's perfect crime is made possible by his knowledge of Western medicine and suggests that his success stems from him being more knowledgeable (Western) than the police who incorrectly diagnose the cause of Kyōhei's death. Ōkawa's perfect crime is made possible by his knowledge of Western detective stories and suggests that his success, too, stems from him being more knowledgeable (Western) than the police, a point that is emphasized by the fact that Ōkawa is stopped by a police officer on the way back from attacking Aono, but he quickly evades further questioning by showing the police officer a fake identification card.

make no room for a hero of such a genre to emerge. The detectives of the Western tradition—exemplified by Sherlock Holmes and Auguste Dupin—take the authority of the state for granted, and the question of morality rarely if ever emerges. But when an individual internalizes as authority something other than the laws of the state to which the individual is subjected, we instead get Raskolnikov, Kitabatake, and Ōkawa, who turn into criminals rather than detectives as a result of such internalization. As the ending of "Futari no geijutsuka" suggests, Tanizaki would continue to seek a world that disavowed such fragmented allegiances through his exploration of masochism and fetishism, revealing how embracing and indulging in disavowal can be a pleasurable, if not legitimate, form of existence. But as we will see in the next section, Satō Haruo sought to present another possibility in his "Shimon," which shows how such a world, constituted in part by its rejection of the detective of the Western tradition, can give rise to another type of detective whose reason for being was found in the kernel of the modern Japanese experience as described in the stories of disavowal by Akutagawa and Tanizaki.

The Birth of a Japanese Detective

Among the stories in the "Himitsu to kaihō" issue of *Chūō kōron*, "Shimon" is no doubt closest to what we might call a detective story.[42] There exists in R. N. a character who occupies the position of the de-

42. "Shimon" tells the story of R. N., a childhood friend of the narrator named Satō. During his studies abroad, R. N. becomes an opium addict, continuing his addiction in Nagasaki after returning to Japan, but he suddenly returns to Tokyo and asks the narrator to let him live with him and his wife in order to beat his addiction. One day, the narrator, his wife, and R. N. go to Asakusa to watch a foreign film called *Nyozoku Rozario*. Encountering a close-up of a fingerprint in the movie, R. N. abruptly leaves the theater and thereafter becomes obsessed with the topic of fingerprints. Ultimately, R. N. reveals to the narrator that he may have killed a person at an opium den in Nagasaki. He tells the narrator, moreover, that near the body he found a watch, on the back of which was a fingerprint identical to the one that they saw in the film. After conducting an investigation at the alleged scene of the crime in Nagasaki with the narrator, R. N. concludes that he did not commit the murder, but rather the murder was committed by the actor in the film named William Wilson. The narrator is incredulous at R. N.'s conclusions, but even after R. N.'s death, the narrator still cannot dispel R. N.'s theories because the fingerprint in the film seems identical to the one on the back of the watch.

tective, and, recounted by the first-person narrator Satō whose shock and awe of R. N.'s actions at every turn evoke the stupefied narrator of Poe's Dupin Trilogy as well as Watson of Sherlock Holmes tales, the story exhibits specific narrative and structural resemblances to the classical detective story format established by these works. The story also includes an investigation of the supposed crime scene in Nagasaki where R. N. shocks the narrator with the accuracy of his 'deductions.' Of course, there is one catch—R. N.'s investigation focuses on exonerating his own guilt for a murder that he may have committed while in an opium daze: R. N., thus, is at once a detective, a criminal, and a witness.

Recalling how he came to discover a dead body lying next to him at the Nagasaki opium den, R. N. tells the narrator of his suspicions that he may have murdered the man during his opium dream because in it he saw "an armored knight" kill a man who was "floating on water."[43] But R. N.'s fear that he is a murderer takes an unexpected turn when he encounters the face of the actor William Wilson in the movie *Gun Moll Rosario* (*Nyozoku Rozario*).[44] R. N. tells the narrator:

> I saw instinctively that that man's face, illuminated by the light that shone from behind him in the picture in front of me, was identical to the face of the knight that basked in the moonlight in that dream of mine. And I recalled in an instant that it was a face that I had frequently seen in an opium den in Shanghai. But I immediately thought at that moment that this instinct of mine was stupid. I rejected myself thinking that I projected my dream into the film as soon as I saw a human face that was as large as in my dream at that time (111).

As this passage reveals, R. N., upon encountering the close-up face of William Wilson on the big screen, makes a connection between the actor and the knight in his opium dream. To support this connection, R. N. also 'realizes' that he has seen the face many times in a Shanghai opium den, thereby making it more plausible for the actor to have been in the Nagasaki opium den as well. But at the same time, R. N. is self-reflective, questioning these connections as a work of projection and of reconstructing the story of his trauma through a convenient foil that was prompted by the likeness of the larger-than-life nature of William Wilson's close-up and the hallucinatory images in his opium dreams.

---

43. Satō, "Shimon," *Teihon Satō Haruo zenshū*, vol. 3, 107. All subsequent references to this source will appear in the text in parentheses.

44. *Gun Moll Rosario* is the English title that is given to *Nyozoku Rozario* by Elaine Gerbert in her discussion of "Shimon" in "Space and Aesthetic Imagination in Some Taishō Writings."

His skepticism gets pushed aside, however, when the close-up of the fingerprint, which is left by Johnson (the character played by the actor William Wilson) on a table, appears on the big screen. Already at this point, as he later reveals to the narrator, R. N. had discovered a gold watch at the murder site with a fingerprint on its back, and, analyzing the fingerprint meticulously, reached the conclusion that it was not his. Thus, upon encountering the fingerprint on the screen, R. N. realizes in a flash that it is identical to the fingerprint on the back of the watch. By obsessively reading various Western literature on fingerprints thereafter to answer the question "In the world, are there two or more fingers that have the identical—or rather, similar—patterned fingerprints?" in the negative, R. N. is able to claim that the actor William Wilson must be the person whose fingerprint is on the back of the watch found at the scene of the crime (112). R. N. tries to confirm his theory by writing to William Wilson through the American film company, stating that the Japanese police are looking for him as a suspect in a murder case, but he receives no reply, learning instead that William Wilson has disappeared just around the time when he would have received R. N.'s letter. Upon this, R. N. concludes: "I escaped to Tokyo thinking that I may have committed a murder in Nagasaki. . . . But don't worry. I was by no means a murderer. The murderer is that man! It is indeed he—William Wilson. That motion picture's Johnson—no, William Wilson" (105).

In such a fashion, R. N.'s hypothesis moves seamlessly from his own exoneration to the identification of the culprit. But as Kawamoto Saburō states, "Shimon" seems to be "a story of mystery-increasing by a 'sickly master detective'" that leaves the reader not with "the feeling of intellectual refreshment" but with "the pleasure of slight perplexity on whether it was real or dream."[45] On the one hand, all physical and circumstantial evidence seem to suggest that the actor William Wilson murdered the man in the Nagasaki opium den. On the other hand, R. N.'s analysis and the resulting story is so fantastic and extraordinary that the narrator can never get himself to fully accept R. N.'s conclusions, even after a body is discovered exactly where R. N. had stated and even after R. N.'s death (details of which are not presented to the reader). In fact, the story ends with the narrator having become entrapped in a perpetual state of uncertainty, inching closer to accepting the identity of the fingerprints but never able to alleviate the need to search for their difference: "Even now,

---

45. Kawamoto, *Taishō gen'ei*, 251.

as I write this, I cannot discover how the fingerprint in that film and the fingerprint inside the lid of the watch are different. Ever more, I cannot doubt my own eyes. Because that would be a bigger blasphemy than not believing in God" (117–18). And such an ending characterized by its uncertainty cannot help trickling down to affect the interpretation of the reader, especially because the certainty and confidence of analysis that R. N. displays are relativized by the narrator's portrayal of R. N. as an opium addict and a madman.

Ultimately, though, it is the identity of the culprit that radically problematizes R. N.'s hypothesis. As discussed in the previous section, William Wilson is the title and the protagonist's name of Edgar Allan Poe's story about the doppelgänger. And importantly, Satō, the narrator, who is an educated writer that actively prompts his conflation with Satō Haruo of the real world through various textual strategies, does not make the connection between the name William Wilson and Poe's work, which was, as previously mentioned, an influential story within Taishō literary circles.[46] In other words, Satō Haruo, the real author and not the narrator, embeds in the story a conscious blindness to a literary connection that would reveal the truth of this story's madness as well as its fictionality, in a similar manner to Tanizaki's "Futari no geijutsuka" also seemingly blind of its likeness to *Crime and Punishment*. In "Shimon," then, the doppelgänger exists on the level of literary reference for the well-read readers familiar with Poe's story (or anyone who read Tanizaki's "Futari no geijutsuka," which mentions William Wilson, in the same issue of *Chūō kōron*) to decode, leaving us with the question: why is it William Wilson and what is the significance of this literary reference?

"Shimon" is a story about the fascination and obsession with fingerprints. Hidden behind this obsession, however, lies the story of the double. On the one hand, we have the fingerprint, a modern technological 'discovery' that enables the identification and differentiation of individuals and, as such, makes possible for the detective to reclaim the lost individual traces in the big city through "capturing the criminal in an act of

46. For example, the narrator refers to the work "Tsuki kage," which Satō Haruo published in reality as an account of R. N.'s opium dream. Also, in explaining why he refrains from describing R. N.'s fascinating views on film, the narrator writes in a parenthetical aside: "I regret that because of the page restrictions and the deadline of this manuscript, I cannot even take a necessary detour" (95).

unconscious revelation."[47] Indeed, it is precisely this "act of unconscious revelation" through the leaving of a fingerprint, the most exemplary of such acts, that "Shimon" describes, for we are led to believe that, in *Gun Moll Rosario*, it is Johnson's inadvertent placing of the fingerprint on the table that brings the gang down.[48] On the other hand, the fingerprint(s) is 'determined' to belong to William Wilson whose name evokes the doppelgänger, also a modern phenomenon but a psychological and literary one, which rejects the very notion of individuality that the fingerprint, as a scientific tool for identification and a proof that each individual is unique, functions to reclaim. Although the fingerprints on the gold watch and the one left by the driver Johnson on the table in *Gun Moll Rosario* may match, the name William Wilson suggests, as Watanabe Masahiko concludes in his *Kindai bungaku no bunshinzō* (The doubling image of modern literature), that the "murderer" is not the same person as the actor who plays Johnson but rather his double.[49] Or as Ubukata Tomoko hypothesizes, "the murderer William Wilson is a person who takes on the territory of R. N.'s 'unconscious'" and, thus, "R. N. as 'detective' and William Wilson as 'criminal' are an entity that shares the 'soul' of one human being despite having two different bodies."[50]

In these ways, the name William Wilson prompts the reader (and critics) to contemplate the identity of the criminal as well as the allegorical significance of the name William Wilson. And naturally, considering that William Wilson appears as a movie actor, these discussions revolve around the question of film as an emergent medium that had

---

47. Gunning, "Tracing the Individual Body," 24. The full passage follows:

> The detective story structures itself around two essential moments: one plays on the possibility of exploiting the loss of the immediate signs of identity and place in society, while the second tries to restore and establish identity and social status beyond a shadow of a doubt. The criminal can use disguise and alias to elude recognition. However, the detective can identify the criminal precisely by focusing on marks that the criminal might not be aware of or would find difficult or impossible to conceal. The drama of this new form of evidence lies less in stripping the criminal of his disguise . . . than in capturing the criminal in an act of unconscious revelation" (ibid., 23–24).

48. The narrator describes this critical scene as follows: "Rosario's band of thieves never took the gloves off from their hands. But the gloves of the driver Johnson had worn out at some moment. Johnson, whose fingers had lost some sense of touch because of his job, did not notice this at all. And he had left his fingerprint carelessly at the crime scene" (96).

49. Watanabe Masahiko, *Kindai bungaku no bunshinzō*, 78.

50. Ubukata, "'Tantei shōsetsu' izen," 175.

significant impact on the experiences of modern life. Drawing on the works of Sigmund Freud and Mary Anne Doane, Ubukata argues: "According to Freud, the unconscious corresponds to the domain where 'the preservation and symbolization of memory traces' take place. And Mary Anne Doane points out that this function of 'the preservation and symbolization of memory traces' is precisely the unique characteristic of cinema."[51] It is this link between the opium dream and cinema as sites of the expressions of the unconscious, as fantasy, that enables Ubukata to hypothesize William Wilson as R. N.'s double, which, in turn, leads to the discussion of the fragmented subject in modern society: "The mystery solving of 'Shimon,' which tries to make sense of the world of the 'unconscious' through the fingerprint, exposes the vulnerability of the concept of individual's 'identity' created by modern authority."[52]

In contrast to Ubukata's argument in which the concept of the double is a product of the connection between opium dream and cinema, Watanabe sees a direct link between cinema and the double. Noting the proliferation of stories of the doppelgänger in the Taishō period, Watanabe singles out the German expressionistic film *Der Student von Prag* (The student of Prague; 1913), which was released in Japan in April 1916, as the most influential work to familiarize the Japanese literati on the subject. Telling the story of Baudin, a poor university student who sells his reflection in the mirror to the devil, the central appeal of *Der Student von Prag* was the simultaneous presentation of Baudin and his double played by the same actor on the screen.[53] Made possible by technological developments within the film medium, namely, superimposition, such presentation produces the sensation that the impossible—the existence of the double showing that an identical person is occupying two different spaces—is possible. Unlike in the case of the novel where such impossibility must be accepted on the symbolic level by the intellect, the film challenges the audience to judge the possibility of this intellectual impossibility for themselves at the level of immediate perception.[54]

---

51. Ibid., 179.

52. Ibid., 180.

53. Baudin sells his reflection to obtain money to court a countess, but to his dismay, he is thwarted at every turn by his own reflection, ultimately leading the horrified Baudin to shoot the reflection, at which point Baudin himself dies.

54. Such comparatist perspective was actively fostered in the film audience from the first days of narrative cinema in Japan. The French film series *Zigomar* about a cat-and-mouse game between a robber and the police that became ex-

The result is that, while the double may be considered impossible by the intellect, the subject nonetheless sees it and, thus, cannot deny its existence. The subject is prompted to give in to the allure of the visual, where the power of the visual forces an override and a disavowal of intellectual knowledge.

Importantly, the significance of *Der Student von Prag* went beyond introducing the theme of the double to the Japanese audience, as the film functions on a meta-level, its content echoing and emphasizing the media-specific effects of cinema on its audience. According to Watanabe, the human images of early films struck their uninitiated viewers as very real and created the sensation that the image is a double of the actor, especially because the image of the same actor appeared inside various stories in multiple movie theaters at any given time. Watanabe concludes: "The audience knows that the person on the screen is a copy of a real human being who lives somewhere in this world. But, as far as feelings go, [the audience] must feel that the same person lives different lives inside multiple stories."[55] Sitting in a dark room with their eyes fixated on the screen, the audience falls under the impression that they are peeping and eavesdropping on the lives of actual human beings existing somewhere in the world, and, thus, when they encounter the same actors playing different roles, they become struck with the sensation of the double, that the same person is leading multiple lives.[56]

The film medium in its early stages of development infected the audience with an eerie sense of the double, imbuing the stories it told with an illusionary quality, one that "Shimon" accentuates by R. N.'s likening of movies to his opium experience and the connection he makes between the murdering knight in his drug-induced daze to William Wil-

---

tremely popular in Japan in the early 1910s utilized the disguise as the primary method by which the robber escaped the detection of the police (and the police infiltrated the gang). Thus, the audience was allowed to detect the disguises of characters on the screen before their identities were unveiled. For plot summaries and discussions of *Zigomar* films, see Nagamine, *Kaitō Jigoma to katsudō shashin no jidai*.

55. Watanabe Masahiko, *Kindai bungaku no bunshinzō*, 72.

56. In her discussion of "Shimon," Elaine Gerbert states on the effect of the cinematic experience: "In the inactive state induced by the darkness and the stationary positioning of the body and the head, the normal sense of self in space is suspended, and in the hypnotic state produced by the illumined image upon the screen, critical analytic activity is temporarily suspended" ("Space and Aesthetic Imagination in Some Taishō Writings," 78).

son in the film *Gun Moll Rosario*. No doubt, such engagement with the new medium of film is one of the major characteristics of "Shimon" that presented itself as being ahead of its time as a literary experiment. But "Shimon" is not only a literary experiment about cinema but also a literary experiment on the literariness of a literary text. As such, to focus the interpretation of "Shimon" solely on the intimate relationship between the emergent film medium and the theme of the double would be to deny the complexity of this story, which is consciously weaved by providing the readers with *excess* clues of a literary nature (with the name William Wilson being the primary clue) to guide and to confuse at the same time.

Nowhere is this clearer than when R. N. shows the narrator a newspaper clipping of an article reporting of William Wilson's disappearance. For R. N., this news is a result of his letter to William Wilson telling him that the Japanese police are searching for him as a murder suspect and, therefore, proves William Wilson's guilt. But if we interpret William Wilson as the double of the criminal in the Nagasaki opium den, as Watanabe does, then his disappearance takes on a new twist: discovering that his double has committed—and may still be committing—crimes around the world, William Wilson, the actor who plays the criminal on the big screen, turns detective to chase after his evil half. But the details of the news reports of William Wilson's disappearance complicate such a reading as well. The news speculates that William Wilson, despite his English-sounding name, is actually of German decent and has disappeared due to this fact in light of a recent situation, namely, World War I (104). This news—no doubt superfluous to the story according to the interpretation above—hints at the possibility that the actor who plays Johnson in *Gun Moll Rosario* has adopted William Wilson as an alias that points to the truth of his identity as a double. And such possibility finds support in the other bit of William Wilson's bio included in the news, namely, that he started out his career as an actor in the film *XYZ*, thus evoking in the readers the name of Anna Katharine Green's detective story, which Tsubouchi Shōyō translated as *Nisegane tsukai*. If we recall the first chapter of this book, the issue of false identity—the detective pretending to be a criminal—played a major role in the story. But *XYZ* as the title of a film has no significance within the story world in terms of William Wilson's real identity, and the significance of this literary reference is once again left for the readers to speculate.

In such ways, we quickly fall into the trap laid out by Satō (the author and not the narrator), finding ourselves in a labyrinth of literary references and myriad interpretations. As the name William Wilson naturally pulls the readers' interpretation toward the supernatural and the symbolic, other details surrounding the actor William Wilson simultaneously suggest the possibility of a more literal interpretation. And a similar antagonistic pull underlies R. N.'s presentation of his analysis of the case as well to confuse the readers further regarding their assessment of the story. For example, in claiming the gold watch as the key piece of evidence, R. N. does not forget to mention that he used to own a similar watch but had misplaced it or given it away, and, thus, raising suspicion in the minds of the readers that the gold watch may be his.[57] But R. N. quickly redirects the discussion to the question of the fingerprint on the watch, stating that it was not his own upon comparison. And indeed, this line of argument by R. N. serves to highlight the obvious and basic fact that, befitting of a story titled "Shimon," the whole of R. N.'s case hinges on the positive match between the fingerprint on the gold watch and that of the driver Johnson in *Gun Moll Rosario*, and thereby, returning to the starting point from which we began our discussion.

But this time, rather than considering the fingerprints within the interpretative framework buttressed by the name of the suspect as a literary reference, I would like to focus somewhere else, namely, that, as a piece of evidence in a detective story, the fingerprint on the gold watch is at best a non-conclusive one regardless of its 'owner,' and the evocation of the double through the name William Wilson echoes the irrelevance of the fingerprint on the gold watch within R. N.'s analysis in the first place. As R. N. tells the narrator, he discovered the gold watch, not next to or on the victim, but inside a wall in near (not immediate) proximity to the victim. But, of course, discovering an object near the corpse does not automatically equal key evidence. It is one thing to discover a foreign object in the victim's house, for example; it is another thing

---

57. R. N. states: "I doubted that the criminal whom I discovered through my subconscious and sixth sense was myself and that the watch, which is material evidence, was mine. In truth, I too had a golden watch. That was lost on some occasion (I have forgotten why. From long ago, I quickly forget trivial and uninteresting things like that. Ever since I started doing opium, it became especially bad. It was either that I gave it to someone, dropped it, sold it, or got it stolen). In order to compare line by line the fingerprint on the back of the watch and my own, I spent most of my good days. That which was on the back of the watch was, indeed, different from mine" (111).

altogether to discover an object where many people gather. And here, R. N.'s comment that he has seen William Wilson several times in the Shanghai opium den functions to undermine his analysis. Not only does this claim raise the possibility that William Wilson had been present in the Nagasaki opium den at some point and had misplaced his watch there, but it also raises the possibility that R. N. could have projected onto the face of the knight in his opium dream a face of a person he had already seen or even interacted, perhaps giving him a gold watch in exchange for something.

The fingerprint on the gold watch is the central evidence of "Shimon," but the watch's link to the murder is thin at best, as it is neither the murder weapon nor was it found in the immediate vicinity of the victim. Yet, despite these issues, there is no doubt in R. N.'s mind that the gold watch is that of the criminal from the moment of its discovery and especially after he encounters the second fingerprint on the movie screen. And the same can be said for the narrator, whose singular focus on the two fingerprints at the story's end clearly indicates that he, too, does not question this connection between the watch and the criminal. In this sense, the obsession with the fingerprints enables R. N. (and the narrator) to disavow all other information that may point to the possibility of having committed a murder, or rather, to not come to terms with the realization that he will never rid himself of the uncertainty surrounding the dead man at the Nagasaki opium den.

As that which was found in proximity to the site of trauma but not necessarily having a fundamental connection with the trauma itself and functioning as an object of obsession that disavows the truth of the trauma, the fingerprint on the gold watch is a fetish object, and R. N. and the narrator are operating within the framework of fetishistic disavowal.[58] And this making of the fingerprint(s) into a fetish is promoted

---

58. Sigmund Freud defines the fetish object as "a substitute for the woman's (mother's) penis that the little boy once believed in and—for reasons familiar to us—does not want to give up" ("Fetishism," 152–53). A fetishist attempts at an unconscious level to maintain his original belief that all humans have a penis. In other words, it is an unconscious disavowal of sexual difference and of the incommensurability between his belief and his visual perception. The need for such disavowal exists because the female body presents itself to a fetishist as a sign of castration and as a reminder that he may also be castrated. Therefore, fetishism is a way in which the female body is made visually pleasurable at an unconscious level through seeing her in conjunction with an object which covers her lack.

by a media-specific characteristic of film that makes the comparison of the two fingerprints possible, namely, the close-up that provides R. N. and the narrator with seemingly infinite details—little squiggly lines that are skin deep yet determine the individual's identity—engrossing them fully to the extent that the narrator by the end of the story has become spellbound.[59] But critical here is the fact that "Shimon" does not allow its readers to partake in this world of the fetish: just as it was the case for the conflation of William Wilson with the knight in R. N.'s opium dream, "Shimon" as a literary work forces its readers to share in the narrator's withholding of judgment precisely because they cannot compare the fingerprints themselves, as it would be the case if this story were a film. In this sense, "Shimon" does not enable the readers to turn detective in the same way that R. N. prompted the narrator to do so by the story's end and, thus, offers linguistic substitution for and resistance against the irresistible allure of the visual in much the same way as the act of eavesdropping did within the sociocultural conditions of 1880s Meiji, as we saw in Chapter 1 of this study.

This is not to say, however, that the story simply ends with uncertainty and mystery, as the aforementioned passage by Kawamoto argues. Rather, "Shimon" is a story about a deferral of such judgment and a rejection of the detective through such process of deferral. Indeed, the key to the mystery of "Shimon," I would argue, is the most conspicuous of the seemingly extraneous information within the dominant reading of the story, namely, the details surrounding R. N.'s gold medal. Revisiting the scene

---

59. On this topic, Tanizaki writes: "The human face—even an ugly face—is such that if you stare at it intently, it seems to conceal a mysterious, solemn, and eternal beauty. When I look at a 'close-up' of a face in a moving picture, this feeling is especially strong. Every individual part of the face or body of a person who ordinarily would escape notice possesses an indescribable energy, and I can feel its compelling force all the more keenly. Perhaps this is not only because film is a magnification of the real object but also because it lacks the sound and color of the real object. Perhaps the lack of color or sound in moving pictures is an asset rather than a limitation. Just as painting has no sound and poems have no shape, the moving pictures, too, because of their limitations, manifest the purification—Crystallization—of nature that is necessary to art. I believe this aspect of the moving pictures will enable them to develop into a more advanced form of art than the theater" ("Katsudō shashin no genzai to shōrai," *Tanizaki Jun'ichrō zenshū*, vol. 20, 16–17. I have used Joanne Bernardi's translation of this passage found in Bernardi, "Tanizaki Jun'ichirō's 'The Present and Future of the Moving Pictures,'" 301).

of the crime with the narrator, R. N. uses his gold medal attached to a string as a way to show that blocked away underneath the floors exists a basement in the house, which he claims was once an opium den. R. N. is successful in his task, but, in so doing, the medal falls into the basement, leading him to comment: "it's dangerous to drop something like that. It will leave a trace" (102). Yet, despite such concern over the gold medal, he quickly drops the subject and heads to the train station to leave Nagasaki. R. N.'s fear is eventually realized, when three years after this incident, a corpse is discovered exactly where R. N. said it would be and, along with it, his gold medal. Engraved and awarded by a literature department at a foreign university, the gold medal will no doubt be tracked to R. N., although R. N. has already died by this point. Important here is the likeness of the expected actions of the Japanese police and that of R. N. His investigation is founded upon the gold watch he discovered near the victim and the fingerprint it contains. The state's investigation, too, will undoubtedly be founded upon the gold medal discovered near the corpse and the fingerprint—R. N.'s—it is likely to contain.

"Shimon" shows how the detective emerges within the framework of disavowal that characterized the 'detective' stories contained in the "Himitsu to kaihō" issue of *Chūō kōron*. But at the same time, the narrator and the story he tells quickly relativize such emergence by suggesting that the state will have the last say regarding the ultimate outcome of the case. In fact, the narrator seems to do more than suggest, as he actively defers the final decision of the case to the state by the publication of "Shimon," which tells the story of R. N.—the likely primary suspect—who can no longer present his analysis that identifies William Wilson as the murderer. In so doing, the narrator releases himself from the agony of perpetual indecision, for it will then be up to the state and not the narrator to make the determination on who the murderer is, whether or not R. N.'s story was true, and whether or not the two fingerprints match. Through its decision—whether correct or not—the state, by exercising its absolute and arbitrary authority, will ensure R. N.'s identity and individuality and 'reclaim,' that is, 'tell' the experiences of R. N., a fragmented subject who has lost grasp of his external reality. And perhaps, R. N.'s choice to use the gold medal—the greatest honor conferred to him in the West and functioning as a symbol of his enlightenment—for such a risky task was an unconscious cry for help to the state to resolve the uncertainty that he could not wipe away regarding his guilt, an uncertainty he hides well but becomes reflected in the narrator by the story's end.

Akutagawa's "Kaika no satsujin" and Tanizaki's "Futari no geijutsuka" explored the power that Western ideals had on Japanese intellectuals and the violence that could erupt when the ideals were understood to be universal and applicable to real life. Thus, they were heirs to the Japanese struggles—introduced in Chapter 3 of this book—with the problematics left by *Crime and Punishment* of the intellectual who found himself outside the confines of a path to productive citizenry, whether by choice or by force. And to the extent that the Japanese student/intellectual was characterized by his contact with Western culture and values, it was fitting that these stories posited him as a subject of fragmented allegiance where Western ideals were pitted directly against the Japanese law, in which the former was understood to be in the position of truth and the latter as preventing the fulfillment of the former. Perhaps this notion of the fragmentary subject explains the difficulty of the emergence of the detective in modern Japan, as suggested by Akutagawa's letter to his friend that expresses his inability to write a detective story despite an explicit request and as intimated by the conspicuous absence of the heroic detective within stories organized under the heading of "new artistic detective novels" of *Chuō kōron*'s special issue "Himitsu to kaihō." If the emergence of the detective as hero required a successful internalization of authority on the level of the general public, the Japanese public was left to wonder which authority they were to internalize.

Fittingly, the question of such fragmentation became paramount in the early Taishō period, precisely because this was the moment when the values, successes, and ills of Japan's modernization process during the Meiji period, understood as a Westernization process, began to be reassessed with the arrival of a new period. No doubt, such reassessment made itself even more keenly felt as it fed into the historical realities both within Japan and abroad during the 1910s, which made it difficult for the Japanese intellectual to hold onto the notions of progress—humanism, cosmopolitanism, and so on espoused by the supporters of Taishō Democracy—as reflecting the actual state of things. And if the stories by Akutagawa and Tanizaki sought to portray the disavowal necessary for the Japanese subject under the spell of Western influence that led him not to productive citizenry but to murder, then Satō's "Shimon" reveals itself as a perverse permutation of these stories. In "Shimon," it is not Western ideals but opium, the ultimate weapon used by England to colonize China, that represents Western influence, thereby suggesting at once its addictiveness and dangers for modern Japanese subjectivity. Befitting such allegorical implications, R. N. becomes addicted to opium in England and continues his habits in Shanghai and Nagasaki, two cities that are characterized by their being integral parts of Asia's encounter with the West.[60]

And if Sōseki, whose *Kokoro* exercised foundational influence on the production of the stories by Akutagawa, Tanizaki, and Satō, hinted at the need for certainty that the detective fiction framework, which connects the past and the present, provides on the imaginary level regardless of whether or not such certainty is illusory, then "Shimon" reiterates this need through R. N.'s—as well as the narrator's—desperate attempts to prove his innocence in the case of the dead man in the Nagasaki opium den. And if Sōseki's work seemed to use the past as a storage place for traumatic secrets that define the individual and thereby disavow the influence of the sociohistorical on the production of the subject, then Satō reintroduces the sociohistorical into the detective fiction framework by developing "Shimon" within the specific context of modernization at whose root lies Japan's encounter with the West. But, of course, insofar as R. N.'s and the narrator's 'solving' of the crime entails a fetishistic focus on the identity of the two fingerprints that may not have anything to do with the case, "Shimon" suggests the difficulties facing the Japanese subject of extricating himself from the web of social relations that produces him as a mystery. It is this task befitting of the Japanese detective—to make sense of a dream-like existence of the deeply fragmented subject—that would be explored in the detective stories of Edogawa Ranpo.

60. But even here, the text must complicate our interpretation of the symbolic significance of its signifiers. After investigating the scene of the crime in Nagasaki, the narrator suggests that they spend a night in Nagasaki. To this, R. N. answers cryptically in the negative: "farther from Nagasaki the better. Actually, there is a truly bad memory for me in Nagasaki" (103). The use of the word "actually" (*jitsu wa*) suggests that this bad memory is something new to the narrator, and, thus, unrelated to the murder in the opium den. Given that Nagasaki is R. N.'s hometown, such comment suggests the possibility of a dark family past, but the text does not elaborate so that we can form an alternate interpretation. Rather, the text only intimates the possibility that our interpretation is wrong.

SIX

Detecting the Unconscious: Edogawa Ranpo and the Emergence of the Japanese Detective

In his essay "Nihon no kindai-teki tantei shōsetsu: toku ni Edogawa Ranpo shi ni tsuite" (Modern detective stories of Japan: especially regarding Edogawa Ranpo) appearing in the April issue of *Shinseinen* in 1925, the foremost social critic of the 1920s Hirabayashi Hatsunosuke (1892–1931) made the following remark on the relationship between detective fiction and science:

> There is no doubt that certain social conditions must exist in order for detective fiction to develop. Until a certain social environment develops, detective fiction will not be born. Broadly speaking, that social condition or environment is the development of scientific civilization, of intellect, of analytic spirit, and of methodical spirit. And narrowly speaking, it is for crimes and their investigations to become scientific, for arrests and trials to be carried out according to reliable physical evidence, and for refined written laws to uphold the order of the nation.[1]

For Hirabayashi, whose optimistic view of modern society rested on the development of a new life founded upon scientific innovations, it was

1. Hirabayashi, "Nihon no kindai-teki tantei shōsetsu," 9. Ranpo reminisced in 1938 that Hirabayashi was "the critic who, more than any other, had guided, cautioned, and encouraged me or brought me happiness and fear in my early years" (cited in Ikeda, *Taishū shōsetsu no sekai to han-sekai*, 143).

only natural that his analysis of detective fiction should focus on its scientific character.[2] The causal connection between "scientific civilization" and detective fiction enabled him at once to explain the late development of detective fiction in Japan as a consequence of the country's scientific immaturity and to welcome the emergence of original detective fiction in early 1920s Japan—which, as the title of the essay leaves no doubt, rested on Edogawa Ranpo—as a sign of its development into a modern civilization comparable to that of the West.

Revolving around the twin axes of science and realism, Hirabayashi's argument reflects the atmosphere of scientific craze brought on in part by Albert Einstein's visit to Japan in 1923 and sheds light on the hope with which the literary critics of the 1920s welcomed detective fiction, in general, and Ranpo's stories, in particular.[3] But such reception of Ranpo was short-lived, as Hirayabashi makes clear in his essay "Tantei shōsetsu dan no shokeikō" (Various trends in detective fiction circles), which appeared in the early spring supplementary issue of *Shinseinen* in 1926. Categorizing Japanese detective fiction into the "healthy" (*kenzen-ha*) and the "unhealthy" (*fukenzen-ha*), the essay criticized the latter category, characterized by its focus on the perverse and the sensational, as

2. For more on Hirabayashi's view on the relationship between modernism and science, see Hamill, "Nihon-teki modanizumu no shisō."

3. Of course, such an understanding of detective fiction was not the only one existing in the mid-1920s, as Satō Haruo's essay "Tantei shōsetsu shōron" (Brief thoughts on detective fiction), which appeared in the supplementary summer issue of *Shinseinen* in 1924, indicates. Despite its similarity to Hirabayashi's in its emphasis on scientific and analytical elements of detective fiction, Satō's departs from Hirabayshi's in its discussion of the secondary nature of science and reason within the production and consumption of detective fiction. Satō writes: "In short, what is called a detective fiction is after all one branch of a fruitful tree called romanticism, a fruit of the bizarre and the curious . . . it would not be a mistake to say that it is a curious admiration of evil common to all people, which takes root upon the strange psychology to want to see what is frightening, but at the same time, it founds itself by relating to the healthy spirit that loves clear thinking." As this passage reveals, Satō believes in the existence of two categories of detective stories, which are characterized by "the reasoning and decisions founded on the mind of a practical person" and by "the pathological sensitivity of a neurotic intuition" ("Tantei shōsetsu shōron," in *Teihon Satō Haruo zenshū*, vol. 19, 275). Yet, at the same time, he subsumes these contrasting categories under the rubric of romanticism, and, in so doing, presents the two types of detective stories as flip sides of a coin where one is not better or more desirable than the other.

deviating from the scientific and analytic spirit upon which truly modern detective fiction must found itself.[4] Hirabayashi writes:

> I for one possess rather unhealthy and morbid interests, and I believe that while there may be some difference in degree, these [interests] seem to be a common phenomenon among all human beings. At the same time, I believe that there exists an antithesis against such interests within all human beings. But I think that the detective story writers of Japan lean too much toward the unhealthy interests, that they chase too eagerly the world of artificiality, grotesque, and the unnatural. Such a tendency is a characteristic of an age of degradation and should be kept away from any art form. . . . I hope for the even greater development of healthy detective fiction.[5]

While admitting that he too enjoys the object of his criticism—stories with "unhealthy and morbid interests"—Hirabayashi makes certain to separate enjoyment from prescription of what art should be and do for people, especially because Japanese writers have a tendency to lean too far "toward the unhealthy interests." Importantly, Hirabayashi, who had called Ranpo "the only true detective fiction writer in Japan" in his 1925 essay, categorizes Ranpo as a representative author of "unhealthy" detective stories, citing in particular his "Yaneura no sanposha" (The wanderer in the attic; August 1925), published about five months before Hirabayashi's essay. In the course of the year separating Hirabayashi's two essays, something had changed. According to Hirabayashi, Ranpo had abandoned his pursuit of modern—that is, scientific and analytical—detective fiction for 'detective' stories that emphasized the perverse and the sensational, stories that would soon earn Ranpo the reputaion of being the forerunner of the *ero guro nansensu* (erotic, grotesque, nonsense) phenomenon in the late 1920s and 1930s.[6]

As history shows, it was not only Hirabayashi who would come to hold this view on the development of Ranpo's fiction, as many critics, both contemporaneous and recent, have identified a shift in Ranpo's works from "healthy" or "scientific" to "unhealthy" or "perverse" detective fic-

---

4. As Kawasaki Kenko points out, Hirabayashi's categorization of detective fiction into "healthy" and "unhealthy" foreshadowed the debate on serious or authentic (*honkaku*) and irregular (*henkaku*) detective fiction that would take place between Ranpo and Kōga Saburō (1893–1945) in the mid-1930s (Kawasaki, "Taishū bunka seiritsuki ni okeru 'tantei shōsetsu' janru no hen'yō," 82).

5. Hirabayashi, "Tantei shōsetsu dan no shokeikō," 347.

6. For extensive discussion on this phenomenon, see Silverberg, *Erotic Grotesque Nonsense*.

tion during the same period.[7] Although important for our understanding of Ranpo's oeuvre, a focus on this shift has also promoted the tendency to subsume Ranpo's transformation as a writer into dualisms such as *honkaku* (serious) and *henkaku* (irregular)—categorizations that would become popular in the 1930s—and consequently veer away from analyzing Ranpo's works as a series of texts with continuing preoccupations and concerns. Indeed, Ranpo's early detective stories, whether Ranpo himself was conscious of it or not, exhibit a specific development of or struggle with what might be called the 'epistemological project,' one that questions and negotiates the methodology of how a person (the detective) can come to hold an objective, that is, certain, knowledge about another (the criminal). This chapter examines the early detective stories of Ranpo—in particular, "Ni-sen dōka" (Two-sen copper coin; April 1923), "Ichimai no kippu" (One ticket; July 1923), "D-zaka no satsujin jiken" (Murder case on D-hill; January 1925), "Shinri shiken" (The psychological test; February 1925), and "Yaneura no sanposha"—all of which appeared in *Shinseinen* during the formative years of the second detective fiction boom in Japan. In so doing, I will consider the significance of these stories within the radical cultural transformation taking place in the aftermath of the Great Kantō Earthquake and of the specific concerns underlying Ranpo's epistemological project, which sought to deal with the growingly tenuous relationship between the Japanese subject and his external environment.

Detective Fiction as Parody

Upon reading the manuscript of Edogawa Ranpo's "Ni-sen dōka," Morishita Uson (1890–1965), the editor-in-chief of *Shinseinen*, wrote a note stating that he experienced "the same joy as Belinksy who upon reading Dostoevsky's first novel pounded the door of his residence in the dead of the night."[8] Uson sent this note along with the manuscript to the doctor and detective fiction enthusiast Kozakai Fuboku (1890–1929), who

7. For example, Ryū Tōun, in his 1931 essay "Edogawa Ranpo ron" (An essay on Edogawa Ranpo), separates Ranpo's fiction into three stages: the first stage, spanning his first story "Ni-sen dōka" and "Muyūbyōsha no shi" (The death of a sleepwalker; July 1925), comprised Ranpo's "healthy and serious detective fiction"; the second stage, from "Yaneura no sanposha" to *Injū* (Shadowy beast; August to October 1928) could be classified his "irregular" detective fiction; and the third stage, from *Nanimono* (Who; December 1929), as his "full-length detective novels" ("Edogawa Ranpo ron," 40–41).

8. Cited in Nakajima Kawatarō, *Nihon suiri shōsetsu shi*, vol. 1, 269.

quickly replied with the same words of excitement and requested to write a recommendation of Ranpo's work upon its publication.[9] The result was his introduction to "Ni-sen dōka" that appeared in the same issue as the story (May 1923), in which he praises the story and, in particular, the secret code presented by Ranpo. Fuboku writes:

> Although he may have got the hint for the copper coin trick from foreign detective novels, his ability to connect Braille and the six-character code is nothing short of remarkable. On this point, even Poe in his grave must be in awe. In the past, there have not been many secret codes in Japanese that are ingenious, and it can be said that this secret code is the finest example of all secret codes that have appeared up to now.[10]

As Fuboku's praise would have us believe, the newness of "Ni-sen dōka" rests on the presentation and deciphering of a secret message written in the ***kanji*** (character) system, rather than in the alphabet system, exhibiting Ranpo's successful effort to adopt and utilize past works of Western detective fiction in a Japanese context. Indeed, direct references appear in "Ni-sen dōka": "If this were French or English, I would have no problem just by searching for the letter 'e' like Poe's 'The Gold-Bug'" and "I am no Sherlock Holmes, but I also know at least 160 ways to write a secret message," alluding to Holmes's comment on his knowledge of

---

9. Beginning in 1922, when he was forced to retire from his position in the Department of Medicine at Tokyo Imperial University due to illness, Fuboku published various articles about medicine as well as detective fiction, including the essay "Kagaku-teki kenkyū to tantei shōsetsu" (Scientific research and detective fiction), published in the supplementary February issue of *Shinseinen* in 1922, which advocated that detective fiction must "found itself first and foremost on contemporary science." Fuboku also published scientific tracts such as "Doku oyobi dokusatsu no kenkyū" (Study of poison and murder by poison; October 1922–January 1923), "Satsujin ron" (Theory on murder; March–November 1923), and "Hanzai bungaku kenkyū" (Study of crime literature; June 1925–June 1926) in *Shinseinen* and set the scientific tone of the magazine during this period.

10. Kozakai, "'Ni-sen dōka' o yomu," 8. In the advance billing to the April 1923 original detective fiction issue of *Shinseinen*, Uson had also expressed a similar sentiment to that of Fuboku: "'Detective fiction that does not fall short of foreign works must arise in Japan'—we have always said. And finally, such a brilliant work has appeared. A work that truly does not fall short of the great foreign works, or rather an utterly original work whose strengths, in some sense, are even more exceptional than the works of foreign writers has been born. This is the work of Edogawa Ranpo that will be introduced in this issue" (Cited in Nakajima Kawatarō, *Nihon suiri shōsetsu shi*, vol. 1, 273).

secret codes in "The Adventure of the Dancing Men" (1903).[11] Such references leave no doubt that Ranpo modeled this story after the secret message stories of Poe and Conan Doyle and sought to compete with their legacy. And it was precisely such an attempt on the part of Ranpo—one-upping Western writers in a literary genre that is emblematic of their culture of science and technology—that led Fuboku to embrace "Ni-sen dōka" as a sign that "there exists in Japan a detective fiction writer who has reached the fort held by the famous foreign writers."[12]

But this is not to say that Fuboku had nothing but praise for Ranpo's story, for he chooses to end a string of high praises in his introduction to "Ni-sen dōka" with the following criticism: "however, it seems a bit 'coincidental' that the secret message spells out '*gojōdan*' (joke, farce) when every eighth word is read."[13] That is, for Fuboku, who believed that in detective fiction "the resolution and the development of the crime must always be natural" and "the coincidental, the supernatural, and the artificial are not permitted," this part of Ranpo's work failed to satisfy the criteria of 'good' detective fiction and represented a 'slip' in his creative process.[14] As it will become clear, however, Fuboku misses the point completely here. There is nothing "coincidental" about this 'slip.' In fact, this 'slip' was not a slip at all but constituted a part of Ranpo's larger narrative strategy in "Ni-sen dōka" that was not a simple bettering of the framework of Western analytical detective fiction introduced by Poe's Dupin trilogy and instituted by Conan Doyle's Sherlock Holmes tales, as Fuboku's review as well as Ranpo's own text may suggest, but a radical problematization of its foundational tenets.

Employing the first-person narration in a memoir format, "Ni-sen dōka" mimics the narrative form and structure found in the detective fiction of Poe and Conan Doyle.[15] Like Watson, who is always confused

---

11. Edogawa, "Ni-sen dōka," in *Edogawa Ranpo zenshū*, vol. 1, 119. All subsequent reference to this source will appear in the text in parentheses.

12. Kozakai, "'Ni-sen dōka' o yomu," 7.

13. Ibid., 8.

14. Ibid.

15. "Ni-sen dōka" begins with the narrator's recounting of a crime that he has read in the newspaper. A man, masquerading as a newspaper reporter, has stolen money from a factory for electrical machinery, but through the persistent legwork of one police detective, the criminal is finally apprehended. However, the criminal, while confessing to the crime, refuses to disclose the whereabouts of the stolen money, and to this day the money has remained undiscovered. After telling this story, the narrator describes the strange behavior of his roommate Matsu-

about Holmes's actions, the narrator appears confused at the strange behavior of his roommate Matsumura at the start of the story—"for some reason, Matsumura became deeply lost in thought" (13); "But Matsumura's behavior in this case was so strange that even I was forced into silence" (14). As the story develops, however, the narrator begins to act suspicious; that is, he appears to know more than he is telling us—"As for this strange behavior of Matsumura, I had a deep interest, the reason for which I have not disclosed to you readers" (15). After Matsumura gives his explanation of how he had come to discover the location of the hidden loot of the so-called gentleman thief, the narrator confirms this suspicion by revealing himself as the one who had orchestrated everything based on the newspaper story on which Matsumura's deductions were based. Disguised as Watson in the course of the narrative, the narrator emerges in the end as Conan Doyle, as a detective fiction writer who manipulates Matsumura, an unknowing actor in a farce authored by the narrator, into playing Sherlock Holmes.[16]

"Ni-sen dōka," thus, is about how the narrator plays on Matsumura's love of detective fiction to lead him through an adventure that he has read many times over, and, in so doing, the narrator, rather than bringing the fictional world of detective fiction to the 'real' world (as a story of the application of the scientific method found in Western detective fiction), reconstructs the 'real' world as the world of fiction (as a story of how the narrator consciously arranged the 'reality' in order to make it applicable to the scientific method found in Western detective fiction).

---

mura who eventually asserts that he found the money that the thief in the newspaper had hidden, delineating in detail how he discovered and decoded a secret message written by the thief. Ultimately, however, the narrator confesses to Matsumura that this is all a farce set up by the narrator himself, that it was he who wrote the secret message and he who had left the fake money at a place designated by the secret message for Matsumura to discover.

16. The basic plot structure of "Ni-sen dōka" bears striking resemblance to Tanizaki Jun'ichirō's "Hakuchū kigo" (The ghost in broad daylight; 1918). In Tanizaki's work, the narrator's friend discovers a code, which he decodes as designating the time and place of a murder. The narrator and his friend arrive at the designated place and witness a murder from a peephole. Becoming enraptured by the female murderer, the friend begins his search for her around Tokyo. While his search is successful, the friend soon realizes that he will be the next victim of this murderess. But before he is murdered, he realizes that another friend of the narrator had paid this woman to dupe the friend into discovering the code and witness the murder.

Matsumura was able to 'solve' the mystery of the hidden loot only because the narrator intended for him to do so. The narrator's farce requires that Matsumura decipher the secret message, just like a detective story requires the detective to solve the crime. If this were not the case, there would be no story. In order to ensure that there will be a 'story,' the narrator must plant various clues to create an artificial world: it is he who places the two-sen copper coin on Matsumura's desk for him to discover and he who tells a false story about the relationship between the tobacconist's daughter and a prison caterer to intimate a possible connection of the copper coin with the gentleman thief.

Given the artificial nature of the secret message and Matsumura's treasure hunting to which its discovery led, it is clear that Fuboku's criticism of "Ni-sen dōka"—"it seems a bit 'coincidental' that the secret message spells out '*gojōdan*' when every eighth word is read"—is wholly unwarranted. The fact that the message spells out "*gojōdan*" is coincidental only if the message was written by the thief with the intention of communicating to his accomplice on the whereabouts of the hidden loot. But this is not the case. It was the narrator who wrote the message, and, as the author of the message, the narrator is free to decide not only what the message says but also how many ways the message can be read. The fact that the message can be read as "*gojōdan*" is not "coincidental" but necessary, precisely because the narrator intended the secret message to be read in two ways so that he can inscribe within it the function of the message within his farce (the whereabouts of the hidden money) as well as its function outside the farce (to reveal that the whole thing was a farce; that the message was just a prop in the farce).

In playing the role of the detective fiction writer to turn Matsumura into a puppet who dances to his tune, moreover, the narrator makes a further claim, as his comments after listening to Matsumura's analysis of the case illustrate:

> Your imagination is truly splendid. You have accomplished a great task. I am sure that my respect for your mind will increase many folds. Indeed, as you say, I cannot compete with your intelligence. But do you believe reality to be that romantic? . . . In other words, do you think that gentleman thief had that sort of wit? I admit that your suppositions are truly impeccable if they were in a novel. But the world is more realistic than a novel (23).

In contrasting the real world with the fictional world, the narrator sets up a dichotomy between the two and locates the place of 'detecting' in the latter. It is not simply that Matsumura's analysis of the case does not hold true because the clues on which it was based were invented by the narrator. Rather, Matsumura's analytical process, modeled after Sherlock Holmes or Legrand in Poe's "Gold-bug," is itself faulty because such models are a product of an author who orchestrates their cases as stories with an imaginative mind and detailed care. The 'real' world, in contrast, is devoid of such authors and thus does not yield the materials for detective fiction.

If "Ni-sen dōka," in its conflation of the narrator and the author, suggested the artificial and fantastical nature of the world where the act of 'detecting' yields actual results, then Ranpo's next story "Ichimai no kippu" goes a step further in its criticism of the world of Western analytical fiction by focusing on one of its fundamental tenets: the truth-value that physical evidence yields through the analysis of the detective.[17] Centering around the student Sōda's refutation of the theories put forth by Detective Kuroda regarding the truth behind the death of a renowned professor's wife, "Ichimai no kippu" can be considered a fairly 'traditional' detective story. The analyses of physical evidence play a crucial role in the investigation of the crime, and the difference between the theories of Sōda and Kuroda, as Sōda readily admits, is not one of quality but quantity: "There was no error in his [Kuroda's] reasoning method. His observations were simply lacking in their materials."[18] That is, while Sōda's refutation of Kuroda's theory implicating the professor in his wife's murder involves the analysis of various physical clues that Kuroda had overlooked, their analyses exist within the same epistemological paradigm, namely, what might be called the positivistic paradigm instituted by the Sherlock Holmes tales, in which the truth is reached based on the analysis of physical evidence, including witness accounts.

Just as the surprising ending of "Ni-sen dōka" required a reinterpretation of the text, however, the ending of "Ichimai no kippu" necessi-

17. In "Ichimai no kippu," a wife of a renowned professor has been killed by a train, and because a suicide note was found on her body, the police determines her death to be a case of suicide. Kuroda, a famous police detective, however, gathers various evidence that ultimately implicates her husband in the murder of his wife. As a result, the professor is arrested, and Kuroda gains a reputation as the Japanese Sherlock Holmes. Sōda, a young man who happened to be present at the scene of the crime, however, believes in the professor's innocence, and through various clues that the police and Detective Kuroda had overlooked but he had discovered, Sōda overturns Kuroda's conclusions and establishes the innocence of the professor.

18. Edogawa, "Ichimai no kippu," in *Edogawa Ranpo zenshū*, vol. 1, 35. All subsequent references to this source will appear in the text in parentheses.

tates a re-reading of the text in terms of its ending as Sōda's response to his friend's commendation of his ability as a detective after the exoneration of the professor makes clear:

"Would you correct that word detective with daydreamer? In fact, I have no idea how far my daydreaming will go. For example, if the suspect was not the professor who I greatly admire, I may even have daydreamed that Professor Tomita was the criminal who killed his wife. And I may have refuted all the powerful evidence I had put forth myself. Do you understand what I mean? If you think deeply, all the evidence I listed as if they were true is ambiguous and can be used to imagine other situations beside this one. The PL Company's ticket is like the only reliable piece of evidence, but that's not true either. For example, what if I did not find it underneath that rock in question but picked it up next to the rock." Sōda stared at the face of the other who could not quite understand and snickered amusedly (40).

Through Sōda's comments revealing his prejudiced motivation for solving the crime that may have led to his tampering of evidence, "Ichimai no kippu" questions the one-to-one relationship between cause and effect whose reinstatement from a state of numerous suspicions and multiple interpretations constitutes the critical function of the detective within the Western analytical detective story paradigm.[19] For Sōda, the interpretation of physical evidence is just one of many possibilities and is founded on his admiration for the suspect, and physical evidence—the scientific source of 'truth' in Western analytical detective fiction—is a rhetorical tool by which he convinces others of the 'truthfulness' of his claim. This is why he is a daydreamer and not a detective: his interpretation is based on a wish and functions to rationally support this wish rather than to rationally explain the evidence. The exoneration of the professor, then, proves not that his interpretations were correct but rather that they were more plausible than the ones that Kuroda offered; that is, Sōda succeeds in letting others partake in his fantasy.

Importantly, Sōda intimates that such a state of things is not simply a result of his personal prejudice but a universal fact—that all interpretations of physical evidence are motivated, confused, and/or arbitrary, being no different epistemologically from a fantasy—by likening Kuroda

19. For example, Franco Moretti writes: "The clue is, therefore, that particular element of the story in which the link between signifier and signified is altered. It is a signifier that always has several signifieds and thus produces *numerous* suspicions. . . . The detective . . . will have to reinstate the univocal links between signifiers and signifieds" ("Clues," 146).

to a novelist ("Mr. Kuroda may be a novelist but he is not a detective" [33]) and thereby to himself who is a "daydreamer." For Sōda, they remain "daydreamers" and "novelists" precisely because they are involved in creating stories and not truths (just as it was the case in "Ni-sen dōka"), never able to escape the fictional world of detective stories and the positivistic paradigm that these stories espouse. (Sōda comments on Kuroda: "he's one of those guys who have read a detective story or two in his days" [30].) As Sōda shows through his utilization of the train ticket for the purpose of convincing the authorities and the world of the professor's innocence, physical evidence can be tampered with and used as a rhetorical tool, and, as such, it always allows for multiple interpretations. In this sense, Sōda, in calling Kuroda a "novelist," is not claiming that Kuroda's theories are false beyond a shadow of a doubt. Rather, his claim is that it is impossible to talk about true and false within the positivistic epistemological paradigm based on the interpretation of physical evidence because this paradigm, at least for 'detectives' like Sōda and Kuroda, has the fictional world of detective stories as its source.

As the above analysis shows, central to Ranpo's early stories was the employment of what can be called a framing technique through which a story is constructed within the story by a surprise ending that demands radical reinterpretation of the preceding text. Through this process, they turn the aim of Western analytical detective fiction on its head by exposing and questioning its ideological and epistemological underpinnings. As the following passage from his essay "Gakuya banashi" (Inside story; 1929) makes clear, such a deconstructive project was prompted by Ranpo's search for the new within the historical condition as a belated experimenter of detective fiction:

> Tricks of detective stories have been exhausted almost completely by foreign writers. Even if one thinks that a trick is new, it is often the case that it had already been used by someone else. So I came up with one way to avoid this; namely, to use a famous trick that are known to many people as a foil by turning them upside down. Therefore, the more commonplace the trick the better. The readers would read in comfort thinking that they know the trick from somewhere else. But then I turn the trick upside down. Precisely because the trick is a famous one, the effect is great. In other words, what I painstakingly thought of was a trick that existed on the reverse side of these tricks.[20]

---

20. Edogawa, "Gakuya banashi," 38. For Ranpo's relationship to the tradition of Western detective stories, see Silver, *Purloined Letters*, 132–35.

As he acknowledges in this and other autobiographical essays and self-criticisms, Ranpo often used famous tricks from past detective stories—that is, Western detective stories—to produce new tricks that cleverly reversed their intentions. Such employment of past detective fiction was motivated by the awareness on the part of Ranpo regarding the 'long' tradition of Western detective stories and the expectations of Japanese readers that had been produced through their encounters with translations of Western works in such magazines as *Shinseinen*. And if we can return to our discussion from the previous chapter, then Ranpo presents us with an alternate way to deal with the belatedness of the Japanese subject within the relationship between Japan and the West, a subject position that became the impetus to turn to crime for the Western educated protagonists of Akutagawa's "Kaika no satsujin" and Tanizaki's "Futari no geijutsuka." In other words, Ranpo, rather than confronting extant detective stories as stumbling blocks in his creative endeavor, utilized them to his advantage—exemplifying how historical circumstances affect literary form—and, in so doing, he maximized the surprise effect of his endings, as seen in "Ni-sen dōka" and "Ichimai no kippu," precisely because they overturned the reader's expectations, which the story had carefully constructed and guided in the course of the narrative.

To the extent that the 'detective' never reveals the 'truth' by employing his method, however, "Ni-sen dōka" and "Ichimai no kippu" are not detective stories at all in the strict sense of the word: Matsumura never discovers the thief's hidden loot, and Sōda never determines whether the professor's wife committed suicide or was murdered. Rather, these stories are about readers of detective fiction and function as metafiction to expose the artificiality of the world of Western analytical detective fiction. These stories describe how the seemingly rational and logical discourse of the detective story can be utilized to manipulate people for comical effect ("Ni-sen dōka") or to convince people of one's biased opinion ("Ichimai no kippu"). But in problematizing detective fiction as rhetoric of deception, does Ranpo kill it off in these stories? Is Ranpo's aim to expose the non-referentiality of all detective fiction and to destroy its myth altogether? According to "Ichimai no kippu," such is not the case. In separating the novelist and daydreamer from the detective, Sōda reserves the word 'detective' to signify someone who exposes the 'truth,' someone who eliminates the possibility that his conclusion may be fiction, and to the extent that this is impossible within the positivistic paradigm, the detective signifies someone who operates within a different epistemological paradigm.

The Psychological Method of Akechi Kogorō and the Burden of Proof

Ranpo's first Akechi Kogorō story—"D-zaka no satsujin jiken," which appeared about a year and a half after "Ichimai no kippu" and the Great Kantō Earthquake—introduces such a detective and begins to reconstruct what he had destroyed in "Ni-sen dōka" and "Ichimai no kippu."[21] Like these two stories, "D-zaka no satsujin jiken" tells a story within a story: the events leading up to the first-person narrator's accusation of his friend Akechi as the murderer of Akechi's childhood acquaintance who had married a used bookstore owner in Tokyo, an accusation based on the positivistic paradigm, and Akechi's rebuttal to the accusation, which problematizes this paradigm and completes its rejection that began with "Ni-sen dōka." What differentiates this work from the other two, however, is that Akechi does not merely deny the validity of the detective's method based on the positivistic paradigm, but he also formulates a new method of detection that operates outside this paradigm.

The narrator's accusation of Akechi is based primarily on two witnesses who claim that they saw a man between the sliding doors of the used bookstore around the time of the crime. Because the sliding door leads to the room where Akechi and the narrator, who had been conversing at a café across the street from the bookstore, discovered the victim's body, the police believe that these witnesses, who entered the bookstore together, have seen the murderer. But they are not much help as witnesses. The only information they can provide about the murderer, beside the fact that it was a man, is what he was wearing, and even on this simple point, their accounts conflict: one witness claims that the man was wearing a black robe and the other claims that the man was wearing a white one. From these conflicting accounts, the narrator, unlike the police who are completely at a loss, reasons that the conflicting accounts are a result of the witnesses' relative position in respect to the gap be-

---

21. "D-zaka no satsujin jiken" tells the story of a murder of a used bookstore owner's wife, a childhood friend of Akechi's, whose body Akechi and the narrator discover. The police are called in, and both Akechi and the narrator are questioned as witnesses. The narrator, an ardent reader of detective fiction, begins to investigate the case on his own and becomes suspicious of Akechi based on several observations. Ultimately, the narrator goes to Akechi's apartment and confronts him about the case, but Akechi disproves the narrator's analysis and proffers a theory of his own, which turns out to be the correct one, as the owner of the noodle shop next door to the used bookstore turns himself in to the police.

tween the sliding doors and comes to the conclusion that the murderer was wearing a striped robe, similar to what Akechi was wearing on the day of the crime. With Akechi surfacing as a suspect, the narrator attributes Akechi's urging to go into the room where they were to discover the body as a ploy to cover up the fingerprints that he had left behind when he committed the murder and interprets his failure to mention to the police that he was a childhood friend of the victim as a sign that he wanted this relationship to remain hidden from the authorities.

When the narrator confronts Akechi with these charges, however, Akechi begins to laugh and states:

> Your ideas are very interesting. I am happy that I have discovered a friend like you. What is regrettable, however, is that your reasoning is too superficial and too materialistic. For example, did you consider internally and psychologically my relationship with that woman [the victim] or what kind of childhood friends we were? Whether I had a romantic relationship with that woman in the past or whether I resent her now? Were you not able to hypothesize on these points?[22]

Here is the first suggestion of Akechi's detective method, which involves a turn away from physical evidence to the psychological. But before he expands on the nature of psychological evidence, Akechi criticizes the eyewitness accounts that form the basis of the narrator's suspicion not by questioning the two eyewitness accounts of this case in particular but by refuting the validity of witness accounts in general. For this purpose, Akechi draws on an experiment conducted by the German psychologist Hugo Münsterberg (1863–1916) and published in his *Psychology and Crime* (1908). In the experiment, a short scuffle between two men and the resulting 'murder' of one man were enacted in front of a group of scientists, after which the description of the murderer's hat is collected from the scientists. The result showed numerous conflicting accounts with only 10 percent of the witnesses able to accurately describe the murderer's hat. After describing this experiment to the narrator, Akechi concludes: "Observations and memories of human beings are something truly unreliable" (111).

In refuting the reliability of eyewitness accounts—central to Western analytical detective stories, in general, and works of Conan Doyle, in particular, where most of Holmes's theories are formed through accounts divulged by his clients at their first meeting—Akechi makes a

22. Edogawa, "D-zaka no satsujin jiken," in *Edogawa Ranpo zenshū*, vol. 1, 109–10. All subsequent references to this source will appear in the text in parentheses.

further claim.[23] Mimicking the words of Sōda in "Ichimai no kippu," Akechi rejects the validity of physical evidence as a whole and suggests a new method of detection. He states: "Physical evidence can mean anything depending on the interpretation. The best detective method is to penetrate psychologically the deepest part of a person's soul" (112). After this articulation of his method of detection, which is highly evocative of Tsubouchi Shōyō's definition of the task of the novelist in *Shōsetsu shinzui*, Akechi describes his investigation of the case. Drawing on his observation that the wives of the used bookstore owner and the noodle shop owner both had fresh wounds on their bodies, Akechi questions the used bookstore owner and discovers that his wife was a masochist. From this discovery, Akechi harbors a suspicion for the noodle shop owner and questions him. It is at this point that Akechi offers more information on his method, which involves a form of questioning that subtly incorporates a word-association test into dialogue.

But in this story, Akechi only offers a vague definition of his method, as he quickly moves to the description of its application, which is just as vague: "I talked to the noodle shop owner about a variety of topics. Very mundane everyday gossip at that. And I examined his psychological responses. This is a very delicate problem of the psyche, and, as such, it's very complicated, so I will give you the details some other time, but the result was that I had reached a firm conviction. That is, I had found the culprit" (113). And true to Akechi's words—"I will give you the de-

---

23. A typical Sherlock Holmes story begins with the arrival of a client to Baker Street, followed by the client's own account of his or her situation. In this recounting by the client, Holmes only judges the honesty of the client, and his or her reliability as a witness is never questioned. For example, in "The Adventure of the Engineer's Thumb" (1891), Holmes and others, after hearing the story of a hydraulic engineer whose thumb has been cut off, travel to the scene of the crime. The only clue to locate the mysterious house where the crime took place is the engineer's word that the house was about twelve miles from Eyford Station and that the horse drawn to the carriage looked "fresh" and "glossy." After others give their opinions on which way they should go, Holmes states that they are all wrong, claiming that the house in question will be found in the immediate vicinity of the station. Here is Holmes's logic: "Six out and six back. Nothing simpler. You say yourself that the horse was fresh and glossy when you got in. How could it be that if it had gone twelve miles over heavy roads?" (Doyle, "The Adventure of the Engineer's Thumb," in *Sherlock Holmes*, vol. 1, 386). Of course, they soon realize that Holmes's theory was correct, but more importantly for the present discussion, so was the engineer's description of the horse.

tails some other time"—Ranpo articulates in detail the psychological method of detection in his next Akechi Kogorō story, "Shinri shiken," which appeared a month after "D-zaka no satsujin jiken."[24]

Focusing not only on the detective but on the criminal Fukiya to follow the events leading up to his arrest, "Shinri shiken" differs from Ranpo's earlier detective stories in narrative structure with its employment of what he calls the inverted detective story (*tōjo tantei shōsetsu*) format, in which the story is told chronologically from the point of view of the criminal.[25] The readers witness the student Fukiya kill the landlady of his friend Saitō's apartment for money and, thus, their focus shifts from the 'whodunit' aspect of detective fiction to its epistemological aspect. To highlight this shift in focus, Ranpo utilizes a mediating figure between the detective and the criminal in Prosecutor Kasamori, who harbors suspicions against Fukiya but is at a loss on how to prove his guilt, leading him to summon the help of Akechi.

---

24. "Shinri shiken" tells the story of a landlady's murder and the ensuing investigation of her killer. The discovery of her body is quickly followed by the arrest of her tenant Saitō, who found the body and reported the murder to the police, because a large sum of money was found in his possession. In police custody, Saitō confesses to stealing the landlady's money but denies that he is her murderer. About a month after the murder, Kasamori, the prosecutor in the case, learns that Saitō's friend, Fukiya, has turned in a large sum of money to the police on the day of the murder. With this new knowledge, Kasamori begins to suspect Fukiya because Fukiya, according to Saitō's testimony, also knew the location of the money. To test his suspicions, Kasamori subjects Fukiya and Saitō to word-association and pulse tests. The results of the tests point to Saitō as the culprit, but Kasamori cannot get rid of his suspicion of Fukiya. It is at this point that Akechi becomes involved in the story, as a friend of Kasamori. Akechi analyzes Fukiya's result of the word-association test and concludes that Fukiya had prepared for the test in advance, and Akechi and Kasamori decide to question Fukiya one more time. It is at this meeting that Akechi succeeds in making Fukiya confess his murder of the landlady.

25. Inverted detective story format was often employed by the detective story writer R. Austin Freeman, who was popular in Japan from the Meiji period. Indeed, it was a lecture in 1922 by the detective fiction fan and literary critic Baba Kochō (1869–1940) on Freeman's inverted detective stories that prompted Ranpo, who attended the lecture, to think seriously about writing and publishing detective stories. For Ranpo's analysis of the inverted detective story format, see Edogawa, "Tōjo tantei shōsetsu" and "Tōjo tantei shōsetsu saisetsu" in *Gen'eijō*, 58–65, 66–85, respectively.

Analyzing the results of word-association test that Kasamori administered to both Fukiya and Saitō, Akechi speculates that Fukiya had prepared for the test in advance, but by shifting his focus from the response time to key words to the responses themselves, Akechi discovers the key to proving Fukiya's guilt. Akechi observes that Fukiya, in the word-association test, has responded to the word "*e*" (painting) with the word "*byōbu*" (folding screen). This response strikes Akechi as peculiar and suggests to him that Fukiya has formed a psychological association between the words "painting" and "folding screen" for some specific reason. Akechi surmises that the source of this association is the folding screen in the landlady's room, which was damaged when she struggled against her murderer. If Fukiya knows about this particular folding screen, Akechi reasons, he must be lying about the fact that he has only visited the victim's room once a few days before the murder because the folding screen was placed in her room only a day prior to the murder.

Based on these observations and conjectures, which the readers do not know at this point in the narrative, Akechi formulates a fake story and tells it to Fukiya, who has been called to Kasamori's house under the false pretense that Saitō has been convicted of the landlady's murder. The false story concerns whether or not the folding screen was damaged during the murder, and Akechi asks Fukiya to make a statement on its condition when he visited her a few days before the murder. Of course, it is a trap, for if Fukiya's statement that he had visited the landlady's room only once is true, then he would have had no opportunity to have known the existence of the folding screen.[26] But Fukiya, feeling at ease from the news of Saitō's conviction, falls into Akechi's hands by stating that there was no damage on the folding screen when he saw it during his visit to the landlady's room. It is at this moment that Akechi reveals his observations and conjectures against Fukiya, including his observation on the psychological association Fukiya has formed between the words "painting" and "folding screen," to expose the falsehood of Fukiya's testimony. Stunned by Akechi's observations, Fukiya signs a statement of confession.

---

26. Befitting the story's similarities to *Crime and Punishment*, this trap laid out by Akechi is highly evocative of the one that Porfiry laids for Raskolnikov in their first conversation, as we saw in Chapter 3 of this book. The difference between the two stories is that Ranpo's requires an extra step, the discovery of the specific associations that Fukiya had formed with the word *byōbu*, which reveals his possible involvement in the crime and informs the suitable subject matter of the trap.

In "D-zaka no satsujin jiken" and "Shinri shiken," Ranpo proposes a detective's method founded upon a new epistemological paradigm, in which the psychological intricacies of the suspect, rather than the physical and circumstantial evidence of the case, take precedence in the determination of the 'truth' of the crime. But as the development from suspicion to confirmation of guilt in these stories intimates, there existed from its inception a fundamental problem in Ranpo's epistemological project that investigates the ways in which the 'truth' surrounding an individual—the 'truth' of the crime—can be known by a third party to the criminal relationship between the criminal and the victim. For example, after Akechi identifies the noodle-shop owner as the culprit in "D-zaka no satsujin jiken," and despite his complete confidence in the accuracy of his analysis, Akechi is quick to point out the crucial shortcomings of his psychological method. He tells the narrator: "But there is not a shred of physical evidence. So, I cannot appeal to the police. Even if I did appeal, they probably will not take me up on it" (113). In other words, with the refutation of physical evidence as unreliable and prone to multiple interpretation and psychological evidence as lawfully impermissible, Akechi's psychological method ultimately requires the confession of the culprit for his or her conviction in a court of law.[27]

At the same time, what is equally important here is that Akechi's method, at least in "D-zaka no satsujin jiken," does not require the confession of the culprit in order to determine the 'truth,' that is, to reach a firm belief on the identity of the criminal, and Akechi's method is not a rhetorical tool, as was the case for Sōda's analysis in "Ichimai no kippu," but an epistemological one: for Akechi, "to penetrate psychologically the deepest part of a person's soul" is to see the 'truth.' In "Shinri shiken," however, Ranpo, in providing a detailed description of Akechi's psychological method in action, is forced to articulate the tenuous relationship between suspicion, knowledge, and conviction that naturally arises from his turn toward the psychological. After examining the word-association test results and observing the peculiar association that Fukiya displays between "painting" and "folding screen," Akechi tells Kasamori: "From the result of the word-association test, I think that Fukiya is the culprit.

27. Although many of the Sherlock Holmes stories also conclude with the confession of the criminal, these confessions are not necessary for the establishment of the criminal's guilt, functioning only to demonstrate the correctness of Holmes's theory to Watson, the police, and the reader.

But I still cannot say for certain that he is."[28] As this passage reveals, the observation of a psychological association is not enough to clear Akechi of all doubt that Fukiya is indeed the culprit, forcing Akechi to fabricate the story of the folding screen. But at least in "Shinri shiken," Ranpo seems to salvage Akechi's psychological method to "penetrate . . . the deepest part of a person's soul," since an argument can be made that Akechi reaches his conclusion regarding Fukiya's guilt prior to his confession when Fukiya makes a false statement to confirm the source of psychological association that he has formed between the words "painting" and "folding screen." As "Yaneura no sanposha," which appeared six months after "Shinri shiken" reveals, however, this separation between epistemological knowledge of the suspect's guilt and his confession is problematic at best, and it is precisely the failure to maintain this separation between belief and conviction and between knowledge and confession that marks the collapse of Ranpo's epistemological project.[29]

Similar in its narrative structure to "Shinri shiken," "Yaneura no sanposha" employs an inverted detective story format to tell Gōda Saburō's murder of his neighbor Endō, but their difference in focus is already clear from the first sentences of respective works. "Shinri shiken" begins: "The details of the reasons why Fukiya Seiichirō had thought of committing the horrible crime which will be told below are unknown. Even if they were known, they do not matter too much to this story."[30] And here is "Yaneura no sanposha": "It was probably one type of mental illness. This world was not fun at all to Gōda Saburō although he tried

---

28. Edogawa, "Shinri shiken," in *Edogawa Ranpo zenshū*, vol. 1, 131.

29. "Yaneura no sanposha" tells the story of the death of Endō, a dental student, and the ensuing investigation. Because Endō died from an overdose of morphine and a bottle of morphine was discovered in his room, the police quickly conclude that his death was a suicide. However, Akechi, who happens to have a friend in the deceased's building, visits this friend and starts investigating. The friend, Saburō, introduces Akechi to Endō's neighbors, and from the testimony that Endō's alarm clock sounded on the morning after his suicide, Akechi begins to harbor a suspicion that Endō was murdered. A few days after his first visit, Akechi surprises Saburō by exiting out of Saburō's closet, which leads to the attic where Saburō had been enjoying his daily 'walks' peeping into the lives of his neighbors. Before Saburō can regain his composure, Akechi interrogates him and ultimately induces his confession of Endō's murder.

30. Edogawa, "Shinri shiken," in *Edogawa Ranpo zenshū*, vol. 1, 117.

various hobbies and jobs."[31] Preparing for the story's exploration of the method of detection through which Fukiya is discovered as the culprit, the opening of "Shinri shiken" de-emphasizes Fukiya's motives, and thus his character; "Yaneura no sanposha" starts by doing the opposite, drawing the attention of the readers to Saburō's peculiar nature.

The rest of the story reflects such a beginning, as "Yaneura no sanposha" devotes most of its pages to Saburō's perverse activities, including the 'walks' that Saburō takes in the attic space of his building and the lives of its denizens that he observes during these 'walks,' and the peculiar format of an inverted detective story becomes a commonplace narrative structure of literature, in which a story is told chronologically through third-person narration.[32] Given such a shift in focus, then, it makes sense that many contemporary and future critics view this story as the turning point in Ranpo's detective fiction, which, as we saw in the introduction to this chapter, Hirabayashi describes as a shift from "healthy" to "unhealthy." This is not to say, however, that Ranpo abandons his exploration of how a detective can reach positive knowledge about the guilt of the criminal in this story. Rather, "Yaneura no sanposha" marks the turning point in Ranpo's detective fiction because this story marks the logical conclusion of the epistemological project that he began in "Ni-sen dōka."

Whereas the importance of "Shinri shiken" within the framework of Ranpo's epistemological project rested on its detailed articulation of Akechi's method of detection, "Yaneura no sanposha" makes its contribution to Ranpo's project by exposing the target site of Akechi's method and its powers. In "Yaneura no sanposha," Akechi becomes suspicious of Saburō as Endō's murderer from an observation of a psychological association that is similar to the one which Fukiya makes. Upon his first visit to Saburō's building during which he asks Saburō to assist him with the investigation, Akechi observes that Saburō has quit smoking cigarettes:

---

31. Edogawa, "Yanuera no sanposha," in *Edogawa Ranpo zenshū*, vol. 1, 249. All subsequent references to this source will appear in the text in parentheses.

32. This is not to say that "Yaneura no sanposha" marks the first work in which Ranpo investigates the criminal mind. In his works such as "Sōseiji" (Twins; October 1924) and "Akai heya" (The red room; April 1925), Ranpo had already depicted the workings of a criminal mind. However, "Yaneura no sanposha," as a work in which his epistemological project fails, signals the end of a period in which a separation between detective fiction and his stories of imagination can be maintained.

"You haven't smoked at all for quite a while, but did you quit?"

"Oh, how strange. I had totally forgotten about it. Even though you are smoking, I had no desire to have one myself."

"Since when?"

"Not for two or three days, I think. Yes, I bought the pack I have here now on Sunday so I haven't smoked a single cigarette in three days. I don't know what's happened."

"Then you haven't smoked since the day that Endō died" (270–71).

It is from this fact, which even Saburō himself cannot explain, that Akechi begins to form his theory about Endō's death. Akechi, who knows that the poison bottle used to kill Endō had spilled on a pack of cigarettes next to his bedding, reasons that Saburō has quit smoking because he has formed a psychological association between cigarettes and poison/death and that this is only possible if he were Endō's killer and witnessed the poison spill on the cigarettes. Unlike in "Shinri shiken," Akechi's conjecture requires an extra step to hypothesize the psychological association, which was verbalized in the word-association test in Fukiya's case, from the change in Saburō's physical behavior.

But instead of devising a trick to confirm the source of the psychological association as in "Shinri shiken," Akechi fabricates a completely unrelated story to induce a confession from Saburō. Emerging from Saburō's closet, which leads to the attic space, Akechi surprises Saburō and states:

> *I was just mimicking you*. . . . Anyway, this is your button isn't it? . . . I checked the other lodgers, but there is no one who is missing this button. Yeah, it's that shirt. Look, the second button is missing. . . . This shirt button is a very peculiar type so it must be yours. In any event, where do you think I found this button? I found it in the attic space and above Endō's room at that. . . . Weren't you the one who murdered Endō? (272; Ranpo's emphasis).

Of course, the button is not Saburō's, but a piece of physical evidence fabricated by Akechi, who had observed a missing button on Saburō's shirt during his prior visit, to induce Saburō's confession. But Saburō, who quickly glances at his shirt only to find a button missing, believes in Akechi's lie and confesses to Endō's murder.

As this course of development reveals, there is no connection between Akechi's observation of a psychological association and the way in which he confirms his suspicion. The connection between the observed psychological association of the suspect and the fabricated story, which functioned to maintain the thin separation between Akechi's knowledge of the criminal's identity and the criminal's confession, has been severed.

In "Yaneura no sanposha," it is Saburō's confession that confirms Akechi's suspicion of Saburō and of the source of observed psychological association. Akechi makes this point clear after Saburō's confession: "The more I investigated, the more the situation pointed in your direction. But unfortunately, there was no conclusive proof. And so I thought up this performance" (274). In the end, Akechi's observation of the psychological association, which represented his detective's method "to penetrate psychologically the deepest part of a person's soul," becomes relegated to one of many kinds of circumstantial evidence that produces his suspicion for a specific suspect: in "Yaneura no sanposha," truth becomes confession.

It is in this sense that "Yaneura no sanposha" marks the collapse of Ranpo's epistemological project. No longer is the detective's focus on the process of detection, the process of arriving at a positive knowledge of the Other, but on the way in which the detective can induce the confession of the criminal. At the same time, however, Ranpo sheds light on "the deepest part of a person's soul" that constitutes the subject—the unconscious—through his description of the psychological association that Saburō has formed. In "Shinri shiken," Ranpo, through Fukiya's psychological association between the words "painting" and "folding screen," describes explicitly the gap that exists between a subject's natural or spontaneous response and his or her intended or conscious response and, in so doing, implicitly exposes the inability on the part of the consciousness to control completely the subject's actions and behavior. But the psychological association in this story involves the unconscious only partially: it is unconscious because Fukiya is not aware that he has made such an association, but it is not unconscious because, as he realizes upon being pointed out by Akechi, he did see the landlady damage the folding screen, the source of the psychological association. Thus, it remains unclear whether the exposure of this psychological association through the word-association test should be interpreted only as a mental slip or as a revelation of the unconscious.

In "Yaneura no sanposha," however, Ranpo leaves no doubt as to the nature of the psychological association that Saburō has formed between cigarettes and poison. Unlike Fukiya, Saburō, even upon being asked specifically, does not recognize the reason that he does not want a cigarette. Whereas "Shinri shiken" describes how a psychological association is formed unconsciously from the experiences of a conscious subject, "Yaneura no sanposha" reveals the possibility of how an unconscious association can form from experiences wholly unknown to consciousness.

The last lines of "Yaneura no sanposha" tell of the importance that Ranpo had placed on the role of the unconscious in this story: "Although he [Saburō] thought that he did not see where the poison bottle landed when he had dropped it through the peephole, he did in fact see the poison pour onto the cigarettes. And this fact, pushed beneath his consciousness had the psychological effect of making him dislike cigarettes" (274). These are not Saburō's words but necessarily the narrator's precisely because Saburō as thinking/conscious subject cannot tell the story of Saburō as corporeal/unconscious subject.

Discourses of Modern Experience from Sōseki to Ranpo

Ranpo's epistemological project, as a re-examination of the way in which an individual can be known regardless of his or her attempts to remain unknown, is a two-fold process: it begins with the rejection of a method of detection based on positivistic science and ends with the articulation of a method of detection based on human psychology. And in positing the unconscious as the ultimate target of detection, it was, as Ranpo readily acknowledges, heavily influenced by Sigmund Freud's psychoanalytical theory, which was quickly gaining currency within intellectual circles in Taishō Japan.[33] A natural extension of other discourses on psychology and abnormal sexuality by the likes of German psychologist Richard von Kraft-Ebbing (1840–1902), whose effect on Tanizaki's fictional works is well documented, the reception and influence of Freudian psychoanalysis in Japan also differed in significant ways from those of previous discourses.[34] First, Freud's theories on dreams and the unconscious provided a broad understanding of the human psyche, the applicability of which was not restricted to the 'abnormal.' Second, befitting a theory that revolves around the understanding of a truth hiding deep behind the surface—that is, a favorite paradigmatic opposition that had guided the development of the mod-

33. For Ranpo's comments on how he became interested in Freudian psychoanalysis, see Edogawa, "Gakuya banashi," 40.

34. For example, see Inoue, "Tanizaki Jun'ichirō no seikimatsu." Concomitant with the spread of such discourses within intellectual circles of the Taishō period (Kraft-Ebbing's *Psychopathia Sexualis* was translated into Japanese in 1914) were new periodicals specifically dealing with the issues of abnormal psychology and sexuality. The most prominent of these examples was the journal *Hentai shinri* (Abnormal psychology), which was founded by Nakamura Kokyō (1881–1952) in October 1917.

ern Japanese novel from Shōyō onwards—Freud's theories were popularized in Taishō Japan predominantly as literary theories.

As Sone Hiroyoshi notes in his overview of the reception of Freud in the 1920s, the essay "Kumon no shōchō" (Agony of the symbol), written by the scholar of English literature Kuriyagawa Hakuson (1880–1923) and published in the January issue of the journal *Kaizō* (Conversion) in 1922, was the most influential in spreading the ideas of Freud to the Japanese reading public.[35] Reflecting Kuriyagawa's background in English literature, this essay, rather than being an introduction to Freud's theories as a scientific examination of human psychology, was an application of Freud's theories to develop his own theory on literature, which was characterized by its "romanticism" and "optimism."[36] Stating that "the root of the literary arts is the agony and anguish that arise when the life force is oppressed" and that "the psychological injury, which arises from the conflict and collision between the power that attempts at any cost to satisfy desire and the suppressive force that operates against this, lurks in the back of the unconscious," Kuriyagawa posits the arts in general and literature in particular as the "only form of living [besides in our dreams] that liberates us from the internal and external oppression that we are always facing in our lives."[37] As these excerpts make clear, Kuriyagawa utilized Freud's notion of repression and the unconscious to legitimize fiction writing as an endeavor that liberated the individual from oppressive forces, both external and internal, and, as such, echoed "the intellectual environment of Taishō Japan that employed words such as 'the self' and 'life' as catchphrases" and were exemplified by the writings of the Shirakaba group that were discussed in the previous chapter.[38]

Given this historical context, does Ranpo's turn to the psychological reveal itself as a shift from one mode of Western scientific discourse/ideology to another? No doubt, Freudian psychoanalysis enabled Ranpo to base his detective stories upon an epistemological system that was not utilized very much in the Western detective fiction tradition. In this sense, Ranpo's choice was similar to his employment of the framing

---

35. Sone, "Furoito no shōkai to eikyō," 82. According to Sone, Kuriyagawa's essay collection that included this essay, which was published posthumously in February 1925 after Kuriyagawa died in the Great Kantō Earthquake, became a bestseller, going through fifty printings in two months (ibid., 84)

36. Ibid.

37. Cited in ibid., 83.

38. Ibid., 84.

technique that developed out of Ranpo's desire to be creative in a later-developing country (in terms of its experimentation with the detective fiction genre) like Japan. At the same time, Freudian psychoanalysis provided Ranpo with a discourse to criticize Japan's modernization process to the extent that it revealed the powerful and hazardous effects of the modernization process on the psychic lives of individuals. In this regard, Ranpo's turn toward the psychological puts him in line with and presents itself as a development of the critical discourses of the 1910s that reconsidered Japan's modernization process and its materialistic emphasis, discourses in which the most prominent voice was that of Natsume Sōseki.[39]

In his essay "Gendai Nihon no kaika" (The civilization of modern-day Japan; 1911), Sōseki criticizes the externally forced modernization of Japan as unnatural and articulates the psychological effect it has on the consciousness of the Japanese population, offering the following metaphor to convey his point: "it is the same as having numerous dishes on the table, but even before you can clearly see them to decipher what sort of delicacies they are, they are withdrawn only to be replaced by new dishes."[40] Described here is a sense of rapid change taking place outside the individual and his or her inability to deal with such changes: the eyes and consciousness are too slow to register and digest the external stimuli that confront the individual at every turn, and the individual is left with "feelings of emptiness," "dissatisfaction," and "anxiety." To the extent that Sōseki describes these stimuli as "dishes" that are believed to be "delicacies," however, they exist as possibilities for 'authentic' experience, and the general feeling of discontentment that afflicts the Japanese stems ultimately from the sense that these experiences are inevitably lost in the flow of history.

In one of his earliest fictional works "Rondon tō" (Tower of London; 1905), Sōseki offers an archetypal example of such a condition when he

---

39. As Minami Hiroshi writes: "Because Meiji's *fukoku kyōhei* (a wealthy nation and a strong army) policy, in order to catch up with and overtake the foreign countries, placed the reform of material conditions first, it [government] focused its energies under the slogan of *bunmei kaika* on imitation and adaptation of the material side of Western life, and it left the all-important modernization of the spiritual side lagging behind to be inherited by the Taishō period. As the Meiji period neared its end, this tardiness of modern culture, concealed under a superficially fashionable civilization, began to be criticized vehemently by those such as Natsume Sōseki and Nagai Kafū who had a good understanding of modern thought" (*Taishō bunka*, 12).

40. Natsume Sōseki, "Gendai Nihon no kaika," in *Sōseki zenshū*, vol. 11, 339.

tells a story of an excursion to the Tower of London by a Japanese narrator who has recently arrived in London. A displaced individual who finds himself in an unknown land ("Unlike other Japanese visitors, I had no letters of introduction to anyone who might show me around"), the narrator is apprehensive and fearful of twentieth-century London, an ever-changing metropolis unlike anything he has experienced.[41] The outside world offers no solace for him: the conveniences of a technologically advanced nation, such as the railway train, the tram, the electric train, and even a hansom cab, confront him only as suspicious forces that might do him harm. And this feeling continues even to his lodgings: "Out on the street I felt I would be carried away by the surging crowd, and in my lodgings I suspected that a railway train might come crashing into my room; night and day I was left without peace of mind."[42] Thoroughly overwhelmed by his new surroundings, the narrator ultimately likens himself to "a hare from Gotenba [the countryside near the foot of Mount Fuji] who finds himself suddenly in Nihonbashi [the center of Tokyo]."[43]

Bearing a striking resemblance to an observation that Walter Benjamin would make several decades later when he described urban life in mid-1800s Paris as "a series of shocks and collisions," Sōseki's description of modern experience in "Gendai Nihon no kaika" and "Rondon tō" suggests his keen awareness of the problems arising from Japan's encounter with and adaptation of Western modernity. In both works, Sōseki describes a Japanese subject who is overwhelmed by his external environment. In "Rondon tō," this sense results from a geographical displacement from the margins of the modernizing world (Japan) to its center (London), and, indeed, I would argue that this physical displacement, which Sōseki experienced in real life when he lived in England in the early 1900s, made him particularly sensitive to the psychological problems of the modern subject. In "Gendai Nihon no kaika," Sōseki suggests how a rapidly changing environment, especially one that is foreign and deviating from a natural course of development, affects the subject in a similar

---

41. Natsume Sōseki, "Rondon tō," in *Sōseki zenshū*, vol. 2, 5.

42. Ibid.

43. Ibid. Sōseki revisits this theme of a displaced individual in his 1908 *Sanshirō*. Just arriving in Tokyo from the country, Sanshirō experiences the city as follows: "There were many things that Sanshirō was shocked about in Tokyo. First, he was shocked that the electric trains made clamoring sounds. And then he was shocked that so many people got on and off the train while it made these clamoring sounds" (*Sōseki zenshū*, vol. 4, 23).

manner. And if Sōseki already observed evidence of such conditions in the social realities of Japan in 1911, then the developments of the 1910s no doubt aggravated these conditions to make his hypothesis more provocative and powerful by the time of Ranpo's emergence.

With the outbreak of World War I in 1914, Japan, whose involvement in the war was minor, saw a period of rapid industrialization to meet the material demands of the warring nations. Consequently, the economy boomed in larger cities, and people flooded into these cities from the country in the hopes of obtaining work and better wages. For example, Tokyo, whose population's rate of increase never exceeded 1 percent in the first five years of Taishō, saw a 14.5 percent increase in population (around 421,900 people) in its sixth year (1917), a figure that is astounding considering that Japan's population only increased by about 384,000 people (0.7 percent rate of increase) during the same year.[44] The result, as Harry Harutoonian notes, was that "by 1920 and the succeeding years, the sharply silhouetted contrast was widely observed in the uneven relationship between the large metropolitan sites like Tokyo/Yokohama and Osaka/Kobe, which literally had been transformed overnight, and a countryside that supplied the cities with a labor force and capital but, according to Yanagita Kunio, received nothing in return."[45]

In addition to the major transformation of large cities that made adjustments to the rapidly shifting environment difficult for urban dwellers, more than half of them had not been 'urban dwellers' for long in the first place. This can be surmised from the rate of population increase in Tokyo during the Taishō period overall as well as the Taishō 9 (1920) survey, which indicated that only 42.5 percent of the Tokyo population was born in Tokyo.[46] Removed from their communities and confronting others as strangers, these 'urbanites' then faced the double task of adapting to a wholly different environment and lifestyle, given the enormous disparity between the country and the city, and of adjusting to the ever-changing urban life. And this situation only grew worse with the Great

---

44. Population numbers are from Tōkyō hyakunen shi henshū iinkai, *Tōkyō hyakunen shi*, 61. Matsuyama Iwao also cites these figures in the chapter entitled "Tantei no me" in Matsuyama, *Ranpo to Tōkyō*, 14–30. In this chapter, Matsuyama discusses Ranpo's "D-zaka no satsujin jiken" as a story that reflects the weakening personal relationships of urban individuals that resulted from the process of mass urbanization in the mid- and late 1910s.

45. Harootunian, *Overcome by Modernity*, 3–4.

46. This figure is from Matsuyama, *Ranpo to Tōkyō*, 21.

Kantō Earthquake and the complete overhaul of the city landscape that followed, which literally transformed the external environment of Tokyo's denizens overnight.

It was against this backdrop of rapid urbanization and radical transformation of the city that *Shinseinen* and the early detective stories of Ranpo emerged and developed as successors to Sōseki's project of dealing with the psychological problematic of modern subjectivity founded upon the tenuous relationship between individuals and their external environment. As the cover drawings during its first year of publication—all idyllic images of rural Japan—are enough to suggest, *Shinseinen* was originally geared toward the young students and workers of rural Japan. Reflecting this target readership, the magazine's content included "cultural and moral tales by journalists, soldiers, educators, and entrepreneurs" and "enlightenment of scientific technology," which sought to educate its young readers on the ways and values of successful men in society and to keep its isolated readers caught up on the new developments around the world.[47] In fact, one of the main attractions of the magazine was the news and advice regarding life in a foreign country that introduced people who had succeeded in immigrating abroad and offered realistic and practical advice to readers' correspondences for doing the same. No doubt serving as "recommendation[s] to go abroad and prosper, which was an inflection of the Meiji period *risshin shusse* ideology," but also suggesting how difficult it had become to find success within the boundaries of the nation, the early *Shinseinen* fueled the dreams of rural youths to leave their homes to make something of themselves out in the city and beyond.[48]

---

47. Kawasaki, "*Shinseinen* no tanjō to sono jidai," 4. In addition, the magazine was characterized by its nationalistic and militaristic concerns. For example, the first issue began the serialization of Higuchi Reiyō's *Nichibei sensō miraiki* (Futuristic tale of the war between Japan and the United States), a fantastic tale about a near-future war between Japan and the United States that had the ominous subtitle of "The Second World War." For an overview of the history and characteristics of *Shinseinen*, see Yamashita, *"Shinseinen" o meguru sakkatachi*, 7–25, and Kimoto, *Zasshi de yomu sengoshi*, 61–64.

48. Kawasaki, "*Shinseinen* no tanjō to sono jidai," 4. Echoing the decision of *Hakai*'s Ushimatsu to move to Texas (discussed in Chapter 3), *Shinseinen*'s 'sincere' recommendation to emigrate abroad and the popularity of articles on this topic suggested at once the undying hold that the ideology of rising in the world had on the magazine's readers and the difficulties of its achievement within the confines of national boundaries, which was exacerbated by the dire conditions of rural Japan in the late 1910s and early 1920s. Significantly, the call to emigrate

But the magazine's style began to change around the time of Ranpo's emergence and with the Great Kantō Earthquake, as signs of rural Japan gradually gave way to the images of the city and more and more pages became dedicated to detective fiction.[49] As Kawasaki Kenko writes: "the physical transformation brought on by the Great Kantō Earthquake became, as a result, the turning point to orient the interests of *Shinseinen* toward the various phenomena of the newly emerging urban civilization."[50] In short, *Shinseinen* began to focus on subjects relating to the rapidly developing urban culture, and the detective story, as a story of exploration into urban life and its darkness, took center stage within this general shift in the magazine's subject matter. This is not to say, however, that such a shift entailed a complete change in the magazine's target audience. In promoting the dreams of rising in the world to youths of rural Japan, who lived under dire economic conditions, and in calling for their participation in the world beyond their peripheral existence, *Shinseinen* reinforced the movement from country to city that was prevalent in the late 1910s and the early 1920s. In this sense, the successfully interpellated readers of the magazine in its early years would have found themselves in the city, if not in some foreign country, confronted, as suggested by Sōseki's description of the modern experience that is distinctly urban, with conditions that would render their external world to be fleeting, ethereal, and dream-like.

Fittingly enough, many if not all prominent characters of Ranpo's early detective stories are young men who have come to Tokyo from the

---

to a foreign country was imbued with the rhetoric of colonialism, exemplified by the article "Nihon minzoku no ijū nōryoku" (The immigrating abilities of the Japanese folk), which appeared in the September issue in 1922. This essay rewrites the ancient folktale of Japan found in *Kojiki* as a history of immigration and colonization, describing the ancient emperor Jinmu as an ideal leader of a colony and the ancient hero Yamato Takeru no Mikoto as a pioneer, to claim that the immigrating ability of the Japanese people is the best in the world.

49. In January 1922, Hakubunkan established *Shin-shumi* (New hobby) as a magazine that was solely devoted to detective fiction. While this event no doubt indicates the growing demand for detective fiction, it also suggests the unwillingness on the part of *Shinseinen* to give up its role as a general magazine geared toward rural youths and to devote its pages to detective fiction. But this attitude changed in 1923, the year of Ranpo's emergence and the Great Kantō Earthquake. In November, *Shin-shumi* was discontinued, and *Shinseinen* began devoting more pages to stories and criticism relating to the detective fiction genre.

50. Kawasaki, "*Shinseinen* no tanjō to sono jidai," 6.

country and, thus, reflect the shift in the readership of *Shinseinen* from rural to urban youths.[51] They are "hares from Gotenba" who found themselves suddenly in Nihonbashi to be confronted with "numerous dishes" that were constantly being "replaced by new dishes." But importantly, it would be a stretch to say that Ranpo's protagonists embody the primary subjects of this urbanization process, namely, the poor that left their farming communities to join the urban labor class. For example, while "Ni-sen dōka" describes the characters' musings and plotting based on the detective fiction worldview as cheap entertainment for the poor urban dwellers fighting to make ends meet, they are clearly educated and present themselves as the student-types, the quintessential subjects of modernization and urbanization in modern Japanese literature.

And here, Akechi and Saburō present themselves as two sides of the same coin. Akechi Kogorō, whose provincial origins are emphasized in his introductory tale "D-zaka no satsujin jiken" through him knowing the victim from his hometown, is educated and well off, having time and money to pursue his interest in detective stories and detective work. Like Akechi in his early days, Saburō is financially independent, and it is his economic condition ("Able to receive some allowance from his parents, he did not have to worry particularly about his life even when he left his job" [249]) that makes possible his peculiar lifestyle switching from job to job, hobby to hobby, and one lodging to another in his search for pleasures in life.[52] Thus, Akechi and Saburō can be classified as *kōtō yūmin* akin to Matsumoto of Sōseki's *Higan sugi made* discussed in Chapter 4. Or to the extent that Saburō, unlike the apolitical con-

---

51. In his discussion of "D-zaka no satsujin jiken," Matsuyama Iwao states: "whether it is Akechi, the 'I' or other youths that appear in Ranpo's short stories, they can be thought of as being superimposed to the image of Ranpo himself, who came to Tokyo alone from Aichi at the age of eighteen" (*Ranpo to Tōkyō*, 19).

52. It is important to note that Saburō (literally, "third man"), as the third son in the family, does not have familial responsibilities to succeed the family name. Moreover, Saburō's relentless search for excitement itself can be considered as being made possible by a modern condition which provides its denizens with time to 'waste,' according to Sōseki's "Gendai Nihon no kaika." As Sōseki states, responsibilities and hobbies are two primary activities of human life, where the time required for the former shortens in modern times thanks to the power of technology (as well as financial independence), leaving the individuals with ample time to spend on pursuing the latter. For details, see Natsume Sōseki, "Gendai Nihon no kaika," in *Sōseki zenshū*, vol. 11, 328.

formist Matsumoto, ends up committing a crime, Saburō is more representative of the vilified *kōtō yūmin* of government and public discourse.

But at the same time, while Akechi shows no indication of being maladjusted to society, which, in turn, may signal his being overwhelmed by his external environment in a manner akin to the narrator in "Rondon tō," the same cannot be said for Saburō, whose condition is emphasized as an illness in the opening lines of the story cited above. And while the text tries to suggest his condition as an extraordinary anomaly by describing the extent to which he goes to remedy it, it is also true that Saburō reeks of modernity. As Sari Kawana has discussed by drawing on Georg Simmel, "the conditions of urban living desensitize the inhabitants," leading to the creation of "bored urbanites" like Saburō.[53] Indeed, his condition can be said to be symptomatic—albeit an extreme version—of what Simmel calls a "blasé Metropolitan attitude," which is "the consequence of those rapidly shifting stimulations of the nerves" to a point where they "can no longer produce any reaction at all."[54] In this sense, the "blasé" or jaded urbanite can be understood as the flipside of the overwhelmed individual as described by Sōseki: Saburō is a jaded individual who seeks out "numerous dishes" but constantly replaces them with "new dishes" on his own accord because he finds none to be "delicacies."

The point of "Yaneura no sanposha," of course, is to show the lengths to which Saburō goes to break out of his jaded shell, a move that becomes a real possibility when he meets Akechi, who introduces him to the fascinating world of crime through various courtroom accounts and detective stories. Saburō's engagement with this world gradually escalates, as he graduates from imagining being a criminal to begin his escapades around town where he pretends to be one. Of his activities, cross-dressing is his favorite, which is fitting for Saburō who yearns to but is unable to commit actual crimes for the fear of being caught: "Despite all consideration, even Saburō did not want to become a criminal by law. He did not yet have the courage to indulge in pleasure by going as far as ignoring the grief and contempt of his parents, siblings, relatives, and acquaintances" (251). If committing a crime is the transgression of the law as the explicit articulation of rules drafted by the government, cross-dressing is the transgression of sociocultural norms that expect the matching of sex and gender. And when we juxtapose this choice of activity with his qualms with his fellow lodgers, we see that his desire to break with social norms

---

53. Kawana, *Murder Most Modern*, 41.

54. Georg Simmel, "The Metropolis and Mental Life," cited in ibid.

is intimately connected with breaking the habits and routines of everyday life. Saburō comments: "What boring creatures human beings are. Wherever it is, they do nothing but present over and over to each other similar thoughts with similar expressions using similar words" (252).

It is precisely this view of human beings that is shattered when Saburō begins the walks in the attic space of his lodging, for what he finds there is an access to the private lives of fellow lodgers, "the inner, rather than outer, colors, the true sentiments of human beings without artifice that come out when they are alone."[55] Importantly, the expression of "true sentiments" is facilitated by the Western construction of the building Tōei-kan, where a clear distinction between private and public space is maintained through "rigid partitions of the walls" and doors with "metal latches" (255). But the Western construction also brings into existence the attic space for Saburō to wander, peeping and eavesdropping through small holes and cracks in the ceiling. The modern/Western construction of Tōei-kan provides its denizens with a seemingly clear demarcation between private and public spheres, thereby making it more 'enticing' for Saburō to transgress the barrier between the two spheres precisely because the denizens can feel free to do as they please without being seen or heard by others. Here again, then, Saburō derives pleasure from transgressing a boundary, but, unlike in the case of cross-dressing, which incorporated the risk of being found out as part of the thrill, the walks in the attic do the opposite. The thrill comes from being completely invisible and from occupying the position of a pure observer who can discern the most private affairs and behaviors of others. As a wearer of an "invisible cloak," he comes to occupy in reality the *imaginary* perspective of Tsubouchi Shōyō's novelist, gaining, so he believes, the ability to "clearly discern the true intentions" of his neighbors (257).[56]

But the way in which Akechi figures out Saburō's involvement in Endō's murder suggests that Saburō's belief that he has discerned "the true intentions" of his neighbors was a false one. By connecting Saburō's involvement in Endō's poisoning to Saburō's sudden dislike for cigarettes, Akechi shows that it is not the things people can hide when in public and

---

55. Matsuyama, *Ranpo to Tōkyō*, 59.

56. As Shōyō writes in the following passage (discussed in Chapter 1): "To freely dissect people's hearts, which would be impossible in reality, to enter the bedroom of a dignitary's wife . . . and write her behavior and actions, or to depict the situations inside [a house] without considering whether the gates or sliding doors are closed—these are the freedoms of a novelist" (*Shōsetsu shinzui*, 149–50).

reveal when in private that constitute the causes of one's behavior, action, and desire. Rather, the connection between effects as observable and palpable experiences of the subject and their true causes is not necessarily known—or necessarily unknown—to the subject himself, for it is only when experience fails to register in the consciousness and slips into the unconscious that the subject experiences a transformation of everyday habits, as was the case with Saburō's smoking. And once again, a Japanese text of modern experience exhibits a striking resemblance to the writings of Walter Benjamin. If Sōseki's overwhelmed subject exists on the flipside of Simmel's blasé urbanite whose tired nerves are a result of constantly responding to external stimuli, then the overwhelmed subject is Benjamin's traumatized subject who fails to fend off external stimuli at the level of consciousness as information, leaving them to fundamentally affect the constitutive core of their unconscious.[57]

And fending off external stimuli must have been made difficult in the latter half of the 1910s and the early 1920s, especially for the likes of Ranpo's characters, who had moved to Tokyo from the country, as it not only "transformed overnight" thanks to rapid industrialization and resulting urbanization in the post–World War I economic boom but also experienced the catastrophic trauma of the Great Kantō Earthquake that

---

57. For details, see Benjamin, "Some Motifs in Baudelaire," especially 109–20. Franco Moretti points out that Freud's text, on which Benjamin's understanding of the shocks of urban experience is based, takes "its cues from traumas undergone in wartime" and questions "whether the category of the traumatic and exceptional event is really the most appropriate for the analysis of the experiences of urban life" ("Homo palpitans," 116). For Moretti, the consciousness of a modern urbanite is much more flexible, enabling him or her to seize external stimuli as opportunities rather than as shocks, because urban life repeats itself and, thus, prepares the consciousness against stimuli. Although convincing, Moretti's argument has as its subject an urbanite who has developed *with* his or her environment, and, as a result, is able to make small adjustments as the environment changes. But there clearly exists another group of modern urbanites for which such adjustments are more difficult. Moretti suggests as much when he writes: "To be suspended between unswerving habit and sudden catastrophe is much more typical of traditional rural societies, villages, and the provinces" (ibid., 117). Those from "traditional rural societies, villages, and the provinces" finding themselves, for one reason or another, in the middle of a metropolis—it is these newcomers to the urban scene, produced en masse during the massive urbanization of 1910s Japan, that Benjamin's theory of urban experience aptly describes. And here, we cannot also forget the Great Kantō Earthquake that is in every sense the exemplar of what constitutes a "sudden catastrophe."

leveled much of the city, leading to a complete overhaul of the urban landscape. Thus, while "Yaneura no sanposha" can be understood as a story of how the traumatic event of murder offers an occasion for a habit-breaking experience for Saburō, such an experience is not necessarily predicated on an extraordinary event. For, whether characterized by our blasé or traumatized exteriors, we are all constituted by precisely what lies beyond the penetrating gaze of the Other and the self alike, resisting observation and self-reflection. Just like our public personae, our private selves made up of desires and fears are nothing but façades masking the true habit-breaking causes—the traumas of modern experience—that remain hidden in the unconscious waiting to be unearthed.

The Power of Confession and the End of a Collusion

Intricately tied to and stemming from the experiences of the metropolis, Ranpo's rejection of the positivistic paradigm is a rejection of the physical and material world whose order and law form the basis of positivistic science precisely because no order or law can be observed in the modern world. The modern metropolis, characterized by rapid change and faceless masses, frustrates the efforts of its inhabitants to process their experiences as meaning, which must be produced through the acts of symbolic reconstruction within the subject. Rather than rejecting the subject as the proper source of 'truth' who preserves his experiences as information, Ranpo posits the unconscious—a notion rapidly gaining currency in the 1920s—as a psychical storage place for information, including those that are unregistered or misrecognized by the conscious mind, and thereby salvages the subject's connection to external reality. But the unconscious is not a mere storage place for experiences as information; it is also a site of symbolic reconstruction as a linguistic link between the subject and his experiences of external reality. And it is precisely because such a link affects the subject at an observable level to reveal what it contains that Akechi's method can understand the existence and the workings of the unconscious. Akechi's method of detection to "penetrate psychologically the deepest part of a person's soul" bases itself not only on the understanding of this dichotomy between the conscious as unreliable and the unconscious as reliable source of 'truth' but also on the power of the unconscious to constitute the subject on the level of consciousness and behavior.

Within this dichotomy between the conscious and the unconscious, moreover, the act of confession, which appeared as a methodological failure within Ranpo's epistemological project in our earlier discussions, reveals its critical function. As Franco Moretti states of the criminal in Western detective fiction: "The criminal is the opposite of Raskolnikov, who *must* confess to his action, bare himself to the world, and demolish his individual shield *by himself*: whence the irrelevance of detection in *Crime and Punishment*. On the contrary, detective fiction always presents the criminal as a self-sufficient watertight consciousness wholly bent on an aim."[58] Although this observation may be true within the Western tradition, we have seen throughout the course of this study that detective fiction in Japan had much to do with the fundamental problem posed by the figure of Raskolnikov, and the same can be said on this topic of confession.

Through its exploration of the notion of the unconscious, "Yaneura no sanposha" negotiates the two extremes of confession, one necessary and willing, the other an afterthought to the detective's determination of the criminal's guilt, problematizing the opposition between confession and detection as well as this definition of the criminal. The criminal may believe himself to be "a self-sufficient watertight consciousness," but he is in actuality never "watertight" because he, like any other subject, is necessarily constituted by what lies beyond consciousness. To the extent that breaking of a habit leads Akechi to grow suspicious of Saburō, Saburō's unconscious betrays his intention to hide his identity as the culprit by sending clues to Akechi to decipher. In direct opposition to the criminal as a conscious agent, the unconsciousness is marked by its desire to confess. Thus, the criminal who desires to hide the truth of his crime is an example *par excellence* of a consciousness whose desire is in absolute opposition to that of the unconscious.

By suggesting the capacity of the unconscious to incorporate experiences that consciousness has failed to register or 'digest,' Ranpo re-claims these 'lost' experiences as 'stored' experiences that retain the possibility of their recovery at a future time and offers Akechi as the 'retriever' who makes this possibility a reality. Akechi aligns the criminal (the conscious) with Raskolnikov who already exists in the unconscious and unites the criminal-as-subject with the fleeting realities of the external world by which the subject is constituted. And to the extent that Akechi's method relies on the criminal's express confession for the proof of guilt, Akechi's incrimination of the criminal entails also the criminal's *imaginary* recuperation of his status as the most suitable narrator of his own experi-

58. Moretti, "Clues," 138. Emphasis in the original.

ences, however fleeting they may be. But in so doing, Ranpo encounters the limitation of detective fiction to accomplish such an ideological task of maintaining the connection between the subject and his experiences within the epistemological quest for the truth of the crime. Although detective fiction as literature cannot focus only on its 'whodunit' aspect but also requires other elements that make itself interesting to the readers, the sole focus of Akechi, as a detective, must remain in his search for the truth of the crime. To satisfy this single objective, Akechi does not need to retrieve the 'lost' experiences of the unconscious at all; he merely has to decipher a single bit of information that pertains to the criminal case at hand. In this sense, detective fiction, or at least Ranpo's early detective stories, was not particularly suited to negotiate the ills of modernization facing the urban readership of *Shinseinen*.

Indeed, for such a task, there was a more suitable literary trend (although to call it a trend is somewhat problematic) rising to prominence in the mid-1920s: the I-novel or *shishōsetsu*. Commonly understood as "an autobiographical narrative in which the author is thought to recount faithfully the details of his or her personal life in a thin guise of fiction," the I-novel has been considered "the most salient and unique form of modern Japanese literature."[59] And within such an understanding, the I-novel often follows a distinct course of development, with Katai's *Futon* as the prototype and the writings of the Shirakaba group, which "advocated the development of the individual self through sincere, direct, and immediate self-expression," as its successor.[60] But as Tomi Suzuki has aptly argued, the I-novel's rise to prominence had as much, if not more so, to do with the critical discourses surrounding the genre as compared to the intrinsic characteristics of its members and, as such, the I-novel is best understood as "a mode of reading that assumes that the I-novel is a single-voiced, 'direct' expression of the author's 'self' and that its written language is 'transparent'" and thus, as "a historically constructed dominant reading and interpretive paradigm" that emerged in the mid-1920s.[61]

As Suzuki's argument makes clear, the I-novel as a literary phenomenon is better characterized as a particular mode of reading that takes what is written on the page as the immediate experiences of the author rather than as a protocol for literary production in which the author faithfully records his experiences. Thus, the I-novel phenomenon in the

---

59. Tomi Suzuki, *Narrating the Self*, 1.

60. Ibid., 92.

61. Ibid., 1, 10.

mid-1920s was a result of a discursive foregrounding of the connection between the writer and the content of his or her endeavor that had already existed in various degrees within the development of modern Japanese literature, including examples prior to Katai's *Futon*, such as Ōgai's *Maihime* and Sōseki's "Rondon tō." Whether supportive or critical of such a connection at the level of literary production, the various essays on the subject functioned to instill within the readers that this connection was a fashionable if not legitimate form of artistic expression. To put it another way, the rise of these essays in the mid-1920s suggests that a reading mode that identifies the content of literary works as depictions of authors' private lives became ideologically significant during this period. And from our previous discussion, it is understandable why such would be the case. The emergence of the I-novel as a discursive phenomenon in the mid-1920s can be seen as a reflection of a growing need on the part of the readers to be able to have faith in the immediate perceptions that make up their everyday lives. In other words, the I-novel discourses functioned to institutionalize a mode of reading through which the value of everyday life could be recuperated precisely because individuals had become unable to make sense of their immediate realities, an inability that rendered their everyday lives phantasmagoric and thus inconsequential.

Of course, what made it possible for this mode of reading to take root was the predisposition of the so-called I-novels themselves to withstand or rather excel within such interpretative paradigm, as illustrated by the writings of Kasai Zenzō (1887–1928) whom the "new I-novel critical discourse designated . . . as the most representative contemporary I-novelist."[62] As the representative work of his later years "Kohan shuki" (Notes from the lakeside; 1924) clearly shows, Kasai's works presented themselves as a dizzying collage of the protagonist's immediate emotions and thoughts that resulted from the intertwining of present impressions with flashbacks from the past in a manner that can be classified as stream of consciousness. And through such a presentation that has the effect of disorienting the readers, Kasai depicts a passive subject who is overwhelmed by his external environment and circumstances, trapped in the mundane problems of everyday life such as money and women and left to wonder if "everything is the doing of what is called delusion."[63] Indeed,

62. Ibid., 7.

63. Kasai, "Kohan shuki," 443. In his insightful analysis of Kasai's works, Edward Fowler writes that "his hero is purely the victim of circumstance, purely at the mercy of outside forces" (*The Rhetoric of Confession*, 257).

the insignificance and triviality of what he wrote were such that they functioned to serve as the defining characteristic of Kasai's writings. As Edward Fowler states in his analysis of Kasai's oeuvre, what set Kasai apart was "the will to write when there is in fact nothing to write about, when life itself has reached a seemingly irreparable impasse."[64]

It is this "will to write," I would argue, that constitutes the central ideological cog of the I-novel phenomenon. In order to affirm the seemingly meaningless life of the reader, it is not enough for the writer to present such a life on a culturally legitimated forum, namely, general-interest magazines such as *Chūō kōron*, *Kaizō*, and *Bungei shunjū* that served as the primary site where the representative 'I-novelists' like Kasai and Makino Shin'ichi (1896–1936) published their works.[65] While the depiction of insignificant life affirms such a life as socially acceptable to the extent that it is published, that is, culturally legitimated, the fictionality of the details—if this is the case—negates the operation of legitimation precisely because a *selection* to be made the subject matter of writing suggests a certain importance and value of that subject matter. It is only through appearing to "faithfully record" the author's autobiographical details—that is, understood by the readers to be as such—that the ideological operation of the I-novel takes full effect. The details of the text present themselves as wholly insignificant in *content* to the readers, leaving only the *form* as significant, for the author tells his or her readers: 'while what I write might not be worth writing, I must write because it is my real life.'

If Ranpo's early detective stories—by criticizing the subject's capacity to accurately observe and digest his external world—probed the painful symptom itself and posited the detective as the cure, then the I-novel functioned to legitimate by virtue of its cultural worth the fleeting and meaningless everyday experiences of its readers like an anesthesia that masks the symptom. In this sense, the I-novel phenomenon represents an inversion of Tsubouchi Shōyō's literary project: whereas Shōyō espoused the importance of private life by depicting the true feelings (*ninjō*) of the average person as an 'authentic' experience that the novelist must unearth, the I-novel 'authenticates' the seemingly meaningless everyday life of the average person by virtue of his identification with the novelist as an established figure of cultural authority. In the process, the Japanese

---

64. Fowler, *The Rhetoric of Confession*, 257.

65. For details on general-interest magazines and their expanding readership during the 1920s, see Nagamine, *Modan toshi no dokusha kūkan*.

novel abandons its rhetoric of truth as something hiding behind the surface—the rhetoric buttressed by its colluder, the detective story—and becomes a site where suitable 'surfaces' as covers are produced for its readers.

As an inversion of the emphasis underlying the literary formations of modern Japan that we have discussed in the course of this study, the I-novel's prominence in the mid-1920s may appear as an instance of the separation of the collusion between the Japanese novel and the detective story. But even so, such separation was short lived, as Ranpo would go the way of the colluder. Soon after "Yaneura no sanposha," Ranpo became the premier writer of the *ero guro nansensu* movement by publishing detective stories that relied heavily on the detailed depictions relating to transgressions of sociocultural norms, in general, and sexual perversions (abnormal sexuality), in particular. In a sense, this shift in focus to represent fantasy, and thereby the unconscious, is continuous with and a necessary result of his early detective fiction because this turn to fantasy, in effect, expands the uncovering of the unconscious, which was previously limited by the detective's single objective of discovering the identity of the criminal. But at the same time, in extending his description of the unconscious, Ranpo abandons it as an object of knowledge and, instead, represents it through its manifestation in the 'real' world as fantasy-come-true: the unconscious no longer exists at an observable level as a secret message to be deciphered but as unbridled desire that explodes in the external world.

This is nowhere clearer than in his full-length novel *Kumo otoko* (Spider man; 1929–1930). Not only is the story about a madman who dreams of constructing a three-dimensional exhibition of his perverse fantasy, including the corpses of 49 girls used as mannequins, but Akechi, who rescues the girls before they are killed, actually helps reproduce the madman's fantasy by using mannequins and undercover police officers despite the fact that he could have easily arrested the madman prior to the time of the exhibition. That the reading public ardently welcomed such works over his early detective stories and that Ranpo gained mass recognition only after this shift (his *Ōgon kamen* [Golden mask] would be serialized in the paradigm-changing mass-circulation magazine *Kingu* from September 1930 to October 1931) are suggestive of the trajectory of literary production as a whole. Toward the end of the 1920s, the rhetoric of truth as something hiding behind the surface—a rhetoric that underlay the profound connection between detective fiction and the Japanese novel—collapses, replaced by the understanding of text as a site where sensational 'surfaces' as expressions of the unconscious are posited as standing in for the subjective core of our being.

In March 1927, just after completing the serialization of *Issun bōshi* (One-inch boy) in *Asahi shinbun*, Edogawa Ranpo left Tokyo to travel around Japan. Self-documented as stemming from "the self-loathing" of the "childishness" of *Issun bōshi*—despite the story's huge popularity (appearing in one of the largest newspapers in Japan and already being made into a film in 1927)—this "aimless wandering," which took him away from writing for over a year, was a period of self-reflection not unlike the one Natsume Sōseki experienced during his absence from writing due to illness prior to his serialization of *Higan sugi made*.[66] And if Sōseki's self-reflection led him to return to a critical and direct engagement with the theme of the detective with which he began his literary career and to the examination of the intimate relationship between the Japanese novel and the detective story, then Ranpo's resulted in a similar endeavor from the side of a professional detective story writer to explore the theoretical issues lying at the heart of this relationship. This endeavor was *Injū* (Shadowy beast), whose serialization in his old home *Shinseinen* began in August 1928 and which sold so quickly that it required the unprecedented reprint of the magazine's issue containing the story's final installment.[67]

Injū is a first-person narrated account of a detective-story writer Samukawa (appearing as the first-person "watashi" for the most of the story) who is asked by Shizuko, the wife of a wealthy man (Oyamada Rokurō), to resolve her real-life troubles with another detective-story writer named Ōe Shundei. Whereas the protagonist-narrator is known for his "healthy" detective stories that explored the analytical and the scientific, the suspect is known for his unhealthy ones that explored the abnormal and the sexual.[68] Importantly, Shundei's criminal actions mimic the stories he has written, which, as any reader of Ranpo would be quick to realize, are all plays on Ranpo's own stories. The primary example is "Yaneura no yūgi," a slight change from "Yaneura no sanposha," the plot line and tricks of which the story revisits in detail. There is also "Ichimai no kitte," which is "Ichimai no kippu," and "B-zaka no satsujin" is, of course,

66. Edogawa, "Jichū jikai," in *Kohan-tei jiken*, 345.
67. Nakajima Kawatarō, *Nihon suiri shōsetsu shi*, vol. 2, 228.
68. Edogawa, *Injū*, in *Edogawa Ranpo zenshū*, vol. 3, 203.

"D-zaka no satsujin jiken." And what's more, the real name of Ōe Shundei, which is a pen name, is Hirata Ichirō, which immediately evokes Ranpo's real name, Hirai Tarō. In these ways, Ranpo constructs the suspect Shundei in the image of himself, perhaps as a sarcastic response to critics like Hirabayashi Hatsunosuke who, as we saw in this chapter's introduction, categorized Ranpo's stories as unhealthy and abnormal from the mid-1920s. And this self-referential dynamic becomes further complicated when the protagonist-narrator determines, in the ensuing investigation after Oyamada Rokurō's murder, that Shundei is, in fact, a phantom created by Shizuko, the supposed victim of his stalking.

As the above summary indicates, ***Injū*** is a highly metafictional work that presents itself as a parody of the I-novel. But the value of the story does not lie simply in its playfulness, mimicking a fashionable genre for the entertainment of the readers. Rather, in telling a story of how a detective story writer is at once a criminal and a woman, ***Injū*** engages in the critical elucidation of the major theme of the Japanese novel, namely, the woman and the criminal as mysteries-to-be-solved for the Japanese student/intellectual. And to the extent that the narrator-detective becomes involved in a sadomasochistic relationship with Shizuko, who is Shundei, who, in turn, is Ranpo, ***Injū*** frames the relationship of the subject-as-detective to the woman and the criminal as a search for the self wherein they assert themselves as narcissistic projections of the self as mystery. Indeed, that abnormal sexuality inserts itself within such linking of the subject to the woman and the criminal seems fitting, for abnormal sexuality offers an instance where the subject's relationship with a woman also entails a transgression of social norms, which, in turn, 'criminalizes' the male subject.

Significantly in this context, moreover, the text posits Shizuko's masochistic predilection as being Western in origin through the riding crop—a symbolic instrument of sadomasochism—brought back from Europe by Shizuko's sadist husband Rokurō.[69] In such a way, ***Injū*** seems to frame Shizuko's masochism in terms similar to R. N.'s opium addiction in

---

69. Mark Silver writes: "It is . . . striking that the novel should trace its characters' sadomasochistic impulses back to a West that is imagined as a perverting influence on Japanese sexuality. This West's influence is most powerfully concentrated in the riding crop, which in the course of the novel comes to take on an almost talismanic significance. . . . Both the riding crop and its associated sadism have, it turns out, been brought back by Mr. Oyamada from Europe" (***Purloined Letters***, 155).

"Shimon," suggesting the dangers and pitfalls of Japan's encounter with the West that corrupts the Japanese subject. But the revelation of Shizuko's identity as Shundei problematizes this understanding of Western influence, for Shundei's writings that vividly portray abnormal sexuality begins with Rokurō's leaving for—not returning from—his trip to Europe. Thus, *Injū* denies the explanatory power of the West as an answer to the question of origin as it relates to one's desires and beliefs as well as a source of criminality, positing itself as a text written by a detective about the criminal-as-woman-as-self in which the source of his/her abnormal and criminal desires is never unearthed.

And fittingly, the story's ending reiterates such a message. *Injū* ends when Shizuko commits suicide after the narrator-detective confronts her with the evidence he has collected on the murder of her husband. Yet, while his deductions and evidence point to her as the culprit, not to mention the effect of suicide as a confirmation of her guilt, the narrator-detective cannot ever get rid of the feeling that Shizuko was not Shundei and that Shundei still exists somewhere in this world as his "horrible suspicions deepen with time."[70] In the context of Ranpo's literary project and on the developmental trajectory of the Japanese novel, the message produced by *Injū*'s ending is clear: the Japanese search for the true self—whose often perverse and sometimes criminal nature is crystallized in its relationship to the West but nonetheless cannot be reduced to the influence of the West—can never reach its destination, always being outside the jurisdiction of the "healthy" and analytical ego that characterizes the student/intellectual.

70. Edogawa, *Injū*, in *Edogawa Ranpo zenshū*, vol. 3, 263.

EPILOGUE

The Detective, the Masses, and the State

As an agent of the state and the embodiment of its powers to police the activities of its citizens, the detective, as Walter Benjamin notes, emerges as a hero in the modern age precisely because such policing becomes difficult with the growth of the metropolis and "the obliteration of the individual's traces in the big-city crowd."[1] In this sense, one of the fundamental antagonisms of the detective fiction genre in general and of Western analytical detective fiction (exemplified by the Dupin trilogy and the Sherlock Holmes tales) in particular is that of the individual and the masses, wherein the position of this distinctively modern genre is clear: detective fiction resists the anonymity of the masses and celebrates individuality, whether through the portrayal of the detective as an eccentric individual with extraordinary powers of observation and analysis or of the criminal as a mastermind behind atrocious and often selfish deeds.

At the same time, the detective's private and academic nature—as an ordinary citizen whose involvement in the criminal case is presented as having nothing to do with the desire to police or punish the criminal but rather deriving from purely personal and asocial interests in the case as a puzzle—functions to preserve the detective story's focus on the antagonism between the individual and the masses by masking the conspiratorial relationship between the detective and the state. Western analytical detective fiction attempts to dissociate its protagonist from the state and its police by presenting the detective's motivation behind his actions as being unrelated to official policing. In so doing, detective fiction not only

1. Benjamin, "The Paris of the Second Empire in Baudelaire," 43.

asserts the capacity of the detective-as-individual to single-handedly combat the masses head-on but also assists in making more acceptable the faceless gaze of the state, which was penetrating deeper and deeper into the everyday lives of its citizens in the course of the nineteenth and early twentieth centuries, whether in Europe or in Japan.

But in the case of Japan, this ideological function of detective fiction—making more acceptable the penetrating gaze of the state by dissociating the individual from the masses—is problematized by the fact that there is no process of picking the individual out of faceless masses in much of Japan's detective stories. There is no placing of a fake ad in the newspaper in order to lure out the owner of the orangutan as Dupin does in "The Murders in the Rue Morgue." Instead, we have Fukiya of "Shinri shiken" who goes through a convoluted line of reasoning based on legal technicality to report the money that he had robbed from the miserly landlady to the police, thereby emerging instantly as a possible suspect in the eyes of the investigating judge and the detective Akechi. Or we have Saburō of "Yaneura no sanposha" who is a friend of Akechi and was, in fact, introduced to the world of crime by the detective himself.

As these examples reveal, Japanese detective stories—including many of Ruikō's translations but especially the early stories of Ranpo—seem to bypass the problem of masses altogether. No doubt, such tendencies have much to do with the intricate relationship between detective fiction and the Japanese novel whose paradigmatic foundations were found in Shōyō's literary theories that described the novel's reason for being as exploring the rifts between internal thoughts/emotions and external appearances/behavior and between private life and public life. By implicating itself within such a worldview that Ruikō's detective stories not only adopted but functioned to popularize, the relationship between the detective and the criminal in Japan developed as a battle of how a detective turns a suspicion held against the criminal into positive knowledge. Similar to that of the novelist/narrator, the detective's task ultimately involved the bridging of the gap between who people seemed/claimed to be and who they actually are, rather than in picking an individual out of a "big-city crowd."

And within this context we can reconsider the significance of the reliance on confession in Ranpo's detective stories, which was discussed in the previous chapter. In requiring the criminal's confession for the purpose of his or her conviction, the early detective stories of Ranpo suggest that the penetrating gaze of the detective as an agent of the state can reach its final destination—the official determination of the truth of the crime—only with the active participation of the criminal as subject. Indeed, Ranpo emphasizes this aspect of the criminal by putting the epistemological validity of the positivist paradigm into question and offering Akechi's psychological method in its stead. In so doing, confession becomes an empowering (albeit paradoxical) act, in which the criminal preempts the total objectification of his being by the state and its regime of social control and policing, and salvages the understanding of the subject as the ultimate source of meaning by participating in his own demise, with the detective emerging as the savior of the symbiotic relationship between the individual and the state in the process.

Of course, the fact that one must commit a crime to become an active participant in the workings of the state is absurd, but one could argue that such absurdity reflected the desperate situation of the declining relevance of the educated class—to which Ranpo's characters invariably belonged—as historical agents and productive subjects, a situation that was brought about by the radical shift in the relationship between the individual, the masses, and the state during the 1920s. In other words, as clearly heralded by Arishima Takeo's 1922 declaration "Sengen hitotsu" (One declaration) that denied the well-off intellectual's ability to understand the rising proletarian class, the early 1920s witnessed the emergence of the masses as an undeniable category of symbolic and social significance. And the significance of the masses in the context of state machinery grew exponentially after the Great Kantō Earthquake, which brought about a sociopolitical atmosphere that seems to reject altogether the notion of the individual as the foundational unit of society, revealing Ranpo's detective stories as site of fictional consolation rather than of ideological negotiation between the individual and the state.

In the immediate aftermath of the earthquake, which resulted in around 100,000 casualties and demolished much of Tokyo and Yokohama, there arose rumors that the Korean residents of Tokyo were using the chaos after the earthquake as a smokescreen to commit various crimes including poisoning of wells. Reacting to these rumors—which, as historians have demonstrated, were wholly unfounded—the citizens of Tokyo took to the streets and brutally beat and murdered over 6,000 Korean residents. Moreover, there arose rumors that behind the supposed rioting of the Korean residents lay the leftist political and labor groups, and various members of these groups, including the anarchist Ōsugi Sakae (1885–1923) and his wife, were murdered by those belonging to the military.

These events following the Great Kantō Earthquake not only reconfirmed the despotic tendencies of the authorities through the violent actions of the military taken against leftist activists but also revealed that such tendencies had reached the level of individual subjects. On the one hand, the violence against leftist activists was executed by the members of the military but without the authority of the law or the government, and, as such, such acts reiterated the fluidity between agents of authority and the criminal-as-individual. On the other hand, to the extent that the brutal murders of Korean residents were carried out for the most part by 'ordinary' citizens acting as a mob, this atrocity revealed the fundamental tenet of detective fiction—that evil is confined in the criminal-as-individual—as nothing but fiction and fantasy by signaling the emergence of the masses as criminals and murderers. In this sense, the violence in the immediate aftermath of the earthquake radically questioned the *reality* of detective fiction, which celebrated individuality by telling the story of the battle of wits between the detective and the criminal.

The significance of the atrocities in the wake of the earthquake within the discourse of detective fiction does not end there but becomes more provocative when we consider the government's reaction to these crimes committed by the masses. In his discussion of the atrocities after the earthquake, Sugamoto Yasuyuki—who posits the primary function of detective fiction as "making legible for the readers = bourgeois the extremely opaque 'masses' and 'metropolis'"—argues that what happened was a radical reversal of this function of detective fiction.[2] He writes:

> The murderers who participated in the earthquake terrorism were not pursued persistently and exposed of their brutal actions like the criminals of detective stories. Indeed, some of the murderers were questioned by the police and ordered to appear before the courts. . . . The court, which is rarely depicted in detective fiction, appeared in this case to lawfully erase the criminal acts of the murderers. . . . By utilizing the unfounded rumors, [the government] guided and connived the terrorism of the masses, and made the criminals who massacred Koreans and Chinese and murdered radical leftist elements disappear into the masses—this was *the terrible and grotesque inversion of detective fiction*.[3]

Rather than discovering "the individual's traces in the big-city crowd"—"the obliteration" of which was "the original social content of the detective story" according to Walter Benjamin—the government and its police did not seek out the individuals among the masses responsible for the

2. Sugamoto, "Tantei shōsetsu, gunshū, Marukusu shugi," 78–79.
3. Ibid., 80. Emphasis in the original.

atrocities to prove their guilt in the court of law but treated the masses as a whole as culprits who by virtue of their faceless and unidentifiable nature were inculpable.[4] In short, the state utilized the opaqueness of the masses to hide and wipe away the crimes that they had committed.

And significantly, it was precisely this inversion of the ideological function of detective fiction that made possible the *actual* materialization of panopticism that is implied in the *fictional* world of the detective story. While Sugamoto describes the citizens who were involved in the massacre of Korean residents in the earthquake's aftermath as "murderers" and "criminals"—and they were—they could also be described as those who took the power of policing and authority into their own hands and became the detective/police, judge, and executioner.[5] Indeed, the government had been fostering such possibilities after the Rice Riots of 1918 by actively organizing vigilante groups among its citizens as a way to combat growing unrest across the country.[6] In this sense, the mass hysteria in the immediate aftermath of the earthquake demonstrated that the government's program of "making police out of the masses" was working.[7] If Ruikō's adaptations of Western detective stories in the late 1880s, in seeking to depoliticize their readers, actively manipulated them into forming a conspiratorial relationship with the authorities, then this relationship finds its ultimate result in the mid-1920s when the people became the pawns of the state, doing its dirty work.

---

4. Benjamin, "The Paris of the Second Empire in Baudelaire," 43.

5. Although there is no doubt that there were mistakes made in the identification of national origin, the citizens functioned as 'detectives' who 'identified' the Korean residents who, in turn, were no different in appearance from the Japanese that formed the masses. In this sense, we could argue that this situation entailed the eruption of the fear that was described in Ruikō's *Muzan*. As we saw in Chapter 2, this story posited the possibility that a Chinese living in Japan can become indistinguishable from a Japanese simply by wearing Japanese clothes and hairstyle.

6. For details on the development of vigilante groups, see Obinata, *Tennōsei keisatsu to minshū*, 139–73.

7. Ibid., 141. Those who became targets of mob violence—the Koreans and the leftists—were precisely the two stereotyped groups of anti-government dissenters who had given the government the most trouble in the late 1910s and the early 1920s, whether demonstrating against Japan's colonization of Korea or for universal male suffrage and better working conditions in the Taishō Democracy movement.

While the extent to which the government was involved in guiding and fueling the violence in the wake of the earthquake has been a topic for debate among historians, it seems indisputable that the citizens of Tokyo as mobs operated and functioned as agents of the state who, just like the detective, exposed its 'enemies.' But unlike the detective, who as an individual can only be in one place at one time and thus must wait for the crime to be committed to showcase his skills, the masses—unlocalizable and ubiquitous—made possible the panoptic gaze that not only discerned and exposed but also preempted 'criminal' activities. And indeed, this state of panopticism characterized Japanese society after the promulgation of the Maintenance of Public Order Act in 1925 when Japanese citizens, inculcated by the government to act as vigilantes, became part of the panoptic gaze to spy on their neighbors and inform the government of any suspicious activity. The effectiveness of this gaze would become clear in the ease with which the state suppressed the Communist Party in the early 1930s as its members—as well as many who had no involvement—were arrested one after another in violation of the Maintenance of the Public Order Act. Significantly enough, these suspects were not simply tried and imprisoned but were forced to confess their crimes against the state and sign a statement that they had 'converted' (*tenkō*) their 'criminal' ways. In the mid-1920s, the detective dissolved into and became incorporated by the masses, making the detective-as-individual—the hero of detective fiction—obsolete, and this union brought about the advent of a modern-day Inquisition.

Reference Matter

Works Cited

Unless otherwise noted, the place of publication of Japanese-language titles is Tokyo.

Akiyama Yūzō. *Hon'yaku no chihei: hon'yakusha to shite no Meiji sakka*. Kanrin shobō, 1995.

Akutagawa Ryūnosuke. *Akutagawa Ryūnosuke zenshū*. 24 vols. Iwanami shoten, 1995–98.

Andō Masami. *Akutagawa Ryūnosuke: kaiga, kaika, toshi, eiga*. Kanrin shobō, 2006.

Ara Masahito. *Natsume Sōseki*. Vol. 3 of *Gendai sakkaron zenshū*. Gogatsu shobō, 1957.

Asano Yō. "Kaika e no manazashi: 'e' aruiwa gakubuchi no guramatorojii." *Kokubungaku: kaishaku to kyōzai no kenkyū* (April 1996): 42–48.

Asaoka Kunio. "Meiji kashihon kashidashi daichō no naka no dokushatachi." *Nihon shuppan shiryō*, no. 4 (March 1999): 1–46.

Asukai Masamichi. *Tennō to Nihon kindai seishinshi*. San'ichi shobō, 1989.

Auslin, Michael R. *Negotiating with Imperialism: The Unequal Treaties and the Culture of Japanese Diplomacy*. Cambridge, MA: Harvard University Press, 2004.

Benjamin, Walter. *Charles Baudelaire: A Lyric Poet in the Era of High Capitalism*. Trans. Harry Zohn. New York: Verso, 1997.

———. "The Paris of the Second Empire in Baudelaire." In *Charles Baudelaire*, 9–106.

———. "Some Motifs in Baudelaire." In *Charles Baudelaire*, 107–54.

Bernardi, Joanne R. "Tanizaki Jun'ichirō's 'The Present and Future of the Moving Pictures.'" In *Currents in Japanese Culture: Translations and Transformations*, ed. Amy Vladeck Heinreich. New York: Columbia University Press, 1997, 293–308.

Bourdaghs, Michael K. *The Dawn That Never Comes: Shimazaki Tōson and Japanese Nationalism*. New York: Columbia University Press, 2003.

Chida Hiroyuki. "'Yomu' koto no sabetsu: Shimazaki Tōson *Hakai*." *Kokubungaku: kaishaku to kanshō* (April 1994): 78–83.

Copeland, Rebecca L. *Lost Leaves: Women Writers of Meiji Japan*. Honolulu, HI: University of Hawai'i Press, 2000.

Copeland, Rebecca L., and Melek Ortabasi, eds. *The Modern Murasaki: Writings by Women of Meiji Japan*. New York: Columbia University Press, 2006.

Deleuze, Gilles. *Coldness and Cruelty*. New York: Zone Books, 1991.

Dostoyevsky, Fyodor. *Crime and Punishment*. Trans. Constance Garnett. New York: Vintage Books, 1950.

Doyle, Sir Arthur Conan. *Sherlock Holmes: The Complete Novels and Stories*. 2 vols. New York: Bantam Books, 1986.

Edogawa Ranpo. *Edogawa Ranpo zenshū*. 25 vols. Kōdansha, 1978–79.

———. "Gakuya banashi." In *Nazo to mahō no monogatari: jisaku ni kansuru kaisetsu*, ed. Shinpo Hirohisa and Yamamae Yuzuru. Kawade shobō, 1995, 34–61.

———. *Gen'eijō*. Futabasha, 1995.

———. *Kohan-tei jiken*. *Ranpo kessakusen*. Vol. 9. Tokyo sōgensha, 1995.

———. "Ruikō no sōsaku *Muzan* ni tsuite." In *Hitori no Bashō no mondai: Nihon misuteri hyōron*, ed. Shinpo Hirohisa and Yamamae Yuzuru. Kawade shobō, 1995, 11–17.

Eguchi Keiichi. *Futatsu no taisen*. Taikei Nihon no rekishi 14. Shōgakukan, 1989.

Emi Suiin. *Jiko chūshin Meiji bundan shi*. Meiji Taishō bungakushi shūsei 12. Nihon tosho sentā, 1982.

Fowler, Edward. *The Rhetoric of Confession:* Shishōsetsu *in Early Twentieth-Century Japanese Fiction*. Berkeley, CA: University of California Press, 1988.

Freud, Sigmund. "Fetishism." In *The Standard Edition of the Complete Psychological Works of Sigmund Freud*, vol. 21, ed. and trans. James Strachey. London: Hogarth Press, 1961, 152–57.

Fujii, James. *Complicit Fictions: The Subject in the Modern Japanese Prose Narrative*. Berkeley, CA: University of California Press, 1993.

Fukaya Masashi. *Ryōsai kenbo shugi no kyōiku*. Nagoya: Reimei shobō, 1981.

Futabatei Shimei. *Ukigumo*. In *Futabatei Shimei shū*. Nihon kindai bungaku taikei 4. Kadokawa shoten, 1971, 37–220.

Gaboriau, Émile. *Within an Inch of His Life*. New York: Charles Scribner's Sons, 1913.

Gaylin, Ann. *Eavesdropping in the Novel from Austen to Proust*. New York: Cambridge University Press, 2002.

Gerbert, Elaine. "Space and Aesthetic Imagination in Some Taishō Writings." In *Japan's Competing Modernities: Issues in Culture and Democracy, 1900–1930*, ed. Sharon A. Minichiello. Honolulu, HI: University of Hawai'i Press, 1998, 70–90.

Girard, René. *Deceit, Desire, and the Novel: Self and Other in Literary Structure*. Trans. Yvonne Freccero. Baltimore, MD: The Johns Hopkins University Press, 1966.

Gluck, Carol. *Japan's Modern Myths: Ideology in the Late Meiji Period*. Princeton, NJ: Princeton University Press, 1985.

Green, Anna Katharine. *XYZ*. New York: G. P. Putnam's Sons, 1883.

Gunning, Tom. "Tracing the Individual Body: Photography, Detectives, and Early Cinema." In *Cinema and the Invention of Modern Life*, ed. Leo Charney and Vanessa R. Schwartz. Berkeley, CA: University of California Press, 1996, 15–45.

Hamill, Barbara. "Nihon-teki modanizumu no shisō: Hirabayashi Hatsunosuke o chūshin to shite." In *Nihon modanizumu no kenkyū*, ed. Minami Hiroshi. Burēn shuppan, 1982, 89–114.

Harootunian, Harry. "Introduction: A Sense of an Ending and the Problem of Taishō." In *Japan in Crisis: Essays on Taishō Democracy*, ed. Bernard S. Silberman and H. D. Harootunian. Princeton, NJ: Princeton University Press, 1974, 3–28.

———. *Overcome by Modernity: History, Culture, and Community in Interwar Japan*. Princeton, NJ: Princeton University Press, 2000.

Haruta Kunio. *Sabakareru hibi: Chichibu jiken to Meiji no saiban*. Nihon hyōronsha, 1985.

Hasegawa Tenkei. "Handō no genshō." *Taiyō* (May 1906): 153–60.

Hasumi Shigehiko. "'Taishō-teki' gensetsu to hihyō." In *Kindai Nihon no hihyō: Meiji Taishō hen*, ed. Karatani Kōjin. Fukubu shoten, 1992, 123–49.

Hibi Yoshitaka, *"Jiko hyōshō" no bungakushi: jibun o kaku shōsetsu no tōjō*. Kanrin shobō, 2002.

Hirabayashi Hatsunosuke. "Nihon no kindai-teki tantei shōsetsu: toku ni Edogawa Ranposhi ni tsuite." In *Edogawa Ranpo: hyōron to kenkyū*, ed. Nakajima Kawatarō. Kōdansha, 1980, 9–13.

———. "Tantei shōsetsu dan no shokeikō." In *Hirabayashi Hatsunosuke bungei hyōron zenshū*, vol. 2. Bunsendō shoten, 1975, 340–47.

Hiraoka Toshio. *Nihon kindai bungaku no shuppatsu*. Hanawa shobō, 1992.

Hirata Yumi. "'Onna no monogatari' to iu seido." In *Nashonariti no datsu kōchiku*, ed. Sakai Naoki, Brett de Bary, and Iyotani Toshio. Kashiwa shobō, 1996, 161–82.

Hirota Masaki., ed. *Sabetsu no soshō*. Vol. 22 of *Nihon kindai shisō taikei*. Iwanami shoten, 1980.

Honda Yasuo. *Shinbun shōsetsu no tanjō*. Heibonsha, 1998.

Huffman, James L. *Creating a Public: People and Press in Meiji Japan*. Honolulu, HI: University of Hawai'i Press, 1997.

Ichiyanagi Hirotaka. "Samayoeru dopperugengā." In *Tantei shōsetsu to Nihon kindai*. Seikyūsha, 2004, 110–31.

Iida Yūko. *Karera no monogatari: Nihon kindai bungaku to jendā*. Nagoya: Nagoya Daigaku shuppankai, 1998.

Ikeda Hiroshi. *Taishū shōsetsu no sekai to han-sekai*. Gendai shokan, 1983.

Imanishi Hajime. *Kindai Nihon no sabetsu to sei bunka: bunmei kaika to minshū shakai*. Yūzankaku, 1998.

Inoue Ken, "Tanizaki Jun'ichirō no sekimatsu." In *Tanizaki Jun'ichirō to seikimatsu*, ed. Matsumura Masaie. Kyoto: Shibunkaku shuppan, 2002, 7–28.

Irokawa Daikichi. *The Culture of the Meiji Period*. Ed. Marius B. Jansen. Trans. Noboru Hiraga. Princeton, NJ: Princeton University Press, 1985.

Ishibashi Ningetsu. "*Imotose kagami* o yomu." In *Ishibashi Ningetsu zenshū*, vol. 3. Yagi shoten, 1995, 3–9.

Ishihara Chiaki. *Hanten suru Sōseki*. Seitosha, 1997.

Ishii Shirō and Mizubayashi Takeshi, eds. *Hō to chitsujo*. Nihon kindai shisō taikei 7. Iwanami shoten, 1992.

Itō Hideo. *Kuroiwa Ruikō: sono shōsetsu no subete*. Tōgensha, 1971.

———. *Kuroiwa Ruikō: tantei shōsetsu no ganso*. San'ichi shobō, 1988.

———. *Meiji no tantei shōsetsu*. Shōbunsha, 1986.

Ito, Ken. "Writing Time in Sōseki's *Kokoro*." In *Studies in Modern Japanese Literature: Essays and Translations in Honor of Edwin McClellan*, ed. Dennis Washburn and Alan Tansman. Ann Arbor, MI: Center for Japanese Studies, University of Michigan, 1997, 3–22.

Itō, Ujitaka. *Kokuhaku no bungaku: Mori Ōgai kara Mishima Yukio made*. Chōeisha, 2002.

Izumi Kyōka. "Obakezuki no iware shōshō to shojosaku." In *Izumi Kyōka shū*. Meiji bungaku zenshū 21. Chikuma shobō, 1966, 347–50.

Jameson, Fredric. *The Political Unconscious: Narrative as a Socially Symbolic Act*. Ithaca, NY: Cornell University Press, 1981.

Jann, Rosemary. *The Adventures of Sherlock Holmes: Detecting Social Order*. New York: Twayne Publishers, 1995.

Jansen, Marius. *The Making of Modern Japan*. Cambridge, MA: Harvard University Press, 2000.

Jauss, Hans Robert. *Toward an Aesthetic of Reception*. Trans. Timothy Bahti. Minneapolis, MN: University of Minnesota Press, 1982.

Jiyū shinbun. 5 vols. San'ichi shobō, 1972.

Kamei Hideo. *Meiji bungaku shi*. Iwanami shoten, 2000.

———. *"Shōsetsu" ron:* Shōsetsu shinzui *to kindai*. Iwanami shoten, 1999.

Karatani Kōjin, ed. *Kindai Nihon no hihyō*, 3 vols. Kōdansha, 1997.

———. *Sōseki ron shūsei*. Daisan bunmei sha, 1992.

Kasai Zenzō. "Kohan shuki." In *Hirotsu Kazuo, Uno Kōji, Kasai Zenzō shū*. Nihon kindai bungaku taikei 40. Kadokawa shoten, 1970, 437–68.

Kawabata Toshifusa. Hakai *no yomikata*. Kyoto: Bunrikaku, 1993.

Kawamoto Saburō. *Taishō gen'ei*. Chikuma shobō, 1997.

Kawana, Sari. *Murder Most Modern: Detective Fiction and Japanese Culture*. Minneapolis, MN: University of Minnesota Press, 2008.

Kawasaki Kenko. "*Shinseinen* no tanjō to sono jidai." In *"Shinseinen" dokuhon: Shōwa gurafiti*, ed. Shinseinen kenkyūkai. Sakuhinsha, 1988, 4–6.

———. "Taishū bunka seiritsuki ni okeru 'tantei shōsetsu' janru no hen'yō." In *Taishū bunka to masu media*, ed. Aoki Tamotsu, Kawamoto Saburō, Tsutsui Kiyotada et al. Iwanami shoten, 1999, 61–92.

Keene, Donald. *Dawn to the West: Japanese Literature of the Modern Era*. New York: Columbia University Press, 1998.

Kimoto Itaru. *Zasshi de yomu sengoshi*. Shinchōsha, 1985.

Kimura Ki. *Maruzen gaishi*. Maruzen, 1969.

Kimura Naoe. *"Seinen" no tanjō*. Shin'yōsha, 1998.

Kinmonth, Earl. *The Self-Made Man in Meiji Japanese Thought*. Berkeley, CA: University of California Press, 1981.

Kitamura Tōkoku. *Kitamura Tōkoku shū*. Meiji bungaku zenshū 29. Chikuma shobō, 1976.

Kokumin no tomo. 23 vols. Meiji bunken, 1966–68.

Komori Yōichi. "Bungaku no jidai." *Bungaku* (Spring 1993): 2–11.

———. *Kōzō to shite no katari*. Shin'yōsha, 1988.

———. "'Watashi' to iu 'tasha'-sei: *Kokoro* o meguru ōto kuritikku." *Bungaku* (October 1992): 13–27.

Kōno Kensuke. *Tōki to shite no bungaku: katsuji, kenshō, media*. Shin'yōsha, 2003.

Kornicki, Peter. *The Reform of Fiction in Meiji Japan*. London: Ithaca Press, 1982.

Kozakai Fuboku. "'Ni-sen dōka' o yomu." In *Edogawa Ranpo: hyōron to kenkyū*, ed. Nakajima Kawatarō. Kōdansha, 1980, 7–8.

Kuroiwa Ruikō. *Hito ka oni ka*. In *Ruikō zenshū*, vol. 2. Kodaira: Takara shuppan, 1979.

———. *Majutsu no zoku*. Shōsetsukan, 1889.

———. *Makkura*. Kin'ōdō, 1889.

———. *Muzan*. In *Kuroiwa Ruikō, Kozakai Fuboku, Kōga Saburō shū*. Nihon tantei shōsetsu zenshū 1. Sōgensha, 1984, 9–49.

———. "Tantei-dan ni tsuite." *Yorozu chōhō*, May 11, 1893. Repr. in *Yorozu chōhō*. Vol. 3. Nihon tosho sentā, 1983.

———. *Yūzai muzai*. Kaishinrō, 1889.

Levy, Indra. *Sirens on the Western Shore: The Westernesque Femme Fatale, Translation, and Vernacular Style in Modern Japanese Literature*. New York: Columbia University Press, 2006.

Lifton, Robert Jay, Shūichi Katō, and Michael R. Reich. *Six Lives, Six Deaths: Portraits from Modern Japan*. New Haven, CT: Yale University Press, 1979.

Maeda Ai. "Gesaku bungaku to *Tōsei shosei katagi*." In *Kindai Nihon no bungaku kūkan*, 116–33.

———. "Kashō no machi." In *Toshi kūkan no naka no bungaku*, 320–38.

———. *Kindai Nihon no bungaku kūkan*. Shin'yōsha, 1983.

———. "Meiji no hyōgen shisō to buntai: shōsetsu no katari o megutte." *Kokubungaku: kaishaku to kyōzai no kenkū*, vol. 25, no. 10 (August 1980): 6–13.

———. "Meiji risshin shusse shugi no keifu." In *Kindai dokusha no seiritsu*. Iwanami shoten, 2001, 114–44.

———. "Mishima Michitsune to Rokumeikan jidai." In *Genkei no Meiji*. Asahi shinbunsha, 1978, 111–36.

———. "Nikai no geshuku." In *Toshi kūkan no naka no bungaku*, 250–77.

———. "Noberu no mosaku." In *Kindai Nihon no bungaku kūkan*, 304–12.

———. *Toshi kūkan no naka no bungaku; rekishi, kotoba, jōkyō*. Chikuma shobō, 1982.

Makihara Norio. "Bunmei kaika ron." In *Iwanami kōza: Nihon tsūshi,* vol. 16. Kindai 1. Iwanami shoten, 1994, 249–90.

Marran, Christine. *Poison Woman: Figuring Female Transgression in Modern Japanese Culture*. Minneapolis, MN: University of Minnesota Press, 2007.

Masaoka Shiki. "Bunkai yatsuatari." In *Masaoka Shiki shū*. Meiji bungaku zenshū 53. Chikuma shobō, 1975, 261–73.

Matsumoto San'nosuke and Yamamuro Shin'ichi, eds. *Genron to media*. Nihon kindai shisō taikei 11. Iwanami shoten, 1990.

Matsumoto Tsunehiko. "Kaika no futari." In *Sakuhinron Akutagawa Ryūnosuke*, ed. Ebii Eiji and Miyasaka Satoru. Sōbunsha, 1990, 121-42.

Matsuo Shōichi. *Kindai tennōsei kokka to minshū/Asia*. Vol. 1. Hōsei Daigaku shuppankyoku, 1997.

Matsuyama Iwao. *Ranpo to Tōkyō*. Chikuma shobō, 1994.

———. *Uwasa no enkinhō*. Seitosha, 1993.

Mertz, John. *Novel Japan: Spaces of Nationhood in Early Meiji Narrative, 1870–88*. Ann Arbor, MI: Center for Japanese Studies, University of Michigan, 2003.

Miller, D. A. *The Novel and the Police*. Berkeley, CA: University of California Press, 1988.

Miller, J. Scott. *Adaptations of Western Literature in Meiji Japan*. New York: Palgrave, 2001.

Minami Hiroshi, ed. *Nihon modanizumu no kenkyū*. Burēn shuppan, 1982.

———. *Taishō bunka*. Keisō shobō, 1965.

Miyoshi Yukio. "Watoson wa haishinsha ka: *Kokoro* saisetsu." *Bungaku* (May 1988): 7–21.

Moretti, Franco. "Clues." In *Signs Taken for Wonders*, 130–56.

———. "Homo Palpitans: Balzac's Novels and Urban Personality." In *Signs Taken for Wonders*, 109–29.

———. *Signs Taken for Wonders: Essays in the Sociology of Literary Forms*. Trans. Susan Fischer, David Forgacs, and David Miller. New York: Verso, 1988.

Morinaga Eizaburō. *Saiban jiyū minken jidai*. Nihon hyōronsha, 1979.

Nagai Kiyotake. *Shizenshugi no retorikku*. Sōbunsha, 2008.

Nagamine Shigetoshi. *Kaitō Jigoma to katsudō shashin no jidai*. Shinchōsha, 2006.

———. *Modan toshi no dokusha kūkan*. Nihon editā sukūru shuppanbu, 2001.

Nagashima Yūko. "'Kōtō yūmin' o megutte: *Higan sugi made* no Matsumoto Tsunezō." In *Natsume Sōseki: hanten suru tekusuto*, vol. 14 of *Nihon bungaku kenkyū shirō shinshū*, ed. Ishihara Chiaki. Yūseidō, 1990, 218–26.

Nakajima Kawatarō, ed. *Edogawa Ranpo: hyōron to kenkyū*. Kōdansha, 1980.

———. *Nihon suiri shōsetsu shi*. Vols. 1–2. Sōgensha, 1993–95.

Nakajima Reiko. "'Zenka mono,' 'Kin to gin,' 'A to B no hanashi' ni tsuite." In *Ronkō Tanizaki Jun'ichirō*, ed. Kōno Toshirō. Ōfūsha, 1980, 75–96.

Nakamaru Nobuaki. "Kindai shōsetsu no tenkai." In *Iwanami kōza: Nihon bungakushi*, vol. 11. Iwanami shoten, 1996, 133–53.

Nakamura Mitsuo. "Tayama Katai ron." *Nakamura Mitsuo zenshū*, vol. 3. Chikuma shobō, 1972, 253–90.

Nakanome Tōru. "Bunmei kaika no jidai." In *Meiji ishin to bunmei kaika*. Nihon no jidaishi 21. Ed. Matsuo Masahito. Yoshikawa kōbunkan, 2004, 213–45.

Nakayama Akihiko, "'Bungakushi' to nashonaritī: waisetsu, Nihonjin, bunka bōei ron." In *Kindai chi no seiritsu 1870–1910 nendai 1*. Iwanami kōza: kindai Nihon no bunkashi 3. Iwanami shoten, 2002, 83–119.

Natsume Kyōko. *Natsume no omoide*. Kaizōsha, 1928.

Natsume Sōseki. *Kokoro*. Trans. Edwin McClellan. Chicago, IL: Regnery Gateway, 1985.

———. *Sōseki zenshū*. 18 vols. Iwanami shoten, 1965–86.

Obinata Sumio. *Nihon kindai kokka no seiritsu to keisatsu*. Azekura shobō, 1992.

———. *Tennō-sei keisatsu to minshū*. Nihon hyōronsha, 1987.

Ochi Haruo. "*Shōsetsu shinzui* no botai." In *Kindai bungaku seiritsuki no kenkyū*. Iwanami shoten, 1984, 254–70.

Ogi Shinzō, Kumakura Isao, Ueno Chizuko, eds. *Fūzoku sei*, Nihon kindai shisō taikei 23. Iwanami shoten, 1990.

Oketani Hideaki. "Akutagawa to Sōseki: Meiji no imi." *Kokubungaku: kaishaku to kyōzai no kenkyū* (May 1981): 26–31.

Oku Takenori. *Bunmei kaika no minshū: kindai Nihon seishin-shi danshō*. Shin hyōron, 1993.

———. *Sukyandaru no Meiji: kokumin o tsukuru tame no ressun*. Chikuma shobō, 1997.

Ōkubo Toshiaki. *Kazokusei no sōshutsu*. Yoshikawa kōbunkan, 1993.

Poe, Edgar Allan. *The Short Fiction of Edgar Allan Poe*. Ed. Stuart Levine and Susan Levine. Urbana, IL: University of Illinois Press, 1990.

Ryū Tōun. "Edogawa Ranpo ron." In *Edogawa Ranpo: hyōron to kenkyū*, ed. Nakajima Kawatarō. Kōdansha, 1980, 39–41.

Sadoya Shigenobu. *Nihon kindai bungaku no seiritsu: Amerika bungaku juyō no hikaku bungaku-teki kenkyū*. Vol. 2. Meiji shoin, 1977.

Sakakibara Takanori. "Dosutoefusukii hon'yaku sakuhin nenpyō." *Hon'yaku to rekishi*, vol. 17 (September 2003): 12–26.

Sakamoto Takao. *Meiji kokka no kensetsu*. Nihon no kindai 2. Chūō kōronsha, 1998.

Satō Haruo. *Teihon Satō Haruo zenshū*. 38 vols. Kyoto: Rinsen shoten, 1998–2001.

Seidensticker, Edward. *Low City, High City: Tokyo from Edo to the Earthquake*. Cambridge, MA: Harvard University Press, 1983.

Serizawa Kazuya. *"Hō" kara kaihō sareru kenryoku: hanzai, kyōki, hinkon, soshite Taishō demokurashī*. Shin'yōsha, 2001.

Shimazaki Tōson. *Hakai*. *Shimazaki Tōson shū*. Vol. 1. Nihon kindai bungaku taikei 13. Kadokawa shoten, 1971, 39–347.

———. *Haru*. In *Shimazaki Tōson shū*. Vol. 2. Nihon kindai bungaku taikei 14. Kadokawa shoten, 1970, 49–301.

Shinseinen. 31 vols. Hon no tomosha, 1990–2003.

Shinseinen kenkyūkai, ed. *"Shinseinen" dokuhon: Shōwa gurafiti*. Sakuhinsha, 1988.

Shiratori Shōgo. "Atarashiki seinen ni gekisuru uta." *Shinseinen* (January 1920): 2–5.

Silver, Mark. *Purloined Letters: Cultural Borrowing and Japanese Crime Literature, 1868–1937*. Honolulu, HI: University of Hawai'i Press, 2008.

Silverberg, Miriam. *Erotic Grotesque Nonsense: The Mass Culture of Japanese Modern Times*. Berkeley, CA: University of California Press, 2006.

Sone Hiroyoshi. "Furoito no shōkai to eikyō: shin-shinri shugi seiritsu no haikei." In *Shōwa bungaku no shomondai*, ed. Shōwa bungaku kenkyūkai. Kasama shoin, 1979, 77–100.

Suga Hidemi. *"Teikoku" no bungaku: sensō to "taigyaku" no aida*. Ibunsha, 2001.

Sugamoto Yasuyuki. "Tantei shōsetsu, gunshū, Marukusu shugi: Hirabayashi Hatsunosuke no tantei shōsetsu ron." *Nihon kindai bungaku*, no. 59 (October 1998): 71–85.

Suzuki Sadami. *"Shōwa bungaku" no tame ni: fikushon no ryōryaku*. Shisōsha, 1989.

Suzuki, Tomi. *Narrating the Self: Fictions of Japanese Modernity*. Stanford, CA: Stanford University Press, 1996.

Takagi Takeo. *Shinbun shōsetsushi kō*. Vol. 1. San'yūsha, 1964.

———. *Shinbun shōsetsushi nenpyō*. Tosho kankōkai, 1987.

Takahashi Osamu. "'Hon'yaku' to iu jiko genkyū: Tsubouchi Shōyō *Nisegane tsukai* no paradokkusu." *Bungaku*, vol. 3, no. 1 (1992): 75–86.

———. "'Tantei shōsetsu' ga inpei suru mono." In *Bungaku no yami/kindai no "chinmoku."* Bungaku nenpō 1. Ed. Nakayama Akihiko, Shimamura Teru, Iida Yūko, Takahashi Osamu, and Yoshida Morio. Yokohama: Seori shobō, 2003, 27–60.

Tanizaki Jun'ichirō. *Tanizaki Jun'ichirō zenshū*. 30 vols. Chūō kōronsha, 1981–83.

Tayama Katai. *Futon*. In *Tayama Katai shū*. Nihon kindai bungaku taikei 19. Kadokawa shoten, 1972, 123–94.

———. *The Quilt and Other Stories by Tayama Katai*. Trans. Kenneth Henshall. University of Tokyo Press, 1981.

Tōkyō hyakunen shi henshū iinkai, ed. *Tōkyō hyakunen shi*. Vol. 4. *Taishō*. Tokyo Prefecture, 1972.

Tsubouchi Shōyō. "Eikoku shōsetsu no hensen." *Shin shōsetsu*, vol. 11 (June 1889): 1–16.

———. *Imotose kagami*. In *Tsubouchi Shōyō shū*. Meiji bungaku zenshū 16. Chikuma shobō, 1969, 164–248.

———. *Nisegane tsukai*. In *Tsubouchi Shōyō senshū*. Supplementary vol. 2. Shun'yōdō, 1927, 657–729.

———. *Shōsetsu shinzui*. In *Tsubouchi Shōyō shū*. Nihon kindai bungaku taikei 3, 39–166.

———. *Tōsei shosei katagi*. In *Tsubouchi Shōyō shū*. Nihon kindai bungaku taikei 3, 221–433.

———. *Tsubouchi Shōyō shū*. Nihon kindai bungaku taikei 3. Kadokawa shoten, 1974.

Tsuchiya Reiko. *Taishūshi no genryū: Meiji-ki koshinbun no kenkyū*. Kyoto: Sekai shisōsha, 2002.

Ubukata Tomoko. "'Tantei shōsetsu' izen: Satō Haruo 'Shimon' ni okeru nazotoki no wakugumi." *Nihon kindai bungaku*, vol. 74 (May 2006): 168–81.

Uchida Roan. *Tsumi to batsu*. In *Meiji hon'yaku bungakushū*. Meiji bungaku zenshū 7. Chikuma shobō, 1972, 141–269.

———. *Tsumi to batsu*. 2 vols. Uchida rōkakuho, 1892–1893.

Uchida Ryūzō. *Tantei shōsetsu no shakaigaku*. Iwanami shoten, 2001.

Ueda, Atsuko. *Concealment of Politics, Politics of Concealment: The Production of "Literature" in Meiji Japan*. Stanford, CA: Stanford University Press, 2007.

Walker, Janet. *The Japanese Novel of the Meiji Period and the Ideal of Individualism*. Princeton, NJ: Princeton University Press, 1979.

Watanabe Masahiko. *Kindai bungaku no bunshinzō*. Kadokawa shoten, 1999.

Watanabe Naomi. *Fukei bungakuron josetsu*. Ōta shuppan, 1999.

———. *Nihon kindai bungaku to "sabetsu."* Ōta shuppan, 1994.

Watarai Yoshiichi. *Meiji no seishin isetsu*. Iwanami shoten, 2003.

Williams, Raymond. *Marxism and Literature*. New York: Oxford University Press, 1977.

Yamada Shunji. *Taishū shinbun ga tsukuru Meiji no "Nihon."* Nihon hōsō shuppan kyōkai, 2002.

———. "*Tōsei shosei katagi* ni okeru 'sakka' no ichi." *Nihon bungaku* vol. 40, no. 1 (January 1991): 1–13.

Yamada Yūsaku. *Gensō no kindai: Shōyō, Bimyō, Ryūrō*. Ōfū, 2001.
Yamamoto Taketoshi. *Shinbun to minshū*. Kinokuniya shoten, 1994.
Yamashita Takeshi. *"Shinseinen" o meguru sakkatachi*. Chikuma shobō, 1996.
Yanagida Izumi. *Seiji shōsetsu kenkyū*. Vol. 3. Shunjūsha, 1967–68.
Yasumaru Yoshio. "'Kangoku' no tanjō." In *Bakumatsu Meiji ki no kokumin kokka keisei to bunka hen'yō*, ed. Nishikawa Nagao and Matsumiya Hideharu. Shin'yōsha, 1995, 279–312.
Yorozu chōhō. 156 vols. Nihon tosho sentā, 1983–93.
Yomiuri shinbun. *Meiji no Yomiuri shinbun*. 37 CD-ROMs. Yomiuri shinbunsha, 1999.
Yoshida Morio, ed. *Tantei shōsetsu to Nihon kindai*. Seikyūsha, 2004.
Yoshida Seiichi et al., eds. *Kindai bungaku hyōron taikei*. 10 vols. Kadokawa shoten, 1971–75.
Zwicker, Jonathan. *Practices of the Sentimental Imagination: Melodrama, the Novel, and the Social Imaginary in Nineteenth-Century Japan*. Cambridge, MA: Harvard University Asia Center, 2006.

Index

Abnormal sexuality, 257, 273, 275–76
Adultery, 36, 63, 90–91, 93, 95, 124, 175, 206n15, 213
Aeba Kōson, 46, 116
Akutagawa Ryūnosuke, 5, 11, 199; and *kaika-mono*, 201, 205–6
—"Kaika no satsujin" (Murder in the age of enlightenment), 200–210, 233; Akutagawa's misgivings in writing of, 200–201; and *bunmei kaika*, 206–7; comparisons to *Kokoro*, 201–2, 205; Girard's triangular structure of desire in, 201–2; ideal of love (*ren'ai*) in, 203–4, 206, 209; moral framework of, 202–5; narrative frame of, 207–9; plot summary of, 201n9
—Other texts: "Futatsu no tegami" (Two letters), 212–14; "Giwaku" (Suspicion), 204n13; "Kaika no otto" (Husband of enlightenment), 206; *Kairaishi* (Puppeteer), 208
Allegorical interpretative framework, 15–16, 60–64; aristocrats-as-peers, 89–91, 95–97; falsely accused-as-political activists, 72, 75–76, 90, 95–97
Andreyev, Leonid: *Der Gedanke*, 172–73
Arishima Takeo: "Sengen hitotsu" (One declaration), 279
Asahi shinbun (newspaper), 274
Assembly Ordinance (Shūkai jōrei), 74
Authority, 200; and detective, 6, 12–13, 54, 220–21, 233; of first-person narrator, 53; of the novelist, 24, 272; of the state, 12–13, 155, 220–21, 232, 280; of third-person narrator, 54, 58; of translator, 56

Baba Kochō, 250n25
Belatedness, sense of, 212, 214–15, 246
Benjamin, Walter, 27, 106, 260, 267, 277
Boissonade, Gustave Emile, 67n17, 74
Bungei shunjū (magazine), 272
Bunmei kaika (civilization and enlightenment), 6, 259n39; and the Japanese intellectual, 6, 206–7; and newspapers, 35, 37–38; and Shōyō's notion of the novel, 20–22; and translation, 56; and Western education, 121

Bunshō sekai (magazine), 139, 146n64
Burakumin, 10, 125n29; and criticism of Meiji government, 130; and detective fiction framework, 132; and Emancipation Edict, 130; literary portrayal of, 125, 131; as the Other, 138, 143n58; and *risshin shusse* ideology, 130–31; and social prejudice, 127, 129, 135, 137, 149n69, 152. *See also* Shimazaki Tōson: *Hakai*

Chida Hiroyuki, 134–35
Chūgaku sekai (magazine), 145–46
Chūō kōron (magazine), 11, 163n11, 199, 272; "Himitsu to kaihō" (Secrets and liberation) issue, 11, 199–200, 208, 232–33
Code of Criminal Procedure (Chizaihō), 67, 74
Confession: and determination of truth, 252–53, 255–56; and dynamic of secret and exposure, 10, 125, 199; and eavesdropping narrator, 28, 35; and first-person narration, 45–46; in *Futon*, 142, 149–50; Japanese detective story's reliance on, 80; in *Hakai*, 128–30, 135, 138–39, 150; in "Kaika no satsujin," 201–2, 205, 208; and the state, 278–79; and the unconscious, 268–69
Conspiratorial relationship, between: authorities and reader, 93, 95, 281; detective and reader, 55, 58, 93; detective and state, 277; masses and state, 281; narrator and reader, 19, 28, 42, 53n59, 55, 58
Constitution, 8, 13n17; Meiji, 1, 13, 14n17, 76, 97n55, 105n69, 192n51
Conway, Hugh: *Dark Days*, 1
Country, and city, 12, 260n43, 261–64, 267. *See also* Urbanization
Crime of disrespect (*fukeizai*), 74, 191
Crime: Meiji understanding of, 123; reporting of, 36, 68, 70; rise in, 68n19
Criminal: and confession, 80, 129, 150, 255–56, 269, 279; detective as, 11, 158, 160; within interior/exterior dichotomy, 23, 83–84; Meiji understanding of, 123; narrative focus on, 18, 68, 115, 250, 254; subject as, 10–11, 110, 114, 122, 173, 185–86, 221, 275–76; and task of the detective, 6, 47, 77, 112, 199, 238, 277
Criminal Code (Keihō), 67, 74, 90, 102
Criminality: foreign, 104, 106, 132, 276; of student/intellectual, 10–11, 123, 152

Deleuze, Gilles, 220
Democracy, 12–13, 122, 197
Der Student von Prag (The student of Prague), 226–27
Desire: of eavesdropper, 20, 34, 37, 39; epistemological (desire to know), 6, 9, 39, 97, 192, 195; fulfillment and non-fulfillment of personal, 206–7, 209, 211; Girard's triangular structure of, 200–202, 205, 206n15, 213; of the novel, 20, 58; vs. reason, 21, 47n55; sexual, 154; to succeed, 144, 150, 151n71; to transgress boundaries, 37, 160–61; of the unconscious, 177, 268–69, 273; West as source of, 276; woman as object of, 33n29, 141, 149
Detective fiction: booms and popularity of, 1, 5–6, 11–12, 108–9, 238, 263n49; and Japanese novel, 2, 4–6, 11–12, 20, 27,

52, 59, 80–81, 96, 109–10, 273–74, 278; Japanese, reception of, 2, 98, 235–38; literary value of, 2–3, 44, 201; and science, 6, 235–36, 239n9; theoretical consideration of, 6, 12–13, 14n18, 15n19, 27, 94, 225n47, 277–78; *tōjo tantei shōsetsu* (inverted detective story) format of, 250; of Western analytical tradition, 6, 98, 100–101, 240, 244–46, 269, 277

Detective: as agent of the state, 12–13, 277–79; ambivalence toward, 9–10, 97–98, 113, 158, 168–69; and confession, 256, 269, 279; and criminal, 9–11, 158, 160–61, 278, 280; as fictional hero in Japan, 9, 11, 64, 77, 97, 233; historical, as enemy of the people, 8–9, 64; as ideal narrator/novelist, 23–24, 46n52, 51, 54, 57, 59; and Japanese student/intellectual, 6–7, 9, 16, 168; Japanese writers' understanding and criticism of, 10–11, 47–48, 157–58, 160–61; as model within Japan's Westernization, 7, 9, 112, 122; modern individual as, 157–58, 161, 168, 176, 182–83, 195; readers as, 180, 188, 231; Western models of, 6, 12–13, 23, 100–101, 221, 277–78

Diet, 1, 8n13, 14n17, 76, 89, 97n55

Dime novels, 1, 65, 91n51

Disavowal, 125, 200, 215, 220–21; detective's emergence from framework of, 232; and the double, 213–14, 227; of egoism and self-interest, 205, 210; fetishistic, 230; and masochism, 220; second-floor room as space of, 112–13; of Western influence, 215–17, 219, 233–34

Dokufu-mono (poisonous women tales), 18, 68–70

Dokusatsu saiban (The trial of poison murder), 69

Doppelgänger. *See* Double

Double: and cinema, 226–27; in "Futari no geijutsuka no hanashi," 212; in "Futatsu no tegami," 212–14; rise in stories about, 212, 213n27, 226; in "Shimon," 224–26, 228–29; and "William Wilson," 212, 224

Dostoevsky, Fyodor, 127, 217, 238; Raskolnikov (character), 114, 116–22, 125–27, 150, 174, 216–17, 269

—*Crime and Punishment*, 4, 10, 114, 121, 125, 139, 233, 251n26, 269; comparisons to *Hakai* and *Futon*, 142, 150, 152; influence on *Hakai* by, 125–27, 129n38; and Japanese intellectual, 173–74; utilization of, in "Futari no geijutsuka no hanashi," 216–17; various translations of, 217. *See also* Uchida Roan: *Tsumi to batsu*

Doyle, Arthur Conan, 6, 13, 98; "The Adventure of Dancing Men," 240; "The Adventure of the Engineer's Thumb," 249n23; Sherlock Holmes (character), 100, 215–17, 221, 239; Sherlock Holmes tales, 23, 104n68, 240, 243, 249n23, 252n27; Watson (character), 51, 54n59, 222

Du Boisgobey, Fortuné, 1, 66n12, 71

Dumas, Alexander: *Taking the Bastille*, 72

Dupin, Auguste (character). *See* Poe, Edgar Allan

E'iri jiyū shinbun (newspaper), 60n1, 62n6, 65–66, 70–71, 73, 76, 83, 87–88, 98n58

Eavesdropper, 20, 50; desire of, 34, 37, 39; detective as, 49, 51, 54; gaze of, 28, 39–40, 54; narrator as, 19, 28, 166–67; novelist as, 40–41, 59, 166–67; and public and private dichotomy, 39; and translator, 56

Eavesdropping: allure of and desire for, 19–20; and cinematic experience, 227; and the detective, 48–49, 51, 57; in *Imotose kagami*, 30–31; and narration, 28, 31, 42; problematization of, 34–35; as resistance against the visual, 39, 231; Shōyō's criticism of, 39–40, 43; structure of, 50; in Western fictions, 29n23; *zappō* columns and, 36–37

Edogawa Ranpo, 5, 11–12, 14n18, 98, 250n25; Akechi Kogorō (character), 11, 181n33, 264–65, 269–70, 279; categorization of and shift in detective stories by, 236–38, 273, 275; as *ero guro nansensu* writer, 237, 273; epistemological project of, 238, 252–54, 256–57; Hirabayashi's reception of, 234–37; framing technique, use of, by, 245–46; and Freudian psychoanalysis, 257–59; positivistic paradigm, criticism and rejection of, by, 243–47, 257, 268; and psychological method of detection, articulation of, by, 248–59 *passim*; urbanization process, portrayal of, by, 263–64; notion of unconscious, use of, by, 268–70, 273

—"D-zaka no satsujin jiken" (Murder case on D-hill), 238, 247–50, 252, 261n44, 264; criticism of witness accounts in, 247–48; detective's method of Akechi in, 249, 252; plot summary of, 247n21

—"Ichimai no kippu" (One ticket), 238, 243–46, 249; criticism of physical evidence in, 243–45; and detective as novelist, 244–45; plot summary of, 243n17

—"Ni-sen dōka" (Two-sen copper coin), 238–43, 246, 264; critical reception of, 238–40; and first-person narration, 240–41; as parody of Western detective fiction, 239–41, 243; plot summary of, 240n15; real vs. fictional world in, 241–42

—"Shinri shiken" (The psychological test), 238, 250–56, 278; and *Crime and Punishment*, 251n26; plot summary of, 250n24; problems of detective's method in, 252–53; use of word-association test in, 251

—"Yaneura no sanposha" (The wanderer in the attic), 237–38, 253–57, 265–69, 278; comparisons to "Shinri shiken," 253–54; as failure of epistemological project, 255–56; and *kōtō yūmin*, 264–65; and modern experience as trauma, 265, 267–68; notion of the unconscious in, 256–57, 269–70; plot summary of, 253n29; and transgression of social norms, 265–66

—Other texts: "Akai heya" (The red room), 254n32; "Gakuya banashi" (Inside story), 245; *Injū* (Shadowy beast), 238n7, 274–76; *Issun bōshi* (One-inch boy), 274; *Kumo otoko* (Spider man), 273; "Muyūbyōsha no shi" (The death of a sleepwalker), 238n7; *Nanimono* (Who), 238n7; *Ōgon kamen* (Golden mask), 273; "Sōseiji" (Twins), 254n32

Einstein, Albert, 236

Emancipation Edict (Kaihō rei), 130–32
Emperor, Meiji, 8, 13, 130n40, 173n24, 195, 198; death of, 191–92; imperial pardon by, 105n69; and peerage system, 89n49
Ero guro nansensu (erotic, grotesque, nonsense), 237, 273
Experience: authentic, 259, 272; cinematic, 226–27; and I-novel, 270, 272; vs. intellectual knowledge, 120, 214; Japanese, 214, 221; modern and urban, traumas of, 260, 263, 267–68; past, power of, 182, 195; vs. scientific reasoning, 100; unconscious, 269–70

Falsely accused, the, 71–73, 75, 77, 84n42, 90, 93n53, 95–97. *See also* Allegorical interpretative framework
Fetishism, 221, 230–31
Film: and close-up, 222, 231; and double, 226–27; as emergent genre, 225
Fingerprint: as fetish, 230–31; in "Shimon," 223–26, 229–32; theoretical consideration of, 224–25
First-person narration. *See* Narration, first-person
Fragmentary (or fragmented): allegiance, 209, 221, 233; identities, 81, 96; nature of Japanese intellectual, 11, 206; subject, 209, 214, 226, 232–34
Framing technique. *See* Narrative frame
Freedom and People's Rights movement, 8, 63–64; and detective fiction boom, 12; as framework for fantasy, 105; falsely accused as allegorical substitute of activists in, 75, 90, 95; frustrated political energies of those involved in, 9, 65, 77, 109, 113; and the Meiji constitution, 14n17; Meiji government's incorporation of activists in, 105fn69; Meiji government's suppression of, 74–75; Meiji government's use of detective in, 8–9, 64; and the political novels, 22n10, 61, 72, 96; and *risshin shusse*, 92; Shōyō's use of rhetoric of, 40; and *sōshi*, 76–77; trials of activists in, 69
Freeman, R. Austin, 98, 250n25
Freud, Sigmund, 226, 230n58, 257–58, 267n57. *See also* Psychoanalysis, Freudian
Fukuzawa Yukichi, *Gakumon no susume* (Encouragement of learning), 7n11, 91
Futabatei Shimei: "Aibiki" (The rendezvous), 52n57; Bunzō (character), 10, 92, 111–13, 116–17, 121–23, 136, 140, 171–73; "Meguriai" (The encounter), 52n57; *Ukigumo* (Drifting clouds), 10, 33n29, 34n30, 91, 111–13, 122

Gaboriau, Émile, 1, 66n12, 71; *File No. 113*, 65; *Other People's Money*, 66; *The Widow Lerouge*, 65; *Within an Inch of His Life*, 70, 90–91
Gaze: of the eavesdropper, 28, 39–40, 54; of the masses, 282; moral and objective, 51, 54, 57; novelistic, 24–26, 30; of social prejudice, 130; of the state, 155, 278; subject's inward, 172–73; Western, 38n39
Girard, René, 200, 202
Great Kantō Earthquake, 12, 261–63, 267–68, 279–82
Great Treason Incident (Taigyaku jiken), 173–74, 198, 219

Green, Anna Katharine, 4, 44
—*XYZ*, 4, 43–44, 57–58, 228; detective's curiosity in, 45, 47, 50–51; as failed detective story, 44–45; as first-person narrative, 45–46, 52–53; plot summary of, 44n49; textual comparison with *Nisegane tsukai*, 48–49; title of, 54. *See also* Tsubouchi Shōyō: *Nisegane tsukai*
—Other texts: *The Leavenworth Case*, 71, 87

Hasegawa Tenkei, 127, 130
Hentai shinri (magazine), 257n34
Hirabayashi Hatsunosuke, 235–37, 275
Holmes, Sherlock (character). *See* Doyle, Arthur Conan
Hototogisu (magazine), 159

Ideal, Western, 9–11, 155, 206, 210, 216; art as, 211, 215; vs. Japanese law, 209, 220–21, 233; *ren'ai* (love) as, 203–4, 206, 209
Iida Yūko, 200–202, 218
Industrialization, 212, 261, 267
Inoue Kaoru, 63, 107
I-novel (*shishōsetsu*), 270–73, 275
Intellectual. *See* Student/intellectual
Interior: conflation with private, 31, 35, 41; and exterior, dichotomy of, 21–25, 28, 31–34, 80–86, 140, 161, 182, 195, 278; as object of the novel, 20n4, 23–25, 51
Ishibashi Ningetsu, 30–31
Itō Hideo, 72n26
Itō Hirobumi, 62–63, 89, 124
Iwamoto Yoshiharu, 115n9, 116, 118n15

Jameson, Fredric, 13–14
Jauss, Hans Robert, 14–15
Jiyū shinbun (newspaper), 72; "Tantei-ron" (On detectives), 8
Jogaku zasshi (magazine), 117, 120, 148n67
Jōkyō shōko gohan roku (Records of wrong judgments based on circumstantial evidence), 67
Judicial system: attachments to premodern, 80; interest in and anxiety over, 68–69; Meiji reality of, 73–75; and Public Order Ordinance, 65n11, 75; Ruikō's criticism of, 66–67, 71, 73, 75–76; Westernization of, 67; in *Yūzai muzai*, 78–79, 82–83, 93–94. *See also* Criminal Code; Code of Criminal Procedure

Kabayama Sukenori, 148
Kaizō (magazine), 258, 272
Kanzen chōaku (encouraging virtue, chastising vice), 19, 41
Kasai Zenzō, 271–72
Katayama Sen, 143, 151
Katsu Kaishū, 63
Kawana, Sari, 5n8, 265
Ken'yūsha, 2
Kikutei Kōsui: *Sanpū hiu: sero nikki* (Walks of life diaries), 91–92
Kingu (magazine), 273
Kinmonth, Earl, 143, 162–63
Kitamura Tōkoku, 116, 126; "Ensei shika to josei" (Disillusioned poets and women), 120–21; reviews of *Tsumi to batsu* by, 117–19, 122
Knowledge: and crime, 86, 90, 208–9; detective's 6–7; disavowal of, 213–14, 227; vs. experience, 120–21, 214; object of, 6, 9, 33n29, 58, 183, 190, 192, 195, 285; within Ranpo's epistemological project, 238, 252–56, 278; reader's sharing of, 28, 95; Western, 7, 27, 56–57, 112–13, 207, 214, 220n41

Kōga Saburō, 237n4
Kokujihan jiken kōhan bōchō hikki (Records of hearings on the incident of the crimes against the state), 69n23
Kokumin no tomo (magazine), 58n64, 76–77, 162; and criticism of detective fiction in "Bungaku shakai no genjō" (Present state of the literary world), 2, 4, 44, 58–59
Komori Yōichi, 25n16, 31n26, 46, 51, 112n2, 146n65, 183–87
Konnichi shinbun (newspaper), 1, 66, 73n27
Koshinbun (small newspaper), 36, 39, 65, 68, 70
Kōtō yūmin (upper-class vagabond), 173–74, 176, 196, 264–65
Kozakai Fuboku, 238–40, 242
Kraft-Ebbing, Richard von, 257
Kravichinsky, S. M.: *Underground Russia*, 72
Kume Masao, 199
Kuriyagawa Hakuson, 258
Kuroiwa Ruikō, 1, 3–5, 9, 62n6, 64–65; classification of adaptations by, 70–71; classification of stories about crime by, 71; and *Crime and Punishment*, 115–17; and criticism of Meiji judicial system, 73–75; early detective stories of, 65–66, 70; emphasis on the falsely accused by, 71–73, 75, 77; function and implications of detective stories by, 109, 122, 154, 175, 278, 281; and Meiji literary and discursive forms, 70; political agenda of, 66–67, 71, 73; and political novels, 72, 77, 96–97; popularity of, 72n26, 108–9; and Tokutomi Sohō, 76–77; and *Yorozu chōhō*, 108, 115, 124, 145, 175
—*Muzan* (Merciless), 65, 68, 97–109, 169, 281n5; comparisons to Western detective fiction, 100–101, 104n68; critical reception of, 98; and *Hakai*, 132; and extraterritoriality clause, 102–5; power of Western learning in, 99–100, 108–9, 112–13, 122; racial/national stereotyping in, 103–4, 106–7; and repressed political energies, 104–5
—*Yūzai muzai* (Guilty, not guilty), 65, 70, 72–73, 77–86, 90–91, 93–96; and adultery, 90–91, 95; allegory of, 95–96; comparisons to the English version, 90–91; dismantling of trial system in, 78–79; interior/exterior dichotomy in, 82–86; narrative structure of, 86, 93; and the newspaper medium, 78–79, 93–94; plot summary of, 78n35; psychological reasoning, use of, in, 83–84; reliance on confession in, 80; role of rumors in, 81–82; role of secrets in, 84–86, 93–95; Ruikō's introduction to, 73–76; as sensational novel, 72–73; significance of aristocrats in, 86–87, 91; and Tsubouchi Shōyō's literary project, 80–81, 85, 96–97
—Other texts: *Baikarō*, 70; *Daitōzoku* (The great thief), 65, 70; *Hito ka oni ka* (Man or devil?), 65–67, 70–72, 84n41, 86, 93n53; *Hōtei no bijin* (A beauty in court), 1, 4, 64–66; "Kaitakushi kanri no shobun o ronzu" (Argument for the punishment of officials of Colonization Bureau), 75n32; *Majutsu no zoku* (Villain of magic), 83, 132; *Makkura* (Utter darkness), 71, 80n37, 86–90, 94n54; *Tanin no*

zeni (Other people's money), 65; "Tantei-dan ni tsuite" (On detective stories), 3, 71n25

Libel Law (Zanbōritsu), 61, 74
Liberal Party (Jiyūtō), 8, 65, 73, 76, 102, 105n69
Loti, Pierre (Julien Viaud), 63

Maeda Ai, 7n11, 25n15, 31n26, 41, 42n46, 60–61, 91–92, 113, 170n20, 176
Maintenance of Public Order Act (Chian iji hō), 12, 282
Masamune Hakuchō, 114n7, 199
Masochism, 220–21, 275
Matsubara Iwagorō: *Saiankoku no Tokyo* (The darkest Tokyo), 124
Matsuyama Iwao, 124n27, 261n44, 264n51
Maupassant, Guy de, 141, 157
Metropolis, 12, 27, 260, 267n57, 268, 277
Miyako no hana (magazine), 112
Miyako shinbun (newspaper), 1n1, 58n64, 73n27, 108
Miyazaki Muryū: *Jiyū no kachidoki* (Torch of freedom), 72; *Kishūshū* (Demons softly crying), 72
Modern individual, 85, 140, 161, 176, 182–83, 190, 195. *See also* Student/intellectual
Modernization: detective as metaphor within, 157; detective fiction as gauge for, 100–101; and phenomenon of the double, 212; and emergence of detective as fictional hero, 9; and social Darwinism, 21; Sōseki's understanding of, 175–76, 259; and student/intellectual, 6, 9, 264; tribulations within Japan's, 175–76, 233–34; as Westernization, 6–7
Moretti, Franco, 244n19, 267n57, 269
Mori Arinori, 63
Mori Ōgai, 124; *Maihime* (The dancing girl), 2, 91, 271; *Seinen* (Youth), 146n65
Morishita Uson, 238, 239n10
Morita Shiken, 46n53, 116, 119n18
Morita Sōhei, 127
Mushanokōji Saneatsu, 218
Mystery: self as, 171, 194, 204, 234, 275; woman as, 33, 140, 171, 275

Nakae Chōmin, 76
Nakamura Hakuyō, 217
Nakamura Kichizō, 199
Nakamura Masanao: *Saigoku risshi-hen* (Success stories of the West), 7n11, 91
Narration, first-person: authority of, 53; and detective fiction, 51–52, 53n59, 222, 240–41; dichotomy between narrating and narrated self in, 45, 165–66, 184, 187; limited perspective of, 51, 165n12; Meiji boom in, 46; and readers, conspiratorial relationship between, 28, 55; self-interest within, 53; and translation, 57
Narration, third-person, 46, 51–52, 180–81; authority of, 54–56, 58
Narrative frame, 207–9, 213–14, 245–46
Narrator: eavesdropping, 28, 35, 41–42; of Edo fiction, 25–28; fundamental immorality of, 166–67. *See also* Detective: as ideal narrator/novelist
Natsume Sōseki, 5, 10–11, 179n31, 274; criticism of detective by, 157–58; and Japanese Naturalism, 158; London experience of, 156–57, 260; mediations on modern experience by, 259-61

—*Higan sugi made* (Until after the equinox), 168–82; comparisons to *Hakai*, 169–70; comparisons to *Kokoro*, 181–82, 187, 195; and *Crime and Punishment*, 172–74; criticism of *risshin shusse* ideology in, 169–70; dynamic of truth-as-secret in, 175–80; and *kōtō yūmin*, 173–74, 264; definition of detective in, 168–69; meditations on the modern Japanese intellectual in, 175–76; and woman as mystery-to-be-solved, 171–72

—*Kokoro*, 181–96, 199, 234; betrayal of the narrator in, 188–89; comparisons to *Higan sugi made*, 181–82, 187, 195; comparisons to "Kaika no satsujin," 200–201, 205–6; and detective fiction paradigm, 191, 194; dynamic of first-person narration in, 183–88; dynamic of traumatic past in, 186–88, 193–94; and General Nogi, 191–94; Komori Yōichi's analysis of, 183–85, 187; meditations on the modern Japanese intellectual in, 182–83; and Meiji emperor, 191, 192n52; as schizophrenic narrative, 190–91

—*Wagahai wa neko de aru* (I am a cat), 158–68, 182, 195; cat as detective in, 163–65; criticism of detective in, 160–61; first-person narration of, 165–66; and monetary success, 144, 162–63; as *shaseibun*, 159; and Shōyō's novelistic worldview, 161, 166–67

—Other texts: *Botchan* (The young master), 167; "Bungei no tetsugaku-teki kiso" (The philosophical foundations of literary arts), 157; "Gendai Nihon no kaika" (The civilization of modern-day Japan), 175n27, 219n39, 259–60, 264n52; *Kusamakura* (Pillow of grass), 167; *Nowaki* (Autumn wind), 167–68; "Rondon tō" (Tower of London), 259–60, 265, 271; *Sanshirō*, 260n43; "Shumi no iden" (The heredity of taste), 167

Naturalism, Japanese, 10, 114, 158

New Criminal Code (Shin-keihō), 123

Newspaper Ordinance (Shinbunshi jōrei), 35, 61, 74

Newspaper, 35–37; and allegorical interpretative framework, 61–63; and *bunmei kaika*, 35–37; circulation numbers for, 39n42; and death of Meiji emperor, 192; Meiji readership of *koshinbun* and *ōshinbun*, 36n34; and literature as institution, 145, 146n65; and novel-writing contests, 145; power of, 8n13; Ruikō's effect on sales of, 1n1, 108; scandal reporting in, 60–63, 108, 124, 153–54; and serialized fiction, 94; as venue for Meiji introduction of detective stories, 1, 65–66; in *Yūzai muzai*, 78–79, 93–94. See also *Koshinbun*; *Ōshinbun*; *Tsuzukimono*; *Zappō*

Ninjō (human feelings), 19–21, 24, 26, 28, 31, 44, 272

Ninjōbon (books on human feelings), 20–21, 25–26, 28

Niroku shinpō (newspaper), 124, 153

Nogi Maresuke, 191–94

Normanton Incident, 69

Novel: Japanese, 5–6, 11, 15, 33n29, 59, 109–10, 111, 273–76, 278; modern, 5, 10, 21, 25, 41, 43, 52, 54, 57, 111, 166; realistic, 16, 26, 42, 44; Western, 26, 29n23, 44

Novel-writing contests, 145–46

Ōi Kentarō, 104–5
Ordinance of Transgressions and Negligence (Ishiki kaii jōrei), 37
Originality, notion of, 212, 215–20
Osaka Incident, 69, 105n69
Ōshinbun (large or prestige newspaper), 36, 39
Ōsugi Sakae, 279
Ōtsuka Kusuoko, 129n38

Peerage, 89–92, 105n69, 108n74
Peerage Ordinance (Kazoku rei), 89, 92
Poe, Edgar Allan, 6, 13; "The Black Cat," 46; Dupin, Auguste (character), 23, 100, 215–17, 221, 278; Dupin trilogy, 51n57, 100, 104n68, 222, 240; "The Gold-Bug," 239, 243; "The Murder in the Rue Morgue," 23, 46, 51n57, 278; "William Wilson," 212, 224
Police, the, 168, 220n41; and detective fiction, 13, 100–101, 113, 277; Japanese, 8n13, 38n41, 62n6, 68, 155n75; masses as, 281
Political novel, 22n10, 61, 63, 65, 72, 75–77, 96–97
Privacy: of Meiji emperor, 191–92; and the novel, 40–41, 58; violation of, 141, 164–65, 169
Private life, 37–38, 271; importance of and respect for, 40, 96; as object of depiction of the novel, 19–20, 24–25, 40–41, 51, 166, 272
Psychoanalysis, Freudian, 257–59
Psychology: criminal, 123; within detective fiction framework, 83–84, 115–16, 248–59 *passim*; and the novel, 23–24
Public and private: conflation with interior and exterior dichotomy, 25; identities, 82, 85, 268; spheres, dichotomy between, 25, 266; spheres, production of, 37–39; spheres, transgression between, 37, 39, 161, 164
Public Order Ordinance (Chian jōrei), 12, 64, 75–77

Reader: private enjoyment of, 51, 94–95, 97; expectation, 14–15, 55, 246
Reason: and detective, 7, 100; within interior/exterior dichotomy, 21–23, 26–27, 31, 33–34, 47n55, 80, 172n23
Ren'ai (love). *See* Ideal, Western
Reportage writings, 124
Revised Law (Kaitei ritsuryō), 67n17
Rice Riots of 1918, 198, 281
Risshin shusse (rising in the world), ideology of, 7, 91–92, 144, 158; alternative modes of, 144–46, 163; and *burakumin*, 130, 139; detective as emblem of success in, 7, 112; fictional negotiation of difficulties within, 112, 150–52; and immigration, 139, 143, 262n43; and middle-school system, 144; and novel-writing contests, 145–46; and peers, 92, 109; and scandal journalism, 124, 154; and *Shinseinen*, 262–63; tribulations of student/intellectual within, 10, 114, 142–43; and woman, 149
Rockwood, Harry: *Donald Dyke*, 83
Rokumeikan: balls, 62–64, 89, 91–92; building, 62; diplomacy, 62–65
Rumors, 63–64, 91, 156–57, 279–80; in fictional works, 48, 81–82, 85, 131, 137, 172n23, 202
Russo-Japanese War, 10, 145, 155

Ryōsai kenbo (good wife, wise mother), ideology of, 147–49, 154–55

Satō Haruo, 5, 11, 199, 233–34
—"Shimon" (The fingerprint), 11, 221–32; as constructed by excessive clues, 228–29, 234n60; and the film medium, 222–23, 225–28, 231; and issue of the double, 224–27; and fetishism, 230–31; plot summary of, 221n42; role of the state in, 232
—Other texts: "Tantei shōsetsu shōron" (Brief thoughts on detective fiction), 236n3; "Tsuki kage" (Moon shadow), 224n46
Satomi Ton, 199
Science: and *bunmei kaika*, 6, 207; and detective, 6–7, 112–13, 122; and detective fiction, 235–36, 239n9, 240; and Meiji intellectual, 207; Ranpo's rejection of positivistic, 257, 268
Secret, 40, 199; adulterous, 85, 91, 175; aristocratic, 86, 92, 97; and crime, 86, 93–95; and exposure, dynamic of, 6, 10, 114, 133, 135, 142, 150, 208–9; harboring of, 84–85; haunting of past, 181, 186–88, 234; truth as, 176–80, 194
Seinen (youth), 76–77
Self-interest: of first-person narrator, 53; and *Kokoro*'s narrator, 187, 190; literary representation of, 161, 174n25; and modern individual, 11, 182–83, 195; and suppression of interior, 32; vs. universal ideals, 205–6, 210–11
Sensational novel, 29n23, 71–73, 98
Shiga Naoya: "Han no hanzai" (Han's crime), 204n13
Shimamura Hōgetsu, 129n38
Shimazaki Tōson, 5, 114, 126–27
—*Hakai* (The broken commandment), 10, 114, 125–39, 169, 174, 262n48; confession scene in, 128–31, 135, 138; and *Crime and Punishment*, 125–27, 150; critical reception of, 127, 129n38; and Emancipation Edict, 130–31; narrative construction of Ushimatsu as criminal in, 133–35; as political criticism, 130–31; and *risshin shusse* ideology, 130–31, 139, 142–43, 150–52; and Ruikō's *Muzan*, 132; and Ushimatsu's immigration to Texas, 138–39, 143. See also *Burakumin*
—Other text: *Haru* (Spring), 126
Shimizu Shikin: "Imin gakuen" (School of émigrés), 126n30
Shinkei suijaku (mental breakdown), 118
Shinseinen (magazine), 197, 235–36, 238, 239n9, 239n10, 246, 262–64, 270, 274
Shin-shumi (magazine), 263n49
Shirakaba group, 218–19, 258, 270
Shiratori Shōgo, 197, 219
Shōnen sekai (magazine), 146n64
Silver, Mark, 5n8, 67n15, 275n69
Simmel, Georg, 265, 267
Sino-Japanese War, 144, 163
Social mobility. See *Risshin shusse*, ideology of
Sōshi (boisterous youth), 76–77, 97, 105, 128
State: authority of, 220–21; and confession, 279, 282; consolidation of Japan as modern, 1; democracy and, 12–13; detective as agent of, 6, 12–13, 277–78; ideology of, 154–55; and masses, 281–82; submission to, 232
Student/intellectual: criminality of, 9–11, 110, 118–19, 122–23, 150, 152, 173–74; detective and, 6–7, 9, 16, 168; as emblematic subjects of Japan's modernization,

6–7, 9–10, 27, 171, 173, 175–76, 264, 279; as *kōtō yūmin*, 173–74; positive model for, 109, 112–13, 122; fantastic projections of, 33n29, 275; Raskolnikov as, 116–19; and *risshin shusse* ideology, 10, 91–92, 151–52; search for self by, 276; from *sōshi* to *seinen*, 77; tribulations of, 10, 111–14, 144, 200; turn away from, as subject of literary exploration, 123–25; and Western ideals, 122, 206, 209, 233. *See also* Western education/learning

Subject: ills of modern Japanese, 260, 267; interpellation by detective fiction framework as, 6–7, 9, 279; within Japan vs. West opposition, 173, 206, 233–34, 246, 276; Meiji, 65, 77, 209. *See also* Modern individual; Student/intellectual

Suehiro Tetchō: *Setchūbai* (Plum blossoms in the snow), 72

Suicide: in fictional works, 30, 93n53, 181, 185–89 *passim*, 194, 201–2, 204-5, 208, 243n17, 246, 253n29, 276; in history, 126, 191–93

Suzuki, Tomi, 114n7, 141n52, 203n12, 218–19, 270

Taishō Democracy, 12, 197–98, 233, 281n7

Taishō period, transition from Meiji: 206, 207n17, 210

Takada Incident, 8n14

Takahashi Oden, 68n21

Takahashi Osamu, 47n55, 52, 55, 100n61, 115

Tamenaga Shunsui, 20, 28n21

Tanizaki Jun'ichirō, 5, 11, 199, 233, 257

—"Futari no geijutsuka no hanashi" (The story of two artists), 210–12, 215–21, 246; and art as ideal, 211, 215, 217; comparison to "Kaika no satsujin," 210–11; and *Crime and Punishment*, 216–17; and the double, 212; mechanism of disavowal in, 215, 217, 219–21; as parody, 216, 218–19; plot summary of, 210n21; Western signifiers in, 215–17

—Other texts: "A to B no hanashi" (A story of A and B), 212n25; "Hakuchū kigo" (The ghost in broad daylight), 241n16; "Katsudō shashin no genzai to shōrai" (The present and future of the moving pictures), 231n59

Tanizaki Seiji, 212

Tantei (detective), use of term, 8–9, 161, 162n9, 167, 199

Tantei shōsetsu (detective novel), use of term, 3, 70

Tayama Katai, 5, 114, 126, 139, 146n64, 199; and novel-writing contests, 145–46

—*Futon* (The quilt), 10, 114, 139–43, 146–55 *passim*, 174; comparisons to *Hakai*, 140, 142; and *Crime and Punishment*, 139, 142, 150; and I-novel discourse, 270–71; and *risshin shusse* ideology, 142–43, 146, 149–50; and *ryōsai kenbo* ideology, 147, 149, 154–55; Tokio as detective in, 140–41; Tokio as model of success in, 152–54; and Western novels, 141; and woman as mystery-to-be-solved, 140; and yellow journalism framework, 153–54

Third-person narration. *See* Narration, third-person

Three major issues petition movement (Sandai jiken kenpaku undō), 63–64, 76

Toda Kindō: *Jōkai haran* (A storm on the passionate seas), 61
Tokutomi Sohō, 2, 76–77
Tōkyō Asahi shinbun (newspaper), 157, 167–68, 181
Tōkyō Nichinichi shinbun (newspaper), 36, 60, 62
Torture, prohibition and practice of, 67n17, 74, 80
Translation, 55; of *Crime and Punishment* in Japan, 4, 115, 217; and introduction of detective fiction in Japan, 1, 4–5, 9, 66n12, 246; Meiji essays on, 55; techniques and strategies of, 46–47, 49–50, 54–57, 90–91, 115
Translator, 55–58, 121
Tsubouchi Shōyō, 4–5, 116, 119n18, 217n34; epistemological paradigm, literary theory, and novelistic worldview of, 81, 96, 123, 140, 161, 166–67, 182, 195, 266, 272, 278; political project of, 96–97; and "Shōyō-esque" clichés, 59, 81
—*Imotose kagami* (Mirror of marriage), 29–43; act of eavesdropping in, 30–31, 33–35, 41; critical reception of, 30–31; criticism of eavesdropping in, 39–40; and the moral author, 43; and paradox of the novel, 40–41; plot summary of, 29n24; and woman as mystery, 32–33; and *zappō* column, 35, 39
—*Nisegane tsukai* (The counterfeiter), 4, 43–44, 46–58, 140, 169, 228; allegorical significance of, 63–64; comparisons to *XYZ*, 46–52; detective as metaphor in, 51, 54; eavesdropping as duty of the detective in, 47–50; role of title in, 54–55; shift of narrative perspective in, 46–48, 51–52, 54; Shōyō's introduction to, 43–44, 47–48, 56, 64; structure of eavesdropping in, 50; as translation, 55–57. *See also* Green, Anna Katharine: *XYZ*
—*Shōsetsu shinzui* (The essence of the novel), 4, 16, 18–25, 80–82; 96–97, 182; criticism of *tsuzukimono* in, 18–19; and didactic framework, 19, 41–42; and focus on the private, 19–20, 25; interior/exterior dichotomy, use of, in, 21–22, 24–25; task of the novelist articulated in, 21–24, 249; and two gazes of the novelist, 24–25
—Other texts: *Daisagishi* (The swindler), 58n64; *Saikun* (The wife), 2, 52n58, 58n64; "Tane hiroi" (Gleaning the seeds), 17, 19–20, 46; *Tōsei shosei katagi* (Manners and lives of contemporary students), 25n16, 26–30, 35, 41–42, 91, 111
Tsuzukimono (serials), 3n5, 17–20, 39, 42, 42n46, 68

Uchida Roan, 4, 115–16, 119n18
—*Tsumi to batsu* (Crime and punishment), 115–19, 121–23, 139; and comparisons between Japan and Russia, 121–22; as detective story, 115–16; Kitamura Tōkoku's review of, 117–19, 122; Meiji reception of, 116; and Meiji understanding of crime and criminals, 123; poor sale of, 115; and *Ukigumo*'s Bunzō, 116–17, 121–23
Uchida Ryūzō, 5n8, 100–101, 157n3, 158n5
Unconscious, 177, 225–26, 230n58, 256–58, 267–70, 273–74
Unequal treaties, 38n40, 62, 105, 107; extraterritoriality clause of, 102–6

Universal male suffrage of 1925, 12, 198
Upper-Girls' School Act (Kōtō jogakko rei), 147–48
Urbanization, 27, 212, 261–62, 264, 267

Voting, 12–13

Waseda bungaku (magazine), 129n38, 154
Watanabe Masahiko, 213n27, 225–28
Watanabe Naomi, 131, 192n52
Western education/learning, 7, 11, 77, 109, 111–13, 122–23, 136, 173. *See also* Student/intellectual
Westernization, 6–7, 9, 21, 62, 67, 92, 196, 233. *See also* Modernization
Williams, Raymond, 7n12
Woman: models of success for, 148; as mystery-to-be-solved, 33, 140, 171, 275

Yanagita Kunio, 129n38
Yanase Keisuke: *Shakai gai no shakai: eta hinin* (Society outside society), 143n58
Yellow journalism. *See* Newspaper: scandal reporting in
Yoda Gakkai, 46n53, 115n9, 117
Yokoyama Gennosuke: *Nihon no kasō shakai* (The lower societies of Japan), 124
Yomiuri shinbun (newspaper), 17, 35–36, 43n46, 44, 46, 55, 69, 127
Yorozu chōhō (newspaper), 1n1, 108, 115, 124, 153, 175; "Chikushō no jitsurei" (The actual examples of keeping a mistress), 124; House of Sōma scandal, 108; and novel-writing contests, 145; "Tantei-dan ni tsuite," 3

Zappō (miscellaneous reports), 35–40, 42n46
Zola, Émile, 114n7, 157

Harvard East Asian Monographs
(*out-of-print)

*1. Liang Fang-chung, *The Single-Whip Method of Taxation in China*
*2. Harold C. Hinton, *The Grain Tribute System of China, 1845–1911*
3. Ellsworth C. Carlson, *The Kaiping Mines, 1877–1912*
*4. Chao Kuo-chün, *Agrarian Policies of Mainland China: A Documentary Study, 1949–1956*
*5. Edgar Snow, *Random Notes on Red China, 1936–1945*
*6. Edwin George Beal, Jr., *The Origin of Likin, 1835–1864*
7. Chao Kuo-chün, *Economic Planning and Organization in Mainland China: A Documentary Study, 1949–1957*
*8. John K. Fairbank, *Ching Documents: An Introductory Syllabus*
*9. Helen Yin and Yi-chang Yin, *Economic Statistics of Mainland China, 1949–1957*
10. Wolfgang Franke, *The Reform and Abolition of the Traditional Chinese Examination System*
11. Albert Feuerwerker and S. Cheng, *Chinese Communist Studies of Modern Chinese History*
12. C. John Stanley, *Late Ching Finance: Hu Kuang-yung as an Innovator*
13. S. M. Meng, *The Tsungli Yamen: Its Organization and Functions*
*14. Ssu-yü Teng, *Historiography of the Taiping Rebellion*
15. Chun-Jo Liu, *Controversies in Modern Chinese Intellectual History: An Analytic Bibliography of Periodical Articles, Mainly of the May Fourth and Post-May Fourth Era*
*16. Edward J. M. Rhoads, *The Chinese Red Army, 1927–1963: An Annotated Bibliography*
*17. Andrew J. Nathan, *A History of the China International Famine Relief Commission*
*18. Frank H. H. King (ed.) and Prescott Clarke, *A Research Guide to China-Coast Newspapers, 1822–1911*
*19. Ellis Joffe, *Party and Army: Professionalism and Political Control in the Chinese Officer Corps, 1949–1964*
*20. Toshio G. Tsukahira, *Feudal Control in Tokugawa Japan: The Sankin Kōtai System*
*21. Kwang-Ching Liu, ed., *American Missionaries in China: Papers from Harvard Seminars*
*22. George Moseley, *A Sino-Soviet Cultural Frontier: The Ili Kazakh Autonomous Chou*

23. Carl F. Nathan, *Plague Prevention and Politics in Manchuria, 1910–1931*
*24. Adrian Arthur Bennett, *John Fryer: The Introduction of Western Science and Technology into Nineteenth-Century China*
*25. Donald J. Friedman, *The Road from Isolation: The Campaign of the American Committee for Non-Participation in Japanese Aggression, 1938–1941*
*26. Edward LeFevour, *Western Enterprise in Late Ching China: A Selective Survey of Jardine, Matheson and Company's Operations, 1842–1895*
27. Charles Neuhauser, *Third World Politics: China and the Afro-Asian People's Solidarity Organization, 1957–1967*
*28. Kungtu C. Sun, assisted by Ralph W. Huenemann, *The Economic Development of Manchuria in the First Half of the Twentieth Century*
*29. Shahid Javed Burki, *A Study of Chinese Communes, 1965*
30. John Carter Vincent, *The Extraterritorial System in China: Final Phase*
31. Madeleine Chi, *China Diplomacy, 1914–1918*
*32. Clifton Jackson Phillips, *Protestant America and the Pagan World: The First Half Century of the American Board of Commissioners for Foreign Missions, 1810–1860*
*33. James Pusey, *Wu Han: Attacking the Present Through the Past*
*34. Ying-wan Cheng, *Postal Communication in China and Its Modernization, 1860–1896*
35. Tuvia Blumenthal, *Saving in Postwar Japan*
36. Peter Frost, *The Bakumatsu Currency Crisis*
37. Stephen C. Lockwood, *Augustine Heard and Company, 1858–1862*
38. Robert R. Campbell, *James Duncan Campbell: A Memoir by His Son*
39. Jerome Alan Cohen, ed., *The Dynamics of China's Foreign Relations*
40. V. V. Vishnyakova-Akimova, *Two Years in Revolutionary China, 1925–1927,* trans. Steven L. Levine
41. Meron Medzini, *French Policy in Japan During the Closing Years of the Tokugawa Regime*
42. Ezra Vogel, Margie Sargent, Vivienne B. Shue, Thomas Jay Mathews, and Deborah S. Davis, *The Cultural Revolution in the Provinces*
43. Sidney A. Forsythe, *An American Missionary Community in China, 1895–1905*
*44. Benjamin I. Schwartz, ed., *Reflections on the May Fourth Movement.: A Symposium*
*45. Ching Young Choe, *The Rule of the Taewŏngun, 1864–1873: Restoration in Yi Korea*
46. W. P. J. Hall, *A Bibliographical Guide to Japanese Research on the Chinese Economy, 1958–1970*
47. Jack J. Gerson, *Horatio Nelson Lay and Sino-British Relations, 1854–1864*
48. Paul Richard Bohr, *Famine and the Missionary: Timothy Richard as Relief Administrator and Advocate of National Reform*
49. Endymion Wilkinson, *The History of Imperial China: A Research Guide*
50. Britten Dean, *China and Great Britain: The Diplomacy of Commercial Relations, 1860–1864*
51. Ellsworth C. Carlson, *The Foochow Missionaries, 1847–1880*
52. Yeh-chien Wang, *An Estimate of the Land-Tax Collection in China, 1753 and 1908*
53. Richard M. Pfeffer, *Understanding Business Contracts in China, 1949–1963*

*54. Han-sheng Chuan and Richard Kraus, *Mid-Ching Rice Markets and Trade: An Essay in Price History*
55. Ranbir Vohra, *Lao She and the Chinese Revolution*
56. Liang-lin Hsiao, *China's Foreign Trade Statistics, 1864–1949*
*57. Lee-hsia Hsu Ting, *Government Control of the Press in Modern China, 1900–1949*
*58. Edward W. Wagner, *The Literati Purges: Political Conflict in Early Yi Korea*
*59. Joungwon A. Kim, *Divided Korea: The Politics of Development, 1945–1972*
60. Noriko Kamachi, John K. Fairbank, and Chūzō Ichiko, *Japanese Studies of Modern China Since 1953: A Bibliographical Guide to Historical and Social-Science Research on the Nineteenth and Twentieth Centuries, Supplementary Volume for 1953–1969*
61. Donald A. Gibbs and Yun-chen Li, *A Bibliography of Studies and Translations of Modern Chinese Literature, 1918–1942*
62. Robert H. Silin, *Leadership and Values: The Organization of Large-Scale Taiwanese Enterprises*
63. David Pong, *A Critical Guide to the Kwangtung Provincial Archives Deposited at the Public Record Office of London*
*64. Fred W. Drake, *China Charts the World: Hsu Chi-yü and His Geography of 1848*
*65. William A. Brown and Urgrunge Onon, translators and annotators, *History of the Mongolian People's Republic*
66. Edward L. Farmer, *Early Ming Government: The Evolution of Dual Capitals*
*67. Ralph C. Croizier, *Koxinga and Chinese Nationalism: History, Myth, and the Hero*
*68. William J. Tyler, tr., *The Psychological World of Natsume Sōseki,* by Doi Takeo
69. Eric Widmer, *The Russian Ecclesiastical Mission in Peking During the Eighteenth Century*
*70. Charlton M. Lewis, *Prologue to the Chinese Revolution: The Transformation of Ideas and Institutions in Hunan Province, 1891–1907*
71. Preston Torbert, *The Ching Imperial Household Department: A Study of Its Organization and Principal Functions, 1662–1796*
72. Paul A. Cohen and John E. Schrecker, eds., *Reform in Nineteenth-Century China*
73. Jon Sigurdson, *Rural Industrialism in China*
74. Kang Chao, *The Development of Cotton Textile Production in China*
75. Valentin Rabe, *The Home Base of American China Missions, 1880–1920*
*76. Sarasin Viraphol, *Tribute and Profit: Sino-Siamese Trade, 1652–1853*
77. Ch'i-ch'ing Hsiao, *The Military Establishment of the Yuan Dynasty*
78. Meishi Tsai, *Contemporary Chinese Novels and Short Stories, 1949–1974: An Annotated Bibliography*
*79. Wellington K. K. Chan, *Merchants, Mandarins and Modern Enterprise in Late Ching China*
80. Endymion Wilkinson, *Landlord and Labor in Late Imperial China: Case Studies from Shandong by Jing Su and Luo Lun*
*81. Barry Keenan, *The Dewey Experiment in China: Educational Reform and Political Power in the Early Republic*
*82. George A. Hayden, *Crime and Punishment in Medieval Chinese Drama: Three Judge Pao Plays*

Harvard East Asian Monographs

- *83. Sang-Chul Suh, *Growth and Structural Changes in the Korean Economy, 1910–1940*
- 84. J. W. Dower, *Empire and Aftermath: Yoshida Shigeru and the Japanese Experience, 1878–1954*
- 85. Martin Collcutt, *Five Mountains: The Rinzai Zen Monastic Institution in Medieval Japan*
- 86. Kwang Suk Kim and Michael Roemer, *Growth and Structural Transformation*
- 87. Anne O. Krueger, *The Developmental Role of the Foreign Sector and Aid*
- *88. Edwin S. Mills and Byung-Nak Song, *Urbanization and Urban Problems*
- 89. Sung Hwan Ban, Pal Yong Moon, and Dwight H. Perkins, *Rural Development*
- *90. Noel F. McGinn, Donald R. Snodgrass, Yung Bong Kim, Shin-Bok Kim, and Quee-Young Kim, *Education and Development in Korea*
- *91. Leroy P. Jones and Il SaKong, *Government, Business, and Entrepreneurship in Economic Development: The Korean Case*
- 92. Edward S. Mason, Dwight H. Perkins, Kwang Suk Kim, David C. Cole, Mahn Je Kim et al., *The Economic and Social Modernization of the Republic of Korea*
- 93. Robert Repetto, Tai Hwan Kwon, Son-Ung Kim, Dae Young Kim, John E. Sloboda, and Peter J. Donaldson, *Economic Development, Population Policy, and Demographic Transition in the Republic of Korea*
- 94. Parks M. Coble, Jr., *The Shanghai Capitalists and the Nationalist Government, 1927–1937*
- 95. Noriko Kamachi, *Reform in China: Huang Tsun-hsien and the Japanese Model*
- 96. Richard Wich, *Sino-Soviet Crisis Politics: A Study of Political Change and Communication*
- 97. Lillian M. Li, *China's Silk Trade: Traditional Industry in the Modern World, 1842–1937*
- 98. R. David Arkush, *Fei Xiaotong and Sociology in Revolutionary China*
- *99. Kenneth Alan Grossberg, *Japan's Renaissance: The Politics of the Muromachi Bakufu*
- 100. James Reeve Pusey, *China and Charles Darwin*
- 101. Hoyt Cleveland Tillman, *Utilitarian Confucianism: Chen Liang's Challenge to Chu Hsi*
- 102. Thomas A. Stanley, *Ōsugi Sakae, Anarchist in Taishō Japan: The Creativity of the Ego*
- 103. Jonathan K. Ocko, *Bureaucratic Reform in Provincial China: Ting Jih-ch'ang in Restoration Kiangsu, 1867–1870*
- 104. James Reed, *The Missionary Mind and American East Asia Policy, 1911–1915*
- 105. Neil L. Waters, *Japan's Local Pragmatists: The Transition from Bakumatsu to Meiji in the Kawasaki Region*
- 106. David C. Cole and Yung Chul Park, *Financial Development in Korea, 1945–1978*
- 107. Roy Bahl, Chuk Kyo Kim, and Chong Kee Park, *Public Finances During the Korean Modernization Process*
- 108. William D. Wray, *Mitsubishi and the N.Y.K, 1870–1914: Business Strategy in the Japanese Shipping Industry*
- 109. Ralph William Huenemann, *The Dragon and the Iron Horse: The Economics of Railroads in China, 1876–1937*
- *110. Benjamin A. Elman, *From Philosophy to Philology: Intellectual and Social Aspects of Change in Late Imperial China*
- 111. Jane Kate Leonard, *Wei Yüan and China's Rediscovery of the Maritime World*

112. Luke S. K. Kwong, *A Mosaic of the Hundred Days:. Personalities, Politics, and Ideas of 1898*
*113. John E. Wills, Jr., *Embassies and Illusions: Dutch and Portuguese Envoys to K'ang-hsi, 1666–1687*
114. Joshua A. Fogel, *Politics and Sinology: The Case of Naitō Konan (1866–1934)*
*115. Jeffrey C. Kinkley, ed., *After Mao: Chinese Literature and Society, 1978–1981*
116. C. Andrew Gerstle, *Circles of Fantasy: Convention in the Plays of Chikamatsu*
117. Andrew Gordon, *The Evolution of Labor Relations in Japan: Heavy Industry, 1853–1955*
*118. Daniel K. Gardner, *Chu Hsi and the "Ta Hsueh": Neo-Confucian Reflection on the Confucian Canon*
119. Christine Guth Kanda, *Shinzō: Hachiman Imagery and Its Development*
*120. Robert Borgen, *Sugawara no Michizane and the Early Heian Court*
121. Chang-tai Hung, *Going to the People: Chinese Intellectual and Folk Literature, 1918–1937*
*122. Michael A. Cusumano, *The Japanese Automobile Industry: Technology and Management at Nissan and Toyota*
123. Richard von Glahn, *The Country of Streams and Grottoes: Expansion, Settlement, and the Civilizing of the Sichuan Frontier in Song Times*
124. Steven D. Carter, *The Road to Komatsubara: A Classical Reading of the Renga Hyakuin*
125. Katherine F. Bruner, John K. Fairbank, and Richard T. Smith, *Entering China's Service: Robert Hart's Journals, 1854–1863*
126. Bob Tadashi Wakabayashi, *Anti-Foreignism and Western Learning in Early-Modern Japan: The "New Theses" of 1825*
127. Atsuko Hirai, *Individualism and Socialism: The Life and Thought of Kawai Eijirō (1891–1944)*
128. Ellen Widmer, *The Margins of Utopia: "Shui-hu hou-chuan" and the Literature of Ming Loyalism*
129. R. Kent Guy, *The Emperor's Four Treasuries: Scholars and the State in the Late Chien-lung Era*
130. Peter C. Perdue, *Exhausting the Earth: State and Peasant in Hunan, 1500–1850*
131. Susan Chan Egan, *A Latterday Confucian: Reminiscences of William Hung (1893–1980)*
132. James T. C. Liu, *China Turning Inward: Intellectual-Political Changes in the Early Twelfth Century*
*133. Paul A. Cohen, *Between Tradition and Modernity: Wang T'ao and Reform in Late Ching China*
134. Kate Wildman Nakai, *Shogunal Politics: Arai Hakuseki and the Premises of Tokugawa Rule*
*135. Parks M. Coble, *Facing Japan: Chinese Politics and Japanese Imperialism, 1931–1937*
*136. Jon L. Saari, *Legacies of Childhood: Growing Up Chinese in a Time of Crisis, 1890–1920*
137. Susan Downing Videen, *Tales of Heichū*
138. Heinz Morioka and Miyoko Sasaki, *Rakugo: The Popular Narrative Art of Japan*
139. Joshua A. Fogel, *Nakae Ushikichi in China: The Mourning of Spirit*

140. Alexander Barton Woodside, *Vietnam and the Chinese Model: A Comparative Study of Vietnamese and Chinese Government in the First Half of the Nineteenth Century*
*141. George Elison, *Deus Destroyed: The Image of Christianity in Early Modern Japan*
142. William D. Wray, ed., *Managing Industrial Enterprise: Cases from Japan's Prewar Experience*
*143. T'ung-tsu Ch'ü, *Local Government in China Under the Ching*
144. Marie Anchordoguy, *Computers, Inc.: Japan's Challenge to IBM*
145. Barbara Molony, *Technology and Investment: The Prewar Japanese Chemical Industry*
146. Mary Elizabeth Berry, *Hideyoshi*
147. Laura E. Hein, *Fueling Growth: The Energy Revolution and Economic Policy in Postwar Japan*
148. Wen-hsin Yeh, *The Alienated Academy: Culture and Politics in Republican China, 1919–1937*
149. Dru C. Gladney, *Muslim Chinese: Ethnic Nationalism in the People's Republic*
150. Merle Goldman and Paul A. Cohen, eds., *Ideas Across Cultures: Essays on Chinese Thought in Honor of Benjamin L Schwartz*
151. James M. Polachek, *The Inner Opium War*
152. Gail Lee Bernstein, *Japanese Marxist: A Portrait of Kawakami Hajime, 1879–1946*
*153. Lloyd E. Eastman, *The Abortive Revolution: China Under Nationalist Rule, 1927–1937*
154. Mark Mason, *American Multinationals and Japan: The Political Economy of Japanese Capital Controls, 1899–1980*
155. Richard J. Smith, John K. Fairbank, and Katherine F. Bruner, *Robert Hart and China's Early Modernization: His Journals, 1863–1866*
156. George J. Tanabe, Jr., *Myōe the Dreamkeeper: Fantasy and Knowledge in Kamakura Buddhism*
157. William Wayne Farris, *Heavenly Warriors: The Evolution of Japan's Military, 500–1300*
158. Yu-ming Shaw, *An American Missionary in China: John Leighton Stuart and Chinese-American Relations*
159. James B. Palais, *Politics and Policy in Traditional Korea*
*160. Douglas Reynolds, *China, 1898–1912: The Xinzheng Revolution and Japan*
161. Roger R. Thompson, *China's Local Councils in the Age of Constitutional Reform, 1898–1911*
162. William Johnston, *The Modern Epidemic: History of Tuberculosis in Japan*
163. Constantine Nomikos Vaporis, *Breaking Barriers: Travel and the State in Early Modern Japan*
164. Irmela Hijiya-Kirschnereit, *Rituals of Self-Revelation: Shishōsetsu as Literary Genre and Socio-Cultural Phenomenon*
165. James C. Baxter, *The Meiji Unification Through the Lens of Ishikawa Prefecture*
166. Thomas R. H. Havens, *Architects of Affluence: The Tsutsumi Family and the Seibu-Saison Enterprises in Twentieth-Century Japan*
167. Anthony Hood Chambers, *The Secret Window: Ideal Worlds in Tanizaki's Fiction*
168. Steven J. Ericson, *The Sound of the Whistle: Railroads and the State in Meiji Japan*
169. Andrew Edmund Goble, *Kenmu: Go-Daigo's Revolution*

170. Denise Potrzeba Lett, *In Pursuit of Status: The Making of South Korea's "New" Urban Middle Class*
171. Mimi Hall Yiengpruksawan, *Hiraizumi: Buddhist Art and Regional Politics in Twelfth-Century Japan*
172. Charles Shirō Inouye, *The Similitude of Blossoms: A Critical Biography of Izumi Kyōka (1873–1939), Japanese Novelist and Playwright*
173. Aviad E. Raz, *Riding the Black Ship: Japan and Tokyo Disneyland*
174. Deborah J. Milly, *Poverty, Equality, and Growth: The Politics of Economic Need in Postwar Japan*
175. See Heng Teow, *Japan's Cultural Policy Toward China, 1918–1931: A Comparative Perspective*
176. Michael A. Fuller, *An Introduction to Literary Chinese*
177. Frederick R. Dickinson, *War and National Reinvention: Japan in the Great War, 1914–1919*
178. John Solt, *Shredding the Tapestry of Meaning: The Poetry and Poetics of Kitasono Katue (1902–1978)*
179. Edward Pratt, *Japan's Protoindustrial Elite: The Economic Foundations of the Gōnō*
180. Atsuko Sakaki, *Recontextualizing Texts: Narrative Performance in Modern Japanese Fiction*
181. Soon-Won Park, *Colonial Industrialization and Labor in Korea: The Onoda Cement Factory*
182. JaHyun Kim Haboush and Martina Deuchler, *Culture and the State in Late Chosŏn Korea*
183. John W. Chaffee, *Branches of Heaven: A History of the Imperial Clan of Sung China*
184. Gi-Wook Shin and Michael Robinson, eds., *Colonial Modernity in Korea*
185. Nam-lin Hur, *Prayer and Play in Late Tokugawa Japan: Asakusa Sensōji and Edo Society*
186. Kristin Stapleton, *Civilizing Chengdu: Chinese Urban Reform, 1895–1937*
187. Hyung Il Pai, *Constructing "Korean" Origins: A Critical Review of Archaeology, Historiography, and Racial Myth in Korean State-Formation Theories*
188. Brian D. Ruppert, *Jewel in the Ashes: Buddha Relics and Power in Early Medieval Japan*
189. Susan Daruvala, *Zhou Zuoren and an Alternative Chinese Response to Modernity*
*190. James Z. Lee, *The Political Economy of a Frontier: Southwest China, 1250–1850*
191. Kerry Smith, *A Time of Crisis: Japan, the Great Depression, and Rural Revitalization*
192. Michael Lewis, *Becoming Apart: National Power and Local Politics in Toyama, 1868–1945*
193. William C. Kirby, Man-houng Lin, James Chin Shih, and David A. Pietz, eds., *State and Economy in Republican China: A Handbook for Scholars*
194. Timothy S. George, *Minamata: Pollution and the Struggle for Democracy in Postwar Japan*
195. Billy K. L. So, *Prosperity, Region, and Institutions in Maritime China: The South Fukien Pattern, 946–1368*
196. Yoshihisa Tak Matsusaka, *The Making of Japanese Manchuria, 1904–1932*

Harvard East Asian Monographs

197. Maram Epstein, *Competing Discourses: Orthodoxy, Authenticity, and Engendered Meanings in Late Imperial Chinese Fiction*
198. Curtis J. Milhaupt, J. Mark Ramseyer, and Michael K. Young, eds. and comps., *Japanese Law in Context: Readings in Society, the Economy, and Politics*
199. Haruo Iguchi, *Unfinished Business: Ayukawa Yoshisuke and U.S.-Japan Relations, 1937–1952*
200. Scott Pearce, Audrey Spiro, and Patricia Ebrey, *Culture and Power in the Reconstitution of the Chinese Realm, 200–600*
201. Terry Kawashima, *Writing Margins: The Textual Construction of Gender in Heian and Kamakura Japan*
202. Martin W. Huang, *Desire and Fictional Narrative in Late Imperial China*
203. Robert S. Ross and Jiang Changbin, eds., *Re-examining the Cold War: U.S.-China Diplomacy, 1954–1973*
204. Guanhua Wang, *In Search of Justice: The 1905–1906 Chinese Anti-American Boycott*
205. David Schaberg, *A Patterned Past: Form and Thought in Early Chinese Historiography*
206. Christine Yano, *Tears of Longing: Nostalgia and the Nation in Japanese Popular Song*
207. Milena Doleželová-Velingerová and Oldřich Král, with Graham Sanders, eds., *The Appropriation of Cultural Capital: China's May Fourth Project*
208. Robert N. Huey, *The Making of 'Shinkokinshū'*
209. Lee Butler, *Emperor and Aristocracy in Japan, 1467–1680: Resilience and Renewal*
210. Suzanne Ogden, *Inklings of Democracy in China*
211. Kenneth J. Ruoff, *The People's Emperor: Democracy and the Japanese Monarchy, 1945–1995*
212. Haun Saussy, *Great Walls of Discourse and Other Adventures in Cultural China*
213. Aviad E. Raz, *Emotions at Work: Normative Control, Organizations, and Culture in Japan and America*
214. Rebecca E. Karl and Peter Zarrow, eds., *Rethinking the 1898 Reform Period: Political and Cultural Change in Late Qing China*
215. Kevin O'Rourke, *The Book of Korean Shijo*
216. Ezra F. Vogel, ed., *The Golden Age of the U.S.-China-Japan Triangle, 1972–1989*
217. Thomas A. Wilson, ed., *On Sacred Grounds: Culture, Society, Politics, and the Formation of the Cult of Confucius*
218. Donald S. Sutton, *Steps of Perfection: Exorcistic Performers and Chinese Religion in Twentieth-Century Taiwan*
219. Daqing Yang, *Technology of Empire: Telecommunications and Japanese Expansionism in Asia, 1883–1945*
220. Qianshen Bai, *Fu Shan's World: The Transformation of Chinese Calligraphy in the Seventeenth Century*
221. Paul Jakov Smith and Richard von Glahn, eds., *The Song-Yuan-Ming Transition in Chinese History*
222. Rania Huntington, *Alien Kind: Foxes and Late Imperial Chinese Narrative*
223. Jordan Sand, *House and Home in Modern Japan: Architecture, Domestic Space, and Bourgeois Culture, 1880–1930*

Harvard East Asian Monographs

224. Karl Gerth, *China Made: Consumer Culture and the Creation of the Nation*
225. Xiaoshan Yang, *Metamorphosis of the Private Sphere: Gardens and Objects in Tang-Song Poetry*
226. Barbara Mittler, *A Newspaper for China? Power, Identity, and Change in Shanghai's News Media, 1872–1912*
227. Joyce A. Madancy, *The Troublesome Legacy of Commissioner Lin: The Opium Trade and Opium Suppression in Fujian Province, 1820s to 1920s*
228. John Makeham, *Transmitters and Creators: Chinese Commentators and Commentaries on the Analects*
229. Elisabeth Köll, *From Cotton Mill to Business Empire: The Emergence of Regional Enterprises in Modern China*
230. Emma Teng, *Taiwan's Imagined Geography: Chinese Colonial Travel Writing and Pictures, 1683–1895*
231. Wilt Idema and Beata Grant, *The Red Brush: Writing Women of Imperial China*
232. Eric C. Rath, *The Ethos of Noh: Actors and Their Art*
233. Elizabeth Remick, *Building Local States: China During the Republican and Post-Mao Eras*
234. Lynn Struve, ed., *The Qing Formation in World-Historical Time*
235. D. Max Moerman, *Localizing Paradise: Kumano Pilgrimage and the Religious Landscape of Premodern Japan*
236. Antonia Finnane, *Speaking of Yangzhou: A Chinese City, 1550–1850*
237. Brian Platt, *Burning and Building: Schooling and State Formation in Japan, 1750–1890*
238. Gail Bernstein, Andrew Gordon, and Kate Wildman Nakai, eds., *Public Spheres, Private Lives in Modern Japan, 1600–1950: Essays in Honor of Albert Craig*
239. Wu Hung and Katherine R. Tsiang, *Body and Face in Chinese Visual Culture*
240. Stephen Dodd, *Writing Home: Representations of the Native Place in Modern Japanese Literature*
241. David Anthony Bello, *Opium and the Limits of Empire: Drug Prohibition in the Chinese Interior, 1729–1850*
242. Hosea Hirata, *Discourses of Seduction: History, Evil, Desire, and Modern Japanese Literature*
243. Kyung Moon Hwang, *Beyond Birth: Social Status in the Emergence of Modern Korea*
244. Brian R. Dott, *Identity Reflections: Pilgrimages to Mount Tai in Late Imperial China*
245. Mark McNally, *Proving the Way: Conflict and Practice in the History of Japanese Nativism*
246. Yongping Wu, *A Political Explanation of Economic Growth: State Survival, Bureaucratic Politics, and Private Enterprises in the Making of Taiwan's Economy, 1950–1985*
247. Kyu Hyun Kim, *The Age of Visions and Arguments: Parliamentarianism and the National Public Sphere in Early Meiji Japan*
248. Zvi Ben-Dor Benite, *The Dao of Muhammad: A Cultural History of Muslims in Late Imperial China*
249. David Der-wei Wang and Shang Wei, eds., *Dynastic Crisis and Cultural Innovation: From the Late Ming to the Late Qing and Beyond*

Harvard East Asian Monographs

250. Wilt L. Idema, Wai-yee Li, and Ellen Widmer, eds., *Trauma and Transcendence in Early Qing Literature*
251. Barbara Molony and Kathleen Uno, eds., *Gendering Modern Japanese History*
252. Hiroshi Aoyagi, *Islands of Eight Million Smiles: Idol Performance and Symbolic Production in Contemporary Japan*
253. Wai-yee Li, *The Readability of the Past in Early Chinese Historiography*
254. William C. Kirby, Robert S. Ross, and Gong Li, eds., *Normalization of U.S.-China Relations: An International History*
255. Ellen Gardner Nakamura, *Practical Pursuits: Takano Chōei, Takahashi Keisaku, and Western Medicine in Nineteenth-Century Japan*
256. Jonathan W. Best, *A History of the Early Korean Kingdom of Paekche, together with an annotated translation of* The Paekche Annals *of the* Samguk sagi
257. Liang Pan, *The United Nations in Japan's Foreign and Security Policymaking, 1945–1992: National Security, Party Politics, and International Status*
258. Richard Belsky, *Localities at the Center: Native Place, Space, and Power in Late Imperial Beijing*
259. Zwia Lipkin, *"Useless to the State": "Social Problems" and Social Engineering in Nationalist Nanjing, 1927–1937*
260. William O. Gardner, *Advertising Tower: Japanese Modernism and Modernity in the 1920s*
261. Stephen Owen, *The Making of Early Chinese Classical Poetry*
262. Martin J. Powers, *Pattern and Person: Ornament, Society, and Self in Classical China*
263. Anna M. Shields, *Crafting a Collection: The Cultural Contexts and Poetic Practice of the* Huajian ji 花間集 *(Collection from Among the Flowers)*
264. Stephen Owen, *The Late Tang: Chinese Poetry of the Mid-Ninth Century (827–860)*
265. Sara L. Friedman, *Intimate Politics: Marriage, the Market, and State Power in Southeastern China*
266. Patricia Buckley Ebrey and Maggie Bickford, *Emperor Huizong and Late Northern Song China: The Politics of Culture and the Culture of Politics*
267. Sophie Volpp, *Worldly Stage: Theatricality in Seventeenth-Century China*
268. Ellen Widmer, *The Beauty and the Book: Women and Fiction in Nineteenth-Century China*
269. Steven B. Miles, *The Sea of Learning: Mobility and Identity in Nineteenth-Century Guangzhou*
270. Lin Man-houng, *China Upside Down: Currency, Society, and Ideologies, 1808–1856*
271. Ronald Egan, *The Problem of Beauty: Aesthetic Thought and Pursuits in Northern Song Dynasty China*
272. Mark Halperin, *Out of the Cloister: Literati Perspectives on Buddhism in Sung China, 960–1279*
273. Helen Dunstan, *State or Merchant? Political Economy and Political Process in 1740s China*
274. Sabina Knight, *The Heart of Time: Moral Agency in Twentieth-Century Chinese Fiction*
275. Timothy J. Van Compernolle, *The Uses of Memory: The Critique of Modernity in the Fiction of Higuchi Ichiyō*

276. Paul Rouzer, *A New Practical Primer of Literary Chinese*
277. Jonathan Zwicker, *Practices of the Sentimental Imagination: Melodrama, the Novel, and the Social Imaginary in Nineteenth-Century Japan*
278. Franziska Seraphim, *War Memory and Social Politics in Japan, 1945–2005*
279. Adam L. Kern, *Manga from the Floating World: Comicbook Culture and the* Kibyōshi *of Edo Japan*
280. Cynthia J. Brokaw, *Commerce in Culture: The Sibao Book Trade in the Qing and Republican Periods*
281. Eugene Y. Park, *Between Dreams and Reality: The Military Examination in Late Chosŏn Korea, 1600–1894*
282. Nam-lin Hur, *Death and Social Order in Tokugawa Japan: Buddhism, Anti-Christianity, and the* Danka *System*
283. Patricia M. Thornton, *Disciplining the State: Virtue, Violence, and State-Making in Modern China*
284. Vincent Goossaert, *The Taoists of Peking, 1800–1949: A Social History of Urban Clerics*
285. Peter Nickerson, *Taoism, Bureaucracy, and Popular Religion in Early Medieval China*
286. Charo B. D'Etcheverry, *Love After* The Tale of Genji*: Rewriting the World of the Shining Prince*
287. Michael G. Chang, *A Court on Horseback: Imperial Touring & the Construction of Qing Rule, 1680–1785*
288. Carol Richmond Tsang, *War and Faith:* Ikkō Ikki *in Late Muromachi Japan*
289. Hilde De Weerdt, *Competition over Content: Negotiating Standards for the Civil Service Examinations in Imperial China (1127–1279)*
290. Eve Zimmerman, *Out of the Alleyway: Nakagami Kenji and the Poetics of Outcaste Fiction*
291. Robert Culp, *Articulating Citizenship: Civic Education and Student Politics in Southeastern China, 1912–1940*
292. Richard J. Smethurst, *From Foot Soldier to Finance Minister: Takahashi Korekiyo, Japan's Keynes*
293. John E. Herman, *Amid the Clouds and Mist: China's Colonization of Guizhou, 1200–1700*
294. Tomoko Shiroyama, *China During the Great Depression: Market, State, and the World Economy, 1929–1937*
295. Kirk W. Larsen, *Tradition, Treaties and Trade: Qing Imperialism and Chosŏn Korea, 1850–1910*
296. Gregory Golley, *When Our Eyes No Longer See: Realism, Science, and Ecology in Japanese Literary Modernism*
297. Barbara Ambros, *Emplacing a Pilgrimage: The Ōyama Cult and Regional Religion in Early Modern Japan*
298. Rebecca Suter, *The Japanization of Modernity: Murakami Haruki between Japan and the United States*
299. Yuma Totani, *The Tokyo War Crimes Trial: The Pursuit of Justice in the Wake of World War II*

300. Linda Isako Angst, *In a Dark Time: Memory, Community, and Gendered Nationalism in Postwar Okinawa*
301. David M. Robinson, ed., *Culture, Courtiers, and Competition: The Ming Court (1368–1644)*
302. Calvin Chen, *Some Assembly Required: Work, Community, and Politics in China's Rural Enterprises*
303. Sem Vermeersch, *The Power of the Buddhas: The Politics of Buddhism During the Koryŏ Dynasty* (918–1392)
304. Tina Lu, *Accidental Incest, Filial Cannibalism, and Other Peculiar Encounters in Late Imperial Chinese Literature*
305. Chang Woei Ong, *Men of Letters Within the Passes: Guanzhong Literati in Chinese History, 907–1911*
306. Wendy Swartz, *Reading Tao Yuanming: Shifting Paradigms of Historical Reception (427–1900)*
307. Peter K. Bol, *Neo-Confucianism in History*
308. Carlos Rojas, *The Naked Gaze: Reflections on Chinese Modernity*
309. Kelly H. Chong, *Deliverance and Submission: Evangelical Women and the Negotiation of Patriarchy in South Korea*
310. Rachel DiNitto, *Uchida Hyakken: A Critique of Modernity and Militarism in Prewar Japan*
311. Jeffrey Snyder-Reinke, *Dry Spells: State Rainmaking and Local Governance in Late Imperial China*
312. Jay Dautcher, *Down a Narrow Road: Identity and Masculinity in a Uyghur Community in Xinjiang China*
313. Xun Liu, *Daoist Modern: Innovation, Lay Practice, and the Community of Inner Alchemy in Republican Shanghai*
314. Jacob Eyferth, *Eating Rice from Bamboo Roots: The Social History of a Community of Handicraft Papermakers in Rural Sichuan, 1920–2000*
315. David Johnson, *Spectacle and Sacrifice: The Ritual Foundations of Village Life in North China*
316. James Robson, *Power of Place: The Religious Landscape of the Southern Sacred Peak (Nanyue* 南嶽*) in Medieval China*
317. Lori Watt, *When Empire Comes Home: Repatriation and Reintegration in Postwar Japan*
318. James Dorsey, *Critical Aesthetics: Kobayashi Hideo, Modernity, and Wartime Japan*
319. Christopher Bolton, *Sublime Voices: The Fictional Science and Scientific Fiction of Abe Kōbō*
320. Si-yen Fei, *Negotiating Urban Space: Urbanization and Late Ming Nanjing*
321. Christopher Gerteis, *Gender Struggles: Wage-Earning Women and Male-Dominated Unions in Postwar Japan*
322. Rebecca Nedostup, *Superstitious Regimes: Religion and the Politics of Chinese Modernity*
323. Lucien Bianco, *Wretched Rebels: Rural Disturbances on the Eve of the Chinese Revolution*
324. Cathryn H. Clayton, *Sovereignty at the Edge: Macau and the Question of Chineseness*
325. Micah S. Muscolino, *Fishing Wars and Environmental Change in Late Imperial and Modern China*

Harvard East Asian Monographs

326. Robert I. Hellyer, *Defining Engagement: Japan and Global Contexts, 1750–1868*
327. Robert Ashmore, *The Transport of Reading: Text and Understanding in the World of Tao Qian (365–427)*
328. Mark A. Jones, *Children as Treasures: Childhood and the Middle Class in Early Twentieth Century Japan*
329. Miryam Sas, *Experimental Arts in Postwar Japan: Moments of Encounter, Engagement, and Imagined Return*
330. H. Mack Horton, *Traversing the Frontier: The* Man'yōshū *Account of a Japanese Mission to Silla in 736–737*
331. Dennis J. Frost, *Seeing Stars: Sports Celebrity, Identity, and Body Culture in Modern Japan*
332. Marnie S. Anderson, *A Place in Public: Women's Rights in Meiji Japan*
333. Peter Mauch, *Sailor Diplomat: Nomura Kichisaburō and the Japanese-American War*
334. Ethan Isaac Segal, *Coins, Trade, and the State: Economic Growth in Early Medieval Japan*
335. David B. Lurie, *Realms of Literacy: Early Japan and the History of Writing*
336. Lillian Lan-ying Tseng, *Picturing Heaven in Early China*
337. Jun Uchida, *Brokers of Empire: Japanese Settler Colonialism in Korea, 1876–1945*
338. Patricia L. Maclachlan, *The People's Post Office: The History and Politics of the Japanese Postal System, 1871–2010*
339. Michael Schiltz, *The Money Doctors from Japan: Finance, Imperialism, and the Building of the Yen Bloc, 1895–1937*
340. Daqing Yang, Jie Liu, Hiroshi Mitani, and Andrew Gordon, eds., *Toward a History Beyond Borders: Contentious Issues in Sino-Japanese Relations*
341. Sonia Ryang, *Reading North Korea: An Ethnological Inquiry*
342. Susan Huang, *Picturing the True Form: Daoist Visual Culture in Medieval China*
343. Barbara Mittler, *A Continuous Revolution: Making Sense of Cultural Revolution Culture*
344. Hwansoo Ilmee Kim, *Empire of the Dharma: Korean and Japanese Buddhism, 1877–1912*
345. Satoru Saito, *Detective Fiction and the Rise of the Japanese Novel, 1880–1930*